The Enduring Classics *of* BILLY GRAHAM

The SECRET *of* HAPPINESS
HOPE *for the* TROUBLED HEART
DEATH *and the* LIFE AFTER

W PUBLISHING GROUP
A Division of Thomas Nelson Publishers
Since 1798

www.wpublishinggroup.com

THE SECRET *of* HAPPINESS

BILLY GRAHAM

W PUBLISHING GROUP
A Division of Thomas Nelson Publishers
Since 1798

www.wpublishinggroup.com

Published by W Publishing Group, a Division of
Thomas Nelson, Inc., P.O. Box 141000, Nashville, TN 37214.

Library of Congress Cataloging-in-Publication Data

Graham, Billy, 1918–
The secret of happiness

1. Beatitudes—Criticism, interpretation, etc.
2. Happiness—Religious aspects—Christianity.
I. Title. BT382.G7 1985 226'.9306 85–16934
ISBN 0-8499-0508-7
ISBN 0-8499-4381-7 (trade paper)
ISBN 0-8499-1478-7 (gift)

Printed in the United States of America

06 07 08 BVG 9 8 7 6 5 4

To my mother and father,
whose dedicated lives taught me
The Secret of Happiness

Contents

Preface

I SAT DOWN to write a book on "The Greatest Sermon Ever Preached"—the Sermon on the Mount—but I got no further than the eight Beatitudes. The more I read them, meditated on them, and studied them, the more I realized that Christ was giving a formula for personal happiness that applied to anyone, no matter what his race, geographical situation, age, or circumstance! I have based my comments on the beautiful and beloved King James Version of the Beatitudes, although I follow the suggestion of scholars and many modern Bible translations who use the word *happy* for "blessed" since it suggests joy in the midst of real life.

When trying to put these thoughts on paper, I consulted with other writers. In these few statements Jesus shares almost the whole depth and scope of His teaching. As someone has said, "The character which we find in the Beatitudes is beyond all question, nothing less than our Lord's own character put into words. It is a description set side by side with an example."

The Beatitudes are revolutionary! Startling! Deeply profound, and yet amazingly simple! If applied on a universal scale, they could transform the world in which we live.

If you apply these simple formulae in your own personal life, you can never be the same!

As I have restudied the Beatitudes to prepare for this revised edition I have been amazed again at the timelessness and universal nature of these teachings of Jesus. I have sensed afresh the depth and challenge of these brief words of our Lord. In this revised edition I have made numerous minor changes to bring the book up to date and make it practical. I also have included some additional insights which I have gathered since the first edition was published in 1955. But the Word of God does not change, nor does its power to change our lives. Just as Christ brought hope and new life to those who first gathered in Galilee to hear the Sermon on the Mount, so He can bring hope and new life to us today as we understand His truth, commit ourselves to it, and live each day in its light.

In the first edition, my friend and assistant Lee Fisher was a tremendous help. In this revised edition, my wife, Ruth, my daughter Gigi Tchividjian, my able research assistant Dr. John Akers, and Word editor Al Bryant have been indispensable. I am deeply grateful also to my administrative assistant Stephanie Wills for her invaluable counsel, advice, and for keeping us on track.

It is my prayer that as you read this book, and as you meditate on the Beatitudes themselves, you will realize that these ancient truths are as modern as tomorrow. They can change your life and point the way to true and lasting happiness—because they will point you to Christ and His timeless principles for living.

One final note: I have used the word *man* in this book, along with the appropriate pronouns that follow it, in the generic sense of the term, to mean the human race in its most inclusive sense.

Billy Graham, Montreat, NC
August 1985

Publisher's Note

SINCE ITS FIRST publication almost fifty years ago, Dr. Billy Graham's *The Secret of Happiness* has offered inspiration to thousands in pursuit of this elusive goal. The eight guideposts Dr. Graham points to have helped us through decades of war, turmoil, and world change and have shown us how to maintain genuine happiness in their midst. While some world situations and statistics have changed since the book's most recent revision, our need to know the secret of happiness has not. W Publishing Group is pleased, therefore, to join Dr. Graham in reaffirming the timeless truths found in the Beatitudes by republishing this devotional classic, as revised in 1985. May you be blessed as you continue your own search for true contentment and joy.

Blessed (happy, to be envied, and spiritually prosperous—with life-joy and satisfaction in God's favor and salvation, regardless of their outward conditions) are the poor in spirit. . . . Matthew 5:3 AMP

CHAPTER ONE

The Search for Happiness

A FRENCH PHILOSOPHER once said, "The whole world is on a mad quest for security and happiness." A former president of Harvard University observed, "The world is searching for a creed to believe and a song to sing."

A Texas millionaire confided, "I thought money could buy happiness—I have been miserably disillusioned." A famous film star broke down: "I have money, beauty, glamour, and popularity. I should be the happiest woman in the world, but I am miserable. Why?" One of Britain's top social leaders said, "I have lost all desire to live, yet I have everything to live for. What is the matter?"

The poet Amy Wilson Carmichael wrote:

The lonely, dreary road he trod.
"Enter into my joy," said God.
The sad ascetic shook his head,
"I've lost all taste for joy," he said.

A man went to see a psychiatrist. He said, "Doctor, I am lonely, despondent, and miserable. Can you help me?" The psychiatrist suggested that he go to a circus and see a famous clown who was said to make even the most despondent laugh with merriment. His patient said, "I am that clown."

A college senior said, "I am twenty-three. I have lived through enough experiences to be old, and I am already fed up with life."

A famous Grecian dancer of a generation ago once said, "I have never been alone but what my hands trembled, my eyes filled with tears, and my heart ached for a peace and happiness I have never found."

One of the world's great statesmen said to me, "I am an old man. Life has lost all meaning. I am ready to take a fateful leap into the unknown. Young man, can you give me a ray of hope?"

The Christian, on the other hand, has a different perspective on the meaning of happiness. C. S. Lewis said, "Joy is the serious business of heaven." He added, "All His biddings are joys." Mother Teresa of Calcutta says, "True holiness consists of doing the will of God with a smile."

Jesus declared, "I am come that they might have life, and that they might have it more abundantly" (John 10:10). Or again He stated, "These things have I spoken unto you, that my joy might remain in you, and that your joy might be full" (John 15:11).

Searching for Happiness in the Wrong Places

Over 2,500 years ago the prophet Isaiah looked out on a people who longed for happiness and security but were looking for it in the wrong places. They were running to the marketplace and to places of amusement, spending their money madly for things which brought them no permanent satisfaction.

He stood before them one day and gave them the Word of God: "Ho, every one that thirsteth, come ye to the waters, and he that hath no money; come ye, buy, and eat; yea, come, buy wine and milk without money and without price. Wherefore do ye spend money for that which is not bread? and your labor for that which satisfieth not? hearken diligently unto me, and eat ye that which is good, and let your soul delight itself in fatness" (Isaiah 55:1–2).

Isaiah didn't speak negatively and berate them for their sins in this particular sermon. He didn't grab the bottle from the drunkard's hand, he didn't lecture them about the evils of gluttony, he didn't shame them for their immoral practices. He overlooked that for the moment. He simply asked them: "Are you getting what you want out of life? Why do you spend your money for that which is not bread and your labor for that which does not satisfy?"

If Isaiah were living today he would probably stand at Forty-second and Broadway in New York, in the Loop in Chicago, or on Market Street in San Francisco, and simply ask the milling, restless throngs: "Are you getting what you want? Are you finding satisfaction?"

He would ask the actress, surfeited with fame and fortune, but peering out on life hungrily: "Are you getting what you want?" He would say to the eminently successful financier who commands his fleets and controls his industries: "Are you getting what you want?"

He would say to the laborers and workmen of America who are enjoying the highest standard of living in history: "Are you getting what you want?" He would ask the youth of America: "Are you getting what you want?"

He would say to the consumers of America who have the best homes, the most comfortable furniture, the finest food, the cleverest gadgets, and the smoothest, most powerful automobiles: "Are you getting what you want?"

God Has the Answer

Isaiah did not leave them with an unanswered question. He went on to tell them that there is a satisfying way of life, if they would seek it. He exhorted them to abandon their vain searching for pots of gold at the end of mythical rainbows, and to start searching for happiness where it is really found, in a right relationship with God.

Our materialistic world rushes on with its eternal quest for the fountain of happiness! The more knowledge we acquire, the less wisdom we seem to have. The more economic security we gain, the more bored and insecure we become. The more worldly pleasure we enjoy, the less satisfied and contented we are with life. We are like a restless sea, finding a little peace here and a little pleasure there, but nothing permanent and satisfying. So the search continues! Men will kill, lie, cheat, steal, and go to war to satisfy their quest for power, pleasure, and wealth, thinking thereby to gain for themselves and their particular group peace, security, contentment, and happiness, and yet in vain.

Yet inside us a little voice keeps saying, "We were not meant to be this way—we were meant for better things." We have a mysterious feeling that there is a fountain somewhere that contains the happiness which makes life worthwhile. We keep saying to ourselves that somewhere, sometime we will stumble onto the secret. Sometimes we feel that we have obtained it—only to find it illusive, leaving us disillusioned, bewildered, unhappy, and still searching.

There are, we need to realize, two kinds of happiness. One kind of happiness comes to us when our circumstances are pleasant and we are relatively free from troubles. The problem, however, is that this kind of happiness is fleeting and superficial. When circumstances change—as they inevitably do—then this kind of happiness evaporates like the early morning fog in the heat of the sun. In addition, even when our outward circumstances are seemingly ideal, we still may be troubled inside by a nagging hunger or longing for something we cannot identify. We say we are "happy"—but down inside we know it is only temporary and shallow at best. Yes, from time to time we may think we have found a degree of happiness, but sooner or later it will vanish. Our search for happiness remains unfulfilled.

But there is another kind of happiness—the kind for which we all long. This second kind of happiness is a lasting, inner joy and peace which survives in any circumstances. It is a happiness which endures no matter what comes our way—and even may grow stronger in adversity. This is the kind of happiness to which Jesus summons us in the Beatitudes. It is happiness which can only come from God. He alone has the answer to our search for lasting happiness.

The happiness which brings enduring worth to life is not the superficial happiness that is dependent on circumstances. It is the happiness and contentment that fills the soul even in the midst of the most distressing of circumstances and the most adverse environment. It is the kind of happiness that survives when things go wrong and smiles through the tears. The happiness for which our souls ache is one undisturbed by success or failure, one which dwells deep within us and gives inward relaxation, peace, and contentment, no matter what the surface problems may be. That kind of happiness stands in need of no outward stimulus.

Near my home is a spring that never varies its flow at any season of the year. Floods may rage nearby, but it will not increase its flow. A long summer's drought may come, but it will not decrease. It is perennially and always the same. Such is the type of happiness for which we yearn.

The Three Things We Search For

First, we search for peace. As we have just seen, the whole human race is consumed with a search for inner peace, happiness, and joy.

The peace we seek is not merely a nondescript, so-called peace of mind which is blind to reality or comes and goes according to our moods or circumstances. The peace every man and woman seeks is one which will free them from the anxiety and frustrations of life's distracting conflicts and problems. It is a peace of soul which permeates one's entire being, a peace that operates through the trials and burdens of life.

Second, we search for purpose. Man is confused and perplexed, wondering where he came from, why he is here, and where he is going. He wants to know if there is truth in this universe—truth which will be like a polar star to guide him and give him meaning.

Some speculate that humanity is an accident on this planet. Accord-ing to their views, man was not put here for a purpose—he just happened. The existentialist philosopher declares that man has no God-given purpose, and is left to make up his own purpose and meaning in life if he can. But down inside we yearn for something more certain. Even the skeptic searches for truth, for man needs truth as the animals do not—not just the truth of the physical sciences and mathematics, but the truth about his being and why he is here.

Third, we search for a relationship with God. Even when men vehemently deny God's existence, they still are searching for something to fill the vacuum in their souls.

But it is a vacuum God, our Creator, placed there—and only He can fill it. Man was created in the image of God. At first, Adam and Eve had perfect fellowship with God. But they turned their backs on God, substituting themselves at the center of their lives instead of God their Creator. Now man is a lost and lonely wanderer upon the earth apart from God. To have a vague knowledge that He exists is not enough. Man yearns to know that he is not alone in this universe, that there is a Higher Power guiding his destiny. He yearns for a relationship with his Creator—even if he does not admit it.

The Beatitudes: God's Key to Man's Search

Yes, every human being ever born yearns for peace, purpose, and God Himself. But can we know these? Can our search be ended? Will our quest for true happiness ever be satisfied? The Bible declares a resounding "Yes!" And in these eight Beatitudes Jesus points the way. In each one of the Beatitudes—which someone has called the "beautiful attitudes"— Jesus used the word *blessed*. This word *blessed is* actually a very difficult word to translate into modern English, because in the original Greek language of the New Testament it has a far richer meaning than the everyday content of our English word. As we noted at the beginning of this chapter, the Amplified Version of the New Testament defines it as "happy, to be envied, and spiritually prosperous . . . with life-joy and satisfaction. . . ." But perhaps the word *happy* comes as close as any single English word to conveying the idea of "blessed" to us today, and that is the word we will use for the most part through this book. But let us never forget that the "blessedness" of which Jesus speaks is far, far deeper than any superficial happiness which comes and goes according to circumstances. That is why the word *blessed* guards well against its reduction and perversion.

Jesus' first words were: "Happy are ye." In those three words He was telling us that there *is* an answer to our search! We can know peace. We can know the truth about our lives. We can know God. And because of that, we can be blessed!

But is that possible, or is Jesus simply speaking some high-sounding words which have no substance? To answer that, look first of all at Jesus Himself. Certainly if anyone had genuine happiness and blessedness, it was Jesus—in spite of the controversy, abuse, and eventual injustice of His death. He knew the secret of true happiness, and in these Beatitudes He unveils it to us.

Who Was This Jesus?

The Beatitudes are not the whole of Jesus' teaching, nor is even the Sermon on the Mount. (You can read the entire Sermon on the Mount in chapters 5 through 7 of the Gospel of Matthew.) There is much else that Jesus taught during the three short years of His public ministry. But Jesus was more than a great teacher. Who was this man Jesus, who never traveled outside His native Palestine and yet changed the entire course of human history?

Some have said that Jesus' main role was as a social reformer, coming to change society and liberate people who were bound by injustice and oppression. Others have said He came merely as an example, showing us by His acts of love how we should live. Still others have dismissed Him as a misguided religious reformer with no relevance to a modern, scientific age.

But none of these are adequate to explain Jesus Christ as we see Him clearly pictured in the New Testament. The Bible, in fact, makes a startling assertion: Jesus was not only a man, but He was God Himself, come down from the glory of heaven to walk on this earth and show us what God is like. Christ "is the image of the invisible

God" (Colossians 1:15). More than that, He is the divinely appointed Savior who died for sinners, bearing their transgressions upon the cross. He died to save all who had disobeyed God and who were slandering Him in their unregenerate natures. And He demonstrated beyond all doubt that He was the Divine Savior and Lord by being raised from the dead. The gospel is the good news of God "concerning his Son Jesus Christ our Lord, which was made of the seed of David according to the flesh; and declared to be the Son of God with power, according to the spirit of holiness, by the resurrection from the dead" (Romans 1:3–4).

The best modern scholarship is discovering once again that even the Sermon on the Mount, and the Beatitudes as well, cannot be isolated from the fact of Jesus' saviorhood. The Old Testament had taught that the Christ was to be meek. He was to turn mourning into joy; righteousness was to be His meat and drink; even upon the cross it was His deepest hunger and thirst.

He also was the One who would show God's mercy to those who were separated from God and in need. He likewise would be pure and without sin. Most of all, He would not flee the persecution that would come His way, but would bring peace—peace with God, peace within the human heart, and peace on earth.

This is another way of saying that, in reality, Jesus Christ is the perfect fulfillment, example, and demonstration of the Beatitudes. He alone, in the history of the human race, experienced fully what He tells us about the happiness and blessedness of life. What He tells us, He tells us as the Savior who has redeemed us and who is teaching His followers. But more than that, He is the One who gives us the power to live according to His teachings. Christ's message when He was upon the earth was revolutionizing and understandable. His words were simple yet profound. And they shook people. His words provoked either happy acceptance or violent rejection. People were never the same after listening to Him. They were invariably better or worse—better if they accepted Him, worse if they rejected Him. They either followed Him in love or turned away in anger and indignation. There was a magic in His gospel which prompted men and women to decisive action. As He clearly said, "He that is not with Me is against Me."

Men Right Side Up in an Upside-Down World

The people who followed Him were unique in their generation. They turned the world upside down because their hearts had been turned right side up. The world has never been the same. History took a sharp turn for the better. People began to behave like human beings. Dignity, nobility, and honor followed in the wake of Christianity. Art, music, and science—sparked by this new interpretation of life's meaning—began to progress and develop. Mankind began at long last to resemble again the "image of God" in which he was created. Society began to feel the impact of the Christian influence. Injustice, inhumanity, and intolerance were dislodged by the tidal wave of spiritual power which was released by Christ. As F. W. Boreham once said, "The Carpenter of Nazareth has encouraged the goldsmiths of the ages." Virtually every significant social movement in Western civilization—from the abolition of slavery to child labor laws—owes its origin to the influence of Jesus Christ.

Centuries have rolled by since that initial surge of spiritual life. The stream of Christianity has flowed unceasingly, sometimes at flood tide but more often at ebb tide.

At times the Church has been gloriously renewed and used of God. Emboldened by the Holy Spirit, and stirred by the truth of the Word of God, men and women throughout the centuries have continued to turn the world upside down for Christ. At other times, however, man-made tributaries have flowed into it, polluting and adulterating it. Deism, Pantheism, and, of late, Humanism and blatant Naturalism have flowed like muddy currents into the mainstream of Christian thought, so that the world has had difficulty in distinguishing the real from the false. In some parts of the world armies have fought and killed supposedly in the Name of Christ—and yet by their actions showed they understood little of His spirit of forgiveness and love.

Yes, Christians are imperfect, and some who have claimed most loudly to follow Him have been the furthest from His teaching. But don't let that divert you or keep you from Christ Himself. At times people have said to me, "Christians are all hypocrites—I don't want anything to do with Christ!" But that is an excuse to keep from having to face the truth that is in Christ. Instead, understand His teaching and examine His life. And if you know Christ and have committed your life to Him, learn from Him and live a consistent life for Him. Do others see something of Christ—His love, His joy, His peace—in your life?

True Christians are supposed to be happy! Our generation has become well versed in Christian terminology, but is remiss in the actual practice of Christ's principles and teachings. Hence, our greatest need today is not more Christianity but more true Christians.

The Impact of Christlike Living

The world may argue against Christianity as an institution, but there is no convincing argument against a person who through the Spirit of God has been made Christlike. Such a one is a living rebuke to the selfishness, rationalism, and materialism of the day. Too often we have debated with the world on the letter of the law when we should have been living oracles of God, seen and read of all people.

It is time that we retrace our steps to the source and realize afresh the transforming power of Jesus Christ.

Jesus said to the woman at Jacob's well: "Whosoever drinketh of the water that I shall give him shall never thirst" (John 4:14). This sin-sick, disillusioned woman was the symbol of the whole race. Her longings were our longings! Her heart-cry was our heart-cry! Her disillusionment was our disillusionment! Her sin was our sin! But her Savior can be our Savior! Her forgiveness can be our forgiveness! Her joy can be our joy!

An Invitation to a Journey

I invite you to go with me on a thrilling, adventuresome journey. The object of our search? The secret of happiness. The place? Galilee! Let us roll back the pages of time almost two thousand years.

It's a hot, sultry day with the sweltering wind spinning little dust whirls and carrying them swiftly down the winding road by the Sea of Galilee. There is an air of expectancy in the atmosphere we breathe. The wind skips happily across the surface of the ancient sea. We hear voices raised in an excited, feverish pitch as friend calls a greeting to friend. Along every trail leading to Galilee little groups of people begin to gather. The word has spread abroad that Jesus is returning to Galilee.

Suddenly He and His little band of followers emerge over the brow of a hill on the road to Capernaum, and immediately in their wake follows a vast multitude of people from Galilee, Decapolis, Jerusalem, Judea, and from beyond the Jordan River.

Quickly the word spreads from mouth to mouth: "Jesus is coming!" Other multitudes from Tiberias, Bethsaida, and Capernaum soon appear and join the others. Together they follow thirteen robed men. As they reach the summit of the hill where the gentle winds from the plains sweep over them, affording relief from the sun, Jesus stops and motions for them to sit down and rest.

The air is tense. It is a moment to be captured and held for eternity. The crowd hushes as Jesus climbs atop a large rock and is seated. In the valley on the deserted road, a lone camel rider wends his way along the trail toward Tiberias. A quiet falls upon the multitude as their faces gaze expectantly at Jesus. Then He begins to speak.

What He said there on that Mount of Beatitudes in faraway Palestine was to go down in history as the most profound, sublime words ever spoken! There in reverent, measured, simple words He revealed the secret of happiness—not a superficial happiness of time and space, but a happiness which would last forever.

His first word was *happy*. Immediately His listeners must have pricked up their ears, as we are prone to do. In the pages to follow it is my prayer that you will do even more: prick up your ears . . . open your heart . . . surrender your will. Then you will begin living life with a capital *L*, find a contentment and joy that crowd the futility and vanity out of the daily walk, and discover the secret of happiness!

Blessed are the poor in spirit: for theirs is the kingdom of heaven. Matthew 5:3

CHAPTER TWO

Happiness Through Poverty

TODAY, THROUGH THE media, we have all been made aware of the abject, hopeless poverty in much of the world. We have seen the starving in Africa, the displaced persons of Southeast Asia.

I myself have traveled in more than sixty countries of the world, many of them hopelessly buried in poverty. I have returned from cities like Calcutta with a heavy heart, wondering if anything can ever be done to alleviate their suffering.

Throughout the world I have found many Mother Teresas. Still, the poverty is virtually untouched. We have sent our own contributions through reliable relief organizations.

Yet under the filth, the starvation, the abject poverty I have sensed an even greater poverty—the poverty of the soul.

A French leader has said that if the whole world had enough to eat, money to spend, and security from the cradle to the grave they would ask for nothing more. And that is something to think about. I have on occasion visited places where the wealthy gather to relax, escape bad weather, or just play—and I have discovered that wealth can be anesthetizing. It is, as Jesus said, easier for a camel to go through the eye of a needle than for a wealthy person to enter the kingdom of heaven (see Matthew 19:24). Surely one reason is that wealth tends to preoccupy a person and dull his sensitivity to his spiritual needs.

I have often asked myself the question: Would wealth make people happy? And I have answered it just as quickly by saying an emphatic "No!" I know too many rich people who are miserable. There are people with everything that money can buy who are tormented, confused, bewildered, and miserable! Yet how many times I have heard people say, "If only I had a little security, I could be happy." Or, "If only I could have a fine home, a new car, and a winter condominium in Florida, I would be content."

There is nothing inherently wrong with being rich. I have been privileged to know some very wealthy people across the years who were humble and generous, seeing their wealth as a God-given means to help others. The Bible, however, warns that riches easily overwhelm a person, distorting his values, making him proud and arrogant, and making him think he does not need God. "But they that will be rich fall into temptation and a snare, and into many foolish and hurtful lusts, which drown men in destruction and perdition. For the love of money is the root of all evil" (1 Timothy 6:9–10). For others, wealth only leads to boredom. King Solomon was unquestionably one of the wealthiest men who ever lived. In his search for happiness he tried everything—possessions, music, sex, great building projects, knowledge—but in the end he declared about them, "I have seen all the works that are done under the sun; and, behold, all is vanity and vexation of spirit" (Ecclesiastes 1:14). Only God could satisfy his deepest longings and give him true happiness.

On the other hand, many great people stay poor all their lives, either through choice (such as a missionary or a person who chooses to live modestly and give away money to help others) or through unavoidable circumstances. There are others, however, who go through life filled with resentment, jealousy, and bitterness because they want "just a little bit more." They may have enough to satisfy their legitimate needs, but instead of being thankful for what they have—which would make them unimaginably wealthy in the eyes of those in poorer nations—they are consumed by a desire for riches. They believe the key to happiness would be found in greater wealth.

But Jesus made it plain that happiness and contentment are not found in possessions or money. He stated that material things and riches do not in themselves bring happiness and peace to the soul.

Happy is that person who has learned the secret of being content with whatever life brings him, and has learned to rejoice in the simple and beautiful things around him.

In the Introduction to his *Anthology* on George MacDonald, C. S. Lewis says of MacDonald: "His resignation to poverty was at the opposite pole from that of a stoic. He appears to have been a sunny, playful man, deeply appreciative of all really beautiful and delicious things that money can buy, and no less deeply content to do without them." In *Annals of a Quiet Neighborbood* MacDonald said of himself, "Let me, if I may, be ever welcomed to my room in winter by a glowing hearth, in summer by a vase of flowers; if I may not, let me then think how nice they would be, and bury myself in my work. I do not think that the road to contentment lies in despising what we have not got. Let us acknowledge all good, all delight that the world holds, and be content without it."

An Unforgettable Day

On that day almost two thousand years ago there were undoubtedly many in that great throng who believed as many today believe—that the key to happiness is to be found in wealth and possessions. As they gathered to listen to Jesus, perhaps they wondered if His words could actually make any difference to them in their search for happiness—as you may wonder. It was soon clear to them, however, that His message was unique, for He was pointing another way to happiness—God's way. And it was a message which applied to every person.

The Sermon on the Mount was delivered to two distinct groups of people: the *multitude* and the *disciples of Christ.* We can therefore assume that it contains significance and meaning for both the disciples and the multitude, else Jesus would not have addressed it to both.

It gave the *disciples* a glimpse into the lofty spiritual Promised Land in which they were to live as the followers of Christ. It revealed the high ethical plane on which they were to live. It showed that to be a Christian was no mere child's play.

As for the *multitude,* the Sermon was an unveiling of what it actually meant to be a follower of Christ. Up to that time Jesus had been to them a fascinating and intriguing miracle worker. His person was magnetic, His manner winsome, His voice compelling. His entire being marked Him as a man of unusual power. He was a master teacher, a formidable debater, a compassionate healer—the gentlest and the sternest of men. Never had they heard anyone like Him.

These people, whose lives were monotonously humdrum in that unromantic faraway land, responded to this Galilean. To spend a day following Him through the villages where He healed the sick, blessed little children, and talked about the kingdom of God was a never-to-be-forgotten experience.

But on this particular day many who followed Him were to be surprised. Religion to them had been little more than superstition and meaningless ceremony. It little occurred to them that there was any relevance between religion and life. They had given up ever being happy; and if they ever knew the meaning of the word *happy,* they had forgotten it.

But Jesus was to put the words *blessed, joyful,* and *happy* back into their vocabularies—and even better, He was to put the words into their very hearts and lives. As Henry van Dyke's grand old hymn puts it: "Joyful, joyful, we adore Thee."

When Jesus opened His mouth, the first word to fall from His lips was *happy.* This word means "blessed, contented, or highly favored." *Happy?* Could any word have been more incongruous? Those who listened that day were far from being blessed or happy. Subdued by the Roman Empire, they were conquered. Poor, dejected, ill-clad, and pawns of an alien government, their lives were without hope and expectation. Happy? How could the meager existence of their lives be highly favored, blessed, and contented?

The Nature of Poverty

Quickly on the heels of that first word followed five others: "Happy are the poor in spirit." If Jesus had omitted the last two words, they would have all rejoiced, for they were all poor—even if they would have been puzzled at how their grinding poverty could possibly make them happy. But Jesus said "the poor in spirit."

Wondering, they listened as He went on. Hidden in these seemingly cryptic words was the first foundational secret of happiness. At first it sounds like a contradiction. We usually think of people who are poor as being unhappy. But Jesus teaches that happiness can be found in spite of poverty.

What kind of poverty did Jesus have in mind? Did He mean those who had very little of this world's goods? No. Certainly they were included. But Jesus was speaking to persons of every type—rich or poor, sick or well, educated or uneducated, young or old. God is concerned about every person on this planet, and Jesus' words were addressed to all persons, in every circumstance, and in every generation. They are addressed to you and me today.

The True Meaning of Spiritual Poverty

What did Jesus mean by being "poor in spirit"? There are at least four dimensions to this crucial question.

FIRST: If we are to be poor in spirit, *we must be aware of our spiritual poverty.*

No man is more pathetic than he who is in great need and is not aware of it. Remember Samson? Standing there in the valley of Sorek, surrounded by the lords of the Philistines, ". . . he wist not that the LORD was departed from him" (Judges 16:20).

The pitiable thing about the Pharisees was not so much their hypocrisy as it was their utter lack of knowledge of how poor they actually were in the sight of God.

Jesus told a dramatic story about a man who had mistaken ideas concerning poverty and riches. This man, in a self-satisfied soliloquy, one night said: "Soul, thou hast much goods laid up for many years; take thine ease, eat, drink, and be merry" (Luke 12:19).

It had never occurred to him that the soul cannot subsist on goods and that the heart cannot be nourished by wine and food. Because of his stupidity and his attaching an undue importance to material things, God said: "Thou fool" (Luke 12:20). And to all those of every age who are tempted to reason falsely as he did, God said: "So is he that layeth up treasure for himself, and is not rich toward God" (Luke 12:21).

Each of us has a body with eyes, ears, nose, hands, and feet. This body has certain legitimate desires and appetites: the appetite for food and drink, the appetite for sex, and the appetite for fellowship. Each of these has been given to us by God, to be used as He intended. At the same time, they can be distorted and misused, eventually bringing sorrow and ruin to our lives.

But the Bible teaches that a person is more than just a body—each of us is actually a living soul! Our souls are created in the image of God. Just as our bodies have certain characteristics and appetites, so do our souls. The characteristics of the soul are personality, intelligence, conscience, and memory. The human soul or spirit longs for peace, contentment, and happiness. Most of all, the soul has an appetite for God—a yearning to be reconciled to its Creator and to have fellowship with Him forever.

In the world in which we live, we give most attention to satisfying the appetites of the body and practically none to the soul. Consequently we are one-sided. We become fat physically and materially, while spiritually we are lean, weak, and anemic. Or we spend enormous amounts of time and money on fad diets, expensive exercise machines, and health clubs. For many people, these things only demonstrate their preoccupation with the physical side of life. To be sure, our bodies have been given us by God, and we are to take care of them in every way possible. But even more important is taking care of our souls. The apostle Paul told Timothy, "Train yourself in godliness; for while bodily training is of some value, godliness is of value in every way, as it holds promise for the present life and also for the life to come" (1 Timothy 4:7–8 RSV).

The soul, created in the image of God, cannot be fully satisfied until it knows God in the proper way. Only God can resolve the deepest longings, desires, and appetites of the soul.

I may have the glamour of a movie queen or I may have the riches of a Texas millionaire and still not find happiness, peace, and contentment. Why? Simply because I have given attention to the body but not to the soul.

The soul actually demands as much attention as the body. It demands fellowship and communion with God. It demands worship, quietness, and meditation. Unless the soul is fed and exercised daily, it becomes weak and shriveled. It remains discontented, confused, restless.

Many people turn to alcohol or drugs to try to drown the cryings and longings of the soul. Some turn to a new sex experience. Others attempt to quiet the longings of their souls in other ways. But nothing but God ever completely satisfies, because the soul was made for God, and without God it is restless and in secret torment.

The First Step

The first step to God is a realization of our spiritual poverty. The poor in spirit do not measure the worth of life in earthly possessions, which fade away, but in terms of eternal realities, which endure forever. Wise is the man who openly confesses his lack of spiritual wealth and in humility of heart cries, "God, be merciful unto me, a sinner."

In God's economy, emptying comes before filling, confession before forgiveness, and poverty before riches. Christ said there is a happiness in that acknowledgment of spiritual poverty which lets God come into our souls.

Now, the Bible teaches that our souls have a disease. It is worse than any dreaded cancer or heart disease. It is the plague that causes all the troubles and difficulties in the world. It causes all the troubles, confusions, and disillusionments in our own lives. The name of the disease is an ugly word. We don't like to use it. But it's a word that the psychiatrists are beginning to use once again. In our desire to be modern, we had almost forgotten it, but once again we are beginning to realize that it is the root of all man's troubles. It is *sin.*

We have sinned against our Creator. God is holy, righteous, and just. He cannot allow sin to enter His Presence. Consequently, sin has come between God and us.

Now, there must be a confession that we have broken His laws and are willing to renounce our sins. We must acknowledge that without His fellowship life has no real meaning. This is not easy! All of us have pride, though it may be expressed in various ways. We do not like to confess that we are wrong or that we have failed. But God says: "All have sinned, and come short of the glory of God" (Romans 3:23). We must confess our sin as the first step to happiness, peace, and contentment!

This generation, encouraged by many second-rate philosophies, has tried in vain to live oblivious to God. The current resurgence of religion in the world is a mass confession that Humanism has failed. Like the Laodiceans of old, we have said, "I am rich, and increased with goods, and have need of nothing" (Revelation 3:17); but we have discovered that our riches, like our beauty, are only skin-deep and not sufficient to satisfy our eternal souls.

Let us face this fact: We came into the world with nothing, and we will leave it with nothing.

Where do we get the notion that our idea of success and God's are the same? You have written a book; you are a clever manager and promoter; you are a talented artist; you are independently wealthy; you have achieved fame and fortune. Without the gifts of intelligence, imagination, personality, and physical energy—which are all endowed by God—where would you be?

Are we not born poor? Do we not die poor? And would we not be poor indeed without God's infinite mercy and love? We came out of nothing; and if we are anything, it is because God is everything. If He were to withhold His power for one brief instant from us, if He were to hold in check the breath of life for one moment, our physical existence would shrivel into nothingness and our souls would be whisked away into an endless eternity.

Those who are poor in spirit recognize their creatureliness and their sinfulness—but more, they are ready to confess their sins and renounce them.

The Cure for Our Spiritual Disease

We have seen that the first dimension of "poor in spirit" is a realization of our spiritual poverty. But can our poverty be overcome? Yes! And that leads us to the second dimension of what Jesus meant by being "poor in spirit."

SECOND: If we are to be poor in spirit, *we must receive the riches that Christ has provided by His death and resurrection.*

Would it not be wonderful if we could find an absolute cure for the troubles of human nature? Suppose we could give a shot in the arm to the whole human race that would fill us with love instead of hate, with contentment instead of greed. This would immediately solve all the problems that the world faces at this moment.

Many years ago two Americans were crossing the Atlantic and on a Sunday night they were singing the hymn "Jesus, Lover of My Soul." They were joined by a third party who had a very rich tenor voice. When the music stopped one of the Americans turned to the third party to ask if he had been in the Civil War. The man replied that he had been a Confederate soldier. Then he was asked if he was at a certain place on a certain night and the man replied, "Yes." And he said that a curious thing had happened that night. This hymn recalled it to his mind. "I was on sentry duty at the edge of the wood. It was dark and very cold. I was frightened because the enemy was supposed to be near. I felt homesick and miserable. About midnight, when everything was still, I was beginning to feel so weary I thought I could comfort myself by singing a hymn and I remembered this hymn. 'All my trust on Thee is stayed/all my help from Thee I bring. / Cover my defenseless head / with the shadow of Thy wing.' After I had sung those words, a strange peace came on me and through the long night I felt no fear."

"Well," said one of the men, "listen to my story. I was a Union soldier and I was in the woods that night with a party of scouts. I saw you standing in the woods. My men focused their rifles on you but when you began to sing, we listened. We could not fire and I told them to put down their rifles. 'We'll go home,' I said."

Our daily papers and television newscasts record discontentment and unhappiness all over the world. They are the result of greed, ambition, lust, prejudice, and evil desire. If people could only be content in whatever state they find themselves; if they could love their fellowmen regardless of the color of their skin or their station in life; if those who "have" would show compassion on the "have-nots"; if the greedy would give up their unholy ambition for power—would not this world be a different place in which to live?

Suppose, also, a cure could be found for the past mistakes, failures, and sins of mankind. Suppose by some miracle all the past could be straightened out, all of life's tangles could be unraveled, and the broken strings of life could be repaired. Such a cure would cause a worldwide stampede!

The most thrilling news in all the world is the fact that there is a cure! A medicine has been provided! People can be forgiven of all sin! The cobwebs that have collected in our lives can be removed!

The sin, confusion, and disillusionment of life can be replaced by righteousness, joy, contentment, and happiness. A peace can be imparted to the soul that is not dependent on outward circumstances. This cure was provided by Jesus Christ two thousand years ago on the cross of Calvary.

The cross has become a symbol in much of the Western world, misused by many rock stars and others who do not comprehend its significance.

The death of Christ on that first Good Friday was no mere accident. It was an act of a loving God to reconcile people to Himself. Sin had come between us and God. We could not be happy and contented apart from God. Therefore, in loving grace God sent His Son to bear our sins and to take the penalty and judgment that we deserved.

However, God requires something of us. We must confess our spiritual poverty, renounce our sins, and turn by faith to His Son, Jesus Christ. When we do that, we are born again. He gives us a new nature. He puts a little bit of heaven down in our souls. Our lives change. Contentment, peace, and happiness come into our souls for the first time.

In my travels I have watched for lastingly contented and happy people. I have found such people only where Christ has been personally and decisively received. There is only one permanent way to have peace of soul that wells up in joy, contentment, and happiness, and that is by repentance of sin and personal faith in Jesus Christ as Savior.

Has such a moment come to your life? Have you had the experience of receiving Christ? It is not simply an emotional experience. It is a simple surrender of the will to Christ. Do you really want happiness? Then you will have to pay the price of humbling yourself at the foot of the cross and receiving Christ as Savior.

Our Dependence on God

We must know our spiritual poverty . . . we must turn to Christ in repentance and faith to receive His riches . . . but there is still more if we are to grasp the true meaning of being "poor in spirit."

THIRD: If we are to be poor in spirit, *we must be conscious of our dependence on God,* our spiritual bankruptcy.

Jesus said we must become like children before we can enter the kingdom of heaven. Children are dependents. That is to say, they depend upon their parents for protection and care. Because of their relationship and position they are not poor; but if it were not for their established relationship with their parents, they could be helpless and poor indeed.

When we come to Christ, a wonderful thing immediately happens to us: We become children of God! We become part of His family, as His sons and daughters! "As many as received him, to them gave he power to become the sons of God, even to them that believe on his name: Which were born, not of blood, nor of the will of the flesh, nor of the will of man, but of God" (John 1:12–13). In fact, the Bible uses the idea of "adoption" to illustrate this great fact. At one time we were alienated from God, with no rights or privileges. But in Christ we were adopted into His family (Ephesians 1:5–6). "For ye are all the children of God by faith in Christ Jesus" (Galatians 3:26).

As God's children, we are His dependents. The Bible says: "Like as a father pitieth his children, so the LORD pitieth them that fear him" (Psalm 103:13).

Dependent children spend little time worrying about meals, clothing, and shelter. They assume, and they have a right to, that all will be provided by their parents.

Jesus said: "Take no thought, saying, What shall we eat? or, What shall we drink? or, Wherewithal shall we be clothed? . . . But seek ye first the kingdom of God . . . and all these things shall be added unto you" (Matthew 6:31, 33).

Because God is responsible for our welfare, we are told to cast all our care upon Him, for He cares for us (1 Peter 5:7). Because we are dependent upon God, Jesus said: "Let not your heart be troubled" (John 14:1). God says, "I'll take the burden—don't give it a thought—leave it to Me."

Dependent children are not backward about asking for things. They would not be normal if they did not boldly make their needs known.

God has said to His dependent children: "Therefore come boldly unto the throne of grace, that we may obtain mercy, and find grace to help in time of need" (Hebrews 4:16). God is keenly aware that we are dependent upon Him for life's necessities. It was for that reason that Jesus said: "Ask, and it shall be given you; seek, and ye shall find; knock, and it shall be opened unto you" (Matthew 7:7).

What is troubling you today? Is your heart burdened because of some problem which threatens to overcome you? Are you filled with anxiety and worry about some problem, wondering what will happen? Listen: As a child of God through faith in Christ, you can turn these over to

Christ, knowing that He loves you and He is able to help you. At times He may take the problem away; other times He may give you strength to bear it. But you can rest in Him. "Have no anxiety about anything, but in everything by prayer and supplication with thanksgiving let your requests be made known to God. And the peace of God, which passes all understanding, will keep your hearts and your minds in Christ Jesus" (Philippians 4:6–7 RSV).

Happy is the person who has learned the secret of coming to God daily in prayer. Fifteen minutes alone with God every morning before one starts the day can change our outlooks and recharge our batteries.

But all of this happiness and all of these unlimited benefits which flow from the storehouse of heaven are contingent upon our relationship to God. Absolute dependency and absolute yieldedness are the conditions of being His child. Only His children are entitled to receive those things that lend themselves to happiness; and in order to be His child, there must be the surrender of the will to Him.

We must admit we are poor before we can be made rich. We must admit we are destitute before we can become children by adoption.

When we realize that all our own goodness is as filthy rags in God's sight and become aware of the destructive power of our stubborn wills, when we realize our absolute dependence upon the grace of God through faith and nothing more, then we have started on the road to happiness.

We do not come to know God through works—we come to know Him by faith through grace. We cannot work our way toward happiness and heaven; we cannot moralize our way, we cannot reform our way, we cannot buy our way. Salvation comes as a gift of God through Christ.

Serving Christ

As God's children we are not just meant to sit back and selfishly enjoy our privileges. Instead, God wants to use us to serve Him and help others. But before we can do that, something else must happen in our hearts if we are truly to know the full meaning of Jesus' words: "Happy are the poor in spirit."

FOURTH: If we are to be poor in spirit, *we must willingly deny ourselves that we might better serve Christ.*

The poor in spirit are those who are willing to sell out their stock in themselves and do as Jesus said: "Deny himself, and take up his cross, and follow me" (Matthew 16:24).

Our modern philosophy of self-reliance and self-sufficiency has caused many to believe that man can make the grade without God. "Religion," they argue, "may be all right for certain emotional people, but you can't beat a man who believes in himself." For example, the Austrian neurologist and founder of psychoanalysis, Dr. Sigmund Freud, said that religion was the universal obsessional neurosis.

But alas, this self-confident generation has produced more alcoholics, more drug addicts, more criminals, more wars, more broken homes, more assaults, more embezzlements, more murders, and more suicides than any other generation that ever lived. It is time all of us, from the intellectuals on down, to begin to take stock of our failures, blunders, and costly mistakes. It is about time that we place less confidence in ourselves and more trust and faith in God.

The rich young ruler who came to Jesus was so filled with his piety, his riches, and his greed that he revolted when Jesus informed him that the price of eternal life was to "sell out" and come and follow Him. He went away sorrowfully, the Bible says, because he could not detach himself from himself. He found it impossible to become "poor in spirit" because he had such a lofty estimate of his own importance.

All around us are arrogance, pride, and selfishness: These are the results of sin. From the heavens comes a voice speaking to a tormented, bankrupt world: "I counsel thee to buy of me gold tried in the fire, that thou mayest be rich; and white raiment, that thou mayest be clothed, and that the shame of thy nakedness do not appear; and anoint thine eyes with eyesalve, that thou mayest see. . . . Behold, I stand at the door, and knock: if any man hear my voice, and open the door, I will come in to him, and will sup with him, and he with me" (Revelation 3:18, 20).

Heaven in this life and heaven in the life to come is not on a monetary standard. Nor can flesh and blood find the door to the kingdom of heaven with its contentment, peace, joy, and happiness. Only those who are poor in spirit and are rich toward God shall be accounted worthy to enter there, because they come not in their own merit but in the righteousness of the Redeemer.

Someone has said, "A man's wealth consists not in the abundance of his possessions, but in the fewness of his wants." "The first link between my soul and Christ," said C. H. Spurgeon, "is not my goodness but my badness, not my merit but my misery, not my riches but my need."

"Happy are the poor in spirit: for theirs is the kingdom of heaven!"

Blessed are they that mourn: for they shall be comforted. Matthew 5:4

CHAPTER THREE

Happiness While Mourning

THERE COMES A time in our lives when good-natured, well-meant encouragement like "Hang in there, pal" and "Cheer up, friend" fail to hoist us out of the doldrums. Because our needs are deeper than psychological, such suggestions only seem to make keener our feeling of helplessness.

The truth is: Regardless of our cleverness, our achievements, and our gadgets, we are spiritual paupers without God.

Christ's message was directed to one specific group—to the "poor," the poor in spirit. Christ said: "The Spirit of the Lord is upon me, because he hath anointed me to preach the gospel to the poor" (Luke 4:18). This did not mean that Christ's message was only for the financially poor, the socially poor, or the intellectually poor. It meant that it was for those who recognized their spiritual poverty. That was the first Beatitude. It was the dominant note upon which this celestial anthem of truth was composed. Of the Macedonian Christians Paul wrote, ". . . in a great trial of affliction the abundance of their joy and their deep poverty abounded unto the riches of their liberality" (2 Corinthians 8:2).

If we would find genuine happiness, we must begin where Jesus began. If we would have meaningful lives, we must live by the Beatitudes.

This second Beatitude, "Happy are they that mourn," at first seems paradoxical. Do crying and joy go together? How can we possibly be happy while we are in the throes of mourning? How can one extract the perfume of gladness from the gall of sorrow?

But rest assured that there is deep and hidden significance here, for remember, Jesus was speaking to all people of all beliefs and of all ages and was revealing to them the secret of happiness.

The Shallowness of Our Lives

This present age is definitely not an age of mourning. Instead, people deliberately turn away from anything unpleasant, determined to fill their lives with those things which will divert their minds from anything serious. In their preoccupation with momentary pleasures and diversions, people settle for shallow and empty substitutes for reality. Millions give more thought to what programs they will watch tonight on TNT or what videotape they will rent for the weekend than they do to the things of eternity.

This century could well go down in history not so much as a century of progress but as "the century of superficiality." The popular exclamation "So what!" aptly describes the attitude of many toward life. Many think that so long as we have sleek automobiles to ride in, TV and movies to entertain us, luxurious homes to live in, and a million gadgets to serve us, what happens to our souls does not matter. "So what! Laugh, and the world laughs with you; weep, and you weep alone." The apostles of mirth therefore put on their grimacing masks, turn the volume up on their TVs or press down the accelerators on their sports cars, and plunge into their superficial living.

But superficial living will never help us stand against the pressures and problems of life. At the end of the Sermon on the Mount Jesus told the story of two men. One decided to build his house on sand; it would, after all, have been easy to do. The other built his house on rock, although that would have involved more work. Outwardly both houses looked the same. But when the storms and floods came the house built on sand was destroyed. Only the house built on rock withstood the pressures of the flood. "Therefore whosoever heareth these sayings of mine, and doeth them, I will liken him unto a wise man, which built his house upon a rock" (Matthew 7:24). Only when our lives are grounded in the eternal truth of God's Word will they be able to withstand the storms of life. A superficial life which neglects God can never give us a firm foundation for true happiness.

The following comment appeared in an issue of the *London Times:* "The grace of final perseverance is that quality of patience that is always equal to the pressure of the passing moment, because it is rooted in the Eternal over which the passing moment has no power."

Beverly Sills, the former opera star and now a producer, has learned some lessons in adversity. Her first child was born almost totally deaf. The little girl was destined never to hear her mother's beautiful voice lifted in song. Her second child, a son, was born mentally retarded.

So great was the sorrow in Mrs. Sills's life that she took off a year from her demanding profession to work with her daughter and son, trying to make peace with the difficult circumstances. Later, when she was asked how she came to terms with the situation she answered, "The first question you ask is, Why me? Then it changes to Why them? It makes a complete difference in your attitude." Her attitude is the opposite of superficiality.

Now, I am not gunning for TV addicts or movie buffs in particular, but I do strongly contend that life is more than "skin-deep." Look at your popular comedians! Underneath the feigned smirks and the pretended smiles are the furrows and lines of seriousness and sobriety. Although it is their business to make you laugh, they are well aware that life is a solemn business.

Recently a dear friend of ours was told she had cancer. "It is amazing," she said to us, "how one day you can be going along smoothly and the next day one little word from the doctor's lips—'cancer'—radically changes everything. Then you know as you never have before that life is serious, and eternity is only a heartbeat away. Suddenly many of the things that seemed so important just a day ago are no longer very important."

Jesus did not mean "Blessed are the morose, the miserable, or the sullen." The Pharisees made a masquerade of religion, rubbed ashes on their faces to appear religious, but He strongly rebuked them for that. "Be not, as the hypocrites, of a sad countenance," He said (Matthew 6:16).

Who was it that said, "Some people's religion is like a man with a headache—he can't afford to give up his head, but it hurts him to keep it"?

The Meaning of Mourning

What did Jesus mean when He said: "Happy are they that mourn"? Certainly He did not mean to imply that a special blessing is promised to "crybabies," "weeping Willies," or the emotionally upset. This verse was not intended to be a comfort for abnormal psychopathic cases, which have somehow become mentally warped and take a morbid view of life. No, it was addressed to normal, average people for the purpose of showing them how to live happier, fuller, richer lives.

Let us begin with the word *mourning* itself. It means "to feel deep sorrow, to show great concern, or to deplore some existing wrong." It implies that if we are to live life on the higher plane then we are to be sensitive, sympathetic, tenderhearted, and alert to the needs of others and the world.

Perhaps we can see its meaning more clearly by thinking about its opposite. What is the opposite of mourning? Some might say it would be joy—and that is correct to a certain degree. But more than that, *the opposite of mourning is insensitivity, lack of caring, unconcern, callousness, indifference.* When I mourn it is because my heart has been touched by the suffering and heartache of others—or even by my own heartache. When I do not care and am indifferent, then I do not mourn. The person who mourns is a person with a tender and sensitive heart.

Kinds of Mourning

Let's list just six kinds of mourning which I believe were implied in this most significant saying of our Lord. The word here employed by Jesus covers such a wide range of attitudes that five shades of meaning are implied. We should ponder each one of them prayerfully.

First, there is *the mourning of inadequacy.* Jeremiah, the weeping prophet who mourned not in self-pity but for a wayward, lost world, said: "O LORD, I know that the way of man is not in himself: it is not in man that walketh to direct his steps" (Jeremiah 10:23).

Now, before I can become strong, I must first realize that I am weak. Before I can become wise, I must first realize that I am foolish. Before I can receive power, I must first confess that I am powerless. I must lament my sins before I can rejoice in a Savior. Mourning, in God's sequence, always comes before exultation. Blessed are those who mourn their unworthiness, their helplessness, and their inadequacy.

Isaiah, the mighty prophet of God, knew by experience that one must bow the knee in mourning before one can lift the voice in jubilation. When his sin appeared ugly and venomous in the bright light of God's holiness, he said: "Woe is me! for I am undone; because I am a man of unclean lips . . . for mine eyes have seen the King, the LORD of hosts" (Isaiah 6:5).

We cannot be satisfied with our goodness after beholding the holiness of God. But our mourning over our unworthiness and sinfulness should be of short duration, for God has said: "I, even I, am he that blotteth out thy transgressions for mine own sake, and will not remember thy sins" (Isaiah 43:25).

Isaiah had to experience the mourning of inadequacy before he could realize the joy of forgiveness. If I have no sense of sorrow for sin, how can I know the need of repentance?

In God's economy, a person must go down into the valley of grief before he or she can scale the heights of spiritual glory. One must become tired and weary of living without Christ before he or she can seek and find His fellowship. One must come to the end of "self" before one can really begin to live.

The mourning of inadequacy is a weeping that catches the attention of God. The Bible says: "The LORD is nigh unto them that are of a broken heart; and saveth such as be of a contrite spirit" (Psalm 34:18).

We have received hundreds of letters from people who tried desperately to "get hold of themselves," who in their own strength tried to shake off their habits, their sins, and their nasty dispositions—but all in vain. Finally in desperation they came to Christ, and in Him they found strength to be more than conquerors.

Experience reveals that we are inadequate. History proves that we are inadequate. The Bible declares that a person is inadequate to save himself. Christ's coming to the world proves the inadequacy of the race.

The happiest day of my life was the day I realized that my own ability, my own goodness, and my own morality were insufficient in the sight of God and I publicly and openly acknowledged my need of Christ. I am not exaggerating when I say that my mourning was turned to joy and my sighing into singing.

Happy are they who mourn for the inadequacy of self, for they shall be comforted with the sufficiency of God.

The Mourning of Repentance

Another kind of mourning is *the mourning of repentance.* Following the consciousness that we are inadequate comes the awareness of the reason for our insufficiency—sin. As individuals we have no control over the fact of sin in the universe, but as creatures of choice we are responsible for its presence in our lives. Because "all have sinned, and come short of the glory of God" (Romans 3:23), all need to mourn the fact of sin in their lives.

One technique of modern psychoanalysis is the association of present conflicts with past experiences. Sometimes when patients of psychiatry confess to past sins, they experience a certain release from their feelings of guilt. But since psychiatry is a science of the mind, it can do nothing for the soul. Only Christ is the Physician of the soul.

God has said: "Turn ye even to me with all your heart . . . with weeping, and with mourning" (Joel 2:12).

The mourning of repentance is not the weeping of self-pity; it is not regret over material losses nor remorse that our sins have been found out. It is entirely possible to be deeply sorry because of the devastation which sin has wrought in our lives—and yet not repent. I have had people pour out their hearts to me with tears, because their sins have been discovered and they are in serious trouble. But true repentance is more than being sorry for our sins and regretting the way we have allowed sin to shatter our lives. True repentance is a turning *from* sin—a conscious, deliberate decision to leave sin behind—and a conscious turning *to God* with a commitment to follow His will for our lives. It is a change of direction, an alteration of attitudes, and a yielding of the will. Humanly speaking, it is our small part in the plan of salvation—although even the strength to repent comes from God. But even so, the act of repentance does not win us any merit or make us worthy to be saved—it only conditions our hearts for the grace of God.

The Bible says: "Repent ye therefore, and be converted, that your sins may be blotted out, when the times of refreshing shall come from the presence of the Lord" (Acts 3:19). Our part is repenting. God will do the converting, the transforming, and the forgiving.

It will not be easy to bend our warped, stubborn wills; but once we do, it will be as though a misplaced vertebra has snapped back into place. Instead of the stress and tension of a life out of harmony with God will come the serenity of reconciliation. Our nerves will sense that our minds and hearts are relaxed, and they will send this happy news over their network to every fiber of our bodies: "Old things are passed away; behold, all things are become new" (2 Corinthians 5:17).

Just as pain precedes birth, mourning over sin comes before spiritual rebirth. I do not mean to imply that in everyone's experience there will be loud, violent weeping over the sin in one's life—sorrow for sin may come quietly, with little or no emotion. But there will be a sincere sorrow for the evils of one's life and a disposition to turn to God for help and salvation. The Bible says: "For godly sorrow worketh repentance" (2 Corinthians 7:10).

The Mourning of Love

There is yet another aspect of this Beatitude, "Happy are they that mourn." There is, third, *the mourning of love.*

In many of the older cars the fuel gauge used to contain a red liquid, and its level in the gauge corresponded to the level of fuel in the tank. As the liquid was in the gauge, so it was in the tank.

If I would know the measure of my love for God, I must simply observe my love for people around me. My compassion for others is an accurate gauge of my devotion to God.

The Bible puts it this way: "Let us love one another: for love is of God; and every one that loveth is born of God, and knoweth God. . . . And this commandment have we from him, That he who loveth God love his brother also" (1 John 4:7, 21).

Some time ago, with some friends, I went through a museum in San Francisco. Among other things, we saw a collection of instruments of torture which were employed by religious people to force other people to believe as they did. History is largely the record of man's inhumanity to man.

This age in which we live could hardly be described as one in which people are honestly sensitive to the needs of others. We have developed a veneer of sophistication—but also cynicism and hardness. Our popular music talks constantly about love, and yet divorce rates skyrocket, child abuse is rampant, and our world is shaken by wars, violence, and terrorism. Major newsmagazines feature cover stories on "The 'Me' Generation." This generation, it seems, would rather see a prizefight than fight for a prize. Not only has the song "Rescue the perishing, care for the dying" disappeared from most of our songbooks, its theme has disappeared from our hearts, except for physical famine, victims of oppressive regimes, and tidal waves. And these are terribly important. It is just that the spiritually perishing need to hear the gospel.

Several years ago we were visiting India. While we were there a terrible tidal wave hit a fifty-mile section of the coast, killing tens of thousands of people and completely destroying hundreds of villages and towns. Indian officials graciously provided a helicopter and accompanied us to the area, and we were among the first to view the devastation. I will never forget the terrible destruction and the stench of death—as if a thousand atom bombs had gone off at the same time. And yet this terrible disaster rated only a few inches in many American newspapers and only a minute or so on the evening news.

Abraham Lincoln once said, characteristically: "I am sorry for the man who can't feel the whip when it is laid on the other man's back."

Much of the world is callous and indifferent toward mankind's poverty and distress. This is due largely to the fact that for many people there has never been a rebirth. The love of God has never been shed abroad in their hearts.

Many people speak of the social gospel as though it were separate and apart from the redemptive gospel. The truth is: There is only one gospel. Divine love, like a reflected sunbeam, shines down before it radiates out. Unless our hearts are conditioned by the Holy Spirit to receive and reflect the warmth of God's compassion, we cannot love our fellowmen as we ought.

Jesus wept tears of compassion at the graveside of a friend. He mourned over Jerusalem because as a city it had lost its appreciation of the things of the spirit. His great heart was sensitive to the needs of others.

To emphasize the importance of people's love for each other, He revised an old commandment to make it read: "Thou shalt love the Lord thy God with all thy heart . . . and thy neighbor as thyself" (Luke 10:27).

St. Francis of Assisi had discovered the secret of happiness when he prayed:

> *O Divine Master, grant that I may not so much seek*
> *To be consoled as to console,*
> *To be understood as to understand,*

To be loved as to love;
For it is in giving that we receive;
It is in pardoning that we are pardoned;
It is in dying that we are born to eternal life!

This generation is rough and tough. I heard a little boy boasting one day about how tough he was. He said, "On the street I live on, the farther out you go the tougher they get, and I live in the last house."

Tears shed for self are tears of weakness, but tears of love shed for others are a sign of strength. I am not as sensitive as I ought to be until I am able to "weep o'er the erring one and lift up the fallen." And until I have learned the value of compassionately sharing others' sorrow, distress, and misfortune, I cannot know real happiness.

The Mourning of Soul Travail

Another kind of mourning which brings comfort is, fourth, *the mourning of soul travail.*

This may seem cryptic, but it represents a very real and a profitable kind of mourning. The Bible says: "As soon as Zion travailed, she brought forth her children" (Isaiah 66:8).

We don't use this phrase "soul travail" very often, not as much as our spiritual forefathers a generation or so ago. *Travail* means "toil, painful effort, labor." "Travail of soul" therefore means spiritual toil—not necessarily outward labor which others will see, but that which takes place within the secret recesses of our souls. It refers to the continual flow of prayer which rises out of the Christian heart for a world which is spiritually unborn. And don't be under any illusions: This kind of soul travail is difficult and costly, because we are involved in spiritual warfare against Satan, the Enemy of Souls. "Pray without ceasing," the Bible says (1 Thessalonians 5:17).

God has worked in a miraculous way in our crusades down through the years. Thousands of men and women have made their decisions for Christ. Their coming was not the result of one man's work or the efforts of a group of men— it was the product of much prayer by many people around the world. God has said: "If my people . . . pray . . . then will I hear from heaven" (2 Chronicles 7:14).

Before three thousand people were brought into the Church on the day of Pentecost, the disciples had spent fifty days in prayer, fasting, and spiritual travail.

John Knox, with an all-consuming soul-concern for his country, prayed: "Give me Scotland, or I die!" His earnest travail was rewarded with a spiritual rebirth in his land. This is what is termed "praying in the Spirit." It is the manifestation of a deep spiritual concern for others, and it is instilled by the Spirit of God.

The Bible says: "For we know not what we should pray for as we ought: but the Spirit itself maketh intercession for us with groanings which cannot be uttered" (Romans 8:26).

This kind of prayer can span oceans, cross burning deserts, leap over mountains, and penetrate jungles to carry the healing, helping power of the gospel to the objects of our prayer.

This kind of mourning, this quality of concern, is produced by the presence of God's Spirit in our lives. That "the Spirit itself maketh intercession" indicates that it is actually God pleading, praying, and mourning through us. Thus we become co-laborers with God, actual partners with Him: Our lives are lifted from the low plane of selfishness to the high plane of creativeness with God.

John Knox travailed in prayer, and the Church in Scotland expanded into new life. John Wesley travailed in prayer, and the Methodist movement was born. Martin Luther travailed, and the Reformation was under way.

God desires that we Christians be concerned and burdened for a lost world. If we pray this kind of prayer, an era of peace may come to the world and hordes of wickedness may be turned back. "As soon as Zion travailed, she brought forth her children" (Isaiah 66:8).

The Mourning of Suffering and Bereavement

Another kind of mourning we shall deal with is, fifth, *the mourning of bereavement.*

Nowhere has God promised anyone, even His children, immunity from sorrow, suffering, and pain. This world is a "vale of tears," and disappointment and heartache are as inevitable as clouds and shadows. Suffering is often the crucible in which our faith is tested. Those who successfully come through the "furnace of affliction" are the ones who emerge "like gold tried in the fire."

The Bible teaches unmistakably that we can triumph over bereavement. The psalmist said: "Weeping may endure for a night, but joy cometh in the morning" (Psalm 30:5).

Self-pity can bring no enduring comfort. The fact is, it will only add to our misery. And unremitting grief will give us little consolation in itself, for grief begets grief. Ceaseless grieving will only magnify our sorrow. We should not peddle our sorrows and bewail our bad fortune—that will only depress others. Sorrow, or mourning, when it is borne in a Christian way, contains a built-in comfort. "Blessed are they that mourn: for they shall be comforted" (Matthew 5:4).

There is comfort in mourning *because we know that Christ is with us.* He has said: "Lo, I am with you alway, even unto the end of the world" (Matthew 28:20). Suffering is endurable if we do not have to bear it alone; and the more compassionate the Presence, the less acute the pain.

How often when a child have you stubbed your toe, bruised a leg, or cut a hand, and, running to the arms of your mother, you there sobbed out your pain? Lovingly caressing you and tenderly kissing the hurt, she imparted the magic of healing; and you went your way half healed and wholly comforted. Love and compassion contain a stronger balm than all the salves and ointments made by man.

Yes, when a loved one dies it is natural for us to feel a sense of loss and even a deep loneliness. That will not necessarily vanish overnight. But even when we feel the pain of bereavement most intensely, we can also know the gracious and loving presence of Christ most closely. Christ—who suffered alone on the cross, and endured death and hell alone for our salvation—knows what it is to suffer and be lonely. And because He knows, He is able to comfort us by His Presence. "Blessed be God, even the Father of our Lord Jesus Christ, the Father of mercies, and the God of all comfort; who comforteth us in all our tribulation, that we may be able to comfort them which are in any trouble, by the comfort wherewith we ourselves are comforted of God" (2 Corinthians 1:3–4).

So, in our lives, there can be a blessedness in the midst of mourning. From suffering and bereavement God can bring into our lives new measures of His strength and love.

Jesus said, "Let not your heart be troubled . . . believe . . . in me" (John 14:1). When faith is strong, troubles become trifles.

There is also comfort in mourning *because in the midst of mourning God gives a song.* God says in Job 30:9: "I am their song." In Job 35:10 Elihu asks, "Where is God my maker, who giveth songs in the night?" His presence in our lives changes our mourning into song, and that song is a song of comfort. Sometimes it must be night to have that song!

This kind of comfort is the kind which enabled a devout Englishman to look at a deep, dark hole in the ground where his home stood before the bombing and say, "I always did want a basement, I did. Now I can jolly well build another house like I always wanted."

This kind of comfort is the kind which enabled a young minister's wife in a church near us to teach her Sunday school class of girls on the very day of her husband's funeral. Her mourning was not the kind which had no hope—it was a mourning of faith in the goodness and wisdom of God; it believed that our Heavenly Father makes no mistakes.

In addition, there can be comfort in mourning *because God can use our sufferings to teach us and make us better people.* Often it takes suffering to make us realize the brevity of life, and the importance of living for Christ. Often God uses suffering to accomplish things in our lives that would otherwise never be achieved.

The Bible puts it succinctly: "Count it all joy, my brethren, when you meet various trials, for you know that the testing of your faith produces steadfastness. And let steadfastness have its full effect, that you may be perfect and complete, lacking in nothing" (James 1:2–4 RSV). Some of the godliest people I have ever known were men and women who had been called upon to endure great suffering—perhaps even being invalids for many years. Many people would have grown bitter and resentful if they had faced such circumstances—and yet because they knew Christ and walked in the joy of His presence every day, God had blessed them and turned them into people who reflected Christ. Often I have gone into a sickroom or hospital room to encourage someone—and have left feeling I was the one who had been encouraged and helped, because God had used their trials to make them more like Christ.

Before the power of the atom was discovered, science had to devise a way to "smash" the atom. The secret of the atom's immeasurable and limitless power was in its being crushed.

Dr. Edward Judson, at the dedication of the Judson Memorial Church in New York City, said, "Suffering and success go together. If you are succeeding without suffering, it is because others before you have suffered; if you are suffering without succeeding, it is that others after you may succeed."

Most of all, there is comfort in mourning *because we know that this life is not all, but we have the hope of heaven.* Paul said, "If in this life only we have hope in Christ, we are of all men most miserable" (1 Corinthians 15:19). But he knew that our hope was not just in this life, but in heaven. Our hope is in the resurrected Christ, who has opened the door to eternal life for all who put their trust in Him. "O death, where is thy sting? O grave, where is thy victory? . . . Thanks be to God, which giveth us the victory through our Lord Jesus Christ" (1 Corinthians 15:55, 57).

I will never forget the last few months of my mother's life, just before she went to be with the Lord. During those months she grew weaker and weaker physically—but her joy and excitement about heaven grew stronger and stronger! Whenever anyone went to visit her they came away marveling at her radiance and sense of expectancy. Yes, when she died there were tears—but in the midst of them, those of us who loved her had a deep sense of joy and comfort because we knew she was with the Lord. "Happy are they that mourn, for they shall be comforted."

This was the apostle Paul's hope—a hope based squarely on the fact of Jesus' resurrection. "We are troubled on every side, yet not distressed. . . . Though our outward man perish, yet the inward man is renewed day by day. For our light affliction, which is but for a moment, worketh for us a far more exceeding and eternal weight of glory; while we look not at the things which are seen, but at the things which are not seen: for the things which are seen are temporal; but the things which are not seen are eternal" (2 Corinthians 4:8, 16–18). Jesus declared, "I am the resurrection, and the life: he that believeth in me, though he were dead, yet shall he live: And whosoever liveth and believeth in me shall never die" (John 11:25–26).

Do you have that hope in your heart? Do you know that if you were to die tonight you would go to heaven to be with Christ forever? You can, if you will trust Christ as your personal Savior and Lord. Jesus promised, "I go to prepare a place for you . . . that where I am, there ye may be also" (John 14:2–3).

"Blessed (happy) are they that mourn." They are happy because they know that their aim, their distress, and their privation are the travail of a new creation, the birth pangs of a better world. They are happy because they are aware that the Master Artist—God—is employing both light and shadow to produce a masterpiece worthy of divine artistry. They are also made to glory in their infirmities, to smile through their tears, and to sing in the midst of their sorrow because they realize that in God's economy, "if we suffer, we shall also reign with him" (2 Timothy 2:12).

The Mourning of Blank Despair

Last, there is *the mourning of blank despair.* "I could not think about my own death," says one young AIDS victim. "I wanted to live forever."

The tragedy of AIDS is obvious. But as C. S. Lewis said of war, "War does not increase death. Death is total in every generation." So it could be said of AIDS; it does not increase death; death is total in every generation.

However, in this present grim situation, a merciful God has given people time. A short time perhaps, torn with frustration, anger, bitterness, and fear—but still time. Time to think of God, His love for a world gone wrong, the sending of His Son to bear in His own body on the cross, all the sins of mankind. Time to come to Him in child-like repentance and to discover the love of Jesus, His transforming power, and the life everlasting that He promises and has gone to prepare for us.

Blessed are the meek: for they shall inherit the earth. Matthew 5:5

CHAPTER FOUR

Happiness Through Meekness

MOST OF US seek shortcuts to happiness. We search for the gold nuggets of spiritual satisfaction on the surface instead of in the depths, where they are found in abundance. It is only natural to follow the line of least resistance, forgetting all the while that heat and light are both products of resistance, a resistance which releases the latent forces of life.

Many of us are like the man out West who had a junkyard. He labored hard and long, buying and selling the old salvage he gathered from the back alleys of the city. But one day he discovered that his junkyard was located on an oil field. He hired a drilling crew, and soon the black gold flowed abundantly from the bosom of the earth. His junkyard was transformed into a veritable mine of wealth which knew no limits.

In these Beatitudes we have a mine of spiritual gold. To many it seems too good to be true, so they go their way, scratching around on the surface of life, picking up salvage in the form of gadgets, gold, and gimmicks. Because they ignore the challenge and the promise of these secrets of happiness, they miss the key to radiant living and remain spiritual paupers, submerged in a misery of their own making.

They forget that what happens *within* them is more important than what happens *to* them. Because they have built no inner fortifications, they fall prey to the Enemy. They become filled with resentments and are baffled by frustration and depressed by disillusionment.

Would God have bothered to send His Son to the world if we had been able to face life and eternity alone? Christ's coming to the world proved that God was not happy with our unhappiness. He sent Him not only that we might have eternal life but that we might have life here and now, and that we might have it more abundantly—Life with a capital *L!*

Jesus' teaching was unique and different. He took religion out of the theoretical realm and placed it in the practical. He used no qualifying statements or phrases in declaring His way of life. He didn't use such phrases as "I venture to say" or "Perhaps it's this way" or "It is my considered opinion."

He spoke with authority! He spoke with finality! He spoke as though He knew . . . and He did! When the Sermon on the Mount was completed we read that "the people were astonished at his doctrine: for he taught them as one having authority, and not as the scribes" (Matthew 7:28–29).

His was not the soft, empty conjecture of the philosopher who professes to search for truth but readily admits he has never found it. It was more the confident voice of the mathematician who gives his answers unhesitatingly because the proof of the answer can be found within the problem.

He taught with authority because He was more than just another religious teacher—He was God Himself, who had come down in human flesh. His words are true, because He is God and God cannot lie. "God . . . hath in these last days spoken unto us by his Son, whom he hath appointed heir of all things, by whom also he made the worlds" (Hebrews 1:1–2). And because He is God incarnate, we can depend totally and absolutely on the trustworthiness of Him and His Word.

In this third Beatitude we have the words "[Happy] are the meek: for they shall inherit the earth." Has it ever occurred to you that there is happiness in meekness?

Searching for the Meaning of Meekness

To most people today the word *meek* brings to mind a picture of someone who is a weak personality, someone who allows everyone to walk over him. Meekness, in fact, in the popular mind is not seen as a desirable personality trait. Our society says, "Get ahead by intimidation" or "Look out for Number One." In the eyes of many people the only way to get ahead is to disregard other people and shove them out of the way. "I want to climb the ladder of success," one woman was quoted as saying, "and I don't care whose fingers I step on as I climb up the rungs."

But what does Jesus mean when He speaks of meekness? Does He, for example, mean that we are to be cringing before God, fearful of Him and slavishly yielding to His will because of fear of what He might do to us if we fail?

Could it be that Christ wanted His followers to be like the subdued puppy that comes crawling into its master's presence whipped and beaten? Is happiness the result of forced submission? Certainly not!

Jesus is not trying to convey the thought that God is an autocrat whose ego can be satisfied only by coerced yielding. Nothing could be further from the truth. There is no happiness in being compelled to do what you do not wish to do. No employees are more miserable than those who constantly resent their position in life. It would be against God's nature, as well as against man's free moral agency, to demand an allegiance which is not freely offered.

God conducts Himself in keeping with His righteousness. He will never violate our freedom to choose between eternal life and spiritual death, good and evil, right and wrong. His ultimate goal is not only to glorify Himself but also to make a happy relationship with His crowning creation—man. Never will He make any demands which encroach upon our freedom to choose.

Or does the meekness to which Jesus refers mean *weakness?* Does it mean that a special blessing is to be given to the feeble, the frail, or the fragile?

Certainly God has a special concern for those who are weak and powerless in this world. "Like as a father pitieth his children, so the LORD pitieth them that fear him. For he knoweth our frame; he remembereth that we are dust" (Psalm 103:13–14). But this is not what Jesus means by meekness here. The disciples were to be meek, but not weak and vacillating. They were to be disciplined, but not subdued and harmless in the face of evil.

Or does Jesus refer to those who are by nature mild-tempered? Some people are born with nicer dispositions than others. Their mild manner is not so much the product of prayer and spiritual grace as it is a matter of heredity. They are mild because their mother or father or grandmother was mild-mannered. This is an admirable trait, but Jesus surely didn't refer to these fortunate few who by nature have good dispositions. That would mean that many who have dispositions like buzz saws could never know this happiness to which He refers.

In His characteristic way, Jesus was saying something quite shocking and quite revolutionary to His listeners in these words: "Happy are the meek." He was saying something quite the opposite to our modern concept of the way to happiness.

We say, "Happy are the clever, for these shall inherit the admiration of their friends"; "Happy are the aggressive, for they shall inherit prosperity"; "Happy are the talented, for they shall inherit a career"; "Happy are the rich, for they shall inherit a world of friends and a house full of modern gadgets."

The True Meaning of Meekness

What, then, did Jesus mean? The dictionary says that the word *meek* means "mild, submissive, and compliant." William Barclay points out that the Greek word for "meek" was the word which was often used to describe an animal which had been tamed to obey the command of its master. It might be a strong animal like a horse or ox, able to do a great deal of work. It was not "weak"—but it was "meek," always obedient to the will of its owner. A tame horse contributes much more to life than a wild one. Energy out of control is dangerous; energy under control is powerful.

That is a vivid picture of what Jesus means by "meekness." When we are apart from Christ we are, in a sense, like a wild animal. We live according to our own desires and wishes, obeying our own instincts and ruling our own lives. But when we come to Christ our goal is different. Now we want to live for Him and do His will. This, after all, is God's will for us, for Christ "died for all, that they which live should not henceforth live unto themselves, but unto him which died for them, and rose again" (2 Corinthians 5:15). We are "meek," submissive to the will of our Master and ready to work for Him. And when our lives and hearts are marked by true meekness, we will know true happiness.

Jesus did not say, "Be meek, and you shall inherit the earth." He, more than anyone else, knew that meekness was a gift of God, a result of a rebirth, a new life within.

Moses was meek, but he was not meek by nature. He slew an Egyptian in anger, and on more than one occasion he showed that he was not naturally meek. When he found the children of Israel turning from the Lord and worshiping idols, he became angry and dashed to the ground the tablets of stone upon which were inscribed the Ten Commandments. His meekness quite obviously was contrary to his nature. It was a miracle of God! Numbers 12:3 says, "Now the man Moses was very meek, above all the men which were upon the face of the earth."

Peter was not meek by nature. He became angry and cut off the ear of a guard who had come to arrest Jesus. (And I think we can safely assume he was aiming for his neck!) He swore profusely and angrily when accused of being one of Jesus' disciples. And yet he became one of the meekest of men and one of the strongest, most virile exponents of Christianity. Where did he get his meekness?

Paul, before his conversion, was not meek. Proudly and brutally he apprehended all Christians and sought to destroy them. He was bigoted, selfish, and boastful. But when he wrote his warm and affectionate letter to the churches of Galatia, he said, among other things: "The fruit of the Spirit is . . . gentleness, goodness . . . meekness" (Galatians 5:22–23). His meekness was something God-given, not something man-made.

It is not our human nature to be meek. On the contrary, it is our nature to be proud and haughty. That is why the new birth is so essential to each of us. That is why Jesus frankly and pointedly said not only to Nicodemus but to every one of us: "Ye must be born again" (John 3:7).

Meekness begins there! You must have a change of nature. Do you want this happiness? Then you must be born again—this is the first step! If you are too proud, stubborn, and willful to take this first step, then you do not qualify to inherit the earth.

When we reject this command of Christ, we automatically forfeit our right to His subsequent promises. We cannot end right when we begin wrong. If there is no rebirth, there can be no imparted meekness. And if there is no meekness, there can be no genuine happiness.

Arrogance has its own built-in misery. Arrogant people may offend others, but they hurt themselves more. My feelings of anger hurt me more than they do the people I'm angry at!

I was once stung by a honeybee. The sting hurt me, but it killed the bee. It died as a result of that thrust, but I didn't. In like manner, I may lash out at someone in anger. Yes, they may be hurt by my action—but like the bee I am the one who is hurt even more.

Muggings and vigilante attacks in retaliation have become commonplace; and they are only the tip of the iceberg. Fathers and mothers wrangle and bicker. Abuse of children and the elderly is rampant. Homes are disintegrating. High government officials in Washington engage in name-calling and in heated disputes not at all in keeping with the dignity of their office.

Why and how has all this savagery crept into our social life? It is because we have forgotten Jesus' words: "Happy are the meek: for they shall inherit the earth."

We have glamorized vice and minimized virtue. We have played down gentleness, manners, and morals—while we have played up rudeness, savagery, and vice. We have reverted to the barbaric era of "tooth and claw," "the survival of the fittest," and the philosophy of "might is right." We are rich in knowledge but poor in wisdom; rich in the know-how of war but sadly lacking in gentleness, meekness, and faith.

Individually, we are mechanisms of resentment, irritation, bitterness, and frustration!

Meekness Means Gentleness

The word *gentle* was rarely heard of before the Christian era and the word *gentleman* was not known. This high quality of character was a direct by-product of Christian faith.

The Bible says: "The wisdom that is from above is first pure, then peaceable, *gentle,* and easy to be intreated, full of mercy and good fruits, without partiality, and without hypocrisy" (James 3: 17, emphasis added).

St. Francis of Sales said: "Nothing is so strong as gentlemen; nothing so gentle as real strength." Charles Dickens wrote: "A man can never be a true gentleman in manner until he is a true gentleman at heart."

I have seen tough, rough, hardened men open their hearts by faith, receive Christ as Savior and become gentle, patient, merciful gentlemen.

I remember, when we were in London, the Ford Motor Company lent us two new Fords and employed two drivers to take our team to their various assignments. One of the chauffeurs was a typical roughneck who had missed little of what this world had to offer. He came to the meetings and looked on the scene perfunctorily with an occupational detachment. But one night he was moved to go to the counseling room and make his decision for Christ. You never saw such a change come over a man! His hardness disappeared; his veneer of sophistication melted away. He was a new creature! He threw away his X-rated literature, began to memorize the New Testament, and took on the true marks of a Christian gentleman. The fruit of the Spirit is ". . . gentleness, goodness . . . *meekness*" (Galatians 5:22–23, emphasis added).

Of Eric Liddell, the missionary and great runner whose story is told in the film *Chariots of Fire,* someone has said, he was ". . . ridiculously humble in victory, utterly generous in defeat." That's a good definition of what it means to be meek.

Meekness Involves Yieldedness

The word *yield* has two meanings. The first is negative and the second is positive. It means "to relinquish, to abandon"; and also "to give." This is in line with Jesus' words: "He that loseth [or abandoneth] his life . . . shall find it" (Matthew 10:39).

We have heard the modern expression "Don't fight it—it's bigger than both of us." Those who are meek do not fight back at life. They learn the secret of surrender, of yielding to God. He then fights for us!

The Bible says: "For as ye have yielded your members servants to uncleanness and to iniquity . . . even so now yield your members servants to righteousness unto holiness" (Romans 6:19).

Instead of filling your mind with resentments, abusing your body by sinful diversion, and damaging your soul by willfulness, humbly give all over to God. Your conflicts will disappear and your inner tensions will vanish into thin air.

Then your life will begin to count for something. It will begin to yield, to produce, to bear fruit. You will have the feeling of belonging to life. Boredom will melt away and you will become vibrant with hope and expectation. Because you are meekly yielded, you will begin to "inherit the earth" of good things which God holds in store for those who trust Him with their all.

Even science teaches in unmistakable terms the Christian concept of entire surrender. Thomas Huxley once wrote to Charles Kingsley: "Science says to sit down before the facts as a little child, be prepared to give up every preconceived notion, be willing to be led to whatever end Nature will lead you, or you will know nothing." S. I. McMillen said: "Surrendering one's will to the divine will may seem a negative procedure, but it gives positive dividends."

Happy are the meek. Happy are the yielded. Happy are those who trustingly put their lives, their fortunes, and their futures in the capable hands of their Creator. Happy are those who "let go and let God."

God does not discipline us to subdue us, but to condition us for a life of usefulness and blessedness. In His wisdom He knows that an uncontrolled life is an unhappy life, so He puts reins upon our wayward souls that they may be directed into the "paths of righteousness." That is what God seeks to do with us: to tame us, to bring us under proper control so we can do His will.

"I beseech you therefore, brethren, by the mercies of God, that ye present your bodies a living sacrifice, holy, acceptable unto God, which is your reasonable service. And be not conformed to this world: but be ye transformed by the renewing of your mind, that ye may prove what is that good, and acceptable, and perfect, will of God" (Romans 12:1–2).

God does in the spiritual realm what science does in the physical realm. Science takes a Niagara River with its violent turbulence and transforms it into electrical energy to illuminate a million homes and to turn the productive wheels of industry.

God took Peter—a zealot, a political reactionary of his day—and diverted his energy and his unbounding enthusiasm to high purposes instead of low, and he helped lead a movement which reshaped the world.

He took Matthew—a suave, tricky politician, who knew the political ropes well enough to keep from dangling from one of them by the neck—and, putting the bridle of grace upon him, changed him into an agent of blessing.

God had to do a job of taming with each of the disciples. Taming was not a matter of doing away with their powers and their energies but of *redirecting* them.

You have a *temper!* There is nothing unique about that. Most people have tempers, in varying degrees of course. God does not ask that you get rid of that temper. But He does say that if you are to be happy, it must be brought under control and rechanneled to proper use. God does not use a person without a temper as well as He does one with a controlled temper. There are too many professed Christians who never get "wrought up" about anything; they never get indignant with injustice, with corruption in high places, or with the godless traffics which barter away the souls and bodies of people. Someone has said, "There are some things that don't improve the longer you keep them. There are others that do. Your temper is one of them." The Bible warns about an uncontrolled temper: "A wrathful man stirreth up strife: but he that is slow to anger appeaseth strife" (Proverbs 15:18).

You have an *ego*—a consciousness of being an individual! Of course you do, and God does not ask you to get rid of that ego. In fact, it is important for us to have a right understanding of our value and importance—what the psychologists call a healthy self-image. But we develop that best when we begin to see ourselves as God sees us—as persons who are so valuable to Him that He wants us to be forgiven and cleansed of sin so we can be His children. But that doesn't mean that you are to worship yourself, to think constantly of yourself, and to live entirely for self. Common sense tells you that your life would be miserable if you followed that course. God is infinitely more concerned about your happiness than you could possibly be. He says, "Deny yourself, and follow Me."

There are people in our mental institutions today who thought excessively about themselves, to the exclusion of God and others. Hypochondriacs who have a fanciful anxiety about their health will never be well regardless of their physical condition. They remind me of the people who have this sign on their desk: "*I* am planning to have a nervous breakdown. *I* have earned it. *I* deserve it. *I* worked for it and nobody is going to keep me from having it!"

Each of us has a *tongue* and a *voice.* These instruments of speech can be used destructively or employed constructively. I can use my tongue to slander, to gripe, to scold, to nag, and to quarrel; or I can bring it under the control of God's Spirit and make it an instrument of blessing and praise. The Bible says, "The tongue is a little member, and boasteth great things. Behold, how great a matter a little fire kindleth! And the tongue is a fire, a world of iniquity" (James 3:5–6). Only God can control it, as we yield it to Him.

The twentieth-century version of James 3:3 says, "When we put bits into the horses' mouths to make them obey us, we control the rest of their bodies also." Just so, when we submit to the claims of Christ upon our lives, our untamed natures are brought under His control. We become meek, tamed, and "fit for the Master's service."

Meekness Denotes Forbearance

Forbearance is a word which has been almost dropped from our modern vocabulary. It means to abstain from condemning others, to refrain from judging the actions and motives of those about us.

The Bible says: "With all lowliness and meekness, with longsuffering, forbearing one another in love" (Ephesians 4:2).

This generation is quick with the deadly thrust but slow with the ointment of healing. The harsh criticism of others and unfair appraisals of those about us may hurt them, but it hurts us more. The unjust condemnation of others has a boomerang effect. I hurl my vindictive indictments with the hope of crippling others, but, alas, I discover that I am hurt more than they are.

Many a person is lonely today because he has driven away by his own bitterness and harsh words the very friends he needs. Many a wife has discovered that scolding and nagging will never win a husband but often result in a divorce situation.

Some people go through their entire lives with a "chip on their shoulder," carrying hurts and resentments over things that were said or done decades ago. Like a poison, their bitterness has made not only their own lives miserable but the lives of those around them. They have never learned the secret of forgiveness and forbearance. The Bible warns us to be on guard "lest any root of bitterness springing up trouble you, and thereby many be defiled" (Hebrews 12:15).

Meekness and forbearance are "musts" if I am to live harmoniously in society and if I want to build a happy family life.

The Bible says: "Speak evil of no man . . . but [be] gentle, showing all meekness unto all men" (Titus 3:2). I cannot be happy as long as I magnify the faults of others and minimize their virtues. This is a good way to frighten away my friends, forfeit my domestic happiness, and fritter away a rosy future.

Here is the Christian answer to neighborhood quarrels, to family fusses, and to community feuds: "Forbearing one another, and forgiving one another, if any man have a quarrel against any: even as Christ forgave you, so also do ye" (Colossians 3:13).

There is a story told of a devout old deacon who, goaded apparently beyond endurance by the persistent malice of an enemy, publicly vowed to "kill him." His enemy heard of his intentions and waited sardonically to see what the harmless old saint would do. Actually, instead of rendering evil for evil, the old deacon sought out every opportunity to do his enemy good. This was at first a source of merriment and some slight annoyance, but when at last the deacon rendered an unquestioned sacrificial service to his enemy by risking his life to save the man's wife from drowning, the deadlock between them was broken.

"All right," said his enemy, "you've done what you said you would do. You've killed me—or at least you've killed the man I was. Now, what can I do for you?"

This world is not yet impervious to a solid Christian act! What the world needs is not more Christianity but more Christians who practice Christian forbearance and forgiveness.

Meekness Suggests Patience

This is a high-strung, neurotic, impatient age. We hurry when there is no reason to hurry, just to be hurrying. This fast-paced age has produced more problems and less morality than previous generations, and it has given all of us a set of jangled nerves. Thomas à Kempis said: "All men commend patience, although few be willing to practice it." John F. Newton wrote: "Be patient enough to live one day at a time as Jesus taught us, letting yesterday go, and leaving tomorrow till it arrives."

Impatience has produced a new crop of broken homes, a million or more new ulcers, and has set the stage for more world wars. In no area of our lives has it been more damaging than on the domestic scene. This homely little couplet bespeaks the rack and ruin modern life has wrought in our homes:

Theirs was a "beef stew" marriage,
And their case was somewhat crude—
The wife was always "beefing,"
And the husband, always "stewed."

But the Bible says: "Let patience have her perfect work, that ye may be perfect and entire, wanting nothing" (James 1:4).

I know of a woman—a professed Christian—who, though good in many respects, was very impatient. Her pastor one day spoke to her husband about his soul, and the man replied, "My wife is a good homemaker, but if religion would make me as impatient as she is, I want no part of it."

The minister had a frank talk with the woman, and in tears and humility she confessed that her sin was the sin of impatience. A few days later her husband came in from fishing. As he walked through the living room with rod in hand, he accidentally knocked over a prized vase that went crashing to the floor. His wife ran into the room, and he braced himself for the second crash—a tirade of words from his nervous wife. But instead, she smilingly said, "Think nothing of it, dear, accidents happen in the best of families."

We will not pursue the story any further except to say that a few weeks later he made his decision for Christ and became a staunch worker in the church. He saw Christianity in practice in the life of his wife!

The apostle Peter declared that some husbands "though they do not obey the word, may be won without a word by the behavior of their wives, when they see your reverent and chaste behavior . . . with the imperishable jewel of a gentle and quiet spirit, which in God's sight is very precious" (1 Peter 3:1–2, 4 RSV).

The world believes that Christianity is a good thing, but Christians have too often failed to "adorn the doctrine" by living meek and patient lives.

"Happy are the meek: for they shall inherit the earth." Only those who are contrite, humble, and submissively dependent upon God can inherit the earth of radiance, joy, and contentment.

Jesus said to Saul: "It is hard for thee to kick against the pricks" (Acts 9:5; 26:14). The pricks He referred to were goads which were in the harness of the oxen to keep them under control. They were not put there to harm the ox but to make him useful, to direct his energies constructively.

Many of you reading these words have been "kicking against the pricks." Your quarrel has not been so much with others, as you thought, as it has been with yourself. God does not want you to live in constant rebellion against life, its seeming injustices, its hurts and its wrongs. He bids you to stop your futile strivings, to surrender your resentments, to yield your will, and to exercise gentleness and patience. Then you will be happy, and others about you will see Christ in you and will be drawn toward Him.

Meekness is not something I can acquire by myself. It is not something I can get in college or in a scientific laboratory. It is not something I inherit. It is God-given! Jesus said: "Take my yoke upon you, and learn of me; for I am meek and lowly in heart: and ye shall find rest unto your souls" (Matthew 11:29).

Happiness and Meekness for You

Go into a television store and notice all the televisions on display. On some of them bright pictures are to be seen, filled with vibrant colors and giving out the sounds of the latest program. But there are others on display which are only sitting there, their screens dark and silent. Your eye naturally goes to the sets that are on; there is nothing particularly interesting about a dark television screen. What is the difference? Only one thing: The dark television sets are not connected to the power. And that can be true of us, if we try to develop true meekness apart from God. We need to have a living relationship with Him.

God is no respecter of persons. Each of us deserves our just share of happiness. Each of us has the same capacity for God. I should not stand back lamenting my bad luck and my bad breaks in life. I should be joined to the source of power. Take Christ's yoke upon you, "and ye shall find rest unto your soul."

"But I can't live it! I would surely fail in the attempt to be a Christian!" you protest.

Jesus said: "Take my yoke upon you." It is His yoke, and I may rest assured that He will bear the heavy part of the load.

Before He left His disciples, Christ promised that He would send a Comforter to help them in the trials, cares, and temptations of life. This word *comforter* means "one that helps alongside." He is the Holy Spirit, the powerful Third Person of the Trinity. The moment we are born again He takes up residence in our hearts.

We may not emotionally feel Him there, but here again we must exercise faith. Believe it! Accept it as a fact of faith! He is in our hearts to help us to be meek!

We are told that He sheds the love of God abroad in our hearts. He produces the fruit of the Spirit: "love, joy, peace, longsuffering, gentleness, goodness, faith, meekness, temperance" (Galatians 5:22–23). We cannot possibly manufacture this fruit in our own cannery. It is supernaturally manufactured by the Holy Spirit, who lives in our hearts!

I must yield to Him . . . surrender to Him . . . give Him control of my life. Then through the meekness I receive from Him I will find happiness!

Blessed are they which do hunger and thirst after righteousness: for they shall be filled. Matthew 5:6

CHAPTER FIVE

Happy Though Hungry

"TWO VERBS HAVE built two empires," wrote St. Augustine, "the verb *to have* and the verb *to be.* The first is an empire of things, material possessions and power. The second is an empire of the Spirit, things that last."

This fourth Beatitude of Christ expresses a crucial, central truth. When Jesus spoke these words: "Happy are they which do hunger and thirst after righteousness," He addressed them to the multitude. It was not enough to be hungry and thirsty. The important question was, "What were they hungry *for?*"

The multitude on that torrid, sultry day in Palestine symbolizes the great parade of men and women down through the centuries. What He said to them, He says to us and has been saying to all people through the years. Most of the people in that throng were deprived spiritually, socially, and economically. Their hungers were very deep, but none would be more important than their spiritual longings and yearnings. How "righteous" is our society at its core? Perhaps a couple of stories from the daily news will help to answer this question.

A Sick Society

Even the interns at San Francisco General Hospital flinched when they saw the injuries of a young policeman who was carried in on a stretcher. His cheek was bloody from an ugly wound, he was in agony from a savage kick to the groin, and his nose was broken after being stomped on by a teenager's foot. Forty minutes earlier he had tried to arrest two drunken rowdies on Market Street in the heart of downtown San Francisco. A crowd had gathered almost at once.

"The people stood around gawking and laughing at me," the officer said. "When other hoodlums tried to take away my prisoners, numbers of the crowd held my arms. One took my gun, and they let the thugs beat me. Some even joined in the assault. Nobody tried to help me."

More mystified than critical, the officer stared up at the hospital ceiling and asked wonderingly, "What's happened to the people these days? Many of them act as if policemen are their enemies."

This injured officer was the victim of a social malady which is threatening the peace of this nation. There is a growing contempt for authority and for law.

In Los Angeles, two officers arrested two boys who were creating a disturbance in an amusement park. Quickly the police were surrounded by a cursing, jeering mob of several hundred people. Bricks were hurled, bats and jack handles were wielded, and the police cars were overturned.

The attitude toward officers is so menacing in New York City that the Police Commissioner has ordered a special tactical patrol force to disperse the taunting, dangerous mobs which try to interfere with the work of the police. The hazards of police work are increasing. In New York City alone, nearly fifteen hundred policemen were attacked by bystanders, youths, and passersby in one recent eight-month period. The Commissioner of Police in New York City says grimly, "The police cannot fight crime and the public at the same time."

There are many contributing causes to the rioting and crime wave in the nation. Certainly one of the contributing elements is poverty. But another contributing element is found in the home.

Much of today's disrespect for authority stems from a disorganized or indifferent family life. Young people reflect the attitudes of their parents. Even though the overwhelming majority of Americans want law, order, peace, and security, an increasingly vocal minority is revolutionary in its attitude. Until the attitude of government, the family, the home, the church, the courts becomes predominantly righteous, our democratic form of government is in danger of being overthrown. What is the answer to our problem?

We can give people social and economic freedom, but if their thirst for fellowship with God remains unquenched, they will still behave like animals. Witness the prosperity of Western civilization at this very moment. We have everything a machine age can provide, yet boredom and unhappiness have reached an all-time high and our morals have plunged to an all-time low. The reason: Our hunger for God has been dulled or wiped out by other things. We have dulled our hunger and quenched our thirst with the desire for money, security, fame, and success.

A man and his wife visited an orphanage where they hoped to adopt a child. In an interview with the boy they wanted, they told him in glowing terms about the many things they could give him. To their amazement, the little fellow said, "If you have nothing to offer except a good home, clothes, toys, and the other things that most kids have—why—I would just as soon stay here."

"What on earth could you want besides those things?" the woman asked.

"I just want someone to love me," replied the little boy.

There you have it! Even a little boy knows that "man shall not live by bread alone" (Matthew 4:4; Luke 4:4).

The heart cannot be satisfied with computers and sophisticated video equipment. We were created "a little lower than the angels" (Hebrews 2:7), and our souls can never subsist on the husks of this pleasure-seeking world. Our deeper yearnings and longings can be met only by a renewed fellowship with the One in whose image we were created: God. As St. Augustine said, "Thou hast made us for Thyself, and our hearts are restless till they find their rest in Thee."

Happiness in Hunger

"Happy are they which do hunger and thirst after righteousness: for they shall be filled."

We can all understand the metaphor which Jesus employed here—hunger. We have all experienced some time in our lives the gnawing pain, the dizziness, and the faint feeling which accompany intense hunger. We know what it is to experience the dry parchedness of thirst. We have also seen the haunting pictures on television of painfully thin mothers bending over little children with swollen bellies and vacant eyes, tragic victims of famine in Africa or other parts of the world. So, quite naturally, we come to attention when He says: "Happy are they which do hunger and thirst."

But what happiness is there in hunger and thirst?

Well, to begin with, hunger is a sign of life. Dead men need no food, they crave no water.

The Bible teaches that it is possible through lack of spiritual earnestness to harden one's heart as Pharaoh did long ago. This is one of the most dangerous processes that can take place in the human soul. It is possible through sin to harden our hearts against God so long that we lose all desire for God. Then the Scripture says: "God gave them up" (Psalm 81:12; Romans 1:24).

If I have the slightest bit of hunger in my heart for God and righteousness, then it is a certain sign that it is not too hardened to be receptive to the voice and message of Christ. I am yet alive and sensitive to the Spirit's voice.

Those who have no cravings for God, no longings for Christ, and no thirst for the things of the Spirit are not only dead in trespasses and sins, but they are also insensitive to the Spirit's promptings. They are like the dead and are in danger of remaining in a state of spiritual stupor that will lead eventually to eternal death.

A man once told me that he nearly froze to death in the far North. His hands lost their feeling, his feet became numb, and he was overcome with an impulse to lie down in the snow and go to sleep when it dawned upon him that he was freezing to death. He jumped up and ran vigorously until his circulation was stimulated. If he had not suddenly become conscious that he was dying and acted upon that consciousness, he would have frozen to death.

Happy are those who respond to the Spirit's warnings. They alone have hope of being filled.

A hungry person is a normal person. Those who are sick and abnormally upset refuse nourishment, but the normal person craves food. In that sense there is a blessedness in hunger. It is a natural reaction.

The normal person also possesses a spiritual hunger—although he may not label it as such. He may think he has filled it, but apart from God there is no lasting quenching of his spiritual hunger and thirst. David said: "As the hart panteth after the water brooks, so panteth my soul after thee, O God" (Psalm 42:1).

Isaiah said: "With my soul have I desired thee in the night; yea, with my spirit within me will I seek thee early: for when thy judgments are in the earth, the inhabitants of the world will learn righteousness" (Isaiah 26:9).

Each of us was created in the image and likeness of God. We were made for God's fellowship, and our hearts can never be satisfied without His communion. Just as iron is attracted to a magnet, the soul in its state of hunger is drawn to God. Though you, like thousands of others, may feel in the state of sin that the world is more alluring and more to your liking, someday—perhaps even now as you read these words—you will acknowledge that there is something deep down inside you which cannot be satisfied by the alloy of earth.

Then with David the psalmist (who had sampled the delicacies of sin and had found them unsatisfying) you will say: "O God, thou art my God; early will I seek thee: my soul thirsteth for thee, my flesh longeth for thee in a dry and thirsty land, where no water is" (Psalm 63:1).

The trouble with most of us is that we make happiness our goal instead of aiming at something higher, loftier, and nobler. Unhappiness is like pain—it is only an effect of an underlying cause. Pain cannot be relieved until the cause is removed. Pain and disease go together: Disease is the cause, and pain is the effect.

Unhappiness is an effect, and sin is the cause. Sin and unhappiness go together. All was blissful happiness in the Garden of Eden until sin crept in. Then happiness crept out. The two just cannot exist together.

Hunger for Righteousness

What is this righteousness we are to desire? Is this righteousness to which Jesus referred in the fourth Beatitude a religious experience? Is it some mysterious ecstasy which comes to only a few people fraught with cataclysmic emotions and spiritual sensations?

Any kind of religious experience which does not produce righteousness in our lives is a counterfeit and not worth seeking. Today there are all kinds of cults and philosophies which claim to have the power to change our lives for the better—but they cannot live up to their claim because they have no power to change the human heart. At worst, they end up enslaving their adherents. But God's will is that we would be righteous in our living. God is holy, and the whole scheme of redemption has holiness for its goal. The apostle Peter declared that Christ was the one "who his own self bare our sins in his own body on the tree, that we, being dead to sins, should live unto righteousness" (1 Peter 2:24).

The kind of religious experience which does not produce righteousness in the life is hardly worth seeking. But religious demonstrations that do not create in us better morals and a Christlikeness of character serve no useful purpose and could certainly do more harm than good. God is holy, and the whole scheme of redemption has holiness for its goal.

Nor is this righteousness to which Jesus referred a perfunctory, mechanical performance of religious rites. Jesus taught the futility of holding to religious theory apart from Christian practice when He said: "Except your righteousness shall exceed the righteousness of the scribes and Pharisees, ye shall in no case enter into the kingdom of heaven" (Matthew 5:20).

Neither is righteousness an abstract, speculative morality so prevalent in the world today. Many people condemn sin in high places but fail to recognize it in their own personal lives. They condemn it in the government and society but condone it in their own hearts.

It is just as sinful in God's sight for an individual to break the marriage vow as it is for a nation to break a treaty.

The Nature of Righteousness

What is this righteousness that Jesus exhorts us to hunger for? The Bible teaches that God is holy, righteous, and pure. He cannot tolerate sin in His presence. However, man has chosen to disregard the divine laws and standards. As a result of man's transgressions, he is called a "sinner." Sin immediately breaks his fellowship with God. Man becomes unrighteous, impure, and unholy in the sight of God. A holy God cannot have fellowship with that which is unholy, unrighteous, and unethical. Therefore, sin breaks off friendship with God. Man is called in the Bible an "alien," an "enemy" to God, and a "sinner" against Him. The only way that man can again have fellowship with God and find the happiness that he longs for is to find some way to possess a righteousness and holiness that will commend him to God.

Many have tried to reform to gain favor with God. Some have mutilated their bodies and tortured themselves, thinking thereby to gain favor with God. Others have thought that if they would work hard and live moral lives, they could somehow justify themselves.

But the Bible teaches that all our righteousness—falling short of the divine standard as it does—is as filthy rags in the sight of God. There is absolutely no possibility of our manufacturing a righteousness, holiness, or goodness that will satisfy God. Even the best of us is impure to God.

I remember what happened one day many years ago when my wife was doing the washing. This was before we had a clothes dryer. The clothes looked white and clean in the house, but when she hung them on the line they actually appeared soiled and dirty in contrast to the fresh-fallen snow.

Our own lives may seem at times to be morally good and decent; but, in comparison to the holiness and the purity of God, we are defiled and filthy.

In spite of our sins and moral uncleanness, God loves us. He decided to provide a righteousness for us. This is the reason that He gave His Son, Jesus Christ, to die on the cross.

Have you ever stopped to think why it is the cross has become the symbol of Christianity? It is because at the cross Jesus purchased our redemption and provided a righteousness which we could not ourselves earn. "The gift of God is eternal life through Jesus Christ our Lord" (Romans 6:23). On the ground of faith in the atoning death and resurrection of His Son, God has provided and ascribed righteousness for all who will receive it.

This means that God forgives all past sin and failure. He wipes the slate clean. He takes our sins and buries them in the depths of the sea and removes them as far as the east is from the west.

To use another illustration from the Bible, in our natural state we are clothed with filthy rags because of our sin, and we cannot come into the presence of God our King. But God in Christ takes away our old filthy garments and clothes us instead with new garments—the pure white garments of Christ! As the old hymn declares:

When He shall come with trumpet sound,
Oh, may I then in Him be found;
Dressed in His righteousness alone,
Faultless to stand before the throne.

Our God Forgets!

The omniscient God has the unique ability that we do not have: He has the ability to forget. The God of grace forgets our sins and wipes them completely from His memory forever! He places us in His sight as though we had never committed one sin.

In theological language, this is called *justification.* The Bible says: "Therefore being justified by faith, we have peace with God through our Lord Jesus Christ" (Romans 5:1).

There is no possibility of true happiness until we have established friendship and fellowship with God. And there is no possibility of establishing this fellowship apart from the cross of His Son, Jesus Christ. God says, "I will forgive you, but I will forgive you only at the foot of the cross." He says, "I will fellowship with you, but I will fellowship with you only at the cross." That is the reason it is necessary for us to come to the cross in repentance of our sin and by faith in His Son to find forgiveness and salvation.

The Goal of Righteousness

As we have noted, when we come to Christ God imparts His righteousness to us. It is almost as if an accounting entry had been made in the books of heaven, declaring us righteous for Christ's sake!

But when we come to Christ by faith and receive Him as our Savior, our "hunger and thirst after righteousness" are not ended. Yes, my sins have been washed away and my salvation is secure in Christ. But I also know that within my soul there still is sin. My motives are not pure; my tongue may not be tamed; my love for others may be dim. It is God's will for this to be changed, however, and for us to exhibit increasingly in our lives the righteousness of Christ. "Let your light so shine before men, that they may see your good works, and glorify your Father which is in heaven" (Matthew 5:16).

Sometimes I have had persons who have not been Christians very long come to me and say that they had decided they must never have been Christians after all. When I have asked them why, they have replied that everything seemed fine for a few weeks after their decision for Christ, but then they found themselves committing sin. They had thought—mistakenly—that if they were Christ's they would never sin again. But that is not true! As long as we are in the flesh we will always be engaged in a continual battle against sin in our lives.

But it is not God's will for us to continue in sin—and in fact, if we are completely indifferent to the presence of sin in our lives the Bible indicates we do not really know Christ. Instead, we are to "hunger and thirst after righteousness"—to pursue righteousness and purity with God's help, so that our lives become increasingly like Christ every day.

Righteousness is something which we do not possess as a natural gift, but it is a God-given gift to be specially received. It is a bit of heaven brought to earth. The righteousness of the God-man is applied to us in justification and in sanctification, so that righteousness is progressively implanted in the believer's heart. It is God's sharing His nature with us. We become partakers of divine life.

Now, God says that only those who hunger after it will receive it. God thrusts this heavenly manna on no one.

We must desire it, above everything else. Our yearning for God must supersede all other desires. It must be like a gnawing hunger and a burning thirst.

There are several things that can spoil our appetite for the righteousness of God.

Stumbling Blocks to Righteousness

FIRST: *Sinful pleasure* can ruin our appetite for the things of God.

Paul had a young co-laborer in the gospel named Demas. Because his appetite for the pleasures of the world was greater than his thirst for God, we hear very little of young Demas. Paul wrote his entire history in nine words: "Demas hath forsaken me, having loved this present world" (2 Timothy 4:10).

Many of us have no appetite for spiritual things because we are absorbed in the sinful pleasures of this world. We have been eating too many of the devil's delicacies.

I once heard the story of a man walking down the road to market. A pig followed behind him. All the other farmers were driving their pigs, struggling to get them to market. A friend called to him and asked him how he got the pig to follow him. He said, "It's very simple. Every step I take, I drop a bean, and the pig likes beans."

Satan goes along the road of life dropping his beans, and we are following him to eternal destruction.

Our sins may be very obvious and open, or they may be very respectable or subtle. Perhaps we are preoccupied with material things which, while not wrong in themselves, have wrapped their tentacles around us and are squeezing out our spiritual hunger and thirst for righteousness. We may be preoccupied with our career or our education, or any of hundreds of other things which can dull our appetite for God and His righteousness.

SECOND: *Self-sufficiency* can impair our hunger after God. No one is so empty as he who thinks he is full. No one is so ill as he who has a fatal disease and yet thinks he is in perfect health. No one is so poor as he who thinks he is rich but is actually bankrupt.

The Bible says: "Thou sayest, I am rich, and increased with goods, and have need of nothing; and knowest not that thou art wretched, and miserable, and poor, and blind, and naked" (Revelation 3:17).

A person who is filled with himself has no room for God in his life. Self-sufficiency can ruin one's appetite for the things of Christ.

THIRD: *Secret sin* can take away our appetite for the righteousness of God.

That secret sin we commit has a price. We may think we've kept our sin a secret, but remorse for it will remain in our hearts. Those evil resentments we harbor in our minds against our neighbor! The failure to forgive those who have wronged us! When the heart is filled with wickedness, there is no room for God. The jealousies, the envies, the prejudices, and the malices will take away our appetite for the things of the Spirit.

Judas was one of the twelve disciples, outwardly a diligent follower of Christ. But in his heart he tolerated greed and evil and they led him to betray Jesus and eventually commit suicide. King Saul outwardly welcomed the young lad David into his palace, but in his heart he was filled with bitterness and jealousy of him. Eventually those secret sins consumed him and destroyed him.

When our lives are filled with the husks of prejudice and the chaff of resentment, we can have no thirst for righteousness. If we allow our hearts to be filled with Satan's rations, we will have no desire for heaven's manna.

FOURTH: *Neglect of our spiritual life* can take away our appetite for the righteousness of God.

All Christians believe in God, but nominal Christians have little time for God. They are too busy with everyday affairs to be concerned with Bible reading, prayer, and being thoughtful to their fellowmen. Many have lost the spirit of a zealous discipleship.

If you ask them if they are Christians, they would probably answer, "I think so," or "I hope so." They may go to church at Easter and Christmas and other special occasions, but otherwise they have little time for God. They have crowded God out of their lives.

The Bible warns us against neglect of our souls. It is possible to harden our hearts and shrivel our souls until we lose our appetite for the things of God. Just like someone who refuses to eat and eventually grows weaker and weaker until he dies, so a person who is "too busy" for God will starve himself and wither away spiritually.

This hunger, then, that we should have is a desire to be always right with God. It is a consciousness that all searching for peace of heart except in Him is in vain. It is an admission of our own futility, our own helplessness, and our complete abandonment to His will.

Like Peter, who stepped out upon the waves of self-sufficiency only to find that they would not bear him up, we cry, "Master, save me, or I perish!"

Like the prodigal son, who sampled the devil's delicacies in the far-off city, we discover that the world's husks fill but do not satisfy. It is then in the knowledge of our real need that we say, "Father, I have sinned against heaven, and before thee. . . . Make me as one of thy hired servants" (Luke 15:18–19).

The prodigal son's "comeback" began down in the swine pen when he said, "How many hired servants of my father's have bread enough and to spare, and I perish with hunger!" (Luke 15:17). The very moment that he began to hunger, God began to "set the table" for spiritual reunion. His deepest yearnings and longings were not for food but for being reconciled to his father. The first thing he said was, "Father, I have sinned against heaven, and before thee, and am no more worthy to be called thy son. . . ."

Neither is our goal to be blessings, experiences, or even answers to our prayers, taken by themselves. These are all the accompaniment of being right with our Heavenly Father.

God, like the prodigal's father, says to all of those who hunger and thirst after righteousness, "Son, all that I have is yours."

But the key to spiritual satisfaction is being right with God. When through faith we are in the position of sonship, then God's riches become our riches; God's abundance, our abundance; God's power, our power. When a proper relationship has been restored between us and God, then happiness, contentment, and peace of mind will be a natural outgrowth of that restored relationship.

The Difference Between Believing and Receiving

You ask, "How can I start? What do I have to do?"

Jesus said: "You must be converted." The word *conversion* means "to turn around," "to change your mind," "to turn back," and "to return."

In many ways conversion is a mystery, for from our viewpoint as humans it is both man's work and God's work. Our responsibility is to turn to Christ in faith and repentance, turning from our sins and asking Him to come into our hearts by faith. We express our desire to change the course of our lives, and we acknowledge our helplessness to do this apart from God's help. We commit ourselves to live in accordance with God's will. And when we do, God the Holy Spirit comes to dwell within us. If our commitment is genuine, God works in our hearts to regenerate us. Then we have truly been converted—we have been born again by the Spirit of God!

But many people immediately argue, "I do believe in Christ. I believe in the Church, and I believe in the Bible. Isn't that enough?"

No! We must *receive* Christ.

I may go to the airport. I have a reservation. I have a ticket in my pocket. The plane is on the ramp. It is a big, powerful plane. I am certain that it will take me to my destination. They call the flight three times. I neglect to get on board. They close the door. The plane taxis down the runway and takes off. I am not on the plane. Why? I "believed" in the plane, but I neglected to get on board.

That's just it! A person may believe in God, Christ, the Bible, and the Church—but neglect to actually receive Him in the heart. That kind of belief is impersonal and speculative. It does not involve complete *commitment* to Him.

The moment we receive Him, the Bible says, we are born again. God's nature enters into our own souls, and we become a child of God in full spiritual fellowship.

This is what we might call the "vertical relationship," the perpendicular companionship between God and man. It is absolutely the first step toward happiness. There is no use reading the rest of this book until you are absolutely sure that you have repented of sin, received Christ by faith, and been born again. The vertical relationship must always precede the "horizontal."

Our sustenance, our supply, our power come from above. Man is like a tram or a streetcar. He must be connected vertically (above) before he can move horizontally. Our relationship must be right with God before it can be right with man. And if this be true, then the converse is equally true—if we are wrong with God, we are wrong with man also.

There is a law in musical tone which says, "Two instruments tuned to the same pitch are in tune with each other." A similar rule in mathematics is: "Two quantities equal to the same quantity are equal to each other."

So two people in tune with God are in tune with each other. Two people in love with Christ have love for each other.

The moment I receive Christ as my Lord and Savior, Christ, through the Holy Spirit, comes to live in my heart. The Scripture says: "Christ in you, the hope of glory" (Colossians 1:27). We may not see Him with the natural eye and we may not feel Him with our emotions, but He is there nevertheless. We are to accept Him by faith!

This aspect of righteousness for which we are to hunger is called, in theological language, *sanctification*. Don't let this word frighten you. It actually means "separated" or "clean." In one sense, sanctification is instantaneous. The moment I receive Christ as Savior, the Holy Spirit comes into my heart.

There is also a sense in which sanctification is progressive. I grow in the grace and knowledge of Jesus Christ. Being a Christian is more than just an instantaneous conversion—it is a daily process whereby I grow to be more and more like Christ. When we start out, we begin as a baby does in physical life. We must be fed on the simple things of the Bible, and we learn to walk in our Christian life gradually. In Elizabeth Goudge's delightful book, *The Dean's Watch,* she describes a part of the saintly Miss Montague's spiritual pilgrimage: "Until now she had only read her Bible as a pious exercise, but now she read it as an engineer reads a blueprint and a traveler a map, unemotionally because she was not emotional, but with profound concentration because her life depended on it. Bit by bit over a period of years, that seemed to her long, she began to get her scaffolding in place." At first we fall down and make many mistakes, but we are to continue growing.

The Dangers of Spiritual Staleness

However, there are many people who have stopped growing. They remain spiritual babes all their lives. I am afraid that this experience is all too common today. Perhaps it is yours.

Do you remember the day when you gave your heart and your life to Christ? You were sure of victory. How easy it seemed to be more than conqueror through Christ who loved you. Under the leadership of a Captain who had never been foiled in battle, how could you dream of defeat?

And yet to many of you, how different has been your real experience!

Your victories have been few and fleeting and your defeats many and disastrous. You have not lived as you feel children of God ought to live.

As Mrs. Hannah Whitall-Smith reminds us in her book *The Christian's Secret of a Happy Life,* "You have had, perhaps, a clear understanding of doctrinal truths but you have not come into possession of their light and power. In your life Christ is believed in, talked about, and served, but He is not filling you hour by hour. You found Christ as your Savior from the penalty of sin, but you have not found Him as your all-sufficient Savior from its power. The joy and thrill of Christian experience is gone."

There is only a dying ember of what used to be a mighty prairie fire for Christ in your soul. In the very depths of your heart you know that your experience is not the scriptural experience. Down through the years it seems that all you can expect from your Christianity is a life of ultimate failure and defeat—one hour failure, and the next hour repenting and beginning again, only to fail again.

Vigor in the Early Church

We read in the Scriptures that the early church was filled with the Holy Spirit. They had no church buildings, no Bibles, no automobiles, no planes, no trains, no television, no radio. Yet they turned their world "upside down" for Christ. They instituted a spiritual revolution that shook the very foundations of the Roman Empire. They were young, vigorous, virile, powerful. They lived their lives daily for Christ. They suffered persecution and even death gladly for their faith in Christ. What was the secret of their success—even in the face of opposition and death? One reason beyond doubt is that they hungered and thirsted after righteousness. And those with whom they came in contact could not help but be impressed by the quality and purity of their lives and their love.

The reason certain false philosophies and religions are making such inroads in the world today is that somewhere along the linc the people who were supposed to live Christian lives failed. We have failed to meet the standards and requirements that Jesus set forth. If we would live for Christ we must be willing to count all else as "nothing but refuse." We must be as dedicated, as committed, and as willing to sacrifice all, as the followers of false religions are.

The great masses of the unbelieving world are confused as they gaze upon the strife within and among religious bodies. Instead of a dynamic, growing, powerful, Christ-centered Church, we see division, strife, pettiness, greed, jealousy, and spiritual laziness—while the world is standing on the brink of disaster.

The great need in Christendom today is for Christians to learn the secret of daily, wholehearted recommitment to Christ.

Paul himself spoke of his struggle. He spoke of desiring to please God, but in himself he found no strength to do so. The things he did not want to do he sometimes did; and the things he wanted to do he did not do. Nearly driven to distraction, Paul shouts out: "Who shall deliver me from the body of this death?" (Romans 7:24).

And in the next verse he records the answer to that all-important, searching, bewildering question when he says: "I thank God through Jesus Christ our Lord" (Romans 7:25).

Christ can be our Deliverer!

Many of us ask the questions: "Why do I, as a Christian, do some of the things I do? Why do I, as a Christian, leave undone the things I ought to have done?"

Many name the Name of Christ, but live in constant defeat. They have unclean hands, unclean lips, unclean tongues, unclean feet, unclean thoughts, unclean hearts—and yet claim to be Christians. They claim Christ, attend church, try to pray—and yet they know there are things in their souls that are not right. There is no joy in their hearts, no love for others. In fact, there is little evidence of the fruit of the Spirit in their lives. The fire in their souls has been quenched.

Yet as we look around, we do know some people who are living different lives. They bear the fruit of the Spirit. But some get only snatches of victory. Once in a while they will have a day that seems to be a victorious day over temptation, but then they slide right back into that same old rut of living, and hunger and long for the righteousness of daily growth.

There are other Christians who have never really learned the biblical truth of separation: separation from unclean thoughts and unclean habits.

There are some Christians who have learned little of a daily devotional life.

Surrender and Devotion

Some time ago a policeman asked me what the secret of victorious living was. I told him that there is no magic formula that can be pronounced. If any word could describe it, I would say *surrender.* The second word I would use would be *devotion.*

Nothing can take the place of a daily devotional life with Christ. The great missionary Hudson Taylor said, "Never mind how great the pressure is—only where the pressure lies. Never let it come between you and the Lord, then the *greater* the pressure, the more it *presses you* to His heart!" Our quiet time, our prayer time, the time we spend in the Word is absolutely essential for a happy Christian life. We cannot possible be happy, dynamic, and powerful Christians apart from a daily walk with Christ.

It is unfortunate that even in Christian circles our conversation is of comparatively small matters. We can quote the batting average of our favorite baseball star, but we are unable to quote a Bible verse other than John 3:16. We are full of talk about our homes, our cars, our television—but we are woefully ignorant of the things of God.

If a sick and dying man should stumble through our door, we would be incapable of guiding him through his problems to Christ the Savior.

Our spiritual intellects have become poverty-stricken; hence the trite verbal interchanges that pass between us. Our daily conversation when we meet each other, whether it be in the office or on the campus or in the shop, should be concerned with the things of God. We should be exchanging spiritual blessings and thoughts that we have received from our daily Bible reading.

It is not enough for us to have been confirmed, or to have made a decision for Christ at an altar, and to hope to walk in the glow of that experience successfully for the rest of our lives. Being human, we have to return and renew our commitment to God. We have to take inventory and get regular spiritual checkups.

Steps to Surrender

Christ is calling Christians today to cleansing, to dedication, to consecration, and to full surrender. It will make the difference between success and failure in our spiritual lives. It will make the difference between being helped and helping others. It will make a difference in our habits, in our prayer life, in our Bible reading, in our giving, in our testimony, and in our church membership. This is the Christian's hour of decision!

But many ask, "How can I begin?" I would like to suggest that you take all of the sins that you are guilty of and make a list of them. Then confess them, and check them off, remembering that Jesus Christ forgives. The Bible says: "If we confess our sins, he is faithful and just to forgive us our sins, and to cleanse us from all unrighteousness" (1 John 1:9).

In addition, ask God to cleanse you from those sins you may not be aware of, and to make you more sensitive to the presence of hidden sins in your life—wrong motives, wrong attitudes, wrong habits, wrong relationships, wrong priorities. It may even be that you will have to make restitution if you have stolen anything, or you may have to seek out someone and ask his forgiveness for a wrong you have committed.

Then, after you have confessed every known sin in your life, yield every area of your life. Yield your girlfriend, your boyfriend, your family, your business, your career, your ambitions, your soul, the innermost thoughts and depths of your heart; yield them all to Christ. Hold nothing back. As the songwriter says: "Give them all to Jesus."

Take your eyes and your ears and your hands and your feet and your thoughts and your heart: Give them completely and unreservedly to Christ. Then by faith believe that God has accepted your surrender.

Paul said: "I am crucified with Christ: nevertheless I live; yet not I, but Christ liveth in me" (Galatians 2:20).

We can reckon ourselves indeed dead unto sin. The Bible says we can be more than conquerors through Him who loved us.

The Secret of Surrender

It has been my privilege to know what it means to walk in the way of Christ. What a thrilling, joyous experience it is to wake up every morning and know His Presence in the room! What a thrilling, joyous experience it is to know in the evening, when the sun is setting, the peace of God as you go to bed and to sleep the sleep of only those who know Christ! What a joy it is to walk in the eternal and permanent experience of Christ!

God is in every tomorrow,
Therefore I live for today—
Certain of finding at sunrise
Guidance and strength for the way.
Power for each moment of weakness,
Hope for each moment of pain.
Comfort for every sorrow,
Sunshine and joy after rain!

ANONYMOUS

And I know what it is to fall flat on my face. As Alexander Whyte, the great Scottish clergyman, said at the turn of the century, "Perseverance of the saints consists in ever new beginnings."

Do you hunger for such a walk? Do you long for such joy, peace, contentment, abandonment, and adventure in your own souls? Do you long to produce the fruit of the Spirit, which is "love, joy, peace, longsuffering, gentleness, goodness, faith, meekness, temperance" (Galatians 5:22–23)? You can if you abide in Christ as the branch abides in the vine.

First, remember that the Christian life is lived by "Christ in you." However, if Christ does not have all of us, it is impossible to live a happy Christian experience. When He has all of us, then He fills us to overflowing and He produces in us the fruit of the Spirit. It is absolutely impossible for any person to manufacture, generate, or produce the Christian life apart from the power of the Holy Spirit. He stands at this moment ready to enter our hearts with a floodtide of blessing if we will surrender every area of our personalities and lives to Him. It is our birthright! We must claim it—believe it—accept it! It's ours *now.*

If this is your hunger and desire, then God will do exactly what He has promised to do: He will fill you. "Happy are they that hunger and thirst after righteousness: for they shall be filled." Every promise God has ever made He has kept. He will fill you now if you are hungry enough to surrender.

The Source of Righteousness

Second, God will fill you with His righteousness, because man has no holy longings, no holy cravings that cannot ultimately be satisfied.

We shall *not* be perfect in thought, word, and deed until we are glorified in the world to come, but the breath of that glory, and a godlikeness of character, is the Christian's proper heritage in this earthly walk. We are *Christians,* and the world should sense to its conviction that, wherever we walk in its midst, a heavenly virtue still goes out from whatever truly bears His Name.

People hunger for food, and God sends the sun and rain upon the golden fields of grain. The grain is made into flour and flour into bread, and our physical hunger is satisfied.

People hunger for love; and ideally they are born into a home where their parents love them. Later, perhaps, God ignites the fire of affection in another heart, and two hearts are made complete in the bonds of holy matrimony.

People hunger for knowledge, and God raises up institutions of learning. He calls out committed instructors and puts it into the hearts of the rich to endow these schools, and students are satisfied in their thirst for knowledge.

People hunger for fellowship, and God allows engineers to build cities. There people can share their industry, their knowledge, and their skills.

Don't tell me that God can supply us with an abundance of everything material and yet will let us starve spiritually!

The Bible says: "Hearken diligently unto me, and eat ye that which is good, and let your soul delight itself in fatness" (Isaiah 55:2).

Again the Bible says: "For the bread of God is he which cometh down from heaven, and giveth life unto the world" (John 6:33).

Satisfaction in Christ

Third, God will satisfy the hunger and thirst of those who desire His righteousness, because He loves the world with an undying affection. He moved heaven and earth to redeem us. Would it seem logical that a father would pay a huge ransom to redeem a son and then forsake him in his hour of hunger? The fact that the initial cost of our salvation was so great helps us know that God certainly does not desire that we shall want for anything. A parent who loves his child will not willingly see him starve.

The Bible says: "But my God shall supply all your need according to his riches in glory by Christ Jesus" (Philippians 4:19).

This promise, "Happy are they which do hunger and thirst after righteousness," is one which makes us responsible to God, and God responsible to us. Our small human part is to hunger and to thirst.

If we have no desire for righteousness, it means only that we have permitted sin and neglect to spoil our desire for fellowship with God. No matter how alluring, attractive, and pleasant the tidbits of the world may seem, they can never satisfy our deeper longings and heart cravings.

We can only know peace of heart and tranquillity of mind when we admit and confess our deeper hungers, when we yield completely to God, and when we are willing to turn from the synthetic substitutes of the world and drink in the "water of life."

Blessed are the merciful: for they shall obtain mercy. Matthew 5:7

CHAPTER SIX

Happiness Through Showing Mercy

THE BIBLE SAYS, "He that hath pity upon the poor lendeth unto the LORD; and that which he hath given will he pay him again" (Proverbs 19:17). A group of businessmen had a hunting lodge. It was their custom to have devotions each evening. One night they called on the godly mountain caretaker to lead in prayer. "O Lord," he prayed, "have mercy on us, 'cause mercy suits our case." In the Bible mercy refers to compassion, to pity for the undeserving and the guilty. Perhaps no more beautiful illustration of it exists in the Bible (apart from God's mercy to us in Christ) than that of Joseph and his undeserving brothers.

You recall how, through jealousy, the brothers sold Joseph into slavery, convincing his father that he had been devoured by wild beasts. In the following years Joseph, through his faithfulness to God and his masters, rose in position in Egypt until he was second in power to Pharaoh himself.

It was famine that drove the unsuspecting brothers down to Egypt to buy food. Read again the incredible story of Joseph recognizing his brothers, his compassionate dealing with them, how he got them to bring his old father and move with their families to Egypt where he could nourish them through the remaining years of famine. Where vengeance and just retribution were certainly justified, Joseph showed only mercy and lovingkindness.

In fact, he says to his apprehensive brothers (in Genesis 50), ". . . ye thought evil against me; but God meant it unto good. . . . Now therefore fear ye not: I will nourish you, and your little ones. And he comforted them, and spake kindly unto them" (vv. 20–21).

What mercy!

So, too, in our lives, we might be prompted to be merciful to those who have wronged us, hurt us, or even done incredibly cruel things to us. If we were submissive and loyal to God we could see behind the unkindness and evil God's love working for our good and His glory.

We have a contrasting story in the rich young ruler who, when told by Jesus to go and sell all he had and give to the poor, then come and follow Him, went away sorrowful for he had great possessions (Matthew 19:22). Here an opportunity to show mercy was held back by greed.

The rich young ruler thought possessions would bring him happiness—but they didn't. And yet he was unwilling to turn to Christ, the only true source of lasting happiness. He could not show mercy to others because of his selfishness and greed—and so he "went away sorrowful," never experiencing true happiness and fulfillment. "Happy are the merciful."

Jesus knew that one of the real tests of our yieldedness to God is our willingness to share with others. If we have no mercy toward others, that is one proof that we have never experienced God's mercy.

Mercy Is Not Self-Centered

To paraphrase this Beatitude we might say, "They which have obtained mercy from God are so happy that they are merciful to others." Our attitude toward our fellowmen is a more accurate gauge of our religion than all of our religious rantings.

Alexander Pope prayed:

Teach me to feel another's woe
To hide the fault I see;
That mercy I to others show,
That mercy show to me.

Emerson must have been reading the gauge of human mercy when he said: "What you are speaks so loud that I cannot hear what you say."

Jesus summed up the whole matter of genuine Christianity when He said: "If any man thirst, let him come unto me, and drink. He that believeth on me, as the scripture hath said, out of his belly shall flow rivers of living water" (John 7:37–38).

Christianity is, first, a coming to Christ—an inflowing of the Living Water; second, it is a reaching toward others—an outflowing. It is to be shared in love, mercy, and compassion with others.

A body of water which has an inlet but no outlet becomes a stagnant pond. When we think of Christianity as *my* experience, *my* emotions, *my* ecstasy, *my* joy, *my* faith—with no desire to share mercifully with others—we can only boast of stagnation. Not living, vital, flowing Christianity!

The Scripture says: "Defend the poor and fatherless: do justice to the afflicted and needy" (Psalm 82:3). "Whoso stoppeth his ears at the cry of the poor, he also shall cry himself, but shall not be heard" (Proverbs 21:13).

Jesus said: "Give to him that asketh thee, and from him that would borrow of thee turn not thou away" (Matthew 5:42). And: "Give, and it shall be given unto you; good measure, pressed down, and shaken together, and running over, shall men give into your bosom" (Luke 6:38).

In this Beatitude, which we could well term the "outflowing" Beatitude, Jesus is emphasizing the fact that we are to be unchoked channels through which His love and mercy flow out to other people.

If we have a religion which does not work effectively in everyday life, one which fails to condition our attitudes toward our fellowmen and one which makes us spiritual introverts, we may be sure that we do not know the Christ who spoke these Beatitudes!

Satan does not care how much you theorize about Christianity or how much you profess to know Christ. What he opposes vigorously is the way you live Christ—the way you become an instrument of mercy, compassion, and love through which He manifests Himself to the world. If Satan can take the mercy out of Christianity, he has killed its effectiveness. If he can succeed in getting us to talk a good case of religion but to live a poor one, he has robbed us of our power.

If we embrace a spiritual, aesthetic gospel only and disregard our obligation to our fellowmen, we annul it all. The gospel of the New Testament can come into full blossom only when the seed of the Spirit is buried in the rich soil of human mercy.

It is first an intaking, and then an outgiving. Jesus said in our outgiving we would find happiness.

Some time ago a lady wrote and said, "I am sixty-five years old. My children are all married, my husband is dead, and I am one of the loneliest people in all the world." It was suggested to her that she find a way of sharing her religious faith and her material goods with those around her. She wrote a few weeks later and said, "I am the happiest woman in town. I have found a new joy and happiness in sharing with others."

That's exactly what Jesus promised!

Mercy in Action

What are some of the areas in today's world toward which we can show mercy?

FIRST: We can show mercy by *caring for the needs of others.* We should look around at our neighbors and see if any are hurting or in need.

Who is my neighbor? He who is closest to me—my husband or wife, child, parent, brother, sister, the person next door, the couple down the street. It is easier to be concerned with the deprived person halfway around the world, and ignore the needs of those closest to me—perhaps only a word of encouragement or appreciation. At the same time, we cannot ignore the needs of our fellowmen on a worldwide scale.

When I go to bed tonight, I must remember that over half of the world's population is hungry, poor, and wretched. Most of these are illiterate people who are unable to read or write. Most use farming methods a thousand years old. Many are little better than slaves to the big landlords who own the land. Others live in countries with corrupt or oppressive governments. Their lives are burdened with injustice or prejudice, and they have little opportunity to get ahead. Their lives are marked by hopelessness and despair. They need food, education, clothes, homes, medical care, and—most of all—love. We have a responsibility to these downtrodden peoples of the world.

Did not Jesus feed the multitudes as well as preach the gospel to them? Did He not point out to us the folly of talking religion and failing to put it into action? Did He not say: "Woe unto you, scribes and Pharisees, hypocrites! for ye shut up the kingdom of heaven against men. . . . For ye devour widows' houses, and for a pretence make long prayer: therefore ye shall receive the greater damnation" (Matthew 23:13, 14)?

A young man from our community is a skilled helicopter pilot. He undoubtedly could make a very high salary working for a major corporation, but instead he has joined a small Christian mission which uses helicopters to reach remote areas of the world with the gospel and with relief supplies. Much of his work has been in some of the drought-stricken areas of Africa, where millions of people live on the brink of starvation every day. Recently he wrote, "I often feel at a loss of words to describe some of the conditions in places here. Some I don't want to describe—just forget." But then he added, "The rewards are high here in seeing our efforts really helping people." In the midst of terrible, heart-breaking conditions he has discovered the truth of Jesus' words: "Happy are the merciful."

How can we theorize about religion and debate doctrinal matters while the world is dying in misery without the necessities of life and, in many cases, without hope?

What a selfish and ingrown people we have become! Little wonder that there is so much boredom, frustration, and unhappiness. The words of Jesus, "Happy are the merciful," are certainly applicable to us.

The late Dr. Frank Laubach once wrote to me, "In my opinion, the United States must make an all-out effort to help the destitute half of the world out of its misery, or we shall find that the world has gone Communist because of our neglect."

Most of us cannot go to these faraway lands, but we can give to missionary and charitable causes that will help build hospitals, educational institutions, and orphanages—and provide the necessities of life to many of these destitute millions.

But let's come closer to home. If we only looked, we would find people near us who are in physical need. One Christmas Eve a friend came to my house and said, "Would you like to go out with me distributing Christmas packages up in the mountains?" I was glad to go. And I was in for one of the greatest surprises of my life! I thought everybody in our community had all the necessities of life. But I was taken back into some little mountain valleys where people did not have enough to wear, enough to eat, and could not even afford soap to wash their bodies. Appalled and humbled, I asked God to forgive me for neglecting the people in my own community. I had not even bothered to look around me to see what people's needs were.

If we will ask God to show us, we will find people in our own communities who need physical help.

There are others in our community who need a friend. There are many lonely people who never know the handclasp of a friend. They never receive a letter. They sit isolated in their loneliness. Having an interested friend willing to write to them and to visit with them would change their entire lives. One of the happiest women in our church lives alone but makes a habit of visiting nursing homes. She reads to the patients, wheels them to the gift shop and cafeteria. When my mother had very few visit her from her church, this dear woman was faithful to her weekly. She is happy in a ministry in nursing homes.

There are others who are lonely and miserable because they perhaps do not have personalities that lend themselves to mixing with other people. I have a friend who went to a social gathering. A harelipped lad with pimples on his face sat over in the corner. No one paid any attention to him. He looked lonely, despondent, and miserable, and completely out of place. My friend went over and spent the evening with him. When he left, the lad was full of smiles. This friend had shown mercy.

There are a thousand little ways that we can be merciful in our daily lives. There may be a hospital nearby which we could visit. There are scores of people on hospital beds who long for someone to call on them, to bring them flowers and a cheery smile. We can show mercy by visiting the sick.

Prejudice—A Barrier to Mercy

SECOND: We can show mercy by *doing away with our prejudices.*

All over the world a new nationalism is rising. Color bars are being broken down while other social barriers are being raised. Prejudice stalks many countries.

I have been privileged across the years to visit many, many countries in every part of the world. However, I have never visited a country which did not have some problem with prejudice. At times it was prejudice against a racial or religious minority within its boundaries. At times it was prejudice against people from other nations. At times it was prejudice or resentment against those who were wealthier or those who were poorer than the average. But prejudice is a universal problem. Why? One reason is because prejudice has its roots in pride—and pride is at the heart of sin. Just as sin is universal, so prejudice is universal as long as our hearts are untouched by God's regenerating power.

The word *prejudice* means "prejudging" or "making an estimate of others without knowing the facts." Prejudice is a mark of weakness, not of strength; it is a tool of the bigot, but never a device of the true Christian. One of our great problems in this complex age continues to grow since modern man has forsaken the pathway of Christian mercy and understanding—and has chosen to walk the road of intolerance and intrigue. Someone has said, "Prejudice is being down on what you're not up on." Lack of awareness along with prejudice stifles mercy.

Edwin Markham referred to the prevailing gentility of yesteryear when he said:

He drew a circle that shut me out,
Heretic, rebel, a thing to flout;

But Love and I had the wit to win,
We drew a circle that took him in.

Prejudice is measured by computing the distance between our own biased opinions and the real truth. If we would all be perfectly honest before God, there would be no prejudice. But since most of us by nature are possessed of biased minds and perverted hearts, prejudice is widespread in the world.

The late Edward R. Murrow once said, "There is no such thing as an objective reporter. We are all slaves of our environment."

All of us have personal biases and prejudices. Despite our improved educational system, our prejudices have grown in the past few years—so we can conclude that education is not the cure for all prejudice.

Even the great Charles Lamb once said: "I am, in plainer words, a bundle of prejudices, made up of likings and dislikings."

Prejudice is a form of robbery, for it robs its victim of a fair trial in the court of reason. It is also a murderer, because it kills the opportunity of advancement for those who are its prey.

Jesus struck at the very core of it when He said: "And why beholdest thou the mote that is in thy brother's eye, but considerest not the beam that is in thine own eye?" (Matthew 7:3). And then He laid down a specific rule against it when He said: "Judge not, that ye be not judged" (Matthew 7:1).

I seriously doubt if we would be prejudiced against anyone if we had all the facts in hand. We are quick to judge and prone to denounce that which we do not understand or know or experience.

Often prejudice would vanish if we had all the facts in hand. We also would be less quick to judge if we would put ourselves in the place of other people, understanding their background, sensing their problems, sympathizing with their weaknesses. Yes, education can do much to neutralize our prejudices—and yet we often find that when we apparently have conquered one type of prejudice, another type crops up in our hearts which is just as strong. I have known people who were able to overcome prejudices against people of another race—and yet their hearts were filled with scorn and prejudice against people of their own race who were of a different social class or a different political party.

The Antidote to Prejudice

But how can we get rid of this murderous prejudice? There is only one way we can get rid of prejudice: by the process of spiritual rebirth through faith in Christ. Only then do we discover God's love for all humanity, and only then will we begin to look at others through the eyes of God and see them as He sees them. Only then does God's love begin to take root in our hearts, pushing out the hate and indifference and selfishness that have resided there. In myself I do not have the capacity to love others as I should, but "the fruit of the Spirit is love" (Galatians 5:22). Yes, Christ can give us a love for others we would never have otherwise, "because the love of God is shed abroad in our hearts by the Holy Ghost which is given unto us" (Romans 5:5). This is an operation which only God can perform.

Listen to the words of Saul of Tarsus, once one of the world's most prejudiced men: "Charity suffereth long, and is kind; charity envieth not; charity vaunteth not itself, is not puffed up. . . . Rejoiceth not in iniquity, but rejoiceth in the truth; beareth all things, believeth all things, hopeth all things, endureth all things" (1 Corinthians 13:4–7).

What the logic of Greece could not do for Saul, the grace of God did. What the culture of Rome could not do, the grace of God accomplished. After his experiences on the Damascus road, Paul found his old prejudices melting away. *Mercy* became the key word of his preaching, the theme of his Epistles, and the pattern for his conduct. "I beseech you therefore . . . by the mercies of God, that ye present your bodies a living sacrifice" (Romans 12:1) was the theme of his pleadings. Having received mercy, he was an exponent of mercy. Having been delivered from his own prejudices, he was eager that all might find release from their destructive power.

How can we be so brazen as to be prejudiced against a person when God in His mercy has been so merciful toward us?

Go with the Gospel

THIRD: We can show mercy by *sharing the gospel of Christ* with others.

Man's spiritual poverty is even more wretched than his physical poverty. His failure to do what he ought to do and be what he ought to be proves that there is something inherently wrong with him.

The Bible puts it this way: "The heart is deceitful above all things, and desperately wicked" (Jeremiah 17:9). All immorality, wantonness, greed, selfishness, prejudice, suffering, hatred, and bigotry stem from one source: the human heart. Nothing in the universe has fallen lower, and yet by the grace of God nothing can rise higher.

Physical poverty, of course, is more visible and apparent to us. We are touched by pictures of those who are starving or who live in rat-infested slums or on the street—and we should be. But spiritual poverty is much more difficult to see, because we only see it as we look at the world through the "spectacles" of God's Word. I have a friend who is extremely nearsighted. Even objects only a few feet away are a blur to him, and if he were to look across a valley, for example, he would be unable to tell you if it had houses or trees on the other side. But when he puts on his glasses it is a different story! Then his vision is almost as sharp as that of an airline pilot. In the same way, the spiritual poverty of the world is not clear or even evident to us until we begin to look at it in the light of God's Word, the Bible. But when we begin to understand God's Word, we realize that the world is lost and under the judgment of God apart from Christ.

Some people have said, "Oh, well, it does not really matter what people believe, just so they are sincere. Somehow all paths lead eventually to God, I guess. And if God is a loving God, then everyone will be saved eventually whether they are trusting Christ or have rejected Him." But the Bible says otherwise: "Neither is there salvation in any other: for there is none other name under heaven given among men, whereby we must be saved" (Acts 4:12).

The fact that after two thousand years of Christianity more than half of the world's population still knows nothing about the saving, transforming grace of Christ should stir us to a renewed dedication to tell a dying world about the mercy of God.

Jesus said: "Go ye into all the world, and preach the gospel to every creature" (Mark 16:15).

Notice the little word *go*. A little word—but worldwide in its sweep! The apostles first had to *come*, and now Jesus commands them to *go*!

We have come in this generation and stopped short, but Christ says, "Go." A little word—but wrapped up in this little word is the whole sum and substance of Christ's gospel. "Go" is the first part of the word *gospel*. It should be the watchword of every true follower of Christ. It should be emblazoned on the banners of the Church. "Go," says the Master. Nearly two thousand years have dragged their weary lengths down the road of time, and yet millions of people are sitting in spiritual darkness.

Is There Any Other Remedy?

There are two opposing concepts about man's true nature. Some assert that human nature is basically good and may rise to higher and higher levels of excellence apart from God. Humanity's basic problem, according to this view, is simply ignorance or unfavorable social or economic conditions. If people can be educated enough and if their social and economic situation is right, then selfishness and conflict will be eliminated. This makes a powerful appeal to our pride, for we do not want to think that we are unable to rise above ourselves. But human experience has repeatedly shown otherwise. Yes, education is important; God, after all, is the author of all truth, and in Christ "are hid all the treasures of wisdom and knowledge" (Colossians 2:3). But lust, greed, and selfishness remain firmly entrenched in our hearts, no matter how much education we have or how ideal our social conditions may be.

The other concept of human nature is that of the Bible. It holds that man was created in the image of God, and as such was originally perfect—exactly the way God intended him to be. But humanity turned its back on God, choosing to be independent of Him. And when they did, something radical and devastating happened to the human heart.

However, today there are statesmen who assume that better organized human government is the remedy for the world's dilemma. They assume that inasmuch as vice and crime flow from ignorance and poverty that virtue could issue from knowledge and competence. Yet history proves this theory inadequate. Constitutional and statutory law lacks the essential element to purify human nature. The power is not within the province of law, whether human or divine.

The Bible says: "By the deeds of the law there shall no flesh be justified in his sight" (Romans 3:20). Again: "What the law could not do, in that it was weak . . . God sending his own Son in the likeness of sinful flesh . . . condemned sin in the flesh" (Romans 8:3).

All of us agree that one form of government may be better than another, but all forms of government have been inadequate to suppress vice and give universal prevalence to virtue to change human nature. Rome was no more pure under the eloquent Cicero than under the cruel Nero.

History proves that it is impossible to solve the problem of human nature by civil law. That is not to say, of course, that laws against evil are unnecessary or unimportant—quite the opposite. The Bible says, in fact, that God has given to civil government the authority to punish wrongdoing, and we are to support justice and the common good of society. "For rulers are not a terror to good works, but to the evil" (Romans 13:3). Good government is also to work for the positive good of society.

But all too often we think that some particular form of government will solve all our problems. Some tyrants and dictators will do all they can to impose their type of government or their political philosophy on other nations, by force or subversion if necessary. Yes, some forms of government are certainly better than others—and one reason is that they have a better understanding of the limitations and possibilities of human nature. Government and civil laws are somewhat like the cages in a zoo—they can restrain evil and keep it from getting out of hand, but they cannot change the basic nature of the human heart.

As an American, I rejoice in our liberties and the legal safeguards we have against those who would seek to destroy society.

But our government is certainly going to fall like a rope of sand if unsupported by the moral fabric of God's Word. The moral structure in our country grew from Judeo-Christian roots. When those values are applied, they produce moral fruits. But if that structure disappears, the moral sentiment that shapes our nation's goals will disappear with it.

Then also, there is the person who claims that the remedy for vice is to be found in a universal system of education. His opinion is that man will be made pure and happy by intellectual culture and mental repose.

Suppose that education is the answer to all the problems that man faces. Develop the intellectual to the maximum; yet do you get virtue? Knowledge did not save Solomon from vice or Byron from immorality. Art and education may refine the taste, but they cannot purify the heart, forgive sin, and regenerate the individual. The Holocaust was carried out by educated people, some brilliantly so. It could well be called a demonstration of educated depravity.

A few years ago my wife and I visited the Nazi death camp of Auschwitz, located in southern Poland. Here some six million people—both Jews and non-Jews from throughout Europe—were brutally imprisoned and murdered. We saw the barbed wire, the instruments of torture, the airless punishment cells, the gas chambers and crematorium. Every square foot of that terrible place was a stark and vivid witness to man's inhumanity to man. We laid a memorial wreath and then knelt to pray at a wall in the midst of the camp where 20,000 people had been shot. When I got up and turned around to say a few remarks to those who had gathered with us, my eyes blurred with tears and I almost could not speak. How could such a terrible thing happen—planned and carried out by people who were often highly educated? The problem is the human heart. Jesus declared, "For out of the heart proceed evil thoughts, murders, adulteries, fornications, thefts, false witness, blasphemies" (Matthew 15:19).

It is not simply education in civilization that the world is wanting today, but civilization with enlightened conscience; not simply institutions and airlines and gigantic corporations, but all these entities free from graft and taint of every kind. Yet today an educated, civilized society is turning its face while thousands of unborn babies are being killed. God Himself, if not history, will judge this greater holocaust.

Where is mercy?

I would rather have a world filled with ignorant savages than with civilized sophisticates without morality. Better the wild, unexplored wilderness than the debauched palace of civilized shame. Better the cannibal of the South Seas than the civilized vultures of our cities.

The mathematician can solve problems on paper, but can he solve his personal problems? The orthopedic surgeon can set broken bones, but what can he do for a broken heart? The engineer can read the blueprints, but where is his blueprint for daily living?

Reformed by Regeneration

Should we drive out civilization? you ask. No, we should pray God to *reform* it *by regeneration.* Starve out graft and put in honesty. Drive out prejudice and put in the Golden Rule. Drive out ruthlessness and put in mercy. This can be done only through an acceptance of Jesus Christ as personal Savior on the part of individuals who make up the society of the world.

We can put a public school and a university in the middle of every block of every city in America—but we will never keep America from rotting morally by mere intellectual education. Education cannot be properly called education which neglects the most important aspects of man's nature. Partial education throughout the world is far worse than none at all if we educate the mind but not the soul.

Turn a half-educated man loose upon the world, put him in the community with inexhaustible resources at his command but recognizing no power higher than his own—he is a monstrosity! He is but halfway educated and is far more dangerous than if he were not educated at all. He is a speeding locomotive without an engineer. He is a tossing ship without a compass, pilot, or destiny.

To think of civilizing people without converting them to Christ is about as wise as to think about transforming wolves into lambs merely by washing them and putting on them a fleece of wool.

"Happy are the merciful: for they shall obtain mercy."

The mercy the world needs is the grace, love, and peace of our Lord Jesus Christ. It is His transforming and regenerating power that the world needs more than anything else.

To be sure, we are to use the world's physical resources, but along with them we are to take the regenerating power of Christ. We are to take a cup of cold water in one hand and regeneration in the other and give them to a physically and spiritually starved world. We have thought that man's needs were entirely physical, but we are beginning to realize that they are also spiritual.

The Gifts of the Gospel

The gospel of Christ provides for our *physical being.* Materialism can see nothing in our bodies except laboratory analyses, but the Bible with stern rebuke exclaims: "What? know ye not that your body is the temple of the Holy Ghost?" (1 Corinthians 6:19).

The gospel provides for our *intellect.* It stimulates the intellect to the highest activity. It commands the complete education of all our intellectual powers. The Bible instructs: "Gird up the loins of your mind" (1 Peter 1:13). It opens before a regenerated person a whole universe of truth.

The gospel also provides for our *sensibilities.* "Let not your heart be troubled" (John 14:1). "Blessed are they that mourn: for they shall be comforted," says Jesus. This is what humanity needs. Humanity wants comfort in its sorrow, light in its darkness, peace in its turmoil, rest in its weariness, and healing in its sickness and diseases: The gospel gives all of this to us.

The gospel provides for our *will.* It provides that we may yoke our will to the omnipotent will of God and thereby strengthen our own will.

The gospel also provides for man's *moral nature.* Its code of morals is acknowledged by any man to be above reproach.

The gospel also provides the only satisfaction in the universe for our *spiritual nature.* The gospel recognizes the tremendous fact of sin and proposes an adequate remedy.

It does not evade the age-old question, "What must I do to be saved?" by saying there is no need of salvation. It does not lift us out of the pit by telling us that we are not bad. It does not remove the sting of our conscience by taking away conscience itself. It does not haunt us.

The gospel shows people their wounds and bestows on them love. It shows them their bondage and supplies the hammer to knock away their chains. It shows them their nakedness and provides them the garments of purity. It shows them their poverty and pours into their lives the wealth of heaven. It shows them their sins and points them to the Savior.

This is the message we are to take to a lost, confused, and bewildered world! This is showing mercy!

There are those near us in our communities who need the regenerating power of Christ. We can call them by name. I suggest that each of us make a list and begin by spending time in prayer for these needy people. We should ask God to show us how to witness to them and how to win them. Their lives can be transformed by the message we give them. We are to share this gospel we have received. If Christ has done anything for us, then we must share it. In so doing, we are showing mercy!

William Shakespeare wrote:

> *The quality of mercy is not strained;*
> *It droppeth as the gentle rain from heaven*
> *Upon the place beneath: it is twice blest*
> *It blesseth him that gives and him that takes:*

'Tis mightiest in the mightiest; it becomes
The throned monarch better than his crown.

No, the path to happiness is not found in selfish living and indifference to others. Instead, when we have experienced the mercy of God then we will show mercy to others. Then we will indeed be "twice blest" because we will both make others happy and experience true happiness ourselves. "Happy are the merciful: for they shall obtain mercy."

Blessed are the pure in heart: for they shall see God. Matthew 5:8

CHAPTER SEVEN

Happiness in Purity

IN THE BIBLE the heart is considered to be something far more complex than a bodily organ. It is called the seat of the emotions. Fear, love, courage, anger, joy, sorrow, and hatred are ascribed to the heart. It has come to stand for the center of the moral, spiritual, and intellectual life of a person. The "heart" is said to be the seat of a person's conscience and life.

Jesus said, "Happy are the pure in heart." Now, we should be able to take that for just what it means. If the heart is the seat of affection, then our love toward God must be pure. If the heart is the center of our motives, then our motives must be pure. If the heart is the residence of our wills, then our wills must be yielded to Christ. We are to be pure in love, pure in motive, and pure in desire.

It might be well to pause at this point to observe just what is meant by being "pure in heart."

The True Meaning of Purity

The word which is translated "pure" here was used in several ways in the original Greek language. For one thing, it was often used to mean something that was unadulterated or unmixed with anything foreign, such as pure gold which has not been mixed with any other metal, or milk which has not been watered down. Or again, it often simply meant "clean," like a dish which had been thoroughly washed or clothes that had been scrubbed.

Now apply those meanings to "pure in heart." If we are truly pure in our hearts, we will have a single-minded devotion to the will of God. Our motives will be unmixed, our thoughts will not be adulterated with those things which are not right. And our hearts will be clean, because we will not tolerate known sin in our hearts and allow it to pollute us. We will take seriously the Bible's promise, "If we say that we have no sin, we deceive ourselves, and the truth is not in us. If we confess our sins, he is faithful and just to forgive us our sins, and to cleanse us from all unrighteousness" (1 John 1:8–9).

There is, however, another dimension to this word *pure.* It also sometimes means something which was purged of wrong so it could be used for right. William Barclay points out that it could be used of an army which had been purged or cleared of soldiers who were cowardly or weak and unable to fight. It would then be a "pure" army, filled with dedicated and trained soldiers ready for battle. This would be like a person's body which is purified of sickness so it is strong and able to work. In the same way, when we are "pure in heart" we are ready to do those good things which God has for us to do.

In other words, purity of heart has both a negative and a positive side. On one hand, our hearts are to be emptied of sin and its dominion over us. On the other hand, we are to be pure in our actions and filled with all that is pure. The Bible illustrates these negative and positive sides to purity: "*Put to death* therefore what is earthly in you: immorality, impurity, passion, evil desire, and covetousness. . . . *Put them all away:* anger, wrath, malice, slander, and foul talk. . . . *Put on then,* as God's chosen ones, holy and beloved, compassion, kindness, lowliness, meekness, and patience. . . . And above all these *put on* love" (Colossians 3:5,8,12,14, RSV emphasis added).

Misconceptions About Purity of Heart

Did Jesus mean that we were to attain a sinless perfection, a spiritual state in which it would be impossible for us to fail again? No.

To be pure in heart does not mean that I must live in a straitjacket, looking pious and retreating periodically into monastic seclusion. Jesus denounced the Pharisees because they had a false conception of heart purity. He said: "Woe unto you, scribes and Pharisees, hypocrites! for ye are like unto whited sepulchres, which indeed appear beautiful outward, but are within full of dead men's bones, and of all uncleanness" (Matthew 23:27).

Jesus' debate with the Pharisees was right at this point. They avowed that the favor of God was gained by making clean the outside of the cup, by observing certain religious rites, and by keeping the letter of the law. In other words, they worked from the "outside in" rather than from the "inside out."

But this was not God's plan. This did not produce purity of heart. This did not bring about happiness of soul.

Their superficial religion was powerless to cleanse their hearts from their moral filth and corruption; hence the Pharisees were not happy men. They were full of resentments, bitternesses, prejudices, and hatreds. Why? Simply because they had lost sight of God's conception of the pure in heart. They thought that as long as they kept the letter of the law that this was enough.

But Jesus taught that God looks deeper than the outside actions of an individual. He searches and ponders the heart. God judges not so much the outside as He does the inside. He looks to the motives, thoughts, and intents of our heart.

We called one of our daughters "Bunny." She was a sweet, loving, cooperative child. At that time, many years ago, she was at the age where she was obsessed with the desire to help Daddy. Whatever I did, she would say, "Daddy, let me help you." Now Bunny meant well, but between you and me, she was seldom of any valuable assistance in a constructive way. If she helped me weed the flowers, she pulled up the flowers instead of the weeds. If she helped me unload the groceries, she invariably dropped something of value and broke it. If she helped me clean my study, she made a mess of things in general. But Bunny's motive was good—she really wanted to help. So I tried to encourage this good, though undeveloped trait, realizing Bunny's motives. Incidentally, she has grown up to be an extraordinarily helpful, caring person.

This is exactly what God does. He does not judge the superficial goodness or the superficial badness of what we do. He goes deeper into the soul and probes as a surgeon! When God is through probing our hearts, He says: "The heart is deceitful above all things, and desperately wicked: who can know it?" (Jeremiah 17:9).

Evil in the Heart

When Jesus had finished probing the hearts of the people with whom He came in contact, He said: "Out of the heart of men, proceed evil thoughts, adulteries, fornications, murders, thefts, covetousness, wickedness, deceit, lasciviousness, an evil eye, blasphemy, pride, foolishness" (Mark 7:21–22). Jesus taught that the human heart was far from God: darkened, unbelieving, blind, proud, rebellious, idolatrous, and stony. He taught that the human heart in its natural state is capable of any wickedness and any crime.

A teenage boy was arrested in New York for having committed one of the most vicious murders of our time. His mother exclaimed, "But he is a good boy!" She had not stopped to realize that an unregenerate human heart is potentially capable of any crime. A certain poet has written:

Quicken my conscience till it feels
The loathsomeness of sin.

That is the reason why many of the peace treaties which have been signed in human history have not been kept and war has ensued. These treaties have been signed in good faith, but they were signed on the basis of trusting the motives of the other party. They have been broken time after time and millions have died on the battlefields of the world because the human heart is deceitful and desperately wicked.

Our hearts are impure! As a result, we are filled with inner tension, pride, frustration, confusion, and a thousand and one other spiritual, mental, and physical ills. The very root of our lives is bad. The theologian William G. T. Shedd said, "Human character is worthless, in proportion as abhorrence of sin is lacking in it."

Jesus says we will never be completely and supremely happy until our hearts are pure. Samuel Rutherford urged us to "labor for a strong and lively sense of sin . . . the more sense of sin, the less sin."

The Cure for a Sick Heart

But if we have bad hearts, what can we do about them? "Should we try to reform or improve our hearts in some way?" someone asks.

Man—ever intent to live independently of God and His transforming grace—claims that environment, education, and right mental attitudes can change the heart and make it pure. "Put people in a wholesome atmosphere and they will be good," the Humanist argument goes.

Although this may sound perfectly logical—like a good many man-made theories—it simply will not hold water. Put an African baboon in a Boston drawing room, and how long will it take for him to act like a human being? "But that is twisting the argument," our Humanist friends will object.

I think not! For we are dealing with the problem of nature as opposed to environment. The nature of an animal is affected by environment but can never be radically and essentially changed by it. An animal trainer may subdue that wild nature to a degree, but the baboon will always have the nature of a baboon, regardless of training and environment. Furthermore, the first crime, Cain's murder of Abel, was committed in a perfect environment!

There are others who say that our mental attitude toward life needs to be changed: "If we *think* right, we *are* right." To them the problem of evil is a psychological one. "Think positively," they say. "As a man thinketh in his heart, so is he."

This is all very good, and I have a great deal of sympathy for those who are trying through psychological means to help bring about better mental attitudes. But this also gives encouragement to the people who say, "Goody, goody. We can help ourselves, just as we had always thought." The "do-it-yourself" rage is spreading everywhere, and people are being told that to be happy all they have to do is think "happiness thoughts." Such thoughts might cheer us, but they will never change us.

However, God says that our need is deeper-seated than the mind. He did not say, "Blessed are they who think happiness thoughts." He said: "Blessed are the pure in heart: for they shall see God."

This heart purity is not produced by mental suggestion, by environment, or by education. It is a miracle wrought by God Himself. God says: "A new heart also will I give you, and a new spirit will I put within you: and I will take away the stony heart out of your flesh" (Ezekiel 36:26).

Purity of heart is a result of a rebirth, a miracle, a new creation. As the Bible says: "Which were born, not of blood, nor of the will of the flesh, nor of the will of man, but of God" (John 1:13).

We need cleansed, forgiven, justified, new hearts! Such can be received only as an act of God on the ground of the death of Christ on the cross.

A Sunday school teacher once told a class of boys and girls that nothing was impossible with God. One little boy objected, saying that he knew one thing God could not do.

"And what could that be?" asked the astonished teacher.

"To see my sins through the blood of Jesus Christ," the youngster wisely answered.

When we have properly confessed and renounced our sins and by faith received Christ into our hearts, then we receive a new heart from God. Only then can we be called "pure in heart." Only then can we know the secret of happiness!

Again, I should like to emphasize that this is not an emotional experience, though emotion may be a factor. I may not "feel" that I have a new heart but I can accept the fact by faith. Faith goes beyond logic, rationalization, and understanding. You may not be able to accept intellectually all that has been said on these pages, but I challenge you to believe and accept by faith that which you cannot understand. There would be no need for faith if we could understand all about God.

Jesus insisted that we must become as little children before we could enter the kingdom of heaven. Each of us must become as a little child and by faith grasp that which we cannot altogether understand. But on the other hand, realize that God can be trusted. Faith is not a blind leap in the dark! It is instead based squarely on what God has done for us in Jesus Christ. Our faith has a firm foundation, because it is not based on speculation or wishful thinking, but upon God and His Word. God can be trusted to keep His promises to us.

Certainly purity of heart is a prerequisite to entering the kingdom of heaven. There is no chance of a person's ever going to heaven until that one has received purity of heart. This purity of heart comes as an act of God after one has renounced sin and received Christ!

Have you received a new heart? If you have, then you stand on the threshold of discovering the secret of happiness!

It is impossible to live pure lives until we have pure hearts. Many people today are trying to put the cart before the horse. They are teaching purity of motives, desires, and actions to old, deceitful hearts! No wonder we have ended up such moral failures in spite of our vaunted knowledge and psychological approaches. Pure motives, desires, and actions stem from pure hearts.

The Nature of the Pure Heart

If we have received a cleansed and pure heart from God we are expected to live a pure life. Theologically (as we have already seen in the chapter on "Happy Though Hungry"), this is called "sanctification."

Pure hearts will be Christlike. It is God's desire that we be conformed to the image of His Son. If Christ lives within us and our bodies become the abode of the Holy Spirit, is it any wonder that we should be like Him? And just what do we mean by Christlike?

The Bible says: "Let this mind be in you, which was also in Christ Jesus" (Philippians 2:5). Jesus had a humble heart. If He abides in us, pride will never dominate our lives. Jesus had a loving heart. If He dwells within us, hatred and bitterness will never rule us. Jesus had a forgiving and understanding heart. If He lives within us, mercy will temper our relationships with our fellowmen. Jesus had an unselfish heart. If He lives in us, selfishness will not predominate, but service to God and others will come before our selfish interests. But even more, Jesus' one desire was to do His Father's will. This is the essence of Christlikeness—eager obedience to the Father's will.

You say, "That's a big order!" I admit that. It would be impossible if we had to measure up to Him in our own strength and with our own natural hearts.

Paul recognized that he could never attain this heart purity by his own striving. He said: "I can do all things *through* Christ which strengtheneth me" (Philippians 4:13, emphasis added).

God hasn't left us alone, out on a limb! Jesus said to His disciples: "Lo, I am with you alway, even unto the end of the world" (Matthew 28:20). They did what they did because He was with them. They were nothing but a group of rough, unlettered men; but with Christ in their hearts they "turned the world upside down" (Acts 17:6).

Christ provided the possibility of purity by His death on the cross. We have seen that the righteousness and the purity of God are imputed to men who confess their sins and receive Christ into their hearts.

Webster defines *purity:* "Freedom from foreign admixture or deleterious matter. Cleanness; freedom from foulness or dirt. Freedom from guilt or the defilement of sin: innocence; chastity. Freedom from any sinister or improper motives or views."

Though all of these ideas are embraced in the term *purity,* they do not set up an absolute standard by which to judge what is foreign and what is not, what is sin and what is not. It is best to regard purity in the all-embracing connotation: complete conformity to the holiness of God.

The Scriptures continually ask us to strive after *physical, mental,* and *moral* purity. God says: "Be ye holy; for I am holy" (1 Peter 1:16). Further, the Scripture says that without holiness, "no man shall see the Lord" (Hebrews 12:14). Again the Scripture says: "Who shall ascend into the hill of the LORD? or who shall stand in his holy place? He that hath clean hands, and a pure heart; who hath not lifted up his soul unto vanity, nor sworn deceitfully" (Psalm 24:3–4).

We are actually commanded in Scripture: "Keep thyself pure" (1 Timothy 5:22).

Physical Cleanliness

God wants us *to be pure in body.* This includes *physical* cleanliness.

Caverno says, "When one realizes that by uncleanness of person or property he may endanger the health or life of family or even of society about him—as in keeping conditions that develop typhoid fever—he begins to realize that there is a close tie between cleanliness and morals."

The ancient Jews strove for physical cleanliness on religious grounds; and although many of the Old Testament laws of purification have been abolished as detailed prescriptions for today, others are incorporated into our own way of life. The principle of physical cleanliness is still in force. In the Middle Ages, however, many Christians felt that not bathing was a sign of humility and the dirtier they became, the more holy they were!

Even in the poorest of circumstances a person can afford some soap and water. There is absolutely no excuse for a Christian's being unclean, unkempt, or slovenly. If you have a pure heart, you will also want to have a pure body.

Physical cleanliness means more than just keeping our bodies washed, however. For example, God has given us our bodies and we are to take care of them in every reasonable way we can. The apostle Paul commanded Christians to be pure in body and to take care of their bodies: "What? know ye not that your body is the temple of the Holy Ghost which is in you, which ye have of God, and ye are not your own? For ye are bought with a price: therefore glorify God in your body, and in your spirit, which are God's" (1 Corinthians 6:19–20).

We need to get proper exercise, and we need to eat properly. We need to realize also that there is a close relationship between our physical health and our spiritual, mental, and emotional outlook. Science is discovering more and more the truth of what the Bible said centuries ago: "A merry heart maketh a cheerful countenance: but by sorrow of the heart the spirit is broken" (Proverbs 15:13). The Bible also states, "A merry heart doeth good like a medicine: but a broken spirit drieth the bones" (Proverbs 17:22). When David sinned against God he was burdened inside with his guilt, but it also affected him physically. Later he wrote, "When I kept silence, my bones waxed old through my roaring all the day long" (Psalm 32:3).

Moral Cleanliness

Being pure in body also includes *chastity.* Thus Paul says: "This is the will of God, even your sanctification, that ye should abstain from fornication. . . ." (1 Thessalonians 4:3).

How often the Scriptures warn against the sins of adultery and fornication. It is significant that in many references Paul mentions "uncleanness" immediately after "fornication."

Our newspapers are filled with stories of immorality in various parts of the nation. In fact, immorality is glorified today. Some of the most popular TV programs are about the decadent rich!

Let me warn you: The Scripture teaches that God hates immorality!

For several centuries our civilization has often been caught in the crosscurrents of a number of different secular philosophies. Often these have gained popular acceptance for a time, and have had a great impact on our institutions, ideas, and values. Some, for example, have taught that there are no firm or absolute moral values by which we are to guide our lives. Instead, morals are relative; we are to do whatever we think is right for us, without worrying about God and His moral law. Such views, however, only lead to moral chaos—and chaos within our society as well. One lawyer told me recently that the vast majority of his clients are not concerned about the fact they have done wrong—all they are interested in is not getting caught!

Many have been convinced that the Bible is not God's revelation, that salvation is to come through man and not through Christ, and that morality is relative and not absolute. We may as well say the rules of the road are relative and not absolute. How would you like to land at an airport where the laws of aviation were relative?

The practical results of this intellectual acceptance of Humanism and Behaviorism have been a degeneration of morals and the abandonment of religious ideals. The wave of behavioristic psychology that swept our college campuses and permeated the high school classrooms is now ingrained in the way our youth are living. The ideal of purity is scorned, immorality is laughed at in school—"God is old-fashioned!" What else can we expect but that thousands of our young people are growing up to be immoral? The Bible warns time after time that no immoral nation can survive and no immoral individual shall enter the kingdom of God.

One of the Ten Commandments says: "Thou shalt not commit adultery" (Exodus 20:14). I am keenly aware that this delicate subject is no longer considered taboo by clergymen. The newspapers mention it, pornographic writers make it the theme of their writings, it is the theme of everyday gossip, children talk about it, and almost every magazine has discussions and pictures about it. And beyond all that, the Bible mentions it over and over again as one of the worst sins! So why in the name of all that is just, proper, and holy should not preachers sound the warning against it?

The Bible says time after time: "Thou shalt not commit adultery." What does this word *adultery* mean? It is derived from the same Latin root from which we get our word *adulterate,* which means "corrupt; to make impure or to weaken."

Sin is not merely the use of that which is corrupt, but more often the misuse of that which is pure and good. So adultery can apply to many things. This sin was so terrible that under Jewish law it was punishable by death. Under the Roman law it was punishable by death. Under the Greek law it was punishable by death. And under God's law, the Bible says, it is punishable by spiritual death.

The Bible says: "She that liveth in pleasure is dead while she liveth" (1 Timothy 5:6), and "The wages of sin is death" (Romans 6:23). The

Bible says we are to keep our bodies pure, we are to abstain from fleshly lust. This sin is a sin not only against the body but against God.

Pure in Our Minds

God also wants us *to be pure in mind.* William Barclay said: "Pure thoughts mean those thoughts which can be examined by the Holy Spirit." Paul said: "Whatsoever things are pure . . . think on these things" (Philippians 4:8).

Returning to the question of chastity, we note that Jesus said: "Ye have heard that it was said . . . Thou shalt not commit adultery: But I say unto you, That whosoever looketh on a woman to lust after her hath committed adultery with her already in his heart" (Matthew 5:27–28).

You can commit immorality by *evil imaginations.* In Genesis 6:5 we read: "And God saw that the wickedness of man was great in the earth, and that every imagination of the thoughts of his heart was only evil continually." God is concerned with our imaginations, for they in a large measure determine what kind of persons we are to be.

Solomon said: "As [a man] thinketh in his heart, so is he" (Proverbs 23:7). If our thoughts are evil, then our acts will be evil. If our thoughts are godly, then our lives will be godly.

Robert Browning said: "Thought is the soul of the act." Ralph Waldo Emerson said: "Thought is the seat of action, the ancestor of every action is thought."

If God destroyed the world during Noah's time for its continual evil imaginations, is it not reasonable to believe that all of the sin, lust, and licentiousness rampant today grieves His heart just as it did in that day?

Many people dream of sin, imagine sin, and if granted the opportunity would indulge in sin. All they lack is the occasion to sin. So in the sight of God they are sinners as great as though they had actually committed immorality. All transgression begins with sinful thinking. We who have come to Christ for a pure heart, must guard against the pictures of lewdness and sensuality which Satan flashes upon the screens of our imaginations. We must select with care the books we read. I must choose discerningly the kind of entertainment I attend, the kind of associates with whom I mingle, and the kind of environment in which I place myself. I should no more allow sinful imaginations to accumulate in my mind and soul than I would let garbage collect in my living room.

Benjamin Franklin said: "It is easier to suppress the first desire than to satisfy all that follow it." St. Augustine said: "Purity of soul cannot be lost without consent." Ask God to cleanse your mind and keep it purified. This can be done through reading the Bible, daily prayer, and association with the right kind of people.

As we have seen, Jesus indicated that one can engage in immorality by a *look*. The Bible places the "lust of the eye" right along with other major sins. Listen: "For all that is in the world, the lust of the flesh, and the lust of the eyes, and the pride of life, is not of the Father, but is of the world" (1 John 2:16).

Peter spoke of having "eyes full of adultery" (2 Peter 2:14). No wonder Job said: "I made a covenant with mine eyes: why then should I think upon a maid?" (Job 31:1).

Our eyes see only what our soul allows them to see. If one's heart is out of harmony with God and he has never been born again, the odds are that he will have a perverted, distorted view of life. Like Paul, the scales of lust and animal passion can fall from our eyes when we catch a vision of Christ. At this moment I can make a covenant with my eyes. I can take my eyes and nail them to the cross until I can say, "They have been crucified with Christ, never again to lust."

Immorality can be engaged in by the *tongue*. The Scripture warns about evil communications that corrupt good manners. The psalmist said: "Set a watch, O Lord, before my mouth" (Psalm 141:3). Off-color jokes and dirty stories have no place in the Christian life. Thousands of people are engaging in immorality by the way they talk. Keep your talk pure. Ask God to purify your tongue.

I can engage in immorality by the way I *dress*. If women purposely dress to entice a man to sin, then they are guilty whether the act is committed or not. A girl said one day, "I came forward in your meeting and accepted Christ. A few nights later I was going to a party. I put on my dress. I looked in the mirror, and it seemed as though Jesus were looking at me. I went to my wardrobe and changed my dress. And now I dress as though Jesus were my escort each evening." Dress to please Christ—in all modesty and good taste.

I can engage in immorality while *reading* unclean books and looking at unclean pictures. Our newsstands today are so indecent that a Christian cannot look upon them without blushing, and yet thousands of people are buying unclean books and the wrong type of magazines. The same is true of our movie and TV screens. By feeding our lusts, we are sinning against God.

Many of you who are reading these pages have committed this terrible sin of breaking the Seventh Commandment. You have been unfaithful to your wife or husband, or you young people have yielded to this temptation of illicit sex. You have become impure in regard to chastity. The prophet Malachi wrote:

> Yet ye say, Wherefore? Because the LORD hath been witness between thee and the wife of thy youth, against whom thou hast dealt treacherously: yet is she thy companion, and the wife of the covenant. And did not he make one? Yet had he the residue of the spirit. And wherefore one? That he might seek a godly seed. Therefore take heed to your spirit, and let none deal treacherously against the wife of his youth. For the LORD, the God of Israel, saith that he hateth putting away: for one covereth violence with his garment, saith the LORD of hosts: therefore take heed to your spirit, that ye deal not treacherously. (2:14–16)

Although the Bible teaches that this sin leads to hell, there is good news! The woman at the well had broken this commandment, but Christ forgave her and met the need of her life. Mary Magdalene had broken this commandment, but Christ wonderfully met the need of her life and cleansed her from sin. The sinful woman who had been taken in adultery was brought to Jesus by the Pharisees, but He said: "Neither do I condemn thee: go, and sin no more" (John 8:11). He did not condone her, but neither did He condemn her, because she had trusted in Him. He sent her away redeemed and forgiven, but commanded her to sin no more. Christ will do the same for you if you will let Him.

Pure in Our Actions

Not only does God want us to be pure in body and pure in mind, but He wants us *to be pure in conduct.*

Paul says: "Let no corrupt communication proceed out of your mouth, but that which is good to the use of edifying, that it may minister grace unto the hearers" (Ephesians 4:29).

Jesus said to the Pharisees: "O generation of vipers, how can ye, being evil, speak good things? for out of the abundance of the heart the mouth speaketh. A good man out of the good treasure of the heart bringeth forth good things: and an evil man out of the evil treasure bringeth forth evil things. But I say unto you, That every idle word that men shall speak, they shall give account thereof in the day of judgment. For by thy words thou shalt be justified, and by thy words thou shalt be condemned" (Matthew 12:34–37).

Cursing, telling smutty stories, smearing the good name of another and referring irreverently to God and the Scriptures may be considered as coming under the expression *corrupt speech.* Our speech is to be clean, pure, and wholesome.

Under this rule of good conduct also come our associations. Paul says that evil companionships corrupt good morals (1 Corinthians 15:33). The Bible warns against being unequally yoked with unbelievers. This condemns all business, social, fraternal, and religious associations in which unchristian principles and practices govern. Concerning the latter, John says: "If there come any unto you, and bring not this doctrine, receive him not into your house, neither bid him God speed:

For he that biddeth him God speed is partaker of his evil deeds" (2 John 10–11).

Christians who are involved in associations that are evil and corrupt are asked to "come out from among them, and be ye separate . . . and touch not the unclean thing" (2 Corinthians 6:17). God promises that if we do this, He will receive us into His most intimate fellowship.

The Bible teaches that purity of conduct includes truthfulness. God's Word teaches that we should be truthful in our representations of ourselves. With what scorn Christ denounced the hypocrisy of the scribes and Pharisees! In the Sermon on the Mount, He rebuked all hypocritical giving, praying, and fasting.

We should also be truthful in speaking of our past achievements in our particular vocation. God does not ask us to understate the facts—that might even be untruthfulness—but neither does He want us to overrate our achievements or our gifts, either in thought or in speech. In the Septuagint (Greek) version of the Old Testament, Proverbs 24:28 says, "Overstate not with thy lips."

Purity in the Marketplace

We are also to be truthful in our business affairs. All misrepresentations of the quality of our merchandise, all false weights and measures, all padding of expense accounts, all forging of checks and other legal papers, and all unjust alterations of accounts are sins of untruthfulness and indicate lack of purity. The farmer who puts his spoiled wheat between two layers of good wheat when he takes it to the market and the fruit grower who puts his best fruit on top in his measure are dishonest. The tourist who misrepresents an article that is subject to duty on entering the country and the taxpayer who does not supply all the desired information are dishonest.

Being pure in conduct also includes *honesty* and *integrity* in dealing with our fellowmen. Employers in business are to give proper wages for work done, while employees are to put in a full hour's honest labor for the wages they receive. A Christian should be known in his or her neighborhood or place of business as an honest person—one who can be trusted.

Purity and Happiness Are Possible

Jesus said: "Blessed are the pure in heart."

Do you want to be happy? All right, apply this Beatitude to your heart. Take it to yourself. The pure in heart are the only ones who can know what it means to be supremely happy. Their hearts are pure toward God and, as a result, are pure toward their fellowmen.

They are happy because in possessing Him who is All and in All, they envy no one's worldly goods. They are happy because they envy not another person's praise or another person's place in the sun. Because they are the enemy of no one, they regard no one as their enemy. The result is peace with God and the world. Because their sins have been freely forgiven, they freely forgive those who have wronged them. They are thus purged of contemptuous malice.

But the greatest happiness that comes to the pure in heart is not only a proper relationship with others but a sublime relationship with God. "For they shall see God." The gates of Eden swing open once more. God and man walk together once again.

Dying to Dirt

From the old magazine *Hi Call* comes this story:

> Visiting in a mining town, a young minister was being escorted through one of the coal mines. In one of the dark, dirty passageways, he spied a beautiful white flower growing out of the black earth of the mine. "How can there be a flower of such purity and beauty in this dirty mine?" the minister asked the miner. "Throw some of the coal dust on it and see," was the reply. The minister did so and was surprised that as fast as the dirt touched those snowy petals, it slid right off to the ground, leaving the flower just as lovely as before. It was so smooth that the dirt could not cling to the flower.

Our hearts can be the same way. We cannot help it that we have to live in a world filled with sin, any more than the flower could change the place where it was growing. But God can keep us so pure and clean that though we touch sin on every side, it will not cling to us. We can stand in the midst of it just as white and beautiful as that flower.

The secret of purity is God! The secret of seeing and knowing God is a pure heart . . . a pure heart comes from God! Get a pure heart, and you can be supremely happy—no matter what the circumstances!

Blessed are the peacemakers: for they shall be called the children of God. Matthew 5:9

CHAPTER EIGHT

Happiness Through Peacemaking

THE PROBLEM OF human strife is as old as man. It had its beginning on the outskirts of Eden when Cain, driven by envy, murdered his more devout brother, Abel. Men fought then as now: primarily because strife was inherent in their natures.

Jesus spoke prophetically of our times when He said: "And ye shall hear of wars and rumors of wars . . . nation shall rise against nation, and kingdom against kingdom . . ." (Matthew 24:6–7).

Someone has pointed out that over the past 4,000 years there have been fewer than 300 years of peace. Yet one wonders, was that universal peace? It is more likely that down through history there has always been a war, or wars, in various parts of the world. Even the most optimistic person is forced to admit that there is something seriously wrong with a world that has such a passion for destruction.

If a man were sent from Mars to report earth's major business, he would in all fairness have to say that war was the earth's chief industry. He would report that the nations of the world were vying with each other in a race to see which could make deadlier weapons and amass bigger nuclear arsenals. He would say that earth's people are too quarrelsome to get along with each other and too selfish to live peacefully together.

Dr. Robert Oppenheimer, who supervised the creation of the first atomic bomb, was asked to appear before a congressional committee.

They asked him if there was any defense against this awesome new weapon of war. "Certainly," the great physicist replied.

"And that is—," someone asked.

The audience awaited the answer in subdued silence. "Peace," the eminent scientist replied softly.

The Search for Peace

But why is it that after these thousands of years of life on this planet we are no nearer peace than were the warring tribes of ancient history?

The world is desperately searching for peace. There are millions of people who would gladly give their right arms to find it. They would like to have peace—deep, inward, satisfying peace.

They also yearn for peace in our world—freedom from conflict and war, freedom from the hatred and strife which divide families and communities, and freedom from fear of the future, wondering when a computer will malfunction or a maniacal dictator will place his finger on the nuclear or biochemical button and wipe out civilization as we know it.

The world thinks peace would come if everyone made a lot of money, but people haven't found peace in possessions. They have thought the world would have peace if all arms were destroyed. Yet Cain killed Abel without a handgun. It is man's heart that is the problem.

Some thought peace could be found in a bottle, but they didn't find it there. It was an artificial peace, frequently leading to death. They thought one would find it in getting and accumulating a lot of knowledge, so they got all the degrees they could get, but still didn't find it. Some have searched the religions of the world, even exotic and mind-warping cults, but haven't found peace even there.

There are a thousand ways we've turned, trying to find peace, but we haven't found it. We've escaped from reality for a few moments, for a few hours, and then it's back there—the old burden, the old suffering, the old emptiness, the old monotony, the old grind. Jesus

Christ is the only One who can give "the peace that passeth all understanding."

The simple fact is: There can be no real peace in the world until we have peace with God.

The motto of the Apollo II flight was, "We come in peace for all mankind." This motto was on the plaque which was left there on the surface of the moon, where the astronauts landed on the Sea of Tranquillity. Astronauts Neil Armstrong and Buzz Aldrin found themselves in a wonderfully peaceful place there on the moon. Do you know why? There had never been any humans there before!

Not long after the development of the atomic bomb, Albert Einstein declared, "The unleashed power of the atom has changed everything except our way of thinking. We shall require a substantially new manner of thinking if mankind is to survive." Later a photographer who had noted the look of immense sadness on Einstein's face asked him, "So you don't believe that there will ever be peace?" "No," the great scientist replied. "As long as there will be man, there will be wars."

Peace is more than a mere cessation of hostilities, a momentary halt in a hot or cold war. Rather, it is something positive. It is a specific relationship with God into which a person is brought. It is a spiritual reality in a human heart which has come into vital contact with the Infinite God.

The Bible says: "But now in Christ Jesus ye who sometimes were far off are made nigh by the blood of Christ. For he is our peace, who hath made both one" (Ephesians 2:13–14).

A Breach Repaired

I saw a painting in England which showed a soldier who had gone to the front to repair the communications lines. The message which was to flow through those lines meant life to hundreds and perhaps thousands of men. He found a breach in the wires but had nothing with which to repair the break. While the enemy shells were bursting around him, he took one broken cable in his left hand and stretching his right hand grasped the other cable and made the connection. The dramatic picture had a one-word title: *Through.*

Christ, in His vicarious death on the cross, repaired the breach between God and man. The Bible says: "He is our peace" (Ephesians 2:14). Those who were afar off are made nigh . . . He has made both one. *Through Him alone* we have peace!

Although God has never been humanity's enemy, we by choice became enemies of God. The revolt began in the Garden of Eden, when Adam revolted against God and allied himself with Satan. It was there that the enmity began. It was there that the abysmal breach was made by humanity, by deliberate choice. *Enmity* and *enemy* come from the same root.

The history of man has been the record of a futile effort to live happily and peacefully apart from God. When Israel turned from the worship of Jehovah to the worship of idols, she lost her peace, and either fell prey to other nations or entered a series of wars. Any step away from the true, living God is a step in the direction of strife.

Hitler felt pretty sure of himself when he denounced the Bible and Christianity and tried to create a "pure Aryan" church with a god who bore a striking resemblance to Thor or Woden, the war gods. We are all acquainted with the record of what happened in Germany. A regime which on the surface looked strong enough to conquer the world crumbled and fell swiftly. Today a new Germany has emerged out of the rubble of World War II. In our tours of Germany we have sensed the heart-hunger of these gifted and virile people for a faith which brings peace and not war.

Jesus said: "Blessed are the peacemakers: for they shall be called the children of God." Notice, He calls for us to be *peacemakers*—not pacifists. There is a world of difference between the two!

Where does peacemaking begin? How can we become peacemakers?

We have pointed out that peace can never come out of war. War is the sire of poverty, depression, suffering, and hatred—it has never given us permanent peace.

Can peace be discovered within ourselves? Psychiatry has told us that peace is but a mental attitude. Cast off our phobias, shed our neuroses, and "voilá!"—we'll have the coveted peace men long for.

Psychiatry Alone Won't Work

I respect psychiatry and psychology for what they can do. One of my sons-in-law is a practicing psychologist and a Christian, and has dedicated his life to helping people who have emotional problems. Many of those problems, he tells me, have a direct relationship to spiritual and moral problems which have caused a person to become insecure and unstable. But emotional stability and peace of mind are no substitute for the lasting inner peace which can only come from God. If psychiatry leaves God out, ultimately we shall see psychiatrists going to each other for treatment. There can be no peace until we find peace with God. The Bible says: "He is our peace" (Ephesians 2:14).

The Bible is not content to leave the nature of the peace Christ purchased for us in doubt. It sketches that peace in the clearest of outlines. Christ made peace by the blood of His cross (Colossians 1:20). He bore the sins of all, so those who know His saviorhood need be troubled by them no longer. He interposed Himself between doomed humanity and the wrath of God. And He stands still between the holy God and fallen man in his strife, rebellion, and conflict. He is the only hope for peace in the inner spiritual warfare of the soul, and for that reason also is the only hope for social stability.

In a materialistic world which has tried to sever diplomatic relations with God, we have nowhere to retreat except within ourselves. We are like turtles in a traffic jam—the best we can do is to pull our heads back into our shells and shut our eyes. But that's a good way to get the life crushed out of you, as any dead turtle can attest.

Where Does It Begin?

Where does peacemaking begin? How can we become peacemakers in our broken, nervous, frightened, and dangerous world?

If we are to be peacemakers, we first must make our peace with God.

The Bible says: "There is no peace, saith the LORD, unto the wicked" (Isaiah 48:22). The same prophet said: "The way of peace they know not; and there is no judgment in their goings: they have made them crooked paths: whosoever goeth therein shall not know peace" (Isaiah 59:8).

Man's conflict with man has been but an expression on the human level of his conflict against God. Until we find an armistice with God, we cannot know peace among ourselves. Both ancient and modern men have discovered the peace of God. David said: "I will both lay me down in peace, and sleep: for thou, LORD, only makest me dwell in safety" (Psalm 4:8).

A former unbeliever, having recently discovered the peace of God, said to me some years ago, "My wife and I used to wake up in the morning quarreling and go to bed at night bickering—but since we have found peace with God, our home is a heaven on earth."

We can have peace with God! "But how can we discover this peace?" you ask.

A Cease-fire Needed

The first step in finding peace with God is to stop fighting Him. Through the Bible, through the Church, through the lives of Christian people, God has been trying to get through to us for years with the message that He wants to give us peace. Christ said to His disciples: "My peace I give unto you" (John 14:27). He is no respecter of persons— He wants to give us peace. But He can't give us His peace as long as we lift high the red flag of rebellion. We must stop resisting God! We must no longer shut Him out of our lives! We must stop fighting! We must give up!

The Solace of Surrender

The second step in finding peace with God is to surrender to Him. We must put down our weapons of war! We must get off the offensive, and stop *being* offensive! The Bible says regarding a people who had no peace with God: "Be ye not stiffnecked, as your fathers were, but yield yourselves unto the LORD" (2 Chronicles 30:8).

When we surrender to a "friendly enemy"—to One who loves us—we are using good sense.

The peace which follows the acceptance of Christ as Savior is more than earthly peace, and it is the greatest of spiritual treasures even though it may not always bring worldly prosperity with it. To know Christ is to have the supremest of riches, a place in the kingdom of God. And men and women who give Him first place find that there is no need for anxiety about this world's goods. "Seek ye first the kingdom of God . . . and all these things shall be added unto you" (Matthew 6:33).

But there is one more aspect of this peace with God. It is not just a passive peace which sits idly under a willow tree strumming a harp. It is a peace of activity and service.

The Secret of Service

The third step in finding peace with God is to serve Him. The Bible told an ancient people who sued for peace not only to yield but to "serve the LORD your God, that the fierceness of his wrath may turn away from you" (2 Chronicles 30:8).

In all of life there is nothing more wonderful than discovering peace with God. Step one to this discovery is realizing God's plan—peace and life. God loves you and wants you to experience peace and life—abundant and eternal.

The Bible says, " . . . we have peace with God through our Lord Jesus Christ" (Romans 5:1). John 3:16 says, "For God so loved the world, that he gave his only begotten Son, that whosoever believeth in him should not perish, but have everlasting life." In John 10:10 Jesus said, ". . . I am come that they might have life, and that they might have it more abundantly."

Since God planned for us to have peace, and the abundant life right now, why are most people not having this experience? Step two is acknowledging man's problem—separation. God created man in

His own image and gave him an abundant life. He did not make him as a robot to automatically love and obey Him, but gave him a will and freedom of choice. Man chose to disobey God and go his own willful way. Man still makes this choice today. This results in separation from God.

The Bible says, "For all have sinned, and come short of the glory of God" (Romans 3:23). In Romans 6:23 the apostle Paul says, "For the wages of sin is death [separation from God]; but the gift of God is eternal life through Jesus Christ our Lord." Man through the ages has tried to bridge this gap in many ways without success.

There is only one remedy for this problem of separation. Step three is recognizing God's remedy—the cross. Jesus Christ is the *only* answer to this problem of separation. When Jesus Christ died on the cross and rose from the grave, He paid the penalty for our sin and bridged the gap from God to man. His *death* and *resurrection* make a new life possible for all who believe.

"God is on one side and all the people on the other side, and Christ Jesus, himself man, is between them to bring them together" (1 Timothy 2:5 TLB).

The Bible says, "But God commendeth [showed] his love toward us, in that, while we were yet sinners, Christ died for us" (Romans 5:8). John writes, "Jesus saith unto him, I am the way, the truth, and the life: no man cometh unto the Father, but by me" (14:6). Paul says, "For by grace are ye saved through faith; and that not of yourselves; it is the gift of God: not of works, lest any man should boast" (Ephesians 2:8–9).

God has provided the only way . . . man must make the choice. Step four is for man to make his response to receive Christ. We must trust Jesus Christ and *receive Him* by personal invitation. The Bible says, "Behold, I stand at the door, and knock [Christ is speaking]: if any man hear my voice, and open the door, I will come in to him" (Revelation 3:20). "But as many as received him, to them gave he power to become the sons of God, even to them that believe on his name," writes the apostle John (1:12).

Is there any good reason why you cannot receive Jesus Christ right now? You must:

1. *Admit your need (I am a sinner).*
2. *Be willing to turn from your sins (repent).*
3. *Believe that Jesus Christ died for you on the cross and rose from the grave.*
4. *Through prayer, invite Jesus Christ to come in and control your life. (Receive Him as Lord and Savior.)*

If we take these steps, we have the assurance that ". . . whosoever shall call upon the name of the Lord shall be saved" (Romans 10:13). If we sincerely ask Jesus Christ to come into our lives, we have this promise: "He that hath the Son hath life [right now]; and he that hath not the Son of God hath not life. These things have I written unto you that believe on the name of the Son of God; that ye may *know* that ye have eternal life, and that ye may believe on the name of the Son of God" (1 John 5:12–13, emphasis added).

Some time ago a Christian workman was fatally injured when he fell from a high scaffolding on a construction job. A minister was called, and when he saw the serious condition of the man, he said, "My dear man, I'm afraid you're dying. I exhort you, make your peace with God!"

"Make my peace with God, sir!" said the man. "Why, that was made nineteen hundred years ago when my Savior paid all my debt upon the cross. Christ *is* my peace, and I do know God—I *do* know God!"

Every person can experience the peace of God through Christ: "For he is our peace" (Ephesians 2:14).

Becoming Peacemakers

To have peace *with* God and to have the peace *of* God is not enough. This vertical relationship must have a horizontal outworking, or our faith is in vain. Jesus said that we were to love the Lord with all our hearts and our neighbor as ourselves. This dual love for God and others is like the positive and negative poles of a battery—unless both connections are made, we have no power. A personal faith is normally useless unless it has a social application. A notable exception would be the thief on the cross and other similar situations.

I once saw a cartoon of a man rowing a boat toward a golden shore labeled "heaven." All around him were men and women struggling in vain to reach the shore and safety, but he was heedless of their peril. He was singing, "I am bound for heaven, hallelujah!" That is not an adequate picture of the Christian life.

If we have peace with God and the peace *of* God, we will become peacemakers. We will not only be at peace with our neighbors, but we will be leading them to discover the source of true peace in Christ.

Christianity increases the scope and area of our lives. It takes us from self-centeredness to multi-centeredness. Conversion takes us from introversion to extroversion.

Our lives take on new dimensions when we find peace with God. To explain this in simpler terms, let us visualize a right-angle triangle sitting on its horizontal base. At the apex or highest point in this triangle write the letter *G*, representing God. At the point where the perpendicular line meets the base write the letter *Y*, representing you. Then, at the opposite end of the horizontal line write the letter *O*, which represents others. There, in geometric form, you have a visual diagram of our relationship with God and man. Our lives (which before we found the peace of God were represented by a single dot of self-centeredness) now take in an area in vital contact with two worlds. Peace flows down from God and out to our fellowmen. We become merely the conduit through which it flows. But there is peace in being just a "channel."

Being Peacemakers in the Home

There are many areas of our lives where we can be peacemakers. There is no part of our lives which is not affected by this peace of God which we are to share with others.

FIRST: We can be peacemakers in the *home*.

In a complicated, mechanized age, it is no easy matter to keep the domestic life on an even keel. Modern gadgets, modern transportation, and modern social changes have all but revolutionized our domestic life. Families are fragmented. The old-fashioned taffy pulls, Sunday afternoon fun times, and family altars seem to have gone out with the horse and buggy.

Many homes today have become little more than dormitories, where the members of the family eat and sleep but otherwise have little communication with each other. One woman wrote to me and stated, "Our home is a war zone." Major newsmagazines carry stories of "latchkey kids," youngsters who come home from school to an empty house, seldom seeing their parents and growing up with little love or discipline. Our society has said, "Get ahead! Do your own thing! Don't worry about anyone else—run your own life!" But in the process family life disintegrates and children grow up emotionally scarred and insecure because they have never known the stability of a happy family.

The divorce rate has escalated drastically in recent decades. The home—which is the basic unit of our social structure—continues to disintegrate at an alarming rate, even among Christians. The breaking of the marriage vow is having an effect upon our other social institutions. A chain reaction has set in that could ultimately destroy the nation.

In the marriage ceremony, after the vows are said, the minister solemnly and reverently remarks: "What God hath joined together let no man put asunder." Is not God the party of the third part in a marriage? Should He not be taken into account in the marriage and in the home that emerges from that marriage? If God joins the couple together at the outset, should not His Presence be recognized in the home continually from that point on?

Many homes are in trouble today because God has been left out of the domestic picture. With the continual clash of personalities in a domestic pattern, there must be an integrating force, and the living God is that Force!

He can give love where there has been hate or indifference. He can make a husband sensitive to the needs of his wife, and the wife sensitive to the needs of her husband—instead of two people constantly clamoring and demanding only to have their own needs met. True self-giving love—the kind God has for us, and the kind He can give us for others—is like a beautiful diamond which sends out flashes of light from its many facets. The Bible gives the most profound and concise summary of love's facets in all of literature: "Love is patient and kind; love is not jealous or boastful; it is not arrogant or rude. Love does not insist on its own way; it is not irritable or resentful; it does not rejoice at wrong, but rejoices in the right. Love bears all things, believes all things, hopes all things, endures all things" (1 Corinthians 13:4–7 RSV).

A gentleman came to me with a serious domestic problem. He and his wife quarreled violently over trifles. Each blamed the other and the domestic stress had built up to the breaking point. I asked him a question to which I already knew the answer, "Do you and your wife go to church, and do you have family prayer?" He answered that they did neither.

"Your trouble in the home, Mr. B.," I said, "is the reflection of your lack of peace with God. Get right with God, and you'll be right with your wife!"

The man did just that. In sincere repentance he confessed his sin to God, and I saw his facial expression change as the peace of Christ came into his heart. The light in his face mirrored the new glow in his soul. A few days later he led his wife to Christ. That home is now a happy one, for Christ is its head.

Many couples think that if they have a more luxurious home, get a better job, or live in a different neighborhood their domestic life will be happier. No! The secret of domestic happiness is to let God, the party of the third part in the marriage contract, have His rightful place in the home. Make peace with Him, and then you can be a real peacemaker in the home.

Peace and Our Community

SECOND: We can be peacemakers in the *community.*

Our society is shot through with slander, libel, and gossip. The strife in many communities is almost unbearable. Here again, the basic cause is a faulty relationship with God.

The Bible says: "The works of the flesh are . . . hatred, variance . . . wrath, strife, seditions . . . envyings" (Galatians 5:19–21). True, we find some of these in the first-century community of Christians. Yet "Behold, how they love one another" was the remark of those who observed the unique peace of the Christian society.

How can I be a peacemaker in my community?

The formula is simple: First, I must make my own peace with God, and then I can make peace in the community. The fruit of human nature is discord and bickering; "but the fruit of the Spirit is love, joy, peace, longsuffering, gentleness, goodness, faith, meekness, temperance" (Galatians 5:22–23).

Our trouble is that we have tried to build a good society without God. In many localities we have taken the Bible out of our schools and God out of our conversation. The result is that decency has disappeared from the community, and bedlam reigns. Peace and decorum will be restored when the individuals in the community give God His proper place once more.

That does not mean it is easy to solve the complex problems that face our communities. But they can be alleviated, and we must not withdraw or refuse to lend our hand in untangling some of the problems and injustices that bring havoc to some communities. Nor must we stand back and let those who peddle evil take over our communities and twist the minds and corrupt the bodies of our young people. Paul spent two years in Ephesus—and the corrupt practices of the magicians and others in that pagan city were reversed. We need more men and women who are willing—for Christ's sake—to become involved in political issues and concerns in their communities, and to be peacemakers in His Name.

In regard to racial peace, let me say that for true Christians there is no race problem! The ground is level at the cross and there are no second-rate citizens with God. Admittedly, the problems are great, and will not be solved overnight; but if all people concerned will make sure that they have made their peace with God, it will then be a simpler matter to make peace with each other. If we approach the problem with a vindictive, intolerant, and unchristian attitude, we are destined to failure and disaster.

Peace in the Church

THIRD: We can be peacemakers in the *church.*

We might as well face it: Strife has even infiltrated our church life. It is true enough that the Church is now the Church militant. But as such its warfare ought to be that of dedication to revealed truth and divine holiness, and not internal bickering and carnal disputes.

We read in the second chapter of Luke that Joseph and Mary lost Jesus one day. Where did they lose Him? They lost Him in the most unlikely place in all the world—in the temple. Strange, I know! But, I have seen many people lose Jesus right in church. I have seen them lose Him in a dispute about who was to be choir director, who was to play the organ, who was to be an elder, or who was to be the minister. Yes, because we are human, though Christian, it is easy to lose sight of Jesus right in the temple!

I know of two deacons who had quarreled over an old line fence, and they had not spoken to each other for a long time. One of them, wanting to make peace, took his Bible and went to visit his neighbor. Handing his Bible to his "old enemy," he said, "John, you read and I'll pray. We must be friends."

But John, fumbling for his glasses, said, "But I can't read. I haven't my spectacles."

"Take mine," said his peace-loving neighbor.

After they had read the Word and prayed together, they arose and embraced each other. John handed back the spectacles to his neighbor and said through his tears, "Jim, that old line fence looks different through your glasses."

When we have the peace of God, we can see things through "the other man's glasses," and by doing that we can make peace.

Working for Peace at Our Work

FOURTH: We can be peacemakers at *work*.

One of the greatest points of tension in our economy is the labor-management relationship. Many industries today are recognizing that disputation is costly on the part of both labor and management and are seeking industrial peace through God and faith in Him.

One minister wrote to us the other day and said that he was chaplain in three industrial plants in Indiana. The managers had found that if they sat down with their employees and listened to the Christian message once each day that everyone was in a better frame of mind.

In London, an industrialist gave his heart to Christ. He wrote to us that he now conducts a chapel service in his plant and that two hundred attend the service regularly. "Never has there been more peace in our factory," he wrote.

Would you like to be an industrial peacemaker? You can be one—whether manager or laborer—if you make your peace with God first, and then seek by His grace to impart this peace to others.

When an employer and employees really know Christ, the lie is given to the Marxist thesis that an opiate religion is for the common people. To know Christ is to have part in His saviorhood and Lordship of life. Godlier employers and godlier employees will find that the right makes a claim upon every life. Where the employer is Christ's servant and the employee is the employer's spiritual partner, they are linked in an eternal vocation.

Peacemaking in Our World

FIFTH: We need peacemakers on the *international scene,* also. Many years ago President Eisenhower knelt in a chapel in Geneva before the Big Four Conference and asked God for divine guidance in the deliberations to follow. I believe that God heard and answered, for President Eisenhower during those days displayed the spirit of a true peacemaker on the international level. Kind, considerate of the opposition's view point, and given to intelligent discussion, he emerged the undisputed hero of the Geneva Conference. This was not because he held a "big stick" but because he convinced the others, at least in a measure, that he wanted peace and not war.

Several years ago I was invited to Moscow to attend an international conference of religious leaders to discuss the subject of world peace. It had been called by Patriarch Pimen, the head of the Russian Orthodox Church. At first I was reluctant to go, knowing that my presence might be misunderstood or I might be accused of being naive or manipulated by Soviet authorities. But after much prayer and thought I went, and one reason was my recollection of Jesus' words: "Happy are the peacemakers." I went as an observer and also as a speaker, delivering an address to the entire conference on "The Biblical Meaning of Peace." Later a leading Western political figure told me, "At first I thought you were wrong to go. But you were right. We must take risks for peace, because the world is too dangerous unless we learn to listen and talk to each other."

As I made clear in Moscow, I am not a pacifist, nor am I for unilateral disarmament; nations have the right to defend themselves against aggressors. Nor am I naive about the very real problems and barriers that exist between nations of different ideologies. But we must do all we can to work for peace, in whatever ways are open to us.

Is it really possible, however, for a single individual to have any impact in a world which often seems out of control? Certainly! First, encourage those who are leaders to seek peace. Second, pray for peace. The Bible commands, "I exhort therefore, that, first of all, supplications, prayers, intercessions, and giving of thanks, be made for all men; for kings, and for all that are in authority; that we may lead a quiet and peaceable life in all godliness and honesty. For this is good and acceptable in the sight of God our Saviour" (1 Timothy 2:1–3). The Bible also reminds us, "The effectual fervent prayer of a righteous man availeth much" (James 5:16).

The only corrective measure in establishing peace is for men as individuals to know the peace of God. Though I am not averse to movements which strive in one way or another for world peace, I have a strong conviction that such peace will never come unless there is a spiritual dynamic at the core. I pray for wars to cease just as I pray for crime to stop; but I know that the basic cause of both crime and war is the inherent sinfulness of human nature.

When Jesus told Nicodemus that he "must be born again," He was addressing not only this great Jewish teacher but all of us, for He saw in Nicodemus a typical representative of the race. The world cannot be reborn until men are born again and are at peace with God.

James asked, "From whence come wars and fightings among you? come they not hence, even of your lusts that war in your members?" (James 4:1).

Peacemaking is a noble vocation. But you can no more make peace in your own strength than a mason can build a wall without a trowel, a carpenter build a house without a hammer, or an artist paint a picture without a brush. You must have the proper equipment. To be a peacemaker, you must know the Peace-Giver. To make peace on earth, you must know the peace of heaven. You must know Him who "is our peace."

Jesus didn't leave a material inheritance to His disciples. All He had when He died was a robe, which went to the Roman soldiers; His mother, whom He turned over to His brother John; His body, which He gave to Joseph of Arimathea; and His Spirit, which returned to His Father.

But Jesus willed His followers something more valuable than gold, more enduring than vast landholdings and more to be desired than palaces of marble—He willed us His peace. He said: "My peace I give unto you: not as the world giveth, give I unto you. Let not your heart be troubled, neither let it be afraid" (John 14:27).

Only as we know Him and the peace He imparts can we be peacemakers . . . and He promised happiness to a maker of peace!

The key is commitment to become peacemakers—to be men and women who actively seek to bring the peace of Christ to others and to our world.

Blessed are they which are persecuted for righteousness' sake: for theirs is the kingdom of heaven. Matthew 5:10

CHAPTER NINE

Happiness in Spite of Persecution

WHO WANTS TO be persecuted? We cannot see happiness in persecution. No one enjoys being maligned. Almost all of us want the goodwill of our neighbors, and it is difficult to see what blessedness there could be in the enmity of others.

Offhand, it would seem that being a Christian should elicit the admiration and acclaim of those about us. A Christian is usually one who lives his life with kindness, honesty, and unselfishness. Such a person should be blessed, not blasted, it would seem. His peers should stand around him and sing, "For he's a jolly good fellow, which nobody can deny!"

It would seem so! But such is not the case. And it is good that this Beatitude gives us the occasion to sit down and rethink this age-old question: "Why are good people persecuted?" Or as a modern-day author has asked, "Why do bad things happen to good people?"

We Are Not Exempt

A Christian was released from a country that had a hostile regime. He eventually got a job working with Christians. He was asked one day how it had felt to be persecuted for his faith. With a surprised look he said, "We thought it was the normal Christian life."

You may have concluded, as have others, that there is usually something wrong with those who are persecuted for righteousness' sake, that there is some quirk in their disposition, some personality peculiarity or some religious fanaticism which causes others to mistreat them. No, that is not always, or let us say that is not usually, the case.

Nowhere does the Bible teach that Christians are to be exempt from the tribulations and natural disasters that come upon the world. It does teach that the Christian can face tribulation, crisis, calamity, and personal suffering with a supernatural power that is not available to the person outside of Christ. Christiana Tsai, the Christian daughter of a former governor of Kiangsu Province in China, wrote, "Throughout my many years of illness [53], I have never dared to ask God why He allowed me to suffer for so long. I only ask what He wants me to do." St. Augustine wrote, "Better is he that suffereth evil than the jollity of him that doeth evil."

The eagle is the only bird which can lock its wings and wait for the right *wind.* He waits for the updraft and never has to *flap* his wings, *just soar. So as we wait* on God He will help us use the adversities and strong winds to *benefit us!* The Bible says, "They that wait upon the LORD . . . shall mount up with wings as eagles" (Isaiah 40:31).

Christians can rejoice in the midst of persecution because they have eternity's values in view. When the pressures are on, they look beyond their present predicament to the glories of heaven. The thought of the future life with its prerogatives and joys helps to make the trials of the present seem light and transient, ". . . for theirs is the kingdom of heaven."

Christians in the People's Republic of China are an illustration of blessings under persecution. In 1949 when the missionaries were forced to leave, there were approximately 700,000 Christians in China. In the beginning, landowners, the educated, and Christians were marked for elimination. Of these three categories, which increased in spite of persecution? Those who were "persecuted for righteousness' sake." Today, reliable estimates range from 30 million to 50 million Christians in China.

The early Christians were able to experience joy in their hearts in the midst of persecution. They counted suffering for Christ not as a burden or misfortune but as a great honor, as evidence that Christ counted them worthy to witness for Him through suffering. They never forgot what Christ Himself had gone through for their salvation, and to suffer for His Name's sake was regarded as a gift rather than a cross.

He Made No False Promises

Jesus Christ spoke frankly to His disciples concerning the future. He hid nothing from them. No one could ever accuse Him of deception. No one could accuse Him of securing allegiance by making false promises.

In unmistakable language He told them that discipleship meant a life of self-denial, and the bearing of a cross. He asked them to count the cost carefully, lest they should turn back when they met with suffering and privation.

Jesus told His followers that the world would hate them. They would be "as sheep in the midst of wolves." They would be arrested, scourged, and brought before governors and kings. Even their loved ones would persecute them. As the world hated and persecuted Him, so they would treat His servants. He warned further, "They will put you out of the synagogues; indeed, the hour is coming when whoever kills you will think he is offering service to God" (John 16:2 RSV).

Many of Christ's followers were disappointed in Him, for in spite of His warning they expected Him to subdue their enemies and to set up a world political kingdom. When they came face to face with reality, they "drew back and no longer went about with him" (John 6:66 RSV). But the true disciples of Jesus all suffered for their faith.

Tacitus, a Roman historian, writing of the early Christian martyrs, said, "Mockery of every sort was added to their deaths. Covered with the skins of beasts, they were torn by dogs and perished, or were nailed to crosses, or were doomed to the flames and burnt, to serve as nightly illumination, when daylight had expired. Nero offered his gardens for the spectacle." How true were the words of Paul to the early Christians:

"Through many tribulations we must enter the kingdom of God" (Acts 14:22 RSV).

Bathed Hands in the Blaze

We are told that the martyrs went rejoicing to their deaths, as if they were going to a marriage feast. They bathed their hands in the blaze kindled for them, and shouted with gladness. One early historian, witnessing their heroism, wrote, "When the day of victory dawned, the Christians marched in procession from the prison to the arena as if they were marching to heaven, with joyous countenances agitated by gladness rather than fear."

We are not surprised that the early Christians rejoiced in suffering, since they looked at it in the light of eternity. The nearer death, the nearer a life of eternal fellowship with Christ. When Ignatius was about to die for his faith in A.D. 110 he cried out, "Nearer the sword, then nearer to God. In company with wild beasts, in company with God."

The Christians of the early church believed that "the sufferings of this present time are not worth comparing with the glory that is to be revealed to us" (Romans 8:18 RSV). Thus they could regard present difficulties as of little consequence and could endure them with patience and cheerfulness.

In all ages Christians have found it possible to maintain the spirit of joy in the hour of persecution. In circumstances that would have felled most people, they have so completely risen above them that they actually have used the circumstances to serve and glorify Christ. Paul could write from prison at Rome, "I want you to know, brethren, that what has happened to me has really served to advance the gospel" (Philippians 1:12 RSV).

In our day millions of Christians in our world live in very difficult situations. For some, life is difficult because they are only a tiny minority in societies in which non-Christians predominate, and they may find themselves discriminated against or scorned. For others, however, there is active oppression or even persecution from governments that do not tolerate religious freedom. It has been estimated that more Christians have suffered and died for their faith in this century than in all previous centuries combined.

In mainland China, for example, thousands of Christians were killed and their churches destroyed or plundered under the Cultural Revolution. Indeed, many Christians had to go underground to worship. Recent reports indicate these restrictions now seem to have been relaxed, but religious faith is still not encouraged. The same is true in many other parts of the world. The resurgence of some of the major non-Christian religions has brought new waves of oppression and persecution for many Christian believers.

That Christians make the best citizens, the most faithful and reliable workers, has begun to dawn on only a few. Until it does, these atheistic regimes are the ultimate losers. The persecuted Christians are definitely on the winning side, if not in this world, then most definitely in the one to come.

There is no doubt that the Bible teaches that every believer who is faithful to Christ must be prepared to be persecuted at the hands of those who are enemies of the gospel. "Indeed all who desire to live a godly life in Christ Jesus will be persecuted," said Paul (2 Timothy 3:12 RSV).

Other Kinds of Persecution

Is persecution, however, only confined to physical torture and death? Or are there other kinds of persecution?

Certainly persecution can take many forms—some of them obvious, but many of them very subtle. We need to realize that a godly person—one who serves Christ, and exhibits purity and integrity in his life—is not necessarily welcomed or admired by those who live differently. They may even react in scorn, or refuse to include a Christian in their social gatherings because his very presence is a rebuke to them. I have known families who disowned a member who took a strong stand for Christ. An employee may find his advancement blocked because a supervisor is prejudiced against Christians. A teenage girl may find herself laughed at because she refuses to join in the immorality of her schoolmates, or a young man may find that his refusal to get involved with alcohol or drugs makes him unpopular with those who do.

But whatever form it takes, the Bible tells us not to give in to the pressures we face, nor are we to lash out at those who oppose us. Instead, we are to do all we can to show Christ's love to them. "Bless them which persecute you: bless, and curse not. . . Recompense to no man evil for evil. . . . If it be possible, as much as lieth in you, live peaceably with all men. Dearly beloved, avenge not yourselves. . . . If thine enemy hunger, feed him; if he thirst, give him drink; for in so doing thou shalt heap coals of fire on his head. Be not overcome of evil, but overcome evil with good" (Romans 12:14, 17, 18–21).

Patience in Persecution

However, Christ told His disciples that they were not to count it a stroke of affliction when they were reviled and persecuted. Rather, they were to count it as a favor and a blessing. They were to "rejoice, and be exceeding glad" (Matthew 5:12). Just as Jesus had overcome the world, so they through His grace and strength would overcome the world. Thus they were to be of good cheer. Here is something to contemplate for those who are persecuted: When the godless plot, God laughs (Psalms 2:4; 37:12–13). When the godless prosper, don't fret (Psalm 37:7).

They were to be "more than conquerors" (Romans 8:37). They were to rejoice in tribulation (Romans 5:3). When beaten and threatened with worse treatment if they continued to preach Christ, Peter and John departed, "rejoicing that they were counted worthy to suffer dishonor for the name. And . . . they did not cease teaching and preaching Jesus as the Christ" (Acts 5:41–42 RSV).

As we read the book of Acts we soon realize that persecution and death intensified the joy of the early Christians.

The apostle Paul could write, "With all our affliction, I am overjoyed" (2 Corinthians 7:4 RSV).

In all his sufferings and sorrows Paul experienced a deep, abiding joy. He writes of being "sorrowful, yet always rejoicing" (2 Corinthians 6:10 RSV). With sincerity he declared that for Christ's sake he was "content with weaknesses, insults, hardships, persecutions, and calamities" (2 Corinthians 12:10 RSV).

I have found in my travels that those who keep heaven in view remain serene and cheerful in the darkest day. If the glories of heaven were more real to us, if we lived less for material things and more for things eternal and spiritual, we would be less easily disturbed by this present life.

In these days of darkness and upheaval and uncertainty, the trusting and forward-looking Christian remains optimistic and joyful, knowing that Christ someday must rule, and "if we endure, we shall also reign with him" (2 Timothy 2:12 RSV). As someone has said, "Patience (*hupomone*) is that quality of endurance that can reach the breaking point and not break."

At the same time I am equally certain that Christians who have spent years at hard labor or in exile, have passed through periods of discouragement—even despair. Those who have had loved ones destroyed have felt deep loss and intense suffering. Victory for such has not come easily or quickly. But eventually the peace of God does come and with it His joy.

An Upside-Down World

Here is a spiritual law which is as unchangeable as the law of gravity: "All that will live godly in Christ Jesus shall suffer persecution" (2 Timothy 3:12).

We must get this fact firmly fixed in our minds: We live in an upside-down world. People hate when they should love, they quarrel when they should be friendly, they fight when they should be peaceful, they wound when they should heal, they steal when they should share, they do wrong when they should do right.

I once saw a toy clown with a weight in its head. No matter what position you put it in, it invariably assumed an upside-down position. Put it on its feet or on its side, and when you let go it flipped back on its head.

In our unregenerate state we are just like that! Do what you may with us, we always revert to an upside-down position. From childhood to maturity we are always prone to do what we should not do and to refrain from doing what we ought to do. That is our nature. We have too much weight in the head and not enough ballast in our hearts so we flip upside down when left alone.

That is why the disciples to the world were misfits. To an upside-down man, a right-side-up man seems upside down. To the nonbeliever, the true Christian is an oddity and an abnormality. A Christian's goodness is a rebuke to his wickedness; his being right side up is a reflection upon the worldling's inverted position. So the conflict is a natural one. Persecution is inevitable.

When Christ's disciples began preaching that Jesus was the Christ, the people cried in consternation, "These that have turned the world upside down are come hither also" (Acts 17:6). Herein lies the fundamental reason for Christian persecution. Christ's righteousness is so revolutionary and so contradictory to man's manner of living that it invokes the enmity of the world.

If we could assume that people were basically upright, then it would be the popularly accepted thing to "live godly in Christ Jesus" (2 Timothy 3:12). But as long as Satan is loose in the world and our hearts are dominated by his evil passions, it will never be easy or popular to be a follower of Christ.

The Bible says: "But ye are a chosen generation, a royal priesthood, an holy nation, a peculiar people; that ye should show forth the praises of him who hath called you out of darkness into his marvelous light: which in time past were not a people, but are now the people of God: which had not obtained mercy, but now have obtained mercy. Dearly beloved, I beseech you as strangers and pilgrims . . ." (1 Peter 2:9–11).

Aliens are rarely shown the "welcome mat." They are often accepted only with a tongue-in-cheek attitude. Being aliens, with our citizenship not in the world but in heaven, we as Christ's followers will frequently be treated as "peculiar people" and as strangers.

Our life is not of this world. "Our conversation is in heaven" (Philippians 3:20). Our interests, primarily, are not in this world. Jesus said: "Lay up for yourselves treasures in heaven . . . for where your treasure is, there will your heart be also" (Matthew 6:20–21). Our hope is not in this world. The Bible says: "We look for the Saviour, the Lord Jesus Christ: who shall change our vile body, that it may be fashioned like unto his glorious body, according to the working whereby he is able even to subdue all things unto himself" (Philippians 3:20–21).

Hence, in every sense we are an enigma to the world. Like a few right-handed persons among a host of left-handed persons, we comprise a threat to their status quo. We cramp their style. We are labeled as "wet blankets," as kill-joys, and as prudes. Like the enemies of Jesus, the world still inquires contemptuously, "Art not thou also one of his disciples?" (John 18:25).

Called Counterfeit

There will be times when the eyes of suspicion will be upon us, because, with people's hearts as they are, they cannot conceive of anyone wanting to live selflessly. Unbelievers will say we have "something up our sleeve," that we have a motive in being so righteous, that it is all a game, that it is sheer hypocrisy. The cry of "counterfeit!" follows the Christian's sincere efforts.

Still another reason for persecution is that there is a war in progress.

The Word of God indicates this! The Bible says: "Fight the good fight of faith, lay hold on eternal life" (1 Timothy 6:12). Again: "No man that warreth entangleth himself with the affairs of this life; that he may please him who hath chosen him to be a soldier" (2 Timothy 2:4).

War in the World

The world, the flesh, and the devil are our enemies. In times of war one can hardly expect the goodwill of the enemy's forces. During World War

II the American journalist Cecil Brown wrote a cover story on the tragedy of the sinking of two British battleships, namely, the *Prince of Wales* and *Repulse.* He said, "There is always the danger of underestimating the enemy to the point where you are *over confident.* Figure him to be *twice* as *good* and *twice* as *smart,* then make preparations in advance!" Though our weapons are not earthly, the enemy's weapons are earthly, and we can expect Satan to use every tool at his command for our persecution and destruction. War atrocities will be committed. They who live godly in Christ *shall* suffer persecution.

All life is a struggle—that is the nature of things. Even within our physical bodies, doctors tell us, a conflict for supremacy is going on. The bacteria in our bloodstream is waging a constant war against alien germs. The red corpuscles fight the white corpuscles constantly in an effort to maintain life within the body. The recent increasingly rampant epidemic of AIDS tragically illustrates this point.

A battle is also raging in the spiritual realm. The Bible says: "We wrestle not against flesh and blood, but against principalities, against powers, against the rulers of the darkness of this world, against spiritual wickedness in high places" (Ephesians 6:12).

"We fight," the Bible says, "against the rulers of the darkness of this world." Darkness hates light. The hymnwriter was writing about war when he asked:

Must I be carried to the skies,
On flowery beds of ease;
While others fought to win the prize,
And sailed through bloody seas?

I once had a dog that would rather have dug up a moldy carcass to chew on than to have the finest, cleanest meal. He couldn't help it—that was his nature.

People cannot help that it is their nature to respond to the lewd, the salacious, and the vile. They will have difficulty doing otherwise until they are born again. And until they *are* changed by the power of

Christ, they will likely be at enmity against those who are associated with Christ.

The Cross for Christians

And, finally, Jesus said that a cross is the Christian's lot. "He that taketh not his cross, and followeth after me, is not worthy of me" (Matthew 10:38).

Does this mean that we are to wear a symbol of the cross around our necks or on the lapel of our coats? Or does it mean that we are literally to carry a wooden cross?

No! It means that the reproach of Christ's cross, which He carried when He was in the world, is ours to carry now. Being at "cross-purposes" with the world is part and parcel of the Christian life. We should not covet or expect the praise of ungodly men. On the contrary, we should expect their enmity. The very fact that they are inclined to persecute us is proof that we are "not of the world," that we are "in Christ." All of the persecution, all of the blasphemy, all of the railing that they would heap on Christ, they hurl against us. He took the reproach of the cross for us; now, it is ours to take for Him.

The Privilege of Persecution

As Paul said: "God forbid that I should glory, save in the cross of our Lord Jesus Christ, by whom the world is crucified unto me, and I unto the world" (Galatians 6:14). This, Paul considered a privilege—the privilege of persecution. In that he gloried, because in a small way he was allowed to share in the sufferings of Christ.

Now, let us remember that this Beatitude says: "Blessed are they which are persecuted for righteousness' sake . . . when men shall revile you, and persecute you, and shall say all manner of evil against you falsely . . ." (Matthew 5:10–11).

Many times we suffer because of our own poor judgment, stupidity, and blundering. There is no blessedness in this. I have known professed

Christians who were dominated by bad dispositions, snap judgments, and poor manners and thought that people were opposed to them because of their "righteousness." It was not their goodness which people resented—it was their lack of it.

We must be careful not to behave offensively, preach offensively, and dress offensively, and, when people are offended and shun us, blame it on the "offense of the cross." Our personal offensiveness is no credit to the gospel we preach.

Shabby Christians are poor advertisements for Christianity. Paul said: "We . . . suffer reproach, because we trust in the living God . . . but be thou an example of the believers, in word, in conversation, in charity, in spirit, in faith, in purity" (1 Timothy 4:10, 12). The reproach we experience is the natural resentment in the hearts of men toward all that is godly and righteous. This is the cross we are to bear. This is why Christians are often persecuted.

Positive Thoughts on Persecution

We have considered the reasons for Christians being persecuted. Now let us see what happiness and blessedness there are in persecution. As George MacDonald puts it, we become "hearty through hardship."

Our Lord instructs the persecuted to be happy. "Rejoice," He said, "and be exceeding glad: for great is your reward in heaven: for so persecuted they the prophets which were before you" (Matthew 5:12).

The word *joy* has all but disappeared from our current Christian vocabulary. One of the reasons is that we have thought that joy and happiness were found in comfort, ease, and luxury. James did not say, "Count it all joy when you fall into an easy chair," but he said, "Count it all joy when you fall into divers temptations" (James 1:2).

The persecuted are happy because they are being processed for heaven. Persecution is one of the natural consequences of living the Christian life. It is to the Christian what "growing pains" are to the growing child. No pain, no development. No suffering, no glory. No struggle, no victory. No persecution, no reward!

The Bible says: "The God of all grace, who hath called us unto his eternal glory by Christ Jesus, after that ye have suffered a while, make you perfect, stablish, strengthen, settle you" (1 Peter 5:10). It is so easy to forget that "all things work together for good to them that love God" (Romans 8:28).

Jesus, in the Sermon on the Mount, had some commandments for us with regard to our attitude toward persecution. We are to:

1. *Rejoice, and be exceeding glad.* (*Matthew 5:12*)
2. *Love our enemies.* (5:44)
3. *Bless them that curse us.* (5:44)
4. *Do good to them that hate us.* (5:44)
5. *Pray for them that despitefully use us and persecute us.* (5:44)

I have a friend who lost his job, a fortune, his wife, and his home. But he tenaciously held to his faith—the only thing he had left. One day he stopped to watch some men doing stonework on a huge church. One of them was chiseling a triangular piece of stone.

"What are you going to do with that?" asked my friend.

The workman said, "See that little opening away up there near the spire? Well, I'm shaping this down here so it will fit in up there."

Tears filled my friend's eyes as he walked away, for it seemed that God had spoken through the workman to explain the ordeal through which he was passing, "I'm shaping you down here so you'll fit in up there."

After you have "suffered a while, make you perfect . . . settle you," echo the words from the Bible.

The persecuted for "righteousness' sake" are happy because they are identified with Christ. The enmity of the world is tangible proof that we are on the right side, that we are identified with our blessed Lord. He said that our stand for Him would arouse the wrath of the world. "And ye shall be hated of all men for my name's sake: but he that endureth to the end shall be saved" (Matthew 10:22).

In a sense, Christ is King in exile, and we who are His followers are often looked upon with derision. To be identified with Him here and now quite naturally entails some "loss of face," some persecution; but some day, we are told, we shall be "kings and priests" and shall be active participators in His kingdom.

Paul must have had this fact in mind when he said: "For I reckon that the sufferings of this present time are not worthy to be compared with the glory which shall be revealed in us. For the earnest expectation of the creature waiteth for the manifestation of the sons of God" (Romans 8:18–19).

Hope Hangs a Halo

If we should be called upon to suffer all our lives, it would not be long compared to eternity. We are in the position of heirs to a large estate who gladly endure a few days of suffering and privation with the hope that we shall soon come into our fabulous inheritance. Such a glorious hope hangs a halo over the drab existence of the here and now.

Life cannot lose its zest when down underneath our present discomfort is the knowledge that we are children of a King. Complaining becomes foolish; behaving in the manner of the world is unworthy; and love, gentleness, and meekness become the hallmarks of God's nobility. "All things" are taken in stride; burdens become blessings in disguise; every wound, like good surgery, is for our good; and etched in every cross is the symbol of a crown.

And last, persecution is blessed because it forms a dark backdrop for the radiance of the Christian life.

The Need for Sunshine and Shadow

All the masterpieces of art contain both light and shadow. A happy life is not one filled only with sunshine, but one which uses both light and shadow to produce beauty. The greatest musicians as a rule are those who know how to bring song out of sadness. Fanny Crosby, her spirit aglow with faith in Christ, saw more with her sightless eyes than most of us do with normal vision. She has given us some of the great gospel songs which cheer our hearts and lives. She wrote some two thousand hymns of which sixty are still in common use.

Paul and Silas sang their song of praise at midnight in a rat-infested jail in Philippi, their feet in stocks, their backs raw from the jailer's whip. But their patience in suffering and persecution led to the conversion of the heathen prison warden. The blood of the martyrs is mixed well into the mortar which holds the stones of civilization together.

The self-sacrifice of God's people through the centuries has contributed immeasurably to our culture, to our ethics, and to our faith. Down deep we know that there are still things worth dying for, that an existence void of faith is still a fate worse than death.

O children of God, despair not at your suffering and persecution. In the words of Thornton Wilder: "Without your wounds, where would your power be that sends your low voice trembling into the hearts of men? The very angels of God in heaven cannot persuade the wretched and blundering children of earth as can one human being broken on the wheels of living. In love's service only wounded soldiers will do."

Messages from the Martyrs

Sanders, the martyr, said, "Welcome the cross of Christ. . . . I feel no more pain in the fire than if I were on a bed of down."

Another martyr said, "The ringing of my chain hath been music in my ears; O what a comforter is a good conscience." Kissing the stake, he said, "I shall not lose my life but change it for better; instead of coals I shall have pearls."

You may not be called upon to suffer as the martyrs suffered, for this is an hour when Satan employs psychological warfare. Jesus said: "Men shall revile you . . . and shall say all manner of evil against you falsely, for my sake" (Matthew 5:11). The tongue often inflicts a more painful wound than does the sword. To be laughed at can be harder to take than to be flogged.

Some in reading this may feel that because they are not at present being persecuted, they are not living godly lives. That is not necessarily so. While there are countries where today to be an active Christian is to court death and worse, we live in a predominantly Christian country where active persecution is at a minimum.

Our environment, as well as the age in which we live, has much to do with the amount of persecution a Christian will be called upon to bear. I have known certain overly eager Christians who actually courted persecution for fear that otherwise they would not be living godly enough lives.

Remember, not all Christians are called upon to suffer at all times. Even our Lord increased in wisdom and knowledge and in favor with God and man. But the periods of popularity did not last. It ended on a cross. The important thing is to walk with Christ. Live for Christ! Have one consuming passion in life—to please Him! And let the chips fall where they may. I believe it was Samuel Rutherford who said, "Never take one step out of the pathway of duty either to take a cross or to escape one."

W. C. Burns of India wrote, "Oh, to have a martyr's heart if not a martyr's crown!"

Popularity and adulation are far more dangerous for the Christian than persecution. It is easy when all goes smoothly to lose our sense of balance and our perspective. We must learn like Paul "how to abound" and "how to be abased." We must learn in "whatsoever state" we are "therewith to be content" (Philippians 4:11).

As we have said, the important thing is to walk with Christ, to live for Christ, and to have one consuming passion to please Him. Then, whatever happens, we know that He has permitted it to teach us some priceless lesson and to perfect us for His service. He will enrich our circumstances, be they pleasant or disagreeable, by the fact of His presence with us. The tomorrows fill us with dread. John 10:4 says, "He putteth forth his own sheep." Whatever awaits us is *encountered* first by Him—like the oriental shepherd always went ahead of his sheep—therefore any attack on sheep has to *deal first* with the shepherd—all the *tomorrows* of our lives have to pass Him before they get to us!

Three Hebrew children were cast into the burning fiery furnace, but the king said: "Lo, I *see four* men loose, walking in the midst of the fire, and they have no hurt; and the form of the fourth is like the Son of God" (Daniel 3:25). Our God is with us in the persecution of this life!

A comforting story comes from some unknown writer. The first convert of a certain missionary was tortured to death for his faith. Years later, the missionary too died. In heaven he met that first convert and asked him how it felt to be tortured to death for his faith. "You know," the man replied with a shrug and looking a bit bewildered, "I can't even remember."

CHAPTER TEN

Steps to Happiness

King George V wrote on the flyleaf of the Bible of a friend: "The secret of happiness is not to do what you like to do, but to learn to like what you have to do."

Too many think of happiness as some sort of will-o'-the-wisp thing that is discovered by constant and relentless searching. Happiness is not found by seeking. It is not an end in itself. Pots of gold are never found at the end of the rainbow, as we used to think when we were children; gold is mined from the ground or panned laboriously from a mountain stream.

Jesus once told His disciples: "Seek ye first the kingdom of God, and his righteousness; and all these things shall be added unto you" (Matthew 6:33). The "things" He spoke of were the basic needs of life: food, drink, clothes, shelter. He told us not to make these the chief goal of our lives but to "seek the kingdom," and these needs would be automatically supplied. And if for some reason only He knows they should be withheld, know that it is for our good and His glory. There have been occasions when Christians have been deprived of one or all these things. They have died of starvation at times—or of thirst or exposure. It is not because He has broken His promise, but because He has something better for us.

There, if we will take it, is the secret of happiness: "Seek ye first the kingdom of God . . . and all . . . shall be added unto you."

Steps to Abundant Living

In the foregoing pages we have tried to interpret Jesus' formula for happiness. We realize that in many ways the interpretation falls short, both in content and clarity. The more we read this introduction to the Sermon on the Mount, the more wisdom we see hidden in it and the more convinced we are that if it is read thoughtfully and prayerfully and applied to life that a richer, fuller happiness will ensue.

In summing up the secret of happiness within the framework of the Beatitudes, we would like to suggest several steps to the abundant life:

We must recognize our spiritual poverty. Don't let pride say, "I am rich, and increased with goods, and have need of nothing" (Revelation 3:17). Remember that our own righteousness is as filthy rags and that salvation is not of works but is the gift of God. We must keep ever in mind the first Beatitude: "Blessed are the poor in spirit: for theirs is the kingdom of heaven."

God measures people by the small dimension of humility and not by the bigness of their achievements or the size of their capabilities.

We must make sure we have received Christ. Remember, it is not creeds, culture, or even respectability that saves us. It is Christ. The Bible says: "But as many as received him, to them gave he power to become the sons of God, even to them that believe on his name" (John 1:12).

Let us say that one day you decide to go to Europe on a jet plane. Perhaps you might contact your travel agency and get all kinds of information about flight schedules and the type of plane you would be flying. You might talk with people who had traveled across the Atlantic on that aircraft. You might even have investigated the airline's safety record and become convinced that the pilot and crew were trustworthy and the aircraft would take you safely. You might have said to yourself, *I believe this airplane is able to take me across the Atlantic.* You might even have gotten a ticket and gone to the airport. You might have done all this and still never have crossed the Atlantic. One thing was lacking: You needed to get on the plane—commit yourself to it and trust it to carry you to your destination.

To know about Christ is not enough. To be convinced that He is the

Savior of the world is not enough. To affirm our faith in Him, as we do in the Apostles' Creed, is not enough. To believe that He has saved others is not enough. We really don't actively believe in Christ until we make a commitment of our lives to Him and receive Him as our Savior.

We can best demonstrate our faith in a bank by putting our money in it. We can best show our faith in a doctor by trusting him with our physical welfare in times of illness. We can best prove our faith in a boat by getting aboard and going some place on it. We can best demonstrate our faith in Christ by trusting Him with our life and receiving Him unconditionally as our Savior.

We must maintain a contrite spirit. The Bible says: "A broken and a contrite heart, O God, thou wilt not despise" (Psalm 51:17). Remember it was to Christians that John wrote: "If we confess our sins, he is faithful and just to forgive us our sins, and to cleanse us from all unrighteousness" (1 John 1:9).

A cultured person is quick with a courteous apology when he has done wrong. If a gentleman stumbles over a lady's foot in a drawing room, he doesn't wait a week to say, "I beg your pardon!" He begs forgiveness immediately.

When we break God's law, utter a hasty, bitter word, or even think an evil thought, immediately we should confess this sin to God. And in accordance with His Word, He will forgive and cleanse our hearts and transform us into His likeness.

We must be sensitive to the needs of others. In the eternal triangle of Christianity, God is first, others are second, and self is last. "Rejoice with them that do rejoice, and weep with them that weep" (Romans 12:15). We should be sympathetic, tolerant, and understanding. Remember the third secret of happiness: "Blessed are they that mourn: for they shall be comforted."

There is no joy in life like the joy of sharing. Don't be content to have too much when millions in the world have too little. I should remember every time I read the Bible that millions have no Bible to read. We should bear in mind when we hear the gospel preached that more than half the world has never heard the gospel story. Let our lives, our means, and our prayers be shared with those millions who at this moment are wondering whether there is any relief from their distress.

Don't be a half-Christian. There are too many of such in the world already. The world has a profound respect for people who are sincere in their faith.

The Bible tells us that we can't serve God and mammon, that no man can serve two masters. Too many Christians, so called, are like the little chameleon which adapts its coloration to that of its surroundings. Even a critical world is quick to recognize a real Christian and just as quick to detect a counterfeit.

We must live surrendered lives. The Bible is explicit at this point. It says: "Know ye not, that to whom ye yield yourselves servants to obey, his servants ye are to whom ye obey; whether of sin unto death, or of obedience unto righteousness?" (Romans 6:16).

A friend of David Livingstone once said: "When I watched Livingstone carry out the 'leave all and follow me' life, I became a Christian in spite of myself." The world knows no greater challenge than the surrendered life.

We should be filled with the Spirit. People who have moved the world have been Spirit-filled. Filled with the Spirit, the first disciples "turned the world upside down." Filled with the Spirit, the Reformers started the spiritual blaze which became the Reformation. Filled with the Spirit, John and Charles Wesley, working out of Oxford University, saved a great nation from moral and political collapse. Filled with the Spirit, Francis Asbury, George Fox, Jonathan Edwards, Charles Finney, and David Brainerd set the mountains and prairies of America aglow with the fires of real Christianity. Filled with the Spirit, D. L. Moody and Ira Sankey shook two continents out of their spiritual lethargy. Corrie ten Boom and Mother Teresa impacted their world greatly.

The tides of civilization have risen, the courses of nations have been changed, and the pages of history have been brightened by people who have been filled with the Spirit of God.

What does it mean to be filled with the Spirit? It is not necessarily an emotional experience, nor will it necessarily bring us some type of spiritual experience that is obvious or open. *To be filled with the Spirit is to be controlled by the Spirit.* It is to be so yielded to Christ that our supreme desire is to do His will. When we come to Christ the Spirit comes to dwell within us—whether we are aware of His presence or not. But as we grow in Christ, our goal is to be controlled by the Spirit. Have you yielded your life to Christ without reserve, asking Him to fill you and use you for His glory?

We should seek to produce the fruit of the Spirit in our lives. The Bible says: "The fruit of the Spirit is love, joy, peace, longsuffering, gentleness, goodness, faith, meekness, temperance" (Galatians 5:22–23, emphasis added).

You say, "I am powerless to produce such fruit. It would be utterly impossible for me to do so!"

With that I agree! That is, we can't produce this fruit in our own strength. Remember, the Bible says: "The fruit of the *Spirit* is love, joy, peace, longsuffering, gentleness, goodness, faith, meekness, temperance" (Galatians 5:22–23, emphasis added). When the Spirit of God dwells in us *He* will produce the fruit. It is ours only to cultivate the soil of our hearts through sincere devotion and yieldedness that He might find favorable ground to produce that which He will.

I might have a fruit tree in my yard; but if the soil isn't enriched and the bugs carefully destroyed, it will not yield a full crop.

As Christians, we have the Spirit of God in us. But ours is the responsibility to keep sin out of our lives so that the Spirit can produce His fruit in us.

We must become grounded in the Bible. As Christians, we have only one authority, one compass: the Word of God.

In a letter to a friend, Abraham Lincoln said: "I am profitably engaged in reading the Bible. Take all of this Book upon reason that you can and the balance upon faith, and you will live and die a better man."

Coleridge said he believed the Bible to be the Word of God because, as he put it, "It finds me."

"If you want encouragement," John Bunyan wrote, "entertain the promises."

Martin Luther said, "In Scriptures, even the little daisy becomes a meadow."

The Bible is our one sure guide in an unsure world.

Great leaders have made it their chief Book and their reliable guide. Herbert J. Taylor, formerly international president of Rotary, told me that he began each day by reading the Sermon on the Mount aloud. President Ronald Reagan revered the Bible so much that he proclaimed 1984 the "year of the Bible."

We should begin the day with the Book, and as it comes to a close let the Word speak its wisdom to our souls. Let it be the firm foundation upon which our hope is built.

Let it be the Staff of Life upon which our spirit is nourished. Let it be the Sword of the Spirit which cuts away the evil of our lives and fashions us in His image and likeness.

We must witness for Christ. Jesus said to us: "Ye are the light of the world. . . . Let your light so shine before men, that they may see your good works, and glorify your Father which is in heaven" (Matthew 5:14, 16).

One faithful witness is worth a thousand mute professors of religion.

The late Tom Allan, Scotland's famous preacher, was brought to Christ while a black soldier was singing "Were You There When They Crucified My Lord?" He said it was neither the song nor the voice, but the spirit in which that soldier sang—something about his manner, something about his sincerity of expression—that convicted him of his wicked life and turned him to the Savior.

Our faith grows by expression. If we want to keep our faith, we must share it—we must witness!

We must practice the Presence of God. Jesus said: "Lo, I am with you alway, even unto the end of the world" (Matthew 28:20). Remember, Christ is always near us. We should say nothing that we would not wish to say in His Presence. We should do nothing that we would not do in His Presence. We should go to no place that we would not go in His Presence. But He is not with us just to judge or condemn us; He is near to comfort, protect, guide, encourage, strengthen, cleanse, and help. He will not only be with us until the "end of the world," but He will be with us "world without end."

He will be with us throughout all eternity.

We must learn the exercise of prayer. Jesus said: "Men ought always to pray, and not to faint" (Luke 18:1). He said on another occasion: "Pray to thy Father which is in secret; and thy Father which seeth in secret shall reward thee openly" (Matthew 6:6).

Prayer is not just asking. It is listening for God's orders. The late Frank Laubach said: "Prayer at its highest is a two-way conversation; and for me, the most important part is listening to God's replies."

The world's great Christians have set regular hours for prayer. John Wesley arose at four in the morning and started the day with prayer, followed by an hour's Bible study.

I suggest an established time for communication with God. Make a date with Him and keep it. The Christian will never regret such a practice, for the "fervent prayer of a righteous man availeth much" (James 5:16).

We must develop a taste for spiritual things. "Happy are they which do hunger and thirst after righteousness: for they shall be filled."

Spiritual tastes, like physical tastes, can be cultivated. I didn't always like yogurt, but they told me that it was good for me, so I kept trying to like it—and now I enjoy it.

It will not perhaps be easy at first to read the Bible, witness, and pray. But after we experience the strength that can come from these means of grace, they will become part of our routine, as much as breathing and eating. These are the things that give strength to the soul.

We must not be critical of others. Habitual criticism can stifle our spiritual growth. We must not build up ourselves at the expense of others. If I praise others, then others will praise me. But if I condemn others, they in turn will condemn me. Criticism begets criticism, but praise begets praise. As Jesus said: "Happy are the merciful: for they shall obtain mercy."

We must not be envious of others. Two of the most devastating sins of today are envy and covetousness. Envying others can work havoc in our spiritual lives and sap us of our spiritual strength. It can also ruin our social batting average and weaken our Christian testimony. We must not be enslaved by this ruinous evil! It can destroy our happiness and rob our lives of their sweetness.

We should love everybody. The Bible says: "Let love be genuine; hate what is evil, hold fast to what is good" (Romans 12:9 RSV). This Scripture says: "*Let* love," as if it were possible for us to hinder love from being all that it should be. The love of Christ, if unhindered and unblocked by our prejudices and our malices, will embrace everyone. Christ in us will go on loving even the unlovely if He is not hindered by our selfishness. We must realize the difference between loving the sinner and hating his sin.

We should stand courageously for the right. Horace Pitkin, the son of a wealthy merchant, was converted and went to China as a missionary. He wrote to his friends in America, saying: "It will be but a short time till we know definitely whether we can serve Him better above or here." Shortly afterward, a mob stormed the gate of the compound where Pitkin defended the women and children. He was beheaded and his head offered at the shrine of a heathen god, while his body was thrown outside in a pit with the bodies of nine Chinese Christians. Sherwood Eddy, writing about him, said: "Pitkin won more men by his death than he ever could have won by his life." The same could be said of the five courageous Christians who died for Christ in Ecuador.

Christ needs people today who are made of martyr stuff! Dare to take a strong, uncompromising stand for Him.

We should learn to relax in Christ. I once watched a little baby learning to walk. As long as it kept its eyes on its mother it was relaxed and in perfect balance. But as soon as it looked down at its little wobbly legs, it failed.

Simon Peter found it possible to walk over the waves of Galilee as long as he kept his eyes on Christ—but when he looked away from the Savior he sank.

These are turbulent times in which we live. People are harassed with tensions, fears, and phobias. Nothing can relieve the tensions of life like a valid faith in Christ.

You, too, can learn to relax in *Christ!*

We must not be victims of paranoia. I am not talking here, of course, about the specific mental illness of paranoia which grips some people and which needs to be treated professionally; I refer here to it in a more general sense. I am talking about an excessive sensitivity to what others say or do about us, which causes us to become overly absorbed in worry and anxiety over what people think about us.

In other words, don't be hypersensitive to criticism or entertain an exaggerated sense of your own importance. This is the secret of unhappiness. Many egocentric people are victims of this terrible disease of the mind. If people never actually criticize them, they at least imagine that they do, and they suffer the agonies of a mental inferno.

Or some people are insecure, lacking in self-confidence, and are therefore easily bruised by what other people say. It may not be easy, but such a person needs to develop more self-confidence by seeing himself the way God sees him. If this is your problem, recognize it for what it is and realize the damage it can cause you. Then ask God to help you overcome it in practical ways.

The paranoid sees two acquaintances talking together somewhat seriously, and immediately he imagines that they are discussing his faults. He retreats into the torture chamber of his own mind where he manufactures misery in wholesale lots. Run from paranoia as you would run from a plague.

We must remember we are immortal and will live forever. To expect absolute, unqualified bliss in this life is expecting a bit too much. Remember, this life is only the dressing room for eternity. In the Beatitudes Jesus said that in this life there are persecution, slander, libel, and deception. But He also said: "Rejoice, and be exceeding glad: for great is your reward in heaven" (Matthew 5:12).

He strongly hinted that relative happiness in this life is related to an absolute happiness in the afterlife. Here we have an "earnest" of our inheritance, a "down payment," but in heaven we come into our full estate of happiness.

Christians think and act within the framework of eternity. They are not embittered when things don't turn out the way they planned. They know that the sufferings of this present world are not worthy to be compared with the glory that shall be revealed hereafter. So rejoice and be exceedingly glad!

In the covered-wagon days when gold was discovered in the Old West, the pioneers endured the sufferings of the prairies, the mountains, and the desert, and the savage attacks of the Indians because they knew that beyond those Sierras lay the promise of gold.

When Bill Borden, son of the wealthy Bordens, left for China as a missionary, many of his friends thought he was foolish to "waste his life," as they put it, trying to convert a few heathens to Christianity. But Bill loved Christ and he loved people! On his way to China he contracted a disease and died. At his bedside they found a note that he had written while he was dying. It read: "No reserve, no retreat, and no regrets."

Borden had found more happiness in his few years of sacrificial service than most people find in a lifetime.

Many thousands of rational, cultured citizens of the earth have found happiness in Christ. You can too! But, remember, you will never find it by searching directly for it. As the Lord of happiness said: "Seek ye first the kingdom of God, and his righteousness; and all these things shall be added unto you" (Matthew 6:33).

Hope *for the* Troubled Heart

Billy Graham

W Publishing Group
A Division of Thomas Nelson Publishers
Since 1798
www.wpublishinggroup.com

HOPE FOR THE TROUBLED HEART

Library of Congress Cataloging-in-Publication Data:

Graham, Billy
Hope for the troubled heart / Billy Graham.
p. cm.
Includes bibliographical references.
ISBN 0–8499–0702–0
1. Theodicy. 2. Consolation. I. Title.
BT160.G66 1991
248.8'6—dc20 91–27705
CIP

Printed in the United States of America

06 07 08 BVG 9 8 7 6 5 4

Contents

Foreword

IN MY TRAVELS over the decades, I have found that people are the same the world over. However, in recent years I find that there is an increasing problem that I would sum up in the word "hopeless." It may be because we get news of troubles, problems, disasters, wars, etc. instantaneously in comparison to years ago when it might have taken weeks, months, or even years to hear of an event. But there's something else even more insidious. People in the most affluent societies are feeling this sense of despair and hopelessness.

Perhaps the greatest psychological, spiritual, and medical need that all people have is the need for hope. Dr. McNair Wilson, the famous cardiologist, remarked in his autobiography, *Doctor's Progress,* "Hope is the medicine I use more than any other—hope can cure nearly anything."

I remember years ago that Dr. Harold Wolff, professor of medicine at Cornell University Medical College and associate professor of psychiatry, said, "Hope, like faith and a purpose in life, is medicinal. This is not exactly a statement of belief, but a conclusion proved by meticulously controlled scientific experiment."

Hope is both biologically and psychologically vital to man. Men and women must have hope, and yet a great part of our world today is living without it. The Apostle Paul wrote two thousand years ago to the Ephesians that the Roman civilization of his day was "without hope."

This is like so much of our world today. We are trying to live normal lives without ultimate hope, and we are finding failures on every hand. I believe that *Hope for the Troubled Heart,* which I have written with the help of several other people, will not only be of help but will be life-transforming for many who may read it. I send it forth with a prayer that it will bring new hope to thousands of sufferers from this terrible disease of hopelessness.

This book has been written with the help especially of my longtime friend Carole Carlson; my beloved wife Ruth, who seems to have unlimited resources for every subject that I write on; my friend Millie Dienert, who was kind enough to go through the manuscript and make suggestions while on our way to Moscow recently; and to my wonderful, small staff at Montreat, especially Stephanie Wills who typed and retyped changes in the manuscript. For their patience, I want to thank Word Publishing, who waited many long months while I finished the book in the midst of other pressing demands.

May God bless this volume to the encouragement of thousands and give hope to the despairing.

Billy Graham, Europe
Summer of 1991

(The royalties from this book will go to East Gates Ministries, a new organization helping to bring about understanding between China and the rest of the world through spiritual understanding.)

CHAPTER ONE

World in Pain

VOICES FROM TROUBLED HEARTS: "Our home is a war zone! Don't talk to me about international war. I want to know how we can find peace in our family!" . . . "I'm a rape victim. How can I ever get over my memories, or my horrible fears?" . . . "I've lost my job and may lose my home. Don't tell me about Wall Street blues!" . . . "How can I raise decent kids when they're surrounded by bad influences?" . . . "I'm more worried about what's polluting the minds of my children. They're the most endangered species!" . . . "We have a nice home and cars—you'd think I would be happy. But I feel empty. I'm not sure of my husband anymore and I'm so lonely."

"This is the generation that will pass through the fire. It is the generation . . . 'under the gun.' This is the tormented generation. This is the generation destined to live in the midst of crisis, danger, fear, and death. We are like a people under sentence of death, waiting for the date to be set. We sense that something is about to happen. We know that things cannot go on as they are. History has reached an impasse. We are now on a collision course. Something is about to give."

I wrote this in 1965.

At that time few of us thought the world could get much worse and survive. I was wrong. In many ways the world has gotten worse, and we have survived. But we are a world in pain—a world that suffers collectively from the violence of nature and man, and a world that suffers individually from personal heartache.

Because we have instant communication today, our planet has shrunk to the size of a television screen. Although husbands and wives, children and parents, have trouble communicating, we can watch a war as it is happening before our eyes. A comfortable room can be turned into a foreign battlefield or a street riot with the push of a button.

Our children have grown and married and we now have (at last count) nineteen grandchildren. I cannot promise them that this present world will get better. With all my heart, I would like to protect them from pain. But what I see is a universal malaise which affects civilization, giving me little hope that man alone can change the course of human events to make a better world.

There have been dazzling achievements in the years since my children were small. Man has landed on the moon, and Patriot missiles have intercepted and destroyed incoming ballistic warheads. From world records in sports to VCR's and microwave ovens, this has been a period of great scientific change.

But how far have we come? Are we better off in the nineties than we were in the sixties? In 1965 I said that most of the current experts, analysts, philosophers, and statesmen agreed that man is sick. Some of them believed we had already passed the point of no return. Has the patient improved or is the diagnosis terminal?

Pain of Wars

We are told by historians that peace has never been achieved at any time in history. Since the early eighteenth century, the world has known only eleven years in which there have been no wars. Even during those eleven years, there may have been small undetected wars in out-of-the-way places in the world.

In 1982 I was invited to address a peace conference in Moscow. After much agony, seeking advice from different people that I trust, but primarily the advice of Scripture, I decided to go. I took a great deal of criticism, but God used it to open many doors in Eastern Europe, which I believe was a contributing factor to the vast changes in the Soviet Union. The speech that I gave there, which was based on the teachings of Scripture concerning peace and war, was quoted over and over throughout the Eastern world.

The United Nations proclaimed 1986 as the International Year of Peace. What happened? The world responded with more than a hundred wars, according to the Center for Defense Information in Washington.

Despite the overwhelming evidence that the absence of peace may be the norm, rather than the exception, one newsman said in December 1989, "Peace on earth seems more possible now than at any time since World War II." This was a hopeful note in a war-weary world, but since then we have had the Persian Gulf War and many other little wars.

Augustine, in the fourth century, believed that achievement of an absolute state of peace on earth was impossible and that war would always claim its place. The weight of history favors Augustine's view over that of the optimistic newsman.

Pain of Lawlessness

Violent crime, often linked with the war against drugs, has accelerated. From every city in the world come stories of drug-related shootings, stabbings, and assaults. A doctor in a Detroit hospital said that the saddest casualties are children. "We have a whole generation of human beings within this urban area who could be so productive and helpful to humanity but are being lost. We have kids thirteen and fourteen years old who are as hardened as anyone in a penitentiary. Look into their eyes, and you see these cold blank stares, void of most moral values."[1]

In Los Angeles, police make drug arrests at a rate of over a thousand a week—and that's less than one-fourth of what they think the real story is.

"Despite the passage of tough anti-drug laws and police dragnets, street crime, much of it drug-related, continues to surge. The nation's violent-crime rate rose 10 percent in the first six months of 1990. Murders were up 8 percent in the first six months of the year and armed robbery rose 9 percent."[2] An FBI report showed that in the last few years, arrests for drug-abuse violations rose dramatically and dangerously.

I love New York and have many friends there, but the stories from that city are heartbreaking. It is reported as having 500,000 drug abusers, an amount almost equal to the population of Boston. In 1952, the city had 8,757 robberies. In 1989 there were 93,387! *U.S. News & World Report* stated in 1990, "Twenty-one cabbies were murdered this year, girls were raped and then thrown off rooftops, a boy was tied up and set afire, and four small children were shot to death in drug wars within three weeks."[3]

Lawlessness is not confined to the city streets. Most law-enforcement officers say the most dangerous calls are those related to domestic arguments. Beatings, rapes, and murder are also happening behind the white picket fences of our suburbs and small towns.

Random violence, without any provocation or reason, is everywhere. No one is safe. We are a nation living behind fences and bars—not only in America, but also in the United Kingdom, Brazil, and many other countries.

Pain of Economic Collapse

Fraud is rampant wherever we are. In the financial world, the cheating touches many of our pocketbooks. When a large savings-and-loan institution collapsed, the American taxpayers probably ended up paying some $2 billion in additional taxes.

Real estate values have so many ups and downs that the financial institutions struggle with bad loans. Is there any doubt that we are a nation in debt?

Part of our problem with debt is that we have confused needs with wants. Yesterday's luxuries are today's necessities.

One of Wall Street's most notorious insider traders summed up this materialistic idolatry in a speech to graduate business school students when he claimed, "Greed is good for you." It wasn't so good for this man, who soon found himself the target of federal indictments for alleged wrongdoing.

"Dark Mood" announced a *Wall Street Journal* headline. The infection spreads, as crisis feeds on itself and fears are expressed for everything from bank failures to global financial panic.

Pain of Family Failure

No subject is closer to my heart than the family. Sometimes I feel that my heart will break when I see the results of divorce, infidelity, and rebellion. The moral foundation of our country is in danger of crumbling as families break up and parents neglect their responsibilities. Isn't it ironic that people cheer and clap for couples who have been married for more than twenty-five years? On a television talk show I announced that my wife and I have been married for nearly fifty years, and we are more in love than ever. The applause was deafening. People seemed surprised, because it is so unusual.

The results of family disintegration are seen all around us. Runaways. Child abuse. Abortions. It is dirty laundry—once hung in the nation's backyard, but now hung shamelessly in front yards—flaunted in headlines and glamorized on television and in films.

One result of family failure has been the loss of dignity. No better example can be found than in the use of language. It's a four-letter world in movies, on television, in comedy routines, and in real life. *Time* magazine asks, "Are the '90s destined to be the Filth Decade?"[4]

Most decent people wonder what impact the raw-language culture will have on this first generation to grow up with it. Music and comedy routines flout human decency in such obscene ways that even reading about them makes us sick.

Are we shock-proof? Parents may still be capable of open-mouthed dismay, but today's youth seems unshockable. This in itself is shocking!

A news commentator said, "Since the traumas of the Kennedy assassination and Vietnam, many Americans have gradually closed off their minds to the nature of atrocity. They cope with the world's horror by numbing themselves to pain. They can shed tears over cute, tender stories of stranded whales or a baby in a well, but all too often everything else—from a politician's promise to the Chernobyl disaster—is so much show biz, ironized with shrugs and sick jokes. Today's children were bred in this atmosphere. With many of their parents past caring, how can the kids not be past shock?"[5]

Pain of a Ravished Earth

The 1990s are appearing to be the decade of environmental concerns. After years of polluting our air and water with little thought about the consequences, many are now trying to be good stewards of the earth that God gave us. Global warming, holes in the ozone layer, tainted water supplies, choking smog layers, and overflowing landfills are just a small part of the concerns.

Over twenty years ago, at a time when environment meant simply the surroundings in which we lived and not an endangered species, Francis Schaeffer wrote in *Pollution and the Death of Man:* "The simple fact is that if man is not able to solve his ecological problems, then man's resources are going to die. . . . So the whole problem of ecology is dumped in this generation's lap."[6]

The problem has truly been dumped upon us. We have made some strides toward its solution, but this ravished earth is like the man who smoked all of his life without any consequences, until one day lung cancer was discovered. Our natural resources have been misused for too many generations, and we are paying the price.

Pain of Affluence

Someone has said that Americans have more wealth, more two-car families, more private homes, and write more books on how to be happy than any other country. If we lived in Bangladesh or in the slums of Calcutta, the thought of suffering in the midst of abundance would sound ridiculous. And yet in America, where the standard of living is one of the highest in the world, the very presence of a life of comparative ease causes a spiritual sickness. A letter from one of the workers for Samaritan Purse, which provides help for hurting people throughout the world and is headed by my son, Franklin, illustrates how affluence can be painful. He wrote:

> One day I was in one of the large camps where Indian nationals from Kuwait were being held waiting repatriation. These people had traveled for days across the burning desert in buses. I noticed a lady with her family of small children who was very distressed, and when I went to her I found that she had given birth to a baby three days before being evacuated from Kuwait. The baby was so dirty and smelly. It was great to be able to buy her all that was needed for the baby, as well as helping the mother with some of her urgent medical problems. The mother's gratitude was profound, and on further conversation with her we found that she had once walked with the Lord. The affluence of living in Kuwait had come between her and God, and her love for Him had grown cold. As we shared with her God's willingness to forgive her, she found new fellowship with Him and was rejoicing in His comfort and care as we left her.
>
> Almost the last thing she said to me was, "I just thank God for allowing my family to lose everything in Kuwait so I could find Him again."

My wife was talking with a young Christian who had just arrived in this country from a regime hostile to Christianity. The woman was suffering from culture shock. She told Ruth, "I think it is more difficult to remain a deeply committed Christian in the midst of prosperity than under persecution."

Materialism may do what a foreign invader could never hope to achieve—materialism robs a nation of its spiritual strength.

Seen or Unseen Pain

In every country and city throughout the world there are people who are suffering from personal pain. Some of it is visible, like the legless war veteran—some is intensely private, like the woman who has lived with the memory of childhood rape.

In my years of global travels, I have seen a world in pain. Some people seem to have more of their share than others. Many can't understand why suffering is their lot.

When Aleksandr Solzhenitsyn described the horrors of torture and death in his book, *The Gulag Archipelago*, a study of the Soviet network of prisons during the Stalin era, he expressed a universal question for all sufferers—"The most sophisticated and the veriest simpleton among us, drawing on all life's experience can gasp out only: 'Me? What for?'"[7]

Me? What For?

When suffering hits us personally, that is the common cry. *Why Me? What's the reason?*

For man without faith in a personal God, reactions to painful situations are as varied as pain itself. In a news release about the deposed Kuwaiti leaders attempting to conduct a government in exile after being ousted from their country by the Iraqi invasion, there was a story of a doctor who had left Kuwait and gone to Egypt. His friend, another Kuwaiti exile, said, "He locked his door and grew his beard, and he did not come out, he just lay on the bed looking at the ceiling. He did not talk to anybody. Probably he saw strange things. When we go back to Kuwait, I think we should bring hundreds of psychiatrists."[8]

The doctor from Kuwait is like many who respond to suffering by retreating into a private world without any solution. Others find bizarre methods of escape. After a serious operation a Hollywood actress was told by her doctor to meditate with pieces of quartz as a therapy to reduce stress.[9]

Without God's guidance, our response to suffering is a futile attempt to find solutions to conditions that cannot be solved. We are plummeting into a world where, in spite of wonder drugs and medical breakthroughs, suffering will become more intense. For all suffering, we know, is not physical. Today, more than ever, we need to know how to find strength to live life to its fullest.

Mirror of Despair

Personal pain has been with us since God told Eve she would have pain in childbirth. However, in spite of the wars and plagues of the past, there has never been a time when a mirror on the world has reflected so much despair.

In 1965, I wrote that the flames of lawlessness, racial unrest, political dilemma, and immorality were out of control. How can I describe that blaze today? It's like the oil wells burning in Kuwait. "Looks like Hell," one observer said. Compared with the 1990s, the 1960s, for all of their rebellion and turmoil, seem almost quaint and placid.

Nothing seems to satisfy. Not politics, not education, not material goods. Some who refuse to turn their hearts toward God have created the New Age movement, with all of its aberrations. This is actually not new but only the latest attempt by man to place something other than Christ inside himself in a futile attempt to satisfy spiritual longings.

As men and women seek to find independence from God, they have lost a sense of purpose in life. The worth of human personality is often equated with what we do for a living. However, a person's occupation, community standing, or bank account is not what is important in God's eyes.

Not only do many not know God, but those who do rarely listen to His voice. It is a tragedy that many of God's people have conformed themselves to the world and its thinking, rather than being transformed by the renewing of their minds. We have become a nation of biblical illiterates. A Gallup survey found that although 90 percent of Americans own Bibles, only 11 percent of Christians read the Bible daily.

As mankind sees its reflection, it is not a pretty sight.

Walking Through the Rubble

While individual suffering has no respite and the collective suffering of our world continues, there are those who have found a refuge in the midst of the rubble. What is the difference between the paraplegic woman with the smile that lights a room and the millionaire with a suicide wish? Or what makes one person accept and keep his balance during a painful time, and another become a self-pitying whiner?

Outside of the Bible, I cannot offer true, unfailing solutions. I do not pretend to be a pop-psychologist or offer pat answers. An old Scottish writer said: "The 'household of faith' has many concerns, and not the least of these are its sorrows. These are the lot of all; and there is no member of the household but has his share in these, either in personal suffering or in helping to bear the burden of others."[10]

We can react with bitterness and hate God, as some do, or we can accept suffering as a natural part of life and a condition that comes with living in this world. We cannot avoid suffering, but we can determine our response to it.

It is my prayer that many voices from troubled hearts may find peace in this world of pain and hope in the midst of hopeless situations.

A unit joined to infinity adds nothing to it, any more than one foot added to infinite length. The finite is annihilated in the presence of God and becomes pure zero. So is our intellect before God.

Blaise Pascal

CHAPTER TWO

His Unfailing Love

AS A LITTLE BOY growing up in the south, my idea of the ocean was very small. The first time I saw the Atlantic I couldn't imagine that any lake could be so big! The vastness of the oceans cannot be understood until they are seen. This is the same with God's love; it is incomprehensible until you actually experience it. No one can describe its wonders to you.

For years Ruth had been trying to secure the release of the last two members of a family still living in the People's Republic of China. The young widowed mother was in America, but her son and daughter had not been able to get out of China.

Ruth and her two sisters and brother were on their way to their old home in China in 1980, but before leaving she made one final call to the State Department to see if the arrangements had been finished for their trip. She was saddened to find out there was no good news for the young mother about her children. They were not granted permits to leave the country and come to America.

My wife stopped in California to see the woman and other members of the family who had escaped. It was then that the lovely young mother told Ruth this story.

There was once in China a kind seller of cherries. A little boy came along, and when he saw the fruit his eyes filled with longing. He had no money, but the seller of cherries asked, "Do you want some cherries?" Of course, he did. But he only ducked his head shyly.

The kind seller of cherries said, "Hold out your hands." But the little boy kept his hands at his sides. The seller said again, "Hold out your hands." The little boy still stood stiffly. The man reached down and gently took the child's hands. Cupping them together, he filled them with cherries.

Later the boy's mother asked, "Why didn't you hold out your hands when he asked you?" The little boy answered, "Because his hands were bigger than mine." Then the mother smiled. "His hands are bigger than ours," she said. "We can wait."

That Chinese family is now reunited in California. Truly, God's hands are bigger than ours, and He is able to fill them to overflowing.

What Is God Like?

Some see God as a harsh father, waiting to punish His children when they do something wrong. Others perceive God as unable to handle the evil on earth, or indifferent to the suffering caused by it.

God's love is unchangeable; He knows exactly what we are and loves us anyway. In fact, He created us because He wanted other creatures in His image upon whom He could pour out His love and who would love Him in return. He also wanted that love to be voluntary, not forced, so He gave us freedom of choice, the ability to say yes or no in our relationship to Him. God does not want mechanized love, the kind that says we must love God because it's what our parents demand or our church preaches. Only voluntary love satisfies the heart of God.

Years ago a friend of mine was standing on top of a mountain in North Carolina and noticed two cars in the distance heading toward each other on a dangerously winding road. He realized neither driver could see the other car approaching. With horror, he watched a third car pull up and begin to pass one of the cars as all three entered a blind curve. My friend shouted a warning, even though he knew he couldn't be heard. The crash was fatal and several were killed. The man standing on the mountain saw it all.

God is a God of love, and He is not blind to man's plight. He doesn't stand on a mountaintop, viewing the wrecks in our lives, without shouting a warning. Since man caused his own crash by his rebellion against the Creator, God could have allowed him to plunge into destruction.

From the very beginning of man's journey, God had a plan for man's deliverance. In fact, the plan is so fantastic that it ultimately lifts each man who will accept His plan far above even the angels. God's all-consuming love for mankind was decisively demonstrated at the cross, where His *compassion* was embodied in His Son, Jesus Christ. The word compassion comes from two Latin words meaning "to suffer with." God was willing to suffer with man.

In His thirty-three years on earth, Jesus suffered with man; on the cross He suffered for man. "God was reconciling the world to himself in Christ" (2 Corinthians 5:19). An important verse to memorize is: "God demonstrates His own love for us in this: While we were still sinners, Christ died for us" (Romans 5:8).

God's love did not begin at the cross. It began in eternity before the world was established, before the time clock of civilization began to move. The concept stretches our minds to their utmost limits.

Can you imagine what God was planning when the earth was "without form and void"? There was only a deep, silent darkness of outer space that formed a vast gulf before the brilliance of God's throne. God was designing the mountains and the seas, the flowers and the animals. He was planning the bodies of His children and all their complex parts.

How could creation be by chance?

Even before the first dawn, He knew all that would happen. In His mysterious love He allowed it. The Bible tells us about the "Lamb that was slain from the creation of the world" (Revelation 13:8). God foresaw what His Son was to suffer. It has been said there was a cross in the heart of God long before the cross was erected at Calvary. As we think about it we will be overwhelmed at the wonder and greatness of His love for us.

That Amazing Love

God's love liberated man from the beginning of time to do his own thing, but whatever his choice, there were to be either benefits or consequences. Adam and Eve enjoyed the benefits for a while, but they forced every generation that would ever be born to face the consequences.

It was the love of God which put the Ten Commandments in the hands of His servant, Moses. It was His love which engraved those laws, not only in stone, but also upon the hearts of all people. Those commandments became the foundation of all civil, statutory, and moral law and the basis of conscience. It was God's love which knew that men were incapable of obeying His law, and it was His love which promised a Redeemer, a Savior, who would save His people from their sins.

It was the love of God which put words of promise into the mouths of His prophets, centuries before Christ came to this planet. It was God's love that planned the political conditions before the coming of Jesus Christ. Greece, as the great power during the four-hundred-year period before the birth of Christ, prepared the way for His message by spreading a common language throughout the world. Then the transportation problem had to be solved, and the great Roman Empire came into power and built a network of roads and developed a system of law and order. So by using the common language and the Roman roads and legal system, God spread His Word through the early Christians. The Scripture says that "when the time had fully come, God sent his Son" (Galatians 4:4).

I believe that God in His love is preparing us now for the Second Coming of Christ, and that time may be nearer than we think.

Like Father, Like Son

The greatest tribute a boy can give to his father is to say, "When I grow up I want to be just like my dad." It is a convicting responsibility for us fathers and grandfathers. Not too long ago I received a handwritten letter from my youngest son, Ned. It is a letter I will always prize. He expressed his appreciation and love for me as his father, and he indicated that he hoped he would be a good role model for his two sons and that he would be able to impact them the way I had been able to impact him. This encouraged me, because I have felt I was a failure as a father due to my extensive absences from home. But Ruth was strong enough and spiritual enough to be both father and mother at the times the children needed it. When I did come home, I tried to spend extra time with them. Now I face the problems and opportunities of trying to be a good grandfather for nineteen grandchildren. Our lives speak loudly to those around us, especially the children in our home.

The Son of God reflects the same selfless compassion for the sick, the distressed, and the sin-burdened as does God the Father. It was God's love which enabled Jesus to become poor, that we might become rich. It was divine love that enabled Him to endure the cross. It was this same love that restrained Him when He was falsely accused of blasphemy and led to Golgotha to die with common thieves.

When a boy is picked on by a bully, he might call for his big brother or his dad to help him. When I was in grammar school, I was constantly being picked on by a bully who must have weighed one-third more than I did. This older boy went out of his way to give me a beating almost every day. One day as we were getting on the school bus and he was slapping me around, a tiny little guy came up and knocked the daylights out of the bully! My defender had taken boxing, wrestling, and karate lessons, and he gave the other boy a sound thrashing. From then on, all three of us were friends.

I remember when my brother, Melvin, was small, and he was picked on by some older boys in our town. I was bigger then and had the chance to defend him.

Jesus could have called on a host of angels to defend Him. They could have drawn their swords and come to His rescue at any time. But His love held Him on the cross and made Him, in a moment of agonizing pain, stop and give hope to a repentant sinner dying beside Him who said, "Jesus, remember me when you come into your kingdom. Jesus answered him, 'I tell you the truth, today you will be with me in paradise'" (Luke 23:42–43).

After terrible torture had been inflicted upon Him by degenerate man, it was love that caused Him to lift His voice and pray, "Father, forgive them, for they do not know what they are doing" (Luke 23:34).

From Genesis to Revelation, from earth's greatest tragedy to earth's greatest triumph, the dramatic story of man's lowest depths and God's most sublime heights can be expressed in twenty-five tremendous words: "For God so loved the world, that he gave his only begotten Son, that whosoever believeth in him should not perish, but have everlasting life" (John 3:16 KJV).

How Can We Comprehend His Love?

On the human level, we frequently love the one who loves us. In the spiritual realm, people do not grasp the overwhelming love of a holy God, but we can understand God's love by getting to know Him through Jesus Christ. No one can grasp the love of the God of the universe without knowing His Son.

Lloyd Ogilvie tells about a conversation with an old friend who said, "Lloyd, I've been a closet agnostic for some time now. I used to be so sure of what I believed, but now I have to admit I've known about God, but never really known God. I've got so many unanswered questions. I guess my mind has finally caught up with my heart."

Ogilvie continues, "Agnosticism is the silent agony of our age. It's not questions about God's existence that trouble most people, but questions about what He is like and how they can know Him. The unanswered questions about God, about His nature, will and ways have surfaced as an honest but very unsatisfying, 'I just don't know!' And this uncertainty troubles people both inside and outside the church."[1]

Speak about the love of God and faces light up, but speak of God as a Judge, and our attitudes change. But God is the Judge of His world; as our Maker, He owns us. He is a Judge who loves righteousness and hates sin, and He is always just.

If we are unfortunate enough to stand before a judge in a court of law, we hope that he or she is fair. God's judgments are based on His wisdom, which is wiser than those of men.

We are not unlike the writer of Psalm 73, who saw the prosperity of the wicked and complained, "They have no struggles, their bodies are healthy and strong. They are free from the burdens common to man." A common cry is "Why do evil men prosper and good men suffer?" In the seventeenth century, John Trapp wrote, "Envy not such a one his prosperity, any more than you would a corpse his flowers."

God is not indifferent to right and wrong. The judgment of a Holy God is as much a part of His nature as His love for us. Judgment means that in the end God's will will be perfectly done. We hear, "How can God love me when I have lived such a despicable life?" "How can God love the world when there is so much needless suffering?" You may have questions of your own which begin with "How can God love . . . ?"

No matter what sin we have committed, no matter how terrible it may be, God loves us.

What God's Love Can't Do

God cannot forgive the unrepentant sinner. The human race is called on throughout the Bible to repent of sin and return to God. This love of God can be entirely rejected. God will not force Himself upon any man against his will. A person can hear a message about the love of God and say, "No, I won't have it," and God will let him go on in his sin to eternity without God.

Francis Schaeffer wrote, "So often people think that Christianity is only something soft, only a kind of gooey love that loves evil equally with good. This is not the biblical position. The holiness of God is to be exhibited simultaneously with love."[2]

When I think about God's love I tend to dwell upon all the good and great things He has done for me. Then I must stop and realize that even when circumstances don't look too bright, God's love still shines. I cannot hide from His love, nor can I escape it.

Shortly after my mother's companion, Rose Adams, lost her husband, Mother wrote a note to her. She said: "Dear precious one: When this storm shall pass, the brightness for which He is preparing you will appear unclouded and it shall be Himself."

No Place to Hide

Escapism seems to be the order of the day. Escape by travelling, go to another city or another country and life will be better. Escape with drugs or alcohol, and the bitterness of living will be blurred. Escape into hobbies or work or television. Reality is too harsh.

We can't escape from God. In Psalm 139:1–5, David said, "O Lord, you have searched me and you know me. You know when I sit and when I rise; you perceive my thoughts from afar. You discern my going out and my lying down; you are familiar with all my ways. Before a word is on my tongue you know it completely, O Lord. You hem me in, behind and before; you have laid your hand upon me."

God's love is called by that theological term *omniscient*. David could not explain the manner of that kind of love any more than we can. However, he could tell how it affected him: "Such knowledge is too wonderful for me, too lofty for me to attain" (v. 6). He goes on to acknowledge that God is in every place. "Where can I go from your presence? If I go up to the heavens, you are there; if I make my bed in the depths, you are there" (vv. 7–8).

If one could climb to the highest heights or descend to the lowest depths, one could not escape the presence of Almighty God. This is what the omniscience and the omnipresence of God means to us in practical terms. "If I rise on the wings of the dawn, if I settle on the far side of the sea, even there your hand will guide me, your right hand will hold me fast" (Psalm 139:9–10).

Every day I read a Psalm to give me strength for the day and a realization of the power of God's love. His love has seen me through sickness, discouragement, and frustration. His love has sustained me during times of disappointment and bewilderment. However, I have never experienced some of the terrible trials of some of my fellow Christians. I have never been in prison or physically tortured for my faith, but I have known those who have been.

In 1948 a Romanian Christian pastor was taken prisoner by the Communists. For sixteen years he was moved from one camp to another, brutally beaten, drugged, and tortured. He underwent brainwashing of the most diabolical kind, but his faith held strong. After years of imprisonment, he almost reached the breaking point. The prisoners were given postcards to invite their families to visit them. Their hopes rose as they shaved, washed, and were given clean shirts. Hour after hour he sat in his cell, but no one came. He did not know then that the postcards were never sent.

As night came, the loudspeakers began to blare: *Nobody loves you now . . . Nobody loves you now . . .* He began to weep. And then the loudspeaker said: *They don't want to know you any more . . . They don't want to know you any more . . .*

The next day he was told that plenty of other wives had come to visit. They told him he was a fool, that his wife was in bed with other men, and they described what was happening with all the obscenity they could. When he had enough of the lecture he was returned to his cell and over the loudspeaker came the chant: *Christianity is dead . . . Christianity is dead . . .*

He began to believe what they had told him all of those months, that Christianity was truly dead. He wrote,

> The Bible foretells a time of great apostasy, and I believed that it had arrived.
>
> Then I thought of Mary Magadalene, and perhaps this thought, more than any other, helped to save me from the soul-killing poison of the last and worst stage of brainwashing. I remembered how she was faithful to Christ even when He cried on the Cross, "My God, why have you forsaken me?" And when He was a corpse in the tomb, she wept nearby and waited until He arose. So when I believed at last that Christianity was dead, I said, "Even so, I believe in it, and I will weep at its tomb until it arises again, as it surely will."[3]

After he was released he wrote: "The prison years did not seem too long for me, for I discovered, alone in my cell, that beyond belief and love there is a delight in God: a deep and extraordinary ecstasy of happiness that is like nothing in this world."

Now the words written by that pastor twenty-three years ago have come true. Christianity has risen again in Romania, and in many other countries in that part of the world. However, Christianity was never dead in those countries, for God was not dead in the hearts of believers. His love will never die.

God is not blind. He knows about you and your problems. He knows of those who are suffering from the loss of a loved one, the knowledge of terminal illness, the memories of childhood abuse, the strain of financial failure, and your particular pain. And His love for His children will never leave in times of trouble.

Lew Wallace distinguished himself as a major general in the Union Army during the Civil War. He was a lawyer who served on the court-martial that tried the assassins of Abraham Lincoln, and he presided over the military court that convicted the superintendent of Andersonville Prison of cruelty in allowing the death of Union prisoners. Wallace was a strong, intelligent man, but he did not know the love of God. However, when he was challenged to read the Bible, to disprove the existence of God, instead, his heart was changed dramatically and he became a believer in Jesus Christ. Subsequently, he penned one of the bestsellers in Christian fiction, *Ben Hur*, which was made into one of the greatest films of all time, starring Charlton Heston.

Wallace, the tough war hero, wrote these words: "Riches take wings, comforts vanish, hope withers away, but love stays with us. God is love."

Before we can grasp any meaning from suffering, we must rest in His unfailing love.

God is preparing His heroes and the time will come when they will appear and the world will wonder where they came from.

A. W. Tozer

CHAPTER THREE

Into Each Life Some Rain . . .

IN MANY CASES, the rain that falls is more like Hurricane Hugo of 1989. The winds of that tempest tore up the lives of thousands in its vicious path. Only in fairy tales do people live charmed lives. We may think that some people have it all, but if we turn the pages of their lives we may see the frog that never turned into a prince or the person who seemed "born to trouble."

Sometimes life touches one person with a bouquet and another with a thorn bush. But the first may find a wasp in the flowers, and the second may discover roses among the thorns.

Who Said Life Was Fair?

Have you ever heard a child wail, "It's not fair!" There are those who have made their fortunes on other people's misfortune. The Bible never promised that life would be fair. Christian living that sounds like an article on the lifestyle page of the newspaper may leave us unprepared for a world where hell does break loose. We are in a battle on this earth, and there is no one who is excused from service.

As we pray and give thanks for the end of the Berlin Wall and the opening of Eastern Europe to democracy and religious freedom, we also realize that new tyrannies challenge the Christian faith. We must not become complacent in our sanctuaries.

I met two Christians from an Eastern Bloc country who worked in a Christian radio station. When asked how it felt to be persecuted for their faith, they replied, "We thought it was the normal Christian life." They were right. It is we who are living abnormally—for the present.

The Popularity Cult

In some churches and religious television programs, we see an effort to make Christianity popular and always positive. This may be a comfortable cushion for those who find the hard facts too difficult. Within the New Testament, there is no indication that Christians should expect to be healthy, wealthy, and successful in this present age. Jesus said, "If the world hates you, keep in mind that it hated me first" (John 15:18). Christ never told his disciples that they would get an Academy Award for their performances, but He did tell them to expect to have troubles.

This age is interested in success, not suffering. We can identify with James and John who wanted choice seats in the kingdom. We might even ask for reclining chairs and soft music.

Our Lord was ridiculed, insulted, persecuted, and eventually killed. In the face of opposition, He went about "doing good." Even His enemies could find no fault in Him. He became the greatest teacher of moral values the world has ever known, but after only three years of public ministry He was executed as a criminal.

"Good" people do not escape suffering in this life. The Bible lists in Hebrews 11 the heroes of the faith, both Jew and Gentile, who were tortured, imprisoned, stoned, torn apart, and killed by the sword. They didn't wear designer jeans but went about in animal skins, destitute and tormented. Those early believers wandered in deserts, crossed mountains, and hid in caves. They were the homeless of that time, without even a cardboard shelter.

In America today, being a Christian is sometimes equated with having good health. Some popular nutrition and psychology publications recommend that a sound body may require a strong spiritual life. Many of these writers lean toward a hybrid of Eastern religious thought and humanistic psychology, but others have been biblically sound. I believe that exercise and proper eating habits are very important, since the Bible says that the body is God's holy temple, but I don't think that superbodies equate with committed Christian discipleship. Some of the greatest saints I've known have been those with physical infirmities.

Joni Eareckson Tada is a living example. Joni cannot walk and has only limited use of her arms. God has used her to touch millions of lives as a result of her handicap. She is a greater testimony to His love than many others who have strong bodies. "For physical training is of some value, but godliness has value for all things" (1 Timothy 4:8).

The Cost of Discipleship

Discipleship is not limited to twelve first-century men. Webster says that a disciple is a pupil or follower of any teacher or school of religion. To be a disciple of Jesus means to learn from Him, to follow Him. The cost may be high.

In the earlier part of His ministry, great crowds followed Jesus. However, the moment He started telling His followers that they must take up their crosses, "many . . . no longer followed him" (John 6:66).

Many forms of suffering are predicted in the Bible. The list sounds like Foxes' *Book of Martyrs*: persecutions for righteousness, reviling and slander, false accusations, rejection, hatred by the world and by relatives, temptations, shame, imprisonments, stonings, beatings, being a public spectacle, and the list continues. Your personal pain may not relate to any of these, because it is unique to you and to your situation. It may not even be comforting to hear of these forms of punishment. In Western democracies, seldom have people been called to endure physical suffering because they were believers. However, there are many other types of suffering.

If you have ever lost your job because you refused to compromise your principles, you know the hurt. If a friend or family member has ever accused you of being a fanatic, you might have felt humiliated. If you're a teenager and your best friends have ever excluded you from a spring break beach party, the rejection may be very painful.

What about the average professing Christian? Is living for the Lord Jesus Christ a priority? Sadly, it may not be. In America, churchgoing has become popular, but attending a service (or a crusade) may not necessarily be accompanied by genuine depth in prayer and Bible study or a change in the way we live.

Christianity is not a spectator sport, it's something in which we become totally involved. The Scripture says, "Therefore, if anyone is in Christ, he is a new creation; the old has gone, the new has come!" (2 Corinthians 5:17). Those who believe are expected to be different from the world about them. They are to be members of the new society and the new community that God has created.

Too many Christian television and radio programs have been geared to please, entertain, and gain the favor of this world. The temptation is to compromise, to make the Gospel more appealing and attractive.

At times in the Crusades we have conducted, I have looked into the cameras and realized that several million people were watching. I know that many of the things I have said from the Scriptures have offended some, but I cannot afford to tone down the message. As Paul said in 1 Corinthians 9:17, "I have a stewardship entrusted to me" (NASB), and that is to preach the pure and simple Gospel in whatever culture I am in.

The Bible says, "Don't let the world around you squeeze you into its own mold, but let God remold your minds from within" (Romans 12:2 PHILLIPS). Charles Colson wrote, "If Christianity is true—then it cannot be simply a file drawer in our crowded lives. It must be the central truth from which all our behavior, relationships, and philosophy flow."[1]

It is easy for Christians to allow themselves to be squeezed into the world's mold. It doesn't mean that we can't be fashionable, or that we have to wear drab clothing and live in hovels. It's the attitude of the world, rather than appearances, that we should not adopt. When nonbelievers see nothing different in the lifestyle of believers, they wonder if our profession of faith is sincere.

Our job in life is not to be successful, but to be faithful. Many Christians would prefer to hear "What a great guy" from the crowd rather than "Well done, good and faithful servant" from the Master.

Dietrich Bonhoeffer was a brilliant young German pastor from an aristocratic family of wealth and education. At the age of thirty-seven he was imprisoned by the Nazi government for his alleged involvement in an attempt to assassinate Hitler. He was never tried, but two years later, near the end of the war, Bonhoeffer was executed. Fellow prisoners who survived reported a message he sent to a friend, "Tell him that for me this is the end, but also the beginning." Bonhoeffer knew the cost of discipleship.

Many Christians want the benefits of their belief, but they hesitate at the cost of discipleship. Again, we have choices to make. Moses had a choice of following God or reveling in the pleasures of Egypt. As heir to the throne of Egypt, he enjoyed luxury; he didn't desire to suffer or sacrifice any more than we do, but he chose to follow God. "He chose to be mistreated along with the people of God rather than to enjoy the pleasures of sin for a short time" (Hebrews 11:25).

Salvation is free, but there is a price to pay in following Jesus. It is never said in Scripture that we can have "Christ and . . ."; it is always "Christ or . . ." Christ or Caesar, Christ or the world, Christ or Antichrist. What is your "or"?

Jesus said, "He who is not with me is against me, and he who does not gather with me scatters" (Matthew 12:30). Following Christ has been made too easy. It is easy to follow Him when our world is safe and comfortable, when we have good health, a contented family, and three meals (plus snacks) a day. But when that world shatters, only a secure faith will sustain us.

In a country where Christians were looked upon with suspicion and disfavor, a government leader said to me with a twinkle in his eye, "Christians seem to thrive under persecution. Perhaps we should prosper them, and then they would disappear."

Gretchen's Story

Gretchen was a woman who had her comfortable world disintegrate in one blinding moment. Without her faith in God, she might have remained for the rest of her life hidden in a dark room.

As she told her story, she was sitting on a California patio, the brilliant sun emphasizing her cruelly disfigured face. It was obvious from the blank socket where one eye should have been, the reconstructed nose, the scarred skin, and the missing arm that she had been in some hideous accident. And yet her beauty was evident. The transcendent glow of her inner strength was not artificial.

Gretchen's world changed one morning in 1982 when a drunk driver forced her car into a fatal spin, hurtling it across the freeway, where it exploded into a burning inferno. Her mother was instantly killed, and Gretchen was miraculously saved from burning to death.

Before that dreadful day, Gretchen had led a sun-filled life. Beautiful, wealthy, with an attentive husband, she seemed to be living every girl's dream. In the following nightmare, she lost everything but gained much more.

She was in a coma for six weeks. When she finally understood that her face was virtually gone, she did not want anyone to see her. Television was her companion, and it was during one of her more than seventy operations that she saw one of our Crusades and gave her life to Christ.

After seven years of seclusion, she realized that she could not stay in hiding. She knew God had saved her for something. She began to volunteer at a rehabilitation center where her own disabilities gave her the credibility to reach out to others. When asked about her greatest joy, she answered, "It's waking up in the morning and knowing that nothing is an accident."

Cross-Bearers with Long Faces

The marks of the cross are not to be confused with self-inflicted austerity or the rigors of the Middle Ages brought up-to-date. We should not intentionally seek suffering with the mistaken idea that we might earn special merit with God. Asceticism is not necessarily a virtue.

Amy Carmichael wrote:

> The narrow thorny path he trod,
> 'Enter into my joy,' said God.
> The sad ascetic shaved his head,
> 'I've lost the taste for joy,' he said.

Christ admonished His followers: "When you fast, do not look somber as the hypocrites do, for they disfigure their faces to show men they are fasting" (Matthew 6:16). This was a clear warning not to boast of trials we have brought upon ourselves.

Bearing our cross does not mean wearing gunny sacks and long faces. Some people we meet imagine that every little headache is a part of their cross. They wear the look of a martyr every time they hear criticism. Sometimes we deserve the criticism we receive; however, we are blessed only when men speak evil against us *falsely* for Christ's sake.

A book was written about me that contained some blatant falsehoods. At first I was offended, but then I began to laugh, because I had just been talking about being blessed for false accusations and God gave me a personal illustration.

Christians should be a foreign influence, a minority group in a pagan world. We are the "light of the world," and light exposes evil. We are the salt, and it adds flavor. If we are at peace with this world, it may be because we have sold out to it and compromised with it.

Dwight L. Moody once said, "If the world has nothing to say against you, beware lest Jesus Christ has nothing to say for you."

Take Heart!

I am not suggesting that we live anticipating trouble at every turn. Some people spend so much time worrying about what might happen that they never enjoy what is happening. Take one day at a time. Today, after all, is the tomorrow you worried about yesterday.

Jesus knew His disciples were worried about the future, and when He talked to them at the end of His ministry, on the very eve of His death, He said, "I have told you these things, so that in me you may have peace. In this world you will have trouble. But take heart! I have overcome the world" (John 16:33).

Trouble is different for all of us—translate it as you will: money, marital, health, social, loneliness. Jesus said His followers would have trouble. But He also promises His presence with us, not to deliver us from our problems, but to be with us in the midst of them and give us the power to overcome whatever circumstances come our way.

Nancy Bates, one of our researchers, is an example of overcoming circumstances. She has a delightful sense of humor and is a joy to be around. Nancy was struck by a car when she was seventeen, and her back was broken. She is a paraplegic. And she is a contagious Christian.

When the Apostle John recorded Christ's message to the church in Smyrna, he wrote, "Do not be afraid of what you are about to suffer. I tell you, the devil will put some of you in prison to test you, and you will suffer persecution. . . . Be faithful, even to the point of death, and I will give you the crown of life" (Revelation 2:10).

Mysterious as it appears to be, true faith and suffering frequently go hand-in-hand. You seldom have one without the other. I think of my dear friend, Corrie ten Boom, who has gone home to be with the Lord. One incident in her last years comes to mind after reading the previous passage from Revelation.

After being a prisoner in Ravensbruk, the infamous women's concentration camp, Corrie traveled throughout the world, telling her story of suffering and joy. For thirty-three years she never had a permanent home. When she was eighty-five years old, her supporters provided her with a lovely house in California. It was a luxury she never dreamed she would have.

One day, as her friend and movie director, the late Jimmy Collier, was leaving her home, he said, "Corrie, hasn't God been good to give you this beautiful place?"

She replied firmly, "Jimmy, God was good when I was in Ravensbruk, too."

Suffering Is Not in Vain

No suffering that one of Christ's own endures for Him is ever in vain. Living for Christ, walking in His way, will not be an easy path. The way of the cross is a hard one, but He never said it would be easy.

The scriptural principles relating to the endurance of pain are just the same today as when they were first written for us in the Word of God. Some of us may have to die, or at least suffer, for our faith. The twentieth century has seen more people tortured and killed for Christ than any other century. Our generation has known its martyrs, like Paul Carlson, the missionary to the Congo who was killed trying to rescue others. Jim Elliot was killed, along with four friends, trying to get the Gospel to the Auca Indians in Ecuador. Bishop Luwum, the archbishop of the Anglican Church of Uganda, was shot in the head at point blank range.

Festo Kivengere was speaking in Asheville, North Carolina, and said this about Luwum's martyrdom: "When a man has lived for God, preaching the Gospel fearlessly, opposing cruelty, injustice, and oppression with courage, yet speaking the truth graciously and in love—when that man seals his testimony with his blood, that is not tragedy, that is glory!"

When Ruth was speaking in Sweden, her interpreter, Gunvar Paulson, told about being in the Salvation Army in Rhodesia when insurgents broke in and murdered many people. Her coworkers were killed. She alone was spared, but after repeated operations has only limited use of her left arm. Impulsively, Ruth said, "What an honor it is to sit beside you—I have never had to suffer for the Lord."

Miss Paulson replied, "Believe me, in spite of all that was going on around me, I felt such a sense of the presence of the Lord Jesus, it was pure joy!"

When David Livingstone returned to his native Scotland after sixteen difficult years as a missionary in Africa, his body was emaciated by the ravages of some twenty-seven fevers that had coursed through his veins during the years of his service. One arm hung useless at his side, the result of being mangled by a lion. He was speaking to the students at Glasgow University and the core of his message to those young people was this: "Shall I tell you what sustained me during the hardship and loneliness of my exile? It was Christ's promise, 'Lo, I am with you always, even unto the end.'"

That promise is ours as well.

A recovery of the old sense of sin is essential to Christianity. C. S. Lewis

CHAPTER FOUR

Pain in Paradise

WHERE DID PAIN BEGIN?

Could God have created a world without suffering?

Yes, He could, and He did.

In millenniums past there was a time when the universe and its undiscovered galaxies were in a state of complete harmony with their Maker. It was an existence beyond the comprehension of our finite minds; we cannot imagine a world that is older than we can even think and which existed without a hint of the suffering to come. However, into this Paradise came Satan, probably the most misunderstood person in the universe. Before Satan there was no sin, and before sin there was no pain.

Who is Satan? He is underestimated and frequently caricatured. Some think he is only a spiritual force, others have imagined him as a goblin or dismissed him as a myth. Today, however, when Satan worship is increasing at an alarming rate, we had better be aware of him, his origin, his aims, his abilities, and his limitations.

Satan was once a dazzling creature. The prophet Ezekiel called him "the model of perfection, full of wisdom and perfect in beauty" (28:12). This incredible person was once one of the "sons of God" (Job 38:7 NASB).

The First Sinner Commits the First Sin

Lucifer (meaning "morning star" in Hebrew) was an angel created to glorify God, but this was not the role he wanted. His heart's desire was to be the chief authority; he wanted to sit on God's throne and rule the universe. Isaiah 14:12–14 tells us: "How you have fallen from heaven, O morning star, son of the dawn! You have been cast down to the earth, you who once laid low the nations! You said in your heart, I will ascend to heaven; I will raise my throne above the stars of God; I will sit enthroned on the mount of assembly, on the utmost heights of the sacred mountain. I will ascend above the tops of the clouds; I will make myself like the Most High."

When Lucifer asserted his desire to be more than God, a great revolution took place in the universe. Many angels joined with Lucifer and became his rebel army. Evidently when God judged Lucifer's crimes, God changed his name to Satan, the Evil One, and sentenced him to eternal exile.

Satan didn't lose any of his beguiling ways when he became the fallen prince. He took his charm, his subtleties, and his clever plots to use on us. When he made his decision to battle God to the death, he took his band of rebel angels with him as his combat soldiers. The battlefield is known as Earth.

The Way It Was

Before the great polluter spread his poison throughout this new territory, God chose to beautify this planet with light and darkness, seas and skies, land and vegetation, sun, moon and stars, air, and land animals.

In a time when we are concerned about our polluted earth, can you imagine what Paradise was like? Every flower that grew was perfect; no blight was on them. The fertilizers and bug sprays we keep in our garden shed were not needed. Visualize a fruit tree laden with juicy apples or pears, without a bug in any piece. Imagine the sky so clear you could see every galaxy and constellation. No trash, no unpleasant odors, no litter. The lakes would have waters so clear you could see the color of every fish. God designed this glorious earth garden for His perfect children. When Adam and Eve were created they brought human beauty into this world of perfection.

The First Perfect Relationship

God wanted someone with whom He could fellowship. So He created Adam and Eve. No couple since then has had the ideal union that those two lovers had.

In the middle of the garden were two special trees, the *Tree of Life* and the *Tree of the Knowledge of Good and Evil.* The Lord God told the man, "You are free to eat from any tree in the garden; but you must not eat from the tree of the knowledge of good and evil, for when you eat of it you will surely die" (Genesis 2:16–17). Monsignor Knox translates it even more emphatically: "Thy doom is death!"

A river flowed out of Eden, dividing into four rivers, two of which were the Tigris and the Euphrates. So the Garden of Eden was somewhere in present-day Iraq. The turmoil and war we have recently witnessed in that part of the world in our time is occurring in the land where God established the first perfect civilization.

It became God's daily practice to walk with man in the garden in the cool of the day (Genesis 3:8). What an idyllic existence! How could anyone want more? And yet the first couple did.

God gave Adam and Eve more than beauty and a perfect environment. He gave them one of the most precious things man can have. Freedom. John Milton said, "When God gave Adam reason, he gave him freedom to choose . . . otherwise, he would have been a mere artificial Adam, such as an Adam in the puppet shows." Adam and Eve could have been created to walk where God directed them, speak the words God gave them—just mere puppets. However, God gave them, just as He has given us, freedom to choose.

Satan's Tactics

Satan entered the garden in the form of a serpent. We can only speculate how this happened, but we do know that he had been on the prowl, searching for ways to destroy God ever since the time of his banishment from Heaven. And here was his opportunity to hurt two who were dear to the heart of God. He started in the same subtle way he uses today.

He cast doubt on what God had said. He worked on Eve first when he said, "Did God really say . . . ?" (Genesis 3:1). The next strategy Satan used was an appeal to the ego. He told Eve she wouldn't die when she ate of that certain tree, she would simply be like God. So Eve took the fatal bite and passed some over to Adam, and he ate. This is called the Fall of man, and it has been a long way down ever since. God said to Adam, "Have you eaten from the tree that I commanded you not to eat from?" (Genesis 3:11). Adam answered by saying, "The woman *you* put here with me—she gave me some fruit from the tree, and I ate it" (Genesis 3:12, emphasis added).

Ever since, man has been passing the blame. A boy sins, his parents are blamed. A person is murdered, his environment is blamed. Someone cheats, the system is blamed. Passing the blame is as old as the Garden of Eden.

Even worse, man keeps asking, *How can a just and loving God allow so much suffering in the world—natural disasters—man's inhumanity to man?* Somehow, like Adam, man tries to blame God.

Beginning of Sorrow

Human nature was now flawed. Man's direct disobedience resulted in the judgment God placed on the human race.

The beginning of all pain and suffering in the world started with one act of disobedience. Christian and non-Christian alike have inherited the consequences from our common ancestors, Adam and Eve—our polluted environment and flawed human nature.

What Is This Thing Called Sin?

Satan exalted himself above God and endeavored to get man to doubt the reliability of God's Word. If Adam and Eve had resisted the devil, he would have fled, defeated. But they didn't (Genesis 3:13). This is where death began! A three-dimensional death:

1. *Instant spiritual death: separation from God.*

2. *Gradual physical death: as soon as we are born we begin to die.*

3. *Ultimate eternal death—but for the saving mercy of Jesus Christ.*

Sin works the same with all of us, whatever our condition, nature, or environment. We are depraved by nature because we inherited it (Romans 3:19), and we must bear the sentence of guilt and the stain of sin. Each person must give an account of himself to God.

One Crisis After Another

One crisis has followed another throughout human history—Cain murdered Abel—the Flood came and only Noah and those in the Ark were saved—confusion fell upon Babel as different languages were introduced—and so on, down through history until today.

Confusion of Good and Evil

We have seen the progression of the "father of lies." He began in Eden. He was behind each of the major crises of faith and obedience down through the centuries. And he still deceives gullible men and women of every age.

An old Scottish clergyman said the devil has two lies that he uses at two different stages. Before we commit a sin, he tells us that one little sin doesn't matter—"no one will know." The second lie is that after we've sinned he tells us we're hopeless. We have all fallen, individually and collectively, and God does not consider this a trifling matter. Judgment hangs over the whole human race because of rebellion and disobedience. The Scripture says, "Sin entered the world through one man, and death through sin, and in this way death came to all men, because all sinned" (Romans 5:12).

The good news is because Jesus Christ came and died on the cross and rose from the dead, we are not in a hopeless position. We can be reconciled to God and put back in right relationship with Him by accepting His provision for sin, His Son Jesus Christ.

As sin has progressed and gained momentum, modern man seems to have lost his ability to be shocked. Behavior that was once considered abominable is now acceptable. One thing is certain, however. There are many new sinners today, but there aren't any new sins, just the old ones clothed in different rags.

Sin invariably hurts the innocent—frequently worse than it does the one committing it.

I have found, however, that most young people really want us to spell out a moral code. They may not accept it or believe it, but they want to hear it, clearly and without compromise. But where can the moral code be found?

The state highway department in Pennsylvania once set out to build a bridge, working from both sides. When the workers reached the middle of the waterway, they found they were thirteen feet to one side of each other. Albert Steinberg, writing some time ago in the *Saturday Evening Post,* went on to explain that each crew of workmen had used its own reference point.

There's a small disc on the Meades Ranch in north central Kansas where the thirty-ninth parallel from the Atlantic to the Pacific crosses the ninety-eighth meridian running from Canada to the Rio Grande. The National Oceanic Survey, a small federal agency whose business it is to locate the exact positions of every point in the United States, uses the scientifically recognized reference point on the Meades Ranch. So far, no mistakes have been made, and none are expected.

All ocean liners and commercial planes come under the survey. The government can build no dams or even launch a missile without this agency to tell it the exact location to the very inch. "Location by approximation," the article goes on to say, "can be costly and dangerous."

In the field of surveying, the word *benchmark* is of ultimate significance. It is the point of reference from which a surveyor takes all his measurements. If the benchmark is wrong, all of his calculations will be wrong. Where you start will determine where you end.

The same thing is true about the compass, the sextant, and the sun and the stars. If the compass is not accurate, you will lose your way. If the sun and the stars were not ordered in their stations, no mariner could depend on them to find his way through the oceans of the world. If there are no absolutes, no fixed reference points, there can be no certainty. The locus of the conflict in the world today rises from the battle between the absolute and the relative.

The reference point from which I approach you today is that of a Christian who believes in the Bible. All my values, judgments, and attitudes must be gauged in relationship to this reference point. If you are coming from another reference point, then you and I may have a very difficult time meeting.

Pain in Paradise: Suffering at Home

Why do we suffer? Why does life seem so unfair, so unjust? One thing is clear. The Bible explains that there is suffering in the world because there is sin in the world. The root of the problem lies in man's alienation from God which began with Adam and Eve. If the separation that sin creates had not entered into the life of man, human suffering would not exist in the world.

In God's original blueprint, suffering was not drawn in the plans. By willful disobedience to God's Word and commandment, man brought suffering upon himself. He has been reaping what he has sown all through the centuries. And he blames God. Repeatedly. Daily. "How could a loving God allow . . . ?" "How can God be just and permit . . . ?" It is always God's fault.

Is it really necessary to know how suffering entered the world? I believe that we need to know the origin of pain, or we would be like the physician prescribing medicine without an examination.

God does not offer Band-Aids when you are bleeding to death, but He gave a life-saving transfusion, the blood of His Son. God is not responsible for sin, but His love led Him to send His Son to die for our sins.

Look, Father, look on His beloved face
And only look on us as seen in Him.
Look not on our misusing of Thy grace
Our prayer so languid and our faith so dim
For, lo, between our sins and their reward,
We place the passion of Thy Son, our Lord.

When I consider my crosses, tribulations, and temptations, I shame myself almost to death, thinking what are they in comparison to the suffering of my blessed Savior Christ Jesus.
Martin Luther

CHAPTER FIVE

Why Jesus Suffered

A GRANDMOTHER IS watching her small grandson when the phone rings. She talks for a few minutes while he climbs the fence and drowns in the pool.

Three high school athletes are hit and killed by a drunk driver.

A beautiful teenager is reported missing. Her distraught parents find her on the streets of San Francisco, living as a prostitute.

Your minister's child is diagnosed with incurable cancer.

Your son is held as a hostage in a foreign land.

Friday comes, and along with your paycheck is a termination notice.

These are anguishing scenarios of human suffering. Perhaps you may have had some heartbreaking times of your own that are worse than these. When we go through some of life's hard trials, it is natural to center upon ourselves. Whether it is physical or mental anguish, personal pain tears us apart.

God did not exclude himself from human suffering. He became man—the Person of Christ—and shared with us all there is to share. Philip Yancey wrote, "God does not, in the comfortable surroundings of heaven, turn a deaf ear to the sounds of suffering on this groaning planet."[1]

God Joined Us

We have read stories, seen many paintings, and sat through numerous Christmas pageants about the birth of Jesus. It never ceases to stir me.

Jesus' life was in peril from the time He uttered His first cry. The most illustrious child ever born was hated by many while He lay in a manger, helpless to defend Himself.

We don't know much about His life as a child, but we do know that He lived with the knowledge of His destiny. His entire life was one of humiliation; He came not as a conquering king, which is what the Jews expected, but as a humble servant.

When He was an adult, the leaders were suspicious of this carpenter from Nazareth, because He was a threat to them. They scorned Him and treated Him with contempt. They said He broke God's law, that He was an unholy person—a drunkard and one who made friends with the scum of society. He had the label of guilt by association stamped upon Him by self-righteous men.

Many people reacted to Him violently. At the beginning of His ministry, His own townsfolk at Nazareth tried to throw Him off a cliff (Luke 4:29). Religious and political leaders often conspired to seize and kill Him. And yet He healed the sick, fed the hungry, loved the unlovely, taught the ignorant, and worked miracles among His people. Ultimately, He was arrested and brought to trial before Pilate and Herod. Though innocent, He was denounced as an enemy of God and man. The frenzied mob incited the religious leaders and cried, "Crucify Him!"

Remember, too, that He knew in advance what was coming, and this increased His suffering. He knew the path of pain He would experience; He foresaw the baptism of blood that awaited Him. He told His disciples very plainly about His coming death by crucifixion, which they could not understand at the time.

The Cross: Symbol of Suffering

Jesus suffered more than any other person in human history. The specifics of how He suffered were predicted in the prophecies of the Old Testament some five hundred to a thousand years before these events occurred.

When we are in trouble, we need a friend. We need someone to understand, to be with us, to hold us close and say, "I'm here to help." When Jesus needed friends, they left Him.

What a devastation! At the end of training the twelve, they failed Him miserably. Anyone who has been deserted knows the terrible feeling of abandonment. Jesus had to appear alone before His accusers. He had to face His trial without a friend.

When Jesus was arrested, it was a religious lynching. False witnesses accused Him, "looking for false evidence against Jesus so that they could put him to death. But they did not find any" (Matthew 26:59–60).

The Jewish authorities were determined to have Him killed, but they needed to get the permission of Pilate, the man appointed by Rome to be in charge of Jerusalem. Jews, under Roman rule, did not have the right to carry out the death penalty. Pilate was convinced that Jesus was not guilty; three times he pronounced Him innocent. Then he had an idea he thought would absolve him of making a decision. It was his custom to release one prisoner at the time of Passover. "Do you want me to release the 'king of the Jews'?" They shouted back, "No, not him! Give us Barabbas!" (John 18:39–40.)

Pilate was disappointed when the crowd chose Barabbas, a common criminal, instead of Jesus. He must have cringed when he led the pitiful, bruised, and bleeding man before the crowd. Instead of sympathy, he heard the shouts, "Crucify! Crucify!"

Pilate was a weak man, and when the chief priests told him that he would be Caesar's enemy if he did not kill this revolutionary, he gave in. Before he handed Jesus over to be crucified, he called for a basin and said, "I am innocent of this man's blood. It is your responsibility." He washed his hands of the whole affair.

All Signs Point to the Cross

The cross of Jesus Christ was the culmination of the one life that held more suffering than any other in human history. His was the suffering of the entire world. And God made Him who had no sin to be sin for us (2 Corinthians 5:21). Since the day of crucifixion, the cross has been the supreme symbol of salvation from sin.

God says there is no hope for the world aside from the cross. We look to the leadership of men, the progress of scientific discovery, or the spread of knowledge and think human beings can find solutions to our problems. But our hope rests not in a system, or a government, or a philosophy, but in the cross of Christ.

To many people, the mention of the blood of Christ is distasteful. However, on my last visit to the Mayo Clinic I noticed that at each reception desk there is a box holding large square pamphlets entitled *A Gift of Life* urging people to donate blood to the blood bank. Anyone who has gone through surgery and looked up to see the bag of blood dripping slowly into his veins, realizes with gratitude the life-giving property of blood.

The message of the blood, the cross, and the work of redemption is still "foolishness" to those who are perishing (1 Corinthians 1:18), but "to us who are being saved, it is the power of God."

Is God on Trial?

In past generations it was thought that mankind was on trial before a holy God. Now it seems that the reverse is true; people imagine God on trial for all the terrible things that happen. At the beginning of this chapter we cited some painful illustrations of real people undergoing real suffering. It is human to question, "Where is God when . . . ?" And you can finish the sentence with your own cry.

When Jesus Christ was on the cross, His blood draining the life from His body, He knew what it was like to be alone, questioning God when He was wracked with pain. But His pain was the suffering of the sins of the ages, the greatest darkness of the soul ever known to man.

Why did Jesus suffer? For you. For me. That we might have life eternal and His peace in the midst of storms. "Peace I leave with you; my peace I give you. I do not give to you as the world gives. Do not let your hearts be troubled and do not be afraid" (John 14:27).

Suffering has no meaning unless we can believe that God understands our pain and can heal it. In the suffering of Jesus we have that assurance.

Few love to hear the sins they love to act.
William Shakespeare

CHAPTER SIX

Who Sinned?

SOME PEOPLE SEE sin in every sickness. They make their friends miserable by probing for hidden sins whenever suffering enters their lives. Although there may be some truth in their questioning, it also could be a cruel response to another's time of pain. They are like Job's so-called friends who pointed out all of his wrongs. Job called them "miserable comforters."

A child was dying of leukemia, and all hope had been abandoned. Her parents received a call from a woman who said she was a "healer." Grasping for any way to help their daughter or prolong her life, they asked the woman to come to their home. When she arrived, she asked a few questions, looked briefly at the weak, bedridden child, and then pronounced, "There's something wrong here. I detect sin in this house." The little girl heard these words and began to cry, "Make her leave, make her leave."

It is unkind to attribute every accident, every illness and sorrow to God's punishment for wrong behavior. It is appalling how many Christians approach suffering friends with that principle. They visit first with words of comfort, and then leave a load of guilt behind ("What could you have done to deserve this?") or pious advice ("Perhaps you need to pray harder.").

Suffering people can be tormented with questions of guilt; however, if all suffering is punishment for sin, then God's signals must be mixed, for accidents occur at random and disease strikes without any relationship to a person's moral or immoral lifestyle.

God's teaching does not attribute all suffering to sin or punishment for human mistakes. I have no right to tell a suffering person that it is because he sinned that his child died, or that he has cancer, or that his house burned.

In John 9, the followers of Jesus pointed to a man born blind and asked, "Who sinned, this man or his parents?" Jesus told them that neither the man nor his parents sinned, "But this happened so that the work of God might be displayed in his life." The disciples wanted to look back, to probe into the behavior of the blind man or his parents, but Jesus pointed them to the future and the hope that even suffering can be used to glorify God.

Who Needs Job's Friends?

Job was one man who endured such incredible suffering that most of us would say, "Don't tell me about Job; I could never relate to him." But in Job's story God has given us great examples of the type of questions or advice well-meaning friends sometimes express. (Is God trying to tell you something, Job? There must be a cause for your suffering. Is there some sin in your life? Repent, Job, that's the way out of your misery.)

Job had his world collapse around him. All of his possessions were wiped out, his seven sons and three daughters were killed in a tornado, and he was inflicted with painful, oozing boils from the top of his head to the bottom of his feet. What did he do to deserve these calamities? It was written that he was a man who was "blameless, upright, fearing God, and turning away from evil."

Yet Satan had to get permission from God before he could touch Job's possessions, much less Job himself. Somehow, all of the reasons for Job's suffering that his friends pointed out to him sound like those offered by Christians today. At one point, Job cried out to the men who berated him with his sins, "If it is true that I have gone astray, my error remains my concern alone" (Job 19:4).

One writer said, "Job is finally satisfied not by having his questions answered, but by a revelation of the incomparable majesty of God."[1] In the end, it was Job's friends who had their self-righteous theories dismissed. God said to Elephaz, one of the friends, "I am angry with you and your two friends, because you have not spoken of me what is right, as my servant Job has" (Job 42:7).

Philip Yancey wrote: "The Book of Job should nail a coffin lid over the idea that every time we suffer it's because God is punishing us or trying to tell us something. Although the Bible supports the general principle that 'a man reaps what he sows' even in this life (see Psalms 1:3; 37:25), the Book of Job proves that other people have no right to apply that general principle to a particular person. Nobody deserved suffering less than Job, and yet few have suffered more."[2]

The Book of Job does not set out to answer the problem of suffering, but to proclaim a God so great that no answer is needed.

Mistaken Thinking About Suffering

Among God's most obnoxious children are those who attribute all suffering to sin or punishment for mistakes. However, there's another error in thinking, and that is to assume that once we come to Christ, it will be almost impossible for sin to dominate us again. We may believe this because the Bible says, "If anyone is in Christ, he is a new creation; the old has gone, the new has come!" (2 Corinthians 5:17).

We think we're OK because our tempers have improved, our souls are calmer, our worldly desires have dwindled. *I'm OK no matter what trials and suffering hit me. I'm ready for them!*

The Trials Come

God's proving ground comes when trouble hits and the evil motives in our lives begin to surface. When you're on a lake where the water is calm and clear, the rainbow ripples of light playing on the surface, everything has an air of peace and beauty. But let the winds rise and the clouds open, and the water churns, bringing up the dredges of dirt and muck from the bottom. So it is with our lives. When calamity hits us, hard thoughts of God may begin to surface. *If God is so loving and wise, why did He allow this to happen?*

Archbishop Leighton said, "Extraordinary afflictions are not always the punishment of extraordinary sins, but sometimes the trial of extraordinary graces. God hath many sharp-cutting instruments and rough files for the polishing of His jewels; and those He especially loves, and means to make the most resplendent, He hath oftenest His tools upon."

Are we immune from evil thoughts and depraved actions when confronted with trials? Even some saints of old, when tried in God's proving grounds, were found not only evil, but many times their depravity was the last we would expect.

King David took one look at Bathsheba, another man's wife, and went after her. When Bathsheba became pregnant, David arranged to have her husband killed. When Peter faced guilt by association, he denied that he knew Jesus. All through the Bible we find occasional illustrations of strong men of old, believing in God, but revealing their innermost evil thoughts and actions in the face of trials.

God Tells Us Our Faults

We are told, "My son, do not make light of the Lord's discipline, and do not lose heart when he rebukes you" (Hebrews 12:5). What does it mean to be rebuked? It's the same word that is used in other passages to indicate that God "tells us our faults." He may begin His rebuke very gently. Simply read what He says to the churches in the Book of Revelation. With most of them He mentions past services and good deeds, but then comes the rebuke. "Yet I hold this against you: You have forsaken your first love," He told the angel of the church in Ephesus.

How do we know when we are being rebuked by God? Some rebukes are light and others are heavier, but when they are light (like the paddle ending in a soft cushion labeled "Grandma's paddle" which hangs in our front hall and has been given as a joke to many doting grandmothers), we tend to pay little attention.

Have you noticed when people tell us our faults, we can become discouraged? But when God points them out, we are not discouraged. With His rebuke comes the longing to do better. It may be that God is whispering to us with some light trial. That "still small voice" may be a warning, a tugging at our conscience.

Stronger Medicine

Can the sin of one or a few cause suffering for many? The answer, of course, is yes, for no sin is isolated in the life of the sinner. It spreads like poison gas into every available crevice. What may have been the rebellion against God of a few men has resulted in the most insidious plague the world has known. The influence of sin touches the innocent as well as the guilty . . . perhaps more.

From the sexually freewheeling culture of the sixties and seventies we inherited the AIDS epidemic. In the early years of its discovery, the response from the Christian community ranged from panic to self-righteousness, mostly wrapped in ignorance.

The Bible clearly teaches that practicing homosexuality is a sin, but to classify AIDS as simply a homosexual disease would be a disastrous public policy. Former Surgeon General C. Everett Koop estimates that by the end of 1991 as many as 270,000 cases of AIDS will have occurred and, in the United States alone, 179,000 people will have died since the disease was reported ten years ago. Because of their sexual practices, homosexual men are efficient transmitters of AIDS, and they make up between 60 and 75 percent of the reported cases. However, one quarter of the cases are intravenous drug users, and one out of every ten victims got the virus through heterosexual sex or blood transfusion. And many are born with AIDS through an infected mother, or through some as yet unidentified way.

If AIDS had never become a disease, practicing homosexuality would still be wrong, according to the Bible. The problems of sexual relations outside of our marriage vows that have caused grief and disease and brokenness would still exist. Our sins catch up with us, and they magnify our capacity to cause suffering.

I believe that many AIDS victims have been graciously given time. When they learn of the seriousness of their affliction, they have a chance to realize the love of God and His grace. The church should be ministering to these people and extending to them the promise of His forgiveness.

Sex: Sin and Not Sin

Some say that the sexual revolution is slowing down. People are seeing the ravages of AIDS and adjusting their lifestyles. Charles Colson said, "There is painful irony in the fact that it took AIDS to accomplish what no amount of pulpit pounding could do. People have a greater fear of disease than of God's judgment!"[3]

A loving God ordained monogamous marriage and the sanctity of what we call the traditional family. Within the bounds of marriage, sex is a gift of God, but when it is misused the possibilities are frightening. This is nothing new in our generation. Sexual immorality has always been a cause of death, judgment, and Hell. AIDS has clearly reminded our society of that, but the reality is not limited to AIDS.

Fatal Attraction, a popular movie of recent years, told the story of a supposedly respectable man who decided one short affair outside his marriage wouldn't hurt. The beautiful woman with whom he slept turned out to be a borderline psychotic who then crosses the border. In the film's terrifying climax, she nearly kills his wife. The story reflects what deep within our hearts we already know; if we want our lives to be good, indulging in what is unholy is risky business, to put it mildly.

The gift of sex is misused with reckless disregard for the consequences. Tragically, within the Christian ministry we see occasional examples of that abuse. What was meant by God to be beautiful within the bounds of marriage is degraded in everything from advertisements for perfume to comic strips. How much further, oh God, can it go?

The Bible shows Jesus dealing with sexual sin in several stories. The woman described in John 8 is one. Jesus had been praying all night before this event took place. He was teaching on the porch of the Temple, and a crowd had gathered. Suddenly there was a rude interruption as the Pharisees dragged before Him a poor woman who had been taken in immorality. She was crying. She expected to be stoned. It was a setup to trap Jesus by asking Him what should be done with the woman.

Jesus' dilemma was this: If He said yes to stone her, He would be in trouble with the Roman authorities, because they alone held the power of capital punishment. If He said not to stone her, He would break the law of Moses. He would be caught either way. So Jesus stooped down and wrote something on the ground. We can only guess what he wrote in the sand that day. Could it have been that He wrote the Ten Commandments?

He said, "If any one of you is without sin, let him be the first to throw a stone at her" (John 8:7). Imagine those religious leaders shifting from one foot to another, their eyes on the ground, not daring to look at one another. None of them could cast the first stone, because they were all guilty. They had dragged themselves to judgment, just as they had dragged the woman. Unfortunately, some Christians have treated those with AIDS in the same way, trying to make a point in an argument, instead of seeing the victim as one more of us sinners needing to be forgiven and cared for.

We understand this story, because we know we are, in our own way, standing in the crowd needing forgiveness, too. We may not be guilty of adultery, but we may be guilty of idolatry, lust, greed, or whatever our private or personal sin is. We may not carry the AIDS virus ourselves, but God forbid as modern-day Pharisees we should condemn others while carrying the virus of our own unconfessed and unrepented sins.

When Sigmund Freud began writing in the early part of this century, he complained of the narrowness of the Victorian era and attributed many neuroses to the sexual repression of his society. But if Freud were to come back today, he might reverse his stand and attribute our modern mania to the license and lack of sexual boundaries.

Historically the church, for the most part, has tried to teach that guilt and suffering are a result of sexual immorality. That is why there is no such thing as "safe sex." It may be sterile and clinically free of disease, but it is not safe from the pain of heartbreak it may cause. However, what right does any church have even attempting to approve of lifestyles or certain acts for which God prescribed the death penalty in the Old Testament?

Why did God make us sexual beings? I was speaking to the cadets at West Point, and as we were driving away, the chaplain said to me, "You know, God gave us one of the most difficult things ever to handle . . . sex." He asked me if I knew why. I said I thought I did. In the first place, God has given us sex to attract us to the opposite sex. That is natural and normal. In the very beginning, He looked at all He had made and called it good.

Second, sex was given for the propagation of the race. None of us would be here if it weren't for sex. That is the way God intended it, and it is the way He meant, within the bonds of matrimony, to produce children.

God has given us our sexuality as a means of expressing our love. This is why sex is not just for playboys to amuse themselves; it is the deepest way we can say to our spouse, "I love you and only you. I give myself completely to you alone."

Human sexuality was given as a glorious contribution to married love. It was given so that a man and a woman could express the unity that binds them together. We find ourselves in emotional quicksand if we go outside those rules of marriage, frequently resulting in depression, despair, or possibly disease.

Sin has a great impact on sex. It follows that if sin affects your sex life, it will also affect the rest of your life. Often it drives people to seek refuge in further sexual activities and other diversions, instead of turning to God.

Rebels against God who have misused the gift of their human sexuality are a growing army during our day. What God has given us as a gift of joy has often been turned into an instrument for our own destruction. But there is the wonderful good news of God's compassion, like that of Jesus speaking to the woman who was dragged before Him for her adulterous acts. Jesus told her to leave her life of sin and that she would not be condemned.

Rebels against God come in many forms. Some believe every disease, every accident, is caused by sin. Their judgmental attitude causes heartache in many lives. Other rebels defy God's laws and cause pain for themselves that may multiply in the lives of others.

Pious and judgmental attitudes will not soothe troubled hearts. The hope is in Jesus Christ, the light sent into this hopeless world.

The explosion of Jesus upon one's life transforms the human personality. It often brings peace of mind, contentment, happiness and joy. But to stop there as many do is like comparing real life to a children's fairy tale in which the heroes and heroines "live happily ever after."
Charles Colson, *Life Sentence*

CHAPTER SEVEN

Why God's Children Suffer

A NEW BELIEVER in Jesus may receive false impressions of the normal Christian life. He may hear a preacher who wants to win his hearers to Christ and therefore glamorizes the Christian experience by making it sound as carefree and positive as he can. Many times believers begin their Christian walk on an emotional high. They see remarkable answers to prayer and experience the world in a rosy glow.

I cannot help comparing this feeling to that of the American public during the first few days of the war in the Persian Gulf. Everything seemed to be going our way as our brave pilots crushed enemy installations with little opposition. However, President George Bush, in a television talk, warned against "euphoria" as a result of these apparent successes.

Marine training is extremely tough. The physical discipline they experience is more than most of them have ever had. Even the most physically fit are left exhausted. In addition, the mental discipline drives them to the limit of their abilities. In actual combat, all of this training is put to use. How much more dangerous it would have been if they were given easy tasks during their training and praised for every accomplishment.

Being a Christian does not exempt us from tough training, which may mean suffering. If the training were easy, we would not be prepared for the tough days ahead.

Tactical Errors

There are two great errors we may make in our response to suffering. The first error is in thinking that the teacher is cruel. Many marines think that about their drill sergeants, until they go into combat.

The second error is to be prepared but to deny the possibility that we might be wounded or captured. The Christian life is a battlefield. The antithesis is the wealth-and-health theology, which says that we deserve God's material and physical blessings just because we are His children. If we fall into either of these two errors in our thinking, we will continually be anguished over the question of why Christians suffer.

I cannot answer why an innocent child dies after a lingering illness, nor why a great minister's life is cut short when his fruitful ministry is so desperately needed. As I write this book, one of my friends is dying of cancer, another had a heart attack, another a brain tumor, and another a stroke.

I do not believe mere suffering teaches us. If that were so the whole world would be wise! However, I do know the Bible shows us some valid reasons that may answer the scoffers who say, "If your God is so great, why doesn't He save you from your pain?"

Because We Are Human

When we are children we hear that goodness has its reward and badness has its punishment. If you're good, you get ice cream; if you're bad, you go to bed early. This can develop into a mushy theological teaching that if you work in the church, attend Bible studies, and support noble causes, you will somehow be rewarded. When rough times come, the victims may think, "After all I've done for the Lord, why is He putting me through this?" We bargain with the Lord, exchanging our good deeds for His blessings. We revert to childish thinking about gold stars on the chart for good behavior.

At the end of the Gulf War I went to Greensburg, Pennsylvania, to speak at a memorial service for those who had been killed in their barracks in Dhahran by a Scud missile. A small area of Pennsylvania lost about one-fourth of all the casualties that we had in that war. The people were asking me, "Why would God allow it?" Disasters, troubles, and illnesses are the common lot of mankind, and Christians and non-Christians are involved in them because we share the human experience.

Because We Sin or Disobey God

If a Christian loses his temper, tells a lie, or commits a sin of any kind, he will suffer God's chastisement or judgment. The Apostle Peter told the believers of his day that judgment must begin first among God's own children (see 1 Peter 4:17). Just as a child needs correcting, so God's children need correcting.

Many children today are growing up without discipline. As they become adults and the discipline of job or family demands are placed upon them, they do not know how to cope. Today's children need discipline to be useful members of society. Likewise, God's children need discipline to be useful members of His family.

The Scripture says the Lord disciplines those He loves, and He punishes everyone He accepts as a son. "Endure hardship as discipline: God is treating you as sons. For what son is not disciplined by his father? . . . No discipline seems pleasant at the time, but painful. Later on, however, it produces a harvest of righteousness and peace for those who have been trained by it" (Hebrews 12:7, 11).

A Christian has tremendous responsibilities to his own family. Husbands and wives are to love each other and to submit to one another. We are to train our children in the way in which they *should* go, not the way they *would* go. My wife and her wonderful parents trained our children as they were growing up, during the difficult times when I was gone so much. God blessed me with a woman who knew how to discipline with love.

If we neglect the responsibilities within our own families, we will suffer the consequences. Perhaps not immediately, but later.

I know of a Christian leader who had been unkind to his wife for years, until she suffered a complete physical and mental breakdown. He became infatuated with his secretary, but he wanted to remain a leader in his community. He wanted it all, but he could not have it all. He suffered a terrible battle within himself until the smile was gone from his face and joy had left his heart. His situation became so obvious that others learned of his circumstances and exposed his sin. His suffering became unbearable, all because of his own sin. As far as I know, he has not yet repented.

If we are unloving or unfaithful in our Christian life, we will pay for it with a guilty conscience or chastisement from God. Many Christians who profess Christ do not live as though they possess Him. There are hypocrites in the church, even in the pulpit and teaching in Bible schools and seminaries. The nonbeliever looks at them and says, "If that's what Christianity is all about, count me out." However, there were hypocrites in Jesus' day, too. He was not gentle with them. He said, "Woe to you . . . you hypocrites! You shut the kingdom of heaven in men's faces" (Matthew 23:13).

To Discipline Us

My brother Melvin tried to describe what I was like as a boy and said that we didn't then know the term "hyper," but if we had, that is what he would have called me. I guess you might say that I crackled with nervous energy. In fact, one of my teachers told my mother, "Billy will never amount to anything."

So I had my share of discipline. My father was not one to spare the rod. However, there is one thing I knew in my heart. My father loved me.

Jesus says, "Those whom I love I rebuke and discipline" (Revelation 3:19). God's discipline is one of love. The life of a Christian may be hard, but God has His divine plan for shaping our lives, and that plan often includes suffering.

I remember visiting Dohnavur, India, which was the home of a remarkable woman. She had written more than forty books. And she spent the last twenty years of her life as a bedridden invalid, but it was during that time that she did most of her writing. That woman was Amy Carmichael.

As I stood in the simple room that had been her personal prison for all that time, the presence of Christ was so very real to me that when I was asked to lead in prayer, I broke down and could not continue. Turning to my traveling companion, the great German industrialist, John Bolton, a very disciplined and apparently unemotional man, I said, "John, you pray." He began, but after a few words he, too, broke down, unable to continue, the tears streaming down his handsome face.

When I talk about suffering, which includes all the elements of pain and anguish known to man, not just physical pain, I'm no different from you. I would like to lead a life free of problems, free of pain, and free of severe personal discipline. However, I have had extreme pressures in my life to the point where I have wanted to run away from reality. I have even been tempted to ask the Lord to take me to Heaven.

C. S. Lewis said in *The Problem of Pain,* "You would like to know how I behave when I am experiencing pain, not writing books about it. You need not guess, for I will tell you; I am a great coward. . . . But what is the good of telling you about my feelings? You know them already; they are the same as yours. I am not arguing that pain is not painful. Pain hurts."[1]

I must admit I feel very inadequate at times when talking about God's discipline through pain. I have been close to those who have lost their children in accidents or lingering illnesses. My own nephew, Sandy Ford, a campus leader at the University of North Carolina, died after an operation for a rare heart disorder. I was with Leighton and Jean in their hour of suffering.

I have been with leaders whose careers were ruined by their own bad choices. I have been in areas devastated by earthquakes, fires, and bombs. When those I love have suffered, I have wished I could take their pain as my own. However, I have lived past the three score and ten, and my wife, my children, grandchildren, and great-grandchildren are all living. How dare I speak of the discipline of suffering? Without God's Word and examples from the lives of believers, I would be as inadequate to write about suffering as a child would be to explain nuclear physics.

God's discipline is one of wisdom. Horatius Bonar says, "What deep wisdom then must there be in all His dealings! He knows exactly what we need and how to supply it. . . . The time and the way and the instrument are all according to the perfect wisdom of God."[2]

When Charles Colson was sent to prison for his participation in the Watergate scandal, it was the wisdom of God that utilized his sentence. A judge may have been the human instrument through whom God worked, but the result was God's plan for the life of a man who has since ministered to thousands inside and outside of prisons around the world.

The wisdom of God's discipline may be obscured when we are in the midst of suffering. In the Faith Chapter in the Bible (Hebrews 11) there is a list of some of God's great heroes. Noah, Abraham, Isaac, Jacob, Joseph, and Moses were some of those old believers. Many were gloriously delivered because of their faith. But others were tortured, flogged, stoned, imprisoned, and lost all their possessions.

In this great roll call of faith, beginning with the second half of verse 35, we have God's "Medal of Honor" list. The last two verses of Hebrews 11 tell us: "These were all commended for their faith, yet none of them received what had been promised. God had planned something better for us so that only together with us would they be made perfect" (vv. 39–40).

The rewards of some may even be greater in the future life because they suffered when there was no relief in sight. They believed and trusted, even when they were not delivered. We need to realize that when God allows these things to happen, there is a reason that will eventually be known to us—perhaps not until we get to Heaven.

Can We Profit from Pain?

Marine Lieutenant Clebe McClary was in a stationary combat observation post deep in enemy-controlled territory in Vietnam. In five months as patrol leader, he hadn't lost a man. He never thought he would be hit. He had no dark premonitions about his mission one night in 1968, but enemy grenades targeted his foxhole. That night he lost his left hand, his left eye, and one leg. As he described it, "Death looked me over—a helpless heap of bleeding flesh and broken bones."

McClary did live, a miracle of God's grace. Although a "religious" man, it was not until he left the hospital on his first leave and went to a stadium in South Carolina, where he heard evangelist Billy Zeoli preach the gospel, that he invited Jesus Christ into his heart. A year later McClary gave his testimony at our Crusade in Anaheim, California, where he shared with fifty-six thousand people what God had done in his life.

Did Clebe McClary profit from the horrible ordeal that left him disabled for life? This is what he wrote: "I don't think my suffering was in vain. The Lord has used my experiences for good by drawing many lives to Him. It's hard to see any good that came from the war in Vietnam, but I don't believe our effort was wasted. Surely some seed was planted for Christ that cannot be stamped out."[3]

The Apostle Peter tells the reason for trials and persecutions: "These have come so that your faith—of greater worth than gold, which perishes even though refined by fire—may be proved genuine and may result in praise, glory and honor when Jesus Christ is revealed" (1 Peter 1:7).

Remember Job? If ever a man had trials, it was this fellow. But this is what he concluded: "When he has tested me, I will come forth as gold" (Job 23:10). That is reacting positively to testing, building on it, rather than criticizing it for interfering with life's normal pattern.

Trials that often come into a Christian's life are the fulfillment of God's gracious purpose as He seeks to make us the sort of person He planned for us to be when He first thought of us. Like a sculptor, He begins with a lump of marble. But He has in mind a picture of what He intends to create. He breaks, cracks, chisels, and polishes until one day there emerges His vision, like Michelangelo's *David*. At the moment, His sculpture of us is incomplete. God has not yet finished with us.

To Lead Us to the Bible

Martin Luther said, "Were it not for tribulation I should not understand Scripture." Bible study may become a routine, dull experience when placed on a daily "things to do" list. But how fast we learn in a day of sorrow or when problems arise! We become aware of how ignorant we are of Bible promises until we are driven to the Scriptures in times of trial.

Joni Eareckson Tada described what she felt as she lay completely helpless in the hospital. She wrote in her book *Joni* that for the first time she saw meaning in the Bible. "My own 'fiery trials' were now a little easier to cope with as I saw how I fit in with God's scheme of things, especially through reading the Psalms." Joni personalized David's words from Psalm 41:3—"The Lord will sustain [me] on [my] sickbed."

A young woman whose younger brother was killed told how she picked up her Bible and, with eyes blurred with tears, read until she came across a certain verse. She called her heartbroken mother and said, "Mom, listen to this verse. 'If we live, we live to the Lord; and if we die, we die to the Lord. So whether we live or die, we belong to the Lord' (Romans 14:8). Mom, it's OK. I know where Bob is."

When we are first hit by pain, disappointment, sorrow, or grief, we may be overwhelmed. We are stunned and unable to see any good out of our disaster. But before long, with patience in reading the Word of God, we may be able to say with David: "The punishment you gave me was the best thing that could have happened to me, for it taught me to pay attention to your laws. They are more valuable to me than millions in silver and gold" (Psalm 119:71–72 TLB).

To Deepen Our Fellowship with God

Nothing will drive us to our knees quicker than trouble. When war was being waged in the Persian Gulf more was heard about prayer than in any recent year. Even hardened newsmen were talking about prayer.

God hears the prayers of those who recognize Jesus Christ as their personal Savior, but our prayers must be in accordance with His will. He knows better what is good for us than we know ourselves.

Too often we neglect the privilege of prayer until we encounter suffering or difficulty. Some of the greatest prayer warriors I know are dear saints in nursing homes or hospital beds. My mother was a wonderful example of a Christian who knew how to pray. In her last years, not able to take care of herself and in constant pain, she believed the only reason the Lord was delaying His coming for her was so she could pray for others. It was an amazing ministry. Whenever she heard of someone in need she would have Rose, her companion, write a note and send a few dollars.

I was in France for a Crusade, and I called my mother's home. Rose said Mother had given her the Scripture for the day, Colossians 1:9. "For this cause we also, since the day we heard it, do not cease to pray for you, and to desire that ye might be filled with the knowledge of his will in all wisdom and spiritual understanding" (KJV). While I was concerned about my dear mother, thousands of miles away on a bed of weakness and pain, she had a verse of encouragement for me.

Suffering Teaches Us Patience

A woman who lived with pain said that she could not live "one day at a time," as her doctor told her. "I live one moment at a time, knowing that I can stand that much pain. When that moment is gone, I can live for another moment."

Helen Keller said, "Face your deficiencies and acknowledge them, but do not let them master you. Let them teach you patience, sweetness, insight. When we do the best we can, we never know what miracle is wrought in our own life or in the life of another."[4]

In Zephaniah 3:17, we find in the margin notes of the King James Version these words from the Hebrew: "He will be silent in His love." Sometimes God seems so quiet. However, when we see the way He works in lives that are imprisoned by walls or circumstances, when we hear how faith can shine through uncertainty, we begin to catch a glimpse of the fruit of patience that can grow out of the experience of suffering.

Peter says, "How is it to your credit if you receive a beating for doing wrong and endure it? But if you suffer for doing good and you endure it, this is commendable before God" (1 Peter 2:20). People suffer and ask God for an explanation. They often quote (or are quoted) one of my favorite verses, Romans 8:28: "We know that in all things God works for the good of those who love him, who have been called according to his purpose." Christians look at the circumstances and say, "How can this possibly work together for my good?" We can't answer that. Only God can make it work for good, and He can't do it unless we cooperate with Him. In all of our praying we must ask that His will be done.

Calvin Thielman, the pastor of the church where we live, illustrated Romans 8:28 this way. Taken individually, the ingredients in a cake may not taste very good. Raw flour is not good! Baking powder, raw eggs, bitter chocolate, or shortening are not good. Any one of these by itself does not taste good, but they work together to make a delicious cake. In the same way, God puts together the individual trials we have and works them for good.

I am not a person who believes we should cancel our newspapers and cut off our televisions so that we do not know what is happening in the world. But when I see the terrible injustice, the cruelty, the numbing madness that exists, we cannot help but ask, "Has the world gone crazy?"

It is reassuring to know that God is still all-powerful, that nothing touches my life without His permission. Things happen to me that I cannot understand, but I never doubt God's love. In the hour of trial I may not be able to see His design, but I am confident it must be in line with His purpose.

The real philosophical stumper is, "Why, in the midst of madness and rebellion in the world, where sin is glorified and good is degraded, why should God send His only begotten Son to love, heal, comfort, and after thirty-three years of teaching and service, to have Him give His life for this very world?"

When the brilliant Swiss theologian Karl Barth was asked by a group of young theologians what was the most important theological fact he had discovered during his lifetime of studies, the old scholar puffed silently on his pipe as he thoughtfully studied the question. The students sat silent, breathless with expectation. Finally, he removed his pipe, paused, and said simply, "Jesus loves me, this I know, for the Bible tells me so!"

The mystery of God's love would not be a mystery if we knew all the answers. Without faith it is impossible to please God. What we do possess are the answers the Bible gives, and from that basis we have the opportunity to share the love of Christ Himself.

It is critical that we either answer or learn to live with these questions, because like the pain that raises them, they are unavoidable. The Apostle Paul lived with these same questions, but he used them to increase his faith rather than allow them to diminish it. He said that now we see as though we were looking through a cloudy mirror, but one day it will be clear to us.

In the first little book she wrote, long before she became known throughout the world, Corrie ten Boom told of her experience in Ravensbruk prison during World War II:

> I did not understand the "why" of suffering, except that of my own suffering in this place. God had brought me here for a specific task. I was here to lead the sorrowing and the despairing to the Savior. I was to see how He comforted them. I was to point the way to Heaven to people among whom were many that would soon be dying. . . . The "why" of my own suffering was no problem to me.
>
> This, too, I had learned: that I was not called upon to bear the grief and the cares of the whole world around me. And so I prayed, "Lord teach me to cast all my burdens upon Thee and go on without them. Only Thy Spirit can teach me that lesson. Give me Thy Spirit, O Lord, and I shall have faith, such faith that I shall no longer carry a load of care."[5]

Where is God when we suffer? He is ever-present and all-knowing, with us in all our struggles and trials. Nothing in our lives takes God by surprise. We are not alone in our suffering, for we have a God who loves us, "a very present help in trouble."

God is in control. He may not take away trials or make detours for us, but He strengthens us through them.

Sometimes the Lord calms the storm; sometimes He lets the storm rage and calms the child. Unknown

CHAPTER EIGHT

What Do I Do When I Hurt?

PAIN CAN DRIVE us in two directions. Either it can make us curse God for allowing our misery, or drive us to Him for relief. There is the expression, "God helps those who help themselves." I think a saying like "God helps us when we are helpless" is infinitely more comforting.

Sickness teaches us that activity is not the only way to serve God. "They also serve who only stand and wait." Man seems to judge active duty, but God shows us that He is also glorified through suffering.

Linda had been poisoned by chemicals, resulting in the destruction of her immune system, making her "allergic to the world." She was like the "boy in the bubble" who lived in a plastic enclosure to guard him from every atmospheric contaminant. Linda was in and out of intensive care and isolation units for five years of her young adult life. She said, "Most of the time I didn't think coherently. I was too busy trying to survive."

Linda struggled with one small goal during those years of intense suffering. She read one verse of Scripture each day and prayed for one minute. "And that was an overwhelming task," she said.

When she was able to leave the prison of hospital isolation, she began to reach out to others. She founded an organization called Direct Link, which links a disabled person to a source of help and support. She said, "The Lord gave me suffering so that I could help the suffering world of the disabled."

Jesus said, "What I tell you in the dark, speak in the daylight" (Matthew 10:27). What does this mean to us? It means, be quiet, listen to God when things are their worst, and you will be able to talk to others when you are better.

Oswald Chambers explained, "Watch where God puts you in darkness, and when you are there keep your mouth shut. . . . Darkness is the time to listen and heed. If you talk to other people, you cannot hear what God is saying. When you are in the dark, listen, and God will give you a very precious message for someone else when you get in the light."[1]

Reactions to pain are as varied as pain itself. Many people say that women can bear more pain than men. In fact, one person wrote: "Man endures pain as an undeserved punishment; woman accepts it as a natural heritage." Having watched women in pain, I believe that is true. Most wives can vouch for that.

Resentment Is a Killer

Resentment leads to bitterness. For example, Lord Byron and Sir Walter Scott were gifted writers and poets who lived in the late eighteenth and early nineteenth centuries. They were both lame. Byron bitterly resented his infirmity and constantly grumbled about his lot in life. Scott was never heard to complain about his handicap.

One day Scott received a letter from Byron that said, "I would give my fame to have your happiness." What made the difference in their reactions to suffering and their attitudes toward their disabilities? Byron was a man who took pride in his dissolute lifestyle. His moral standards were doubtful. Scott, on the other hand, was a Christian believer whose courageous life exemplified his standards and values.

A friend of ours, whose husband had left her after fifty years of marriage for a girl young enough to be his granddaughter, asked us once, "What does one do with bitterness?" Bitterness is like an abscess. It festers and grows, and has to come to a head, which is an extremely painful process. But once it is ripe, it will either burst or require lancing, which will get rid of all the poison. Even so, it still takes time for the wound to heal, and there will always be a scar.

Bitterness can strangle a human being. It can turn those who are in pain into complaining, self-pitying people who eventually drive others away. The Bible says, "See to it that no one misses the grace of God and that no bitter root grows up to cause trouble and defile many" (Hebrews 12:15).

Betty was a tiny woman, but her influence upon her daughter and grandchildren was profound. From the time her husband died, she was sick. She diagnosed herself with every ailment in her home medical guide. Her daughter was kept constantly in tension, because Betty would call her with emergencies night and day. Her grandchildren never enjoyed her visits. She resented the fact that her sicknesses, real or imaginary, made her dependent upon her family. And she drove her family away from her.

If we are living self-centered lives and something happens to disrupt our carefully laid plans, our natural tendency is to react with impatience and resentment. We tend to blame God when things go wrong and take credit when things seem to be going right. This may become a way of life with us, as it was with Betty, and the result is unattractive and repelling.

Resentment and bitterness develop when we persist in resisting what God has allowed to happen to us. Christians who are strong in the faith grow as they accept whatever God allows to enter their lives. Resentment can compound physical pain. The steps are short from stress to tension, and pain becomes more severe.

To resent and resist God's disciplining hand is to miss one of the greatest spiritual blessings we Christians can enjoy this side of Heaven. Though Job suffered as few others have, he never lost sight of God's presence with him in the midst of suffering. He emerged victorious on the other side of sorrow, because he never allowed resentment to cloud his relationship with God.

Resentment leaves us with an embittered personality, but there is another response that sounds so noble and pious. This is heard in the sighs of the self-made martyr!

Suffering with a Sigh

With a deep breath, the sufferer approaches daily living with doleful resignation. Let's admit it, most of us feel this way at some point in our lives. "It's just something I have to live with," we say with a forced smile. But resignation is not a distinctly Christian virtue. The Stoics of ancient Greece accepted calamity with resignation as the hallmark of their philosophy. Often resignation is the easy way out, a sort of painkiller—anesthesia where there should be action.

We've probably all experienced times when we feel we should "keep a stiff upper lip," or wear a happy face button on our lapel when we're crying on the inside. I'm glad David didn't live on a perpetual high. Think of the Psalms we would have missed if he had said, "Don't worry about me, folks, everything is just great." David complained, cried, and felt abandoned, but not perpetually.

Christians seem to be programmed to keep suffering to themselves. But God will hear our complaints, and the wonderful thing is that He won't hold them against us.

David refused to resign himself to the defeats that sometimes threatened to flatten him. More than once, in his personal as well as his public life, he seemed to be "down for the count"—but he always looked beyond the obstacle or problem to God Himself. When we're "in the pits," we don't need to resign ourselves to fate or tough luck, but say, "I lift up my eyes to the hills—where does my help come from? My help comes from the Lord, the Maker of heaven and earth" (Psalm 121:1–2).

If we have our eyes upon ourselves, our problems, and our pain, we cannot lift our eyes upward. A child looks up when he's walking with his father, and the same should be true for the Christian.

Unfortunately, in our society there is little tolerance for another's sickness or pain. We put sick people out of sight, or at least out of mind. Resentment builds when we are not treated as someone of value. Many people with long-term illnesses tell how they get cards and calls in the first few days or weeks of their sickness. But too soon the mailbox is empty, the phone silent, and the visitors dwindle. Loneliness is foisted upon someone who is suffering because those who are healthy don't want to be bothered.

Sometimes our burdens seem too big for anyone to handle. We are buried in the quicksand of physical and emotional pain. Jesus reaches out with a love that never fails, never forgets, and is always available and says, "Come to me, all you who are weary and burdened and I will give you rest. Take my yoke upon you and learn from me, for I am gentle and humble in heart, and you will find rest for your souls. For my yoke is easy and my burden is light" (Matthew 11:28–30).

Come. Take. Learn. What powerful words! They contain an invitation to accept and take advantage of our burdens and our hurts. A muscle becomes weak if it is not used. To become strong, a muscle must push against something. To reach the greatest heights as an individual, a person must learn how to take advantage of difficulty.

Dave Dravecky, former star pitcher for the San Francisco Giants, made a remarkable comeback after cancer surgery and was giving speeches around the country about overcoming adversity. After having 50 percent of the major pitching muscle removed from his left arm, he used that arm to throw eight strong innings and defeat the Cincinnati Reds, 4–3. At the time a tearful Dravecky said, "It's a miracle."

Five days after this triumph, his left arm broke. He was out for the season, but he thought he could make another comeback. That dream was shattered when the doctors discovered a mass in his arm that resembled another cancerous tumor.

Dravecky said, "Nobody ever promised that life would be fair. Everybody is going to have adversity. The only way to handle it is to take our eyes off our own circumstances and put them on the Lord."[2]

Comfort and prosperity have never enriched the world as much as adversity has done. Out of pain and problems have come the sweetest songs, the most poignant poems, and the most gripping stories. When we have visited our oldest daughter, who married a Swiss, we have taken chairlifts high up in the Alps to see the scenery. I am not a skier, so our trips are usually in the summer. We gaze down from dizzying heights and see some of the most beautiful flowers found anywhere. It's hard to believe that just a few weeks before, these flowers were buried under many feet of snow. The burdens of ice and winter storms have added to their luster and growth.

Our burdens can have the same effect on our lives. As Christians face the winds of adversity and the storms of trouble, they may rise with more beauty. They are like the trees that grow on the mountain ridges of North Carolina—battered by winds, yet trees in which we find the strongest wood.

Resentment and resignation are not the answer to the problem of suffering. Accepting our lot in life and clinging to the Lord and His strength will ease our pain. There is another step beyond acceptance, and that is acceptance with joy. Is it possible?

It's All in the Attitude

When Jeff Steinberg limped onstage, the audience seemed to suck in its breath. His body was tragically misshapen, and it was difficult for him to walk. His head was disproportionately large for his body, and he held a microphone with the hooks he used for hands. But his smile was bigger than his disability. Jeff Steinberg had a song and a slogan that was uniquely his: "I'm a masterpiece in progress."

Instead of focusing on his physical problems, he looked at the gifts God had given him and used them fully. He could laugh, he could sing, and he could tell about God's love.

We don't have a magic shield to protect us from problems. Ultimately, it's our attitude that counts—attitude toward ourselves and toward God. We can turn burdens into blessings, or we can let those burdens bury us.

James said, "Consider it pure joy, my brothers, whenever you face trials of many kinds, because you know that the testing of your faith develops perseverance. Perseverance must finish its work so that you may be mature and complete, not lacking anything" (James 1:2–4).

Joy is one of the marks of a true believer. This is not a gushy emotion or a forced grin, but the security of knowing God's love. I read a news story about soldiers in the Persian Gulf watching videotapes from their families back home. In a gloomy tent, sipping coffee to ward off the morning chill, the soldiers listened in silence as one wife held herself erect and sang a gospel hymn that her husband could think of whenever he felt alone. Joy is not just jumping up and down when your team makes a touchdown, it's that deep, abiding emotion that gives a lonely soldier's wife the ability to reach out to an equally lonely man and touch him with God's presence. The ability to rejoice in any situation is a sign of spiritual maturity.

Paul sang and shouted his way through his trials. His greatest victories came out of his persecution. To the Romans he wrote, "We also rejoice in our sufferings, because we know that suffering produces perseverance. . . . Who shall separate us from the love of Christ? Shall trouble or hardship or persecution? . . . Be joyful in hope, patient in affliction, faithful in prayer" (Romans 5:3; 8:35; 12:12).

Grady Wilson was one of my closest friends, as well as associate and traveling companion. He was always able to see the funny side of things and make me laugh. He was a person who radiated joy, and anyone he ever met would quickly find out that "count it all joy" was his favorite expression.

We all know people who are not Christians who seem to possess the key to joy, but that soon evaporates when the tough times come. On the other hand, we know professing Christians who look as if they habitually eat lemons. These are the people who fight God's will for their lives and complain that life has dealt them unfair blows. Christ Himself is the Christian's secret of joy: "Though you have not seen him, you love him, and even though you do not see him now, you believe in him and are filled with an inexpressible and glorious joy" (1 Peter 1:8).

I remember visiting an elderly man who spent most of his life in China as a missionary. He had always enjoyed good health and was an unusually strong man. His deep dedication to Christ and the love between him and his wife made people love and admire him. However, he contracted cancer, and it spread to many parts of his body. I went to minister to him, but, instead, he ministered to me. There was a joy and radiance about him that I have rarely seen. He got up out of his bed and walked me to the car when I left. I shall never forget my last glimpse of him. With a great smile and cheery wave, he said, "Keep on preaching the Gospel, Billy. The older I get, the better Christ is to me."

When we are so wedded to the world that we lose sight of eternity, we can lose our joy. My father-in-law, Nelson Bell, held on to the things of this world so loosely that when he died and we opened his closet, there were only two suits hanging there. Things were not that important to him.

In my travels I have found that those who keep Heaven in view remain serene and cheerful in the darkest day. If the glories of Heaven were more real to us, if we lived less for material things and more for things eternal and spiritual, we would be less easily disturbed by this present life.

A friend told me about stopping on a street corner in London and listening to a man play the bagpipes. He was playing "Amazing Grace" and smiling from ear to ear. My friend asked him if he was from Scotland, and he answered, "No sir, my home is in Heaven. I'm just traveling through this world."

Closer My God to Thee or Farther Away?

How do we respond to crisis or suffering? We can resent suffering, resign ourselves to it, or accept it with joy because we know God is in control of our lives.

Amy Carmichael, who lived in almost constant pain, is a striking example of a Christian whose physical suffering enabled her to reflect the character of Christ. She lived her life rejoicing in the midst of tribulation. She wrote this poem:

Before the winds that blow do cease,
Teach me to dwell within Thy calm:
Before the pain has passed in peace,
Give me, my God, to sing a psalm.

Let me not lose the chance to prove
The fullness of enabling love.
O Love of God, do this for me:
Maintain a constant victory.[3]

Rewards Here and Later

We're living in a time of spiritual darkness and political upheaval. Only the forward-looking Christian remains sincerely optimistic and joyful, knowing that Christ will win in the end and "if we endure, we will also reign with him" (2 Timothy 2:12).

God works in unexpected ways to bring us strength and joy in the midst of suffering. The Scriptures say, "Now is your time of grief, but I will see you again and you will rejoice, and no one will take away your joy" (John 16:22), and "For our light and momentary troubles are achieving for us an eternal glory that far outweighs them all" (2 Corinthians 4:17).

There is a joy to be discovered in the midst of suffering. I truly believe that the lot of those that suffer is more enviable than the people who seem to be set apart, untouched, like a piece of fine china in a locked cabinet. Without dark clouds in our lives we would never know the joy of sunshine. We can become callous and unteachable if we do not learn from pain.

It is said that if your cup seems too bitter, if your burden seems too heavy, be sure that it is the wounded hand that is holding the cup and that it is He who carried the cross that is carrying the burden with us. "Come unto me, all ye that labour and are heavy laden," He says, "and I will give you rest. Take my yoke upon you, and learn of me. . . . For my yoke is easy, and my burden is light" (Matthew 11:28–30 KJV).

I will search for the lost and bring back the strays.
I will bind up the injured and strengthen the weak.
Ezekiel 34:16

CHAPTER NINE

When Your Heart Is Breaking

IT WAS THE message she most feared. The young wife of a corporal serving in the Persian Gulf was told that her husband had been instantly killed in Saudi Arabia by a missile. She said, "I'll never forget the nauseating feeling when I opened my door and heard that news."

Your heart may be breaking with grief over the death of a loved one. You may have a child with a long-term illness or one who has left home in open rebellion. Perhaps you have lost your job or experienced a crushing failure in your personal life. Maybe you just want to help relieve someone else's pain.

In *Hope for the Hurting,* Doug Sparks wrote about the griefs we encounter: "If you don't have one now, you will. If you live long enough, there'll come a time when you have to keep going even though your heart is pierced through."[1] Somehow we have to keep on keeping on.

My wife grew up in China, but I have never been able to master the language. The Chinese system of writing contains pictographs, characters that represent mental images, and I have been told that the Chinese word picture for perseverance is represented by a knife and a heart. How true that is in our personal experiences. What do you do when you feel ripped in half? How do you continue (persevere) with a knife in your heart?

Many Faces of Grief

Barbara Johnson's Marine son was killed in Vietnam. Five years later, her oldest boy was hit and killed by a drunk driver. Two years later, on the eve of another son's graduation from a junior college, where he had been voted the most outstanding student, he told his mother he was a homosexual. Grief compounded upon grief. The knife in her heart was so sharp she thought she would die. She wrote: "I think I'm having a heart attack. I don't know what you call it, but I think I'm dying. I can't breathe, and I'm choking. It feels as if I've got a rug in my throat and my teeth itch."[2]

When Barbara Johnson described her reactions as a Christian, she said, "All the promises of God are there, and they're real, and they're true, but right now you're bleeding, you're raw and hurting, and you have to hang on to those promises even if they don't seem to work for you at the moment."[3]

Responses to grief are as varied as grief itself. While some people want to die, others blow up. They shout and curse the world and blaspheme God. Sociologists have tried to grade the types of grief according to their severity, but no one can put a magnifying glass on another's hurts, except God.

Many times grief is accompanied by guilt; whether real or false, guilt compounds grief. With false guilt, we fall into the trap of "if only's." "If only we had been home, we might have been able to get the paramedics in time." "If only we hadn't said she could stay out until midnight." These thoughts are normal emotions when we feel guilty about something over which we have no control.

Then there is real guilt. Emotions become raw when we know we have disobeyed man's or God's laws or have become careless with what God has given us.

One vivid example of guilt due to carelessness was the news story about the man who was driving his family to the market, a few blocks from his home. His wife was holding their baby instead of having him confined to a car seat. The father made a left turn and accidentally ran into an oncoming car, resulting in a crushing impact. The baby was thrown against the windshield, killing him instantly. Soon after the accident, the distraught father was charged with manslaughter, because he hadn't obeyed the law requiring safety seats for children under the age of four. Imagine the amount of grief compounded by guilt in that poor father's heart.

How can we understand the grief of others unless we have been in their shoes? Jesus was no stranger to grief. It was foretold by Isaiah that He would be a "man of sorrows and acquainted with grief." Our greatest hope is that people may know Him before an hour of severe grief.

Some people may have an outward appearance of serenity and peace after a tragedy or severe loss, but inside they may be hemorrhaging. Grief may drive them to resentment or blaming others. We can almost imagine the tone of Martha's voice when, after her brother Lazarus died, she said to Jesus, "Lord, if you had been here my brother would not have died" (John 11:32). She was indulging in the "if only's" that plague many of us.

Jesus didn't try to reason with Martha or argue with her. He understood her frustration. If there is something we need more than anything else during grief, it is a friend who stands with us, who doesn't leave us. Jesus is that friend.

The faces of grief may be filled with anger. Anger is debilitating if it runs unchecked. Non-Christians may vent their anger like animals with snarling, destructive, cruel acts. Before we put on faces of piety, we must realize that Christians are not above some of these attitudes. They often can be just as vehement as their non-Christian neighbors.

King David cried out, "Why are you downcast, O my soul? Why so disturbed within me?" (Psalm 42:5). David was distraught. His very soul was in turmoil. Have you ever felt that way? Have you ever been so down in the dumps that you couldn't see a way to climb out? Grief can kill a person emotionally and physically. If not counteracted with God's strength and power, our personal weakness may debilitate us.

Another face of grief is panic. "I imagine all sorts of terrible things. I think I'm losing my mind." The grief-stricken person seems to lose the ability to concentrate, which adds to his panic. Panic may lead to emotional paralysis.

Guilt, anger, resentment, panic. These are just some of the faces of grief. None of these reactions are abnormal. Like soldiers going into battle, we need to be prepared for grief.

A clipping from the war in the Persian Gulf explained how a veteran officer prepared his troops for the possibility of a bloody ground war. Until that time none of these soldiers, except the battalion commander, had ever seen real combat. He told them, "I want to talk about fear. You will be afraid. If you're not afraid, there's something wrong with you . . . you'll know when you're afraid, guys . . . you will taste a metal taste in your mouth like you had maybe a half-dozen nails. It is going to happen. Understand it. Cope with it. Talk to each other about it. Understand with each other that all of you are afraid . . . all you can do is have faith in the guys around you. I have faith in you. I know you'll do the best you can. Have faith in me to do my best."[4]

That officer was preparing his men for combat, just as our Lord prepares us for life's combat. I don't know how anyone overcomes personal grief without His directions. He says to have faith in Him. He has told us that He will be with us always and never leave or forsake us (Hebrews 13:5).

Often it takes that "knife in our heart" to drive us to Him. Our faith, our very lives, depend on God, and when we enter the valley of grief, we need His help or we will never climb another mountain.

Wounded Hearts

Remember how we used to chant, "Sticks and stones will break my bones, but words will never hurt me?" That's not true. Probably some of the worst pain is caused by wounds from others, words or actions that break our lives into fractured pieces.

Henry had worked for the same company for more than thirty years. He had been a valuable member of the firm, loyal to the core, and dependable. He was close to retirement, and his pension was going to be the major part of his living expenses. Henry was given his severance notice due to a change in company management. He went home, a broken man, too shocked to know what to do next.

We have been given the ability to hope and dream, to set goals and make plans for what we want our lives to be. What do we do when someone else takes our dreams and smashes them into pieces?

Our children may wound us and twist the knife in our heart until we believe we will never be able to heal. David Jeremiah wrote about the painful time he experienced when his daughter was caught experimenting with cocaine at the Christian school where he was president. He wrote, "The feelings that overwhelmed me . . . were unlike anything in my previous experience . . . nothing in my life had prepared me for the initial shock and the resulting pain of the days and months to follow."[5]

When we think we've done our best as parents and things go wrong, the wounds we receive may turn to guilt. "Where did we go wrong?" we cry. I have met godly men and women who have suffered heartache as a result of wounds from their children. The healing of these wounds can only come when we love our children unconditionally, release the guilt feelings, and get on with the recovery.

People cause wounds, and usually we don't blame God when we have people problems. A friend divulges a confidence or spreads an untruth about us. A promise is broken or words are spoken to us in anger. Let's face it, so many of our problems are caused by people who take advantage of us, misuse us, or are just plain hard to get along with.

Does Jesus understand these wounds? He was misunderstood, scorned, ignored, and finally betrayed. Remember the old spiritual, "Nobody knows the troubles I've seen . . . nobody knows but Jesus?" He said, "Whatever you did for one of the least of these brothers of mine, you did for me" (Matthew 25:40). I believe that applies to the problem people in our lives, as well as the hungry, the thirsty, the stranger, the naked and sick, and the imprisoned. "One of the least of these brothers" may be the very person who has been a thorn in your side and who needs your unconditional love.

Many Faces of Persecution

Persecution may wear an insulting face. Insults may come as a result of a Christian's lifestyle, which should be different from that of the secular world. Peter said: "If you are insulted because of the name of Christ, you are blessed, for the Spirit of glory and of God rests on you" (1 Peter 4:14).

If the Bible says, "Thou shalt not . . . ," then there's no doubt. However, if the Bible is not explicit, then we should weigh the pros and cons and ask God to give us wisdom to do what would please Him under the circumstances.

Christians are being persecuted today for holding their basic beliefs, and even in the United States they are persecuted for their stands on moral issues. If your heart is wounded by insults, know that Jesus blesses you. He said, "Blessed are you when people insult you, persecute you and falsely say all kinds of evil against you because of me" (Matthew 5:11).

It's a small step "from insult to injury," and one of the worst wounds we can receive or give is done with words. Snide words, critical words, unkind words, untrue words. The twin ills caused by the tongue can infect Christian and non-Christian alike. If a Christian makes a mistake in his life, he is more vulnerable than a non-Christian. Churches have been split by gossip. Families have been broken by slander. Ministries have been destroyed by the indiscretions of a few.

Christians may be slandered because they hold to their beliefs. A Christian student at a high school or college is verbally abused because he wouldn't join his peers in a drinking or sex party. The Christian businessman loses an account because he wouldn't take a kickback. The Christian salesman was honest in his expense accounts and was laughed at by his fellow salesmen. It costs in a thousand subtle ways to be a true disciple of Christ. Peter expressed it so well: "They think it strange that you do not plunge with them into the same flood of dissipation, and they heap abuse on you" (1 Peter 4:4).

If we are living according to what we believe, we may be falsely accused. It is not to our credit, however, if we are accused because our conduct as believers is inconsistent. Jesus was falsely accused at His trial. The Apostles Peter and John were falsely accused when they were brought before the Council. Stephen was falsely accused and lost his life. If the apostles and other early church leaders were falsely accused because of their faith, how can we expect to escape false accusations and the hurt that such attacks can bring into our lives?

Have you ever been rejected? Probably one of the forms of persecution that hurts the most is rejection. Basically, we all want to be accepted and loved. But there are very few people I have known who haven't had some rejection in their lives. The hardest to take is when it comes from a member of your family, a close friend, or perhaps worst of all, from your husband or wife.

During the Persian Gulf War many young men and women accepted Christ. The chaplains have told of unprecedented numbers of soldiers attending services, making commitments, and being baptized. When these new Christians return to their homes, they may be accused of "foxhole religion" by the ones they love.

I was on an airliner in the Far East when one of the stewards asked if he could talk to me. He had a big smile on his face when he said, "I have been a Christian for two years. I came from a non-Christian background. My family belonged to a religious sect that was quite opposed to Christianity. Yet for years I had been searching for something. I didn't know what it was. One day I listened to a tape of a preacher who told about Jesus Christ. I knew this was what I had been searching for all my life. I accepted Christ, went home and told my parents, brothers, and sisters about my newfound faith. They threw me out of the house. However, I continued to witness to them and now, I am glad to say, they are all Christians."

Recently I met a man with a strong, but tragic face. It was just a year ago, I was told, that his son had been shot to death in front of his home by religious extremists. The man's eyes filled, and as the tears coursed down his cheeks, I suggested we pray. I, who have suffered so little and nothing like he has, felt unworthy to pray. Later, I learned he could not return home as these same extremists had threatened to kill him. Out of fear, his wife has rejected both him and the Christian faith. He had no job, no money, no home. That is what persecution is like.

Jesus told His disciples that the "world," meaning the world system, the political and social order organized apart from God, will despise Christians. He said, "If the world hates you, keep in mind that it hated me first. If you belonged to the world, it would love you as its own" (John 15:18–19).

Can You Relate to Paul?

When we're hurting from what could be called the subtle suffering of life, we may find little comfort that others are experiencing or have experienced the same trials. The Apostle Paul was in the major leagues when it comes to all types of suffering. What a list he had:

> For it seems to me that God has put us apostles on display at the end of the procession, like men condemned to die in the arena. We have been made a spectacle to the whole universe, to angels as well as to men. We are fools for Christ, but you are so wise in Christ! We are weak, but you are strong! You are honored, we are dishonored! To this very hour we go hungry and thirsty, we are in rags, we are brutally treated, we are homeless. We work hard with our own hands. When we are cursed, we bless; when we are persecuted, we endure it; when we are slandered, we answer kindly. Up to this moment we have become the scum of the earth, the refuse of the world.
>
> *1 Corinthians 4:9–13*

Paul had devastating physical sufferings, but he described even greater pressure as he thought about his responsibilities as a Christian missionary. "I face daily the pressure of my concern for all the churches" (2 Corinthians 11:28).

If any of you are leaders in your churches or Christian organizations, you know the kind of pressure Paul is describing. Humanly speaking, it can lead to loneliness, depression, and often discouragement. Only God's illimitable grace and peace can carry us through times of trial.

In my own life, the pressures at times, mentally, physically, and spiritually, have become so great that I felt like going to the Cove and lying down in the cemetery to see how I fit. God has called me to my responsibilities, and I must be faithful. I am constantly concerned about being quoted in the press and perhaps saying the wrong thing or having what I say misinterpreted and bringing reproach to the name of Christ. People put well-known Christians on a pedestal, and if the slightest thing goes wrong, they are immediately blamed and often ridiculed.

At times we do make mistakes. Unintentionally, we offend others. Remember, "we're not offering people Christians, we're offering them Christ." I have wondered what would have happened in the ministry of the Lord Jesus Christ if television had been in existence. What would the media have done, for example, when He drove the moneychangers from the Temple, or when He denounced the Sadducees and Pharisees, or when He raised Lazarus from the dead, or when He fed the five thousand?

Paul's attitude was not that of self-pity, but one of triumph. We can have the same attitude. He said: "We are hard pressed on every side, but not crushed; perplexed, but not in despair; persecuted, but not abandoned; struck down, but not destroyed" (2 Corinthians 4:8–9). God has never sent any difficulty into the life of His children without His accompanying offers of help in this life and reward in the life to come.

David Jacobsen was a hostage in Beirut for seventeen months. He was head of the largest hospital in West Beirut when, one day in 1985, three men in hoods and wielding machine guns took him captive. Bound and gagged, he was taken from one hideout to another. He spent most of his time on a cold, dirt floor, chained to the wall. Once a day he was fed a tepid, unpalatable mush of watery rice and lentils.

As an American, Jacobsen was hated by his captors. He was just a political pawn and treated cruelly. Instead of breaking his spirit, however, he became stronger. He wrote: "I discovered that no one's faith was weakened by the hell we found ourselves in. . . . We hostages, with the guidance of Father Jenko, a captive Catholic priest, and Rev. Benjamin Weir, founded the Church of the Locked Door, a name we chose with some ruefulness. Grasping hands, we'd quote Scripture and pray. Oddly, our guards seemed to respect this ritual. Our togetherness in prayer showed me that when the Holy Comforter is called, He answers."

Jacobsen was released in November 1986, but in his final forty-five days of captivity he was alone in a six-by-six-by-six cell, his muscles and joints cramped by confinement and the damp, aching cold. Yet he said, "The presence of God, the Great Comforter, was stronger than ever, especially when I recited Psalms 27 and 102."[6]

The Pain of Personal Failure

After reading about other people's triumphs and hearing success stories, we may become more depressed than ever. Even hearing about successful marriages may be bitter if yours is rocky or disintegrating. Success stories may be great motivational material for sales seminars, but we are not always successful. Many people have learned to hide their failures and defeats, not wanting to "bother anyone with my troubles."

Mrs. Charles E. Cowman, in *Streams in the Desert,* says, "Many of us would nurse our grief without crying if we were allowed to nurse it. The hard thing is that most of us are called to exercise our patience, not in bed, but in the street. We are called to bury our sorrows not in lethargic quiescence, but in active service—in the exchange, in the workshop, in the hour of social intercourse, in the contribution to another's joy. There is no burial of sorrow so difficult as that; it is the 'running with patience.'"[7]

Jay Kesler told about a man whose son had been arrested for armed robbery. The story appeared in newspapers and on television. The Christian parents of the boy were so ashamed that they didn't leave their home for several days. Over and over again they asked God how this could happen in their family. They didn't know if they could face people again, particularly those in their church.

The parents finally went to church, and their shame and fear made them stick together like burrs. But something wonderful happened. A constant stream of people started coming to them for spiritual help. The father told Kesler, "It seems to me that when people take a superspiritual pose in church, pretending they have no problems, all the other church people are afraid to be honest with them for fear that they will look like failures. It's really strange that when we were trying our best and, on the surface at least, succeeding in our Christian lives, we didn't touch any other lives. Now that we have had so many problems with our own child, everyone wants our help—everyone wants to know how the Lord is working out our problems."[8]

We hear so many times, "He is a strong Christian." Inside, that person may be very weak, plagued by insecurities, wounded by others. Not knowing, we should encourage each one we meet. The Lord told Paul: "My grace is sufficient for you, for my power is made perfect in weakness. . . . That is why," Paul wrote, "for Christ's sake, I delight in weaknesses, in insults, in hardships, in persecutions, in difficulties. For when I am weak, then I am strong" (2 Corinthians 12:9–10).

We can persevere with a "knife in our heart" when we allow the Lord to lead us, even carrying us in His arms when we are wounded, to the time and place where we will be healed. The young widow of the soldier mentioned at the beginning of this chapter said that time had helped her look at her situation from a stronger perspective. "You can look at this like the worst thing that ever happened or you can look for something good in this," she said. Someone has said, "You go through it, but you don't get over it." Yet time softens memories, and the presence of Christ helps us not only to survive but to help others. Yes, time does help the broken heart.

Helping others is a great step toward healing. Barbara Johnson now has a ministry that grew out of her own heartbreak. In helping others, she also saw her son denounce his homosexual lifestyle and rededicate his life to Christ. David Jeremiah's daughter was loved through her problems and became a great witness to the healing powers of God.

When we are weak and powerless, God is there to give us strength. When we lack wisdom, He will supply it. Healing is not instantaneous;

it is a process. When we admit that we cannot heal ourselves, and we fall to our knees and ask God to take over, we will be on the road to spiritual health. Why wait?

Ruth, who loves the poetry of Amy Carmichael, gave me this one:

Will not the end explain
The crossed endeavor, earnest purpose foiled,
The strange bewilderment of good work spoiled,
The clinging weariness, the inward strain,
Will not the end explain?

Meanwhile He comforteth
Them that are losing patience. 'Tis His way:
But none can write the words they hear Him say
For men to read; only they know He saith
Sweet words, and comforteth.

Not that He doth explain
The mystery that baffleth; but a sense
Husheth the quiet heart, that far, far hence
Lieth a field set thick with golden grain
Wetted in seedling days by many a rain;
The end—it will explain.

When you pass through the rivers,
they will not sweep over you.
When you walk through the fire,
you will not be burned;
the flames will not set you ablaze.
Isaiah 43:2

CHAPTER TEN

The Fourth Man in the Fire

IN A LAND that is now called Iraq, there was an arrogant, despotic ruler who wanted to be worshiped as a god. He had a golden image of himself erected outside of the capital city of Babylon. He called in his guard and ordered his military band to play for the great ceremony where everyone was ordered to worship his statue. This command was accompanied by a sinister warning. King Nebuchadnezzar gave orders that anyone who didn't bow down would be thrown into a red-hot furnace.

Three Jewish refugees from Jerusalem refused to obey the order. They worshiped their God, not man. They said, "If we are thrown into the blazing furnace, the God we serve is able to save us from it . . . but even if he does not, we want you to know, O king, that we will not serve your gods or worship the image of gold you have set up" (Daniel 3:17–18).

The king was enraged. His order was carried out by his elite guards, and the three Hebrews were thrown into the blazing furnace. But a strange thing happened. The guards were burned to death, and the Jews didn't even have their hair singed. The crowd gasped, the king was shocked, for in the midst of that blazing furnace were seen not three, but four men, walking around unharmed. God was the fourth man in the fire.

God has promised that if we call upon Him, He will be with us in times of trouble. He will walk through our trials with us. He promises to be the other Person with us in the tough times of life, which does not always mean deliverance.

Think of those Christian martyrs who have been burned at the stake, someone who has lost a loved one in a house fire, or an airplane that exploded and crashed in flames. Our Lord could have claimed that promise, "He will give His angels charge over thee." But He was willing, for our sakes, to forgo the promise, saying instead, "Thy will be done." For the sake of others, we too at times must be willing to relinquish the promise for His glory and the good of others.

A Book of Promises

The Bible is a book of promises, and unlike the books of men, it doesn't change or get out of date. The message I have been proclaiming for many years is basically the same—and God does not lie!

The Bible makes it clear that no problems in our lives are too great or too small for His concern. He cares about everything that affects His children.

If we have no knowledge of God's promises to us, we will not be able to appropriate them. The three Hebrews, Shadrach, Meshach, and Abednego, had studied their Old Testament Scriptures. Of course, we don't know what promises they claimed when they defied Nebuchadnezzar's order, but it could have been from the Psalms. They might have remembered, "The Lord is my light and my salvation—whom shall I fear?" (27:1). Their words to the king were, "Our God is able to deliver us—*but* if not, we still won't worship your image." They certainly knew some of the promises of God to give them the strength and faith they exhibited.

We cannot possibly cover all the promises of the Bible in this chapter. It would take a book, since figures on the number of biblical promises range from eight thousand to thirty thousand. We just need to know, claim, and memorize a few for the times when we will need them. When it comes to the subject of pain and suffering, there are some promises that God has given us both in the Old and the New Testaments.

When I think of some of the promises, certain people come into my mind. You may have some special promises that the Lord has given you. Hold onto them, cling to them, for you never know when you will need them.

God Promises Us a Refuge

"God is our refuge and our strength, an ever-present help in trouble" (Psalm 46:1). What a great and simple promise! This does not imply that we huddle and are panic-stricken behind a protective wall. It pictures a person actively involved in life, for the psalmist says that God is "ever-present." He goes with His people into the scene of suffering and onto the platform of pain to sustain them in the midst of it.

Refuge means a hiding place, and that always reminds me of a long-time friend whom we met in Switzerland. At one time she was imprisoned by the Nazis and placed in solitary confinement for four months. The cell was dark, with dirty water standing on the floor. When she heard the piercing cries of other prisoners, she knew that she was also under the constant threat of being tortured.

She said: "Once I stood with my back against the wall with my hands spread out, as if to try to push away the walls that were closing in on me. I was dead scared. I cried out, 'Lord, I'm not strong enough to endure this. I don't have the faith.'"

Some of us look at people who have suffered and say, "I wish I had your faith." Corrie admitted to a weak faith, but God spoke to her in an unusual way. She noticed an ant on the floor. The moment that ant felt the water, he ran straight to his tiny hole in the wall.

"Then it was as if the Lord said to me, 'What about that ant? He didn't stop to look at the wet floor or his weak feet—he went straight to his hiding place. Corrie don't look at your faith. It is weak. . . . I am your hiding place, and you can come running to Me just like that ant disappeared into that hole in the wall.'"

From the depths of her despair, Corrie pulled up a verse. She continued her story by speaking to all of us: "I know there are moments for you when you lose all courage. You feel as a prisoner that you don't exist in the eyes of the people around you, in the eyes of God, or in your own eyes. Then you can read in the Bible a promise from Jesus: 'Come to me, all you who are weary and burdened, and I will give you rest' (Matthew 11:28)."[1]

God is our rest, our refuge, our hiding place. In Psalm 91:15 God promises, "He will call upon me, and I will answer him; I will be with him in trouble." Again Scripture says, "Trust in him at all times, O people; pour out your hearts to him, for God is our refuge" (Psalm 62:8).

Sometimes we allow bitterness to replace trust and we can't seem to find God through our pain. We can't seem to pour out our hearts, because they have become so hardened.

A young Irish immigrant, Joseph Scriven (1820–86) was deeply in love with a girl, and their marriage plans had been made. Not long before their wedding day, however, she drowned. For months Scriven was bitter, in utter despair. At last he turned to Christ, and through His grace, he found peace and comfort. Out of this tragic experience he wrote the familiar hymn that has brought consolation to millions of aching hearts: "What a Friend we have in Jesus, all our sins and griefs to bear!"

Sometimes our lives are very bright, as it was for Scriven as he approached his wedding day. But like him, we may find that our path also leads through some dark shadows. Business losses, pensions that don't pay the bills, loss of work, inflation, sickness that lays us low, sorrows that rob our homes of their light, children who rebel—all may be turned into blessings for those who find a hiding place in His love.

He Is Our Shield and Our Refuge

When Moses was about to die, he gave his blessings to the tribes of Israel. To Benjamin he said, "Let the beloved of the Lord rest secure in him, for he shields him all day long, and the one the Lord loves rests between his shoulders" (Deuteronomy 33:12). When children play war they sometimes take the lids off garbage cans and use them for shields. Whatever is thrown at them will bounce off, as long as they use this protection. There will be times in your life when you know the Lord has given you Divine protection.

God is our refuge. He shelters us, just as the eagle spreads its magnificent wings over the nest where the baby birds have been hatched. The eagle is not only protective, but he is strong and courageous. It is no coincidence that the official seal of the United States carries a spread-winged bald eagle.

What an illustration this is for the way God cares for His children! Psalm 91:4 says: "He will cover you with his feathers, and under his wings you will find refuge; his faithfulness will be your shield and rampart."

God Is Our Strength

Dale and Roy Rogers have been friends of mine for many years. They have had many tragedies in their lives, with the deaths of three of their children and setbacks that would stagger most people. In her book, *Trials, Tears, and Triumphs,* Dale tells a story about having two speaking engagements for large groups on the same day. By the time she had spoken once, she was so emotionally and physically drained that she was sure she would not be able to go on the second time. (I can relate to this!)

Before her second appearance, Dale was overcome with a spell of weakness. She didn't feel she could continue, so she prayed, "Lord, take over, I've had it." That may not be a very profound prayer, but I'm sure many of you have felt the same way. I know I have.

She said, "As I walked into the pastor's study, three young men took my hands and said, 'Let's pray.' We prayed, and strength flowed into me like a mighty river. It sustained me through the entire service. How true it is what Isaiah says: 'They that wait upon the Lord shall renew their strength; they shall mount up with wings as eagles; they shall run, and not be weary; and they shall walk, and not faint' (Isaiah 40:31)."[2] I have heard Dale say that she intends to wear out in His service and not rust out.

Strength. How we need it. Moses told the children of Israel in Deuteronomy 33:25, "Your strength will equal your days." This is a promise for strength in all areas of life. He is our source to go on, not only in the tough times, but for the daily grind. He adds meaning and joy to our days and gives us the strength to go on, or sit still peacefully. Without Him our daily routine would become tiresome and tedious, a drudgery rather than a joy.

He is my strength to go up. The psalmist says, "By my God have I leaped over a wall" (Psalm 18:29 KJV). I cannot literally leap over a wall, unless it's about as high as a curb, but when there are obstacles that look like mountains, He will give us the strength for the climb.

A few good friends who will support us, without a critical attitude, will give us strength when we are down. Having a support group is a valuable asset to carry us when we are buried under a load of troubles. But what if we don't have friends like this? What if we have moved, or there does not seem to be anybody with whom we can be frank and open. What then? Remember, the Holy Spirit is praying (Romans 8:26–27, 34).

Lucinda was going through a very difficult time. She had been sexually abused as a child, and many years later the memory of that terrible time surfaced. She went to a counselor, who helped her with her severe depression and nightmares. But Lucinda moved to another country when her husband's job changed. She was thousands of miles from her counselor and found it difficult to function without the counselor's help and her support group.

She called one of her Christian friends and said, "I need a simple verse to help me. Can you give me one that's not hard to remember?" Her friend said a quick prayer and went to the Psalms. "Here's one . . . it's Psalm 56:4. 'In God I trust; I will not be afraid. What can mortal man do to me?'" Later, when Lucinda returned to the States, she went back to her counselor. Every time the memories of her abuse surfaced, she repeated that verse.

No matter where we are, God is as close as a prayer. He is our support and our strength. He will help us make our way up again from whatever depths we have fallen.

We don't often consider that sometimes Jesus is our strength simply to sit still. "Be still, and know that I am God" (Psalm 46:10). Our natural tendency when we have a painful happening in our lives is to go into action—do something. Sometimes it is wiser to wait and just be still. The answers will come.

When her husband died, one woman immediately started on a buying spree until most of the life insurance money was gone. Someone else, upon receiving bad news, may react by making other rash and senseless decisions. The Lord is our strength when we allow Him to calm us. "I wait for the Lord, my soul waits, and in his word I put my hope" (Psalm 130:5). "He that hasteth with his foot misses his way" (Proverbs 19:2 ASV).

He Promises to Shepherd Us

The picture of God as a shepherd is found in many places in the Old Testament. What a comfort it is to know that the God of the universe comes down into the hills and valleys of our lives to be our Shepherd.

In the most famous Psalm, David, a former shepherd himself, cries out, "The Lord is *my* shepherd, I shall not be in want" (Psalm 23:1, emphasis added). Our Shepherd leads us, He guides us along the right paths, and He is with us in the dark valley. No wonder David testifies, "My cup overflows" (v. 5). Isaiah describes how the Lord "tends his flock like a shepherd: He gathers the lambs in his arms and carries them close to his heart" (40:11).

In the New Testament Jesus applies the image of the shepherd to Himself. He says, "I am the good shepherd. The good shepherd lays down his life for the sheep. The hired hand is not the shepherd who owns the sheep. So when he sees the wolf coming, he abandons the sheep and runs away. Then the wolf attacks the flock and scatters it. . . . I am the good shepherd; I know my sheep and my sheep know me" (John 10:11–14).

If Jesus lives in the heart, the Good Shepherd owns the sheep; they belong to Him. He guards the sheep; He never leaves them in time of trouble. He knows the sheep by name, and His love is so great that He lays down His life for His sheep.

We need to keep close to our Shepherd, to listen to His voice and follow Him, especially in times of spiritual peril. Jesus tells us not to be misled by the voices of strangers. There are so many strange voices being heard in the religious world of our day. We must compare what they say with the Word of God.

When Jesus Was Jenny's Shepherd

Shame and embarrassment have kept many people from revealing their suffering as the result of sexual abuse and incest. In recent years more and more of these tragic stories have surfaced. All treatment does not fall into the category of psychological counseling, such as Lucinda underwent.

Jenny's mother was a drug dealer. Her parents were divorced, and there was no religious influence in her home. However, when Jenny was three years old, a woman in the apartment building took her to a Good News Club. Jenny began to understand that she had a best friend, and His name was Jesus.

Jenny's mother moved to a large house in an expensive part of the city. Jenny said, "There were as many as thirty people living there at one time. The activities in that house were wicked beyond description, but somehow I felt detached from them, as if there were a shield around me that would not allow me to be touched with this evil."

When her mother was arrested, Jenny was taken to juvenile hall and after that went to live with her father and stepmother in abject poverty. "However, I sought out any church I could find on Sundays and went alone to the services. I loved my Friend so much, and the time spent with Him were my happiest hours."

At the age of twelve, Jenny was sexually abused by a music teacher. She was forced to go to these music lessons, and one time hid in a dumpster to avoid going into the studio. Years later, after pouring herself into her work and putting herself through college, one day the memory of that music teacher flooded over her. "For ten years it had been buried in my subconscious, and when it resurfaced it almost killed me."

Jenny struggled with hatred and guilt, thinking that somehow she was responsible for the molestation, not the victim. She retreated into her house, pulled the blinds, and spent months in solitude. Unlike Lucinda, she did not have the money to pay for a counselor. Instead of seeking outside help, she went into seclusion. During that time she read her Bible and prayed. She said:

> My constant friend was Jesus. One day I knew I had to confront the music room that had me in the grips of severe depression. I had a vivid impression of walking into that room, with Jesus by my side. His arms were wrapped around me. I saw the room, and I was wearing a dress of pure white satin, virginal in appearance.
>
> Jesus, my Friend, my Good Shepherd, cleansed me of my bitter and tainted memories. It was only then that I was prepared to be the bride of the man I loved.

The stories of Lucinda and Jenny are true, although their names have been changed, and the circumstances could be repeated in more sordid detail in thousands of other lives.

I do not believe that most non-Christian counselors, no matter how skilled and sympathetic they may be, have the complete solution to such desperate problems. Jesus is the answer, and as we point to Him, those who are crying for help will find the Shepherd who will lead them out of the valleys of despair.

Sometimes I watch Oprah Winfrey's show. I admire her because she listens. However, sometimes when I see the people on the show and the desperate problems they face, I want to cry out to the screen and say to them, "Turn to God!"

He Promises to Provide Superabundantly

God promises "to do immeasurably more than all we ask or imagine, according to his power that is at work within us" (Ephesians 3:20). We need to believe that He can do even more than what we ask. Paul told the Philippians, "My God will meet all your needs according to his glorious riches in Christ Jesus" (4:19). What a promise this is for the Christian! The supply is inexhaustible.

We once had a well dug at our home. We reached one layer of water at a hundred feet and another layer of water at three hundred feet, then another at six hundred feet. We asked the well diggers how much water they thought there was. They said there was no way to compute it, but that it would last forever!

God gives us supplies of His power that will never run out. No matter what my need, He is more than able to meet it.

When Do We Need Him?

I find that I need Christ just as much, and sometimes more, in the times when everything seems to be going right as I do in times of trouble. We make the mistake of thinking that Christ's help is needed only for sickrooms, or in times of overwhelming sorrow and suffering. This is not true. When life is going smoothly, we may begin to think it is entirely due to our own goodness, our own power, our own strength. In our triumphs we may forget that Jesus wants to rejoice with us, as well as to weep with us. He went to the wedding at Cana and celebrated with the guests, as well as to the home of Mary and Martha and wept with them after Lazarus had died.

It has been said, "There are just as many stars in the sky at noon as at midnight, although we cannot see them in the sun's glare."

God Promises to Send His Angels

At times in my life I have felt protected in a supernatural way. We have been promised, "For he will command his angels concerning you to guard you in all your ways" (Psalm 91:11).

We face dangers every day of which we are not even aware. Often God intervenes on our behalf through the use of His angels. The Bible is full of the accounts of angels. Psalm 34:7 teaches us that angels protect us and deliver us: "The angel of the Lord encamps around those who fear him, and he delivers them."

Evidence from the Bible, as well as personal experience, convinces us that guardian angels surround us at times and protect us. Many Christians can remember when a near car wreck, a severe accident, or a fierce temptation was averted in some unusual manner. Angels may bring unexpected blessings, like a check in the mail for the exact amount needed, or some food on the doorstep when the cupboards are empty.

Once when I was going through a dark period I prayed long and earnestly, but there was no answer. I felt as though God was indifferent and that I was all alone with my problem. It was what some would call "a dark night of the soul." I wrote my mother about the experience, and I will never forget her reply: "Son, there are many times when God withdraws to test your faith. He wants you to trust Him in the darkness. Now, Son, reach up by faith in the fog and you will find that His hand will be there." Relieved, I knelt by my bed and experienced an overwhelming sense of God's presence. Whether or not we sense and feel the presence of the Holy Spirit or one of the holy angels, by faith we are certain God will never leave us nor forsake us.

He Walks with Us Through the Fire

When the three Hebrews were thrown into the fire, they didn't know they were going to come out unscathed. They only trusted God that whatever happened to them, it was His will for their lives.

Incredible as it may seem, God wants our companionship; He wants to be close to us. Unlike friends on earth, who may leave us when the going gets rough, He wants to shield us, to protect us, and to guide us in our way through life.

The story has been told about a lone survivor of a shipwreck who was marooned on an uninhabited island. He managed to build a hut in which he put everything he had saved from the wreck. He prayed to God for rescue, and anxiously scanned the horizon every day to signal any passing ship.

One day he returned to his hut and to his horror found it in flames and all of his possessions gone. What a tragedy! Shortly after, a ship arrived. "We saw your smoke signal and hurried here," the captain explained. The survivor had only seen his burnt hut, but out of disaster, God worked a blessing. The shipwrecked man fell to his knees to thank God for the fire that caused his rescue.

When we walk through our fires, He will be with us. He will be our "fourth man in the fire."

Groanings which cannot be uttered are often prayers which cannot be refused.
Charles Haddon Spurgeon

CHAPTER ELEVEN

How to Pray Through the Pain

PRAYER IS AN embarrassment to some. To bow in a restaurant and give thanks, to kneel in a place where others might see you, are outward demonstrations of personal faith. But many people consider them public shows of excessive religiosity. The commitment of the Muslims, in this respect, should be a challenge to us.

In the hard times of life, prayer is no longer awkward, but openly displayed. When the Marines returned to Camp Pendleton, California, after their service in the Persian Gulf War, it was reported that as soon as they spilled out of the airplane, fifteen of the servicemen formed a circle and prayed unashamedly.

Prayer is for every moment of our lives, not just for times of suffering or joy. Prayer is really a place; a place where you meet God in genuine conversation.

Have you ever said, "Well, all we can do now is pray"? Instead of beginning with prayer, we sometimes resort to it after all other resources have been used. When we come to the end of ourselves, we come to the beginning of God. We don't need to be embarrassed that we are needy. God doesn't demand that we pray in King James English, or even with eloquence. Every feeble, stumbling prayer uttered by a believer is heard by God. A cry, a sigh, a "Help!" are all prayers, according to the Psalms.

Frank Laubach, my old friend and a great humanitarian missionary, said, "Prayer at its highest is a two-way conversation—and for me the most important is listening to God's replies." "The polite part of speaking," Edward Gloeggler said, "is to be still long enough to listen."

Many people pray only when they are under great stress or in danger. I have been in airplanes when an engine died; believe me, you could see people praying. I have talked to soldiers who told me that they never prayed until they were in the midst of battle. There seems to be an instinct in man to pray in times of danger. If we are to depend on prayer during tough times, we should be people of prayer before the crisis hits.

Amy Carmichael wrote, "We must learn to pray far more for spiritual victory than for protection from battle-wounds, relief from their havoc, rest from their pain. . . . This triumph is not deliverance from, but victory in trial, and that not intermittent but perpetual."[1]

Our Prayer Model

Jesus is the supreme model of a person devoted to prayer. He was constantly in an attitude of prayer, and never more urgently than in the face of suffering. One of the most amazing things in all the Scriptures is how much time Jesus spent in prayer. He had only three years of public ministry, but He was never too hurried to spend hours in prayer. He prayed before every difficult task and at every crisis in His ministry. No day began or closed in which He was not in communion with His Father.

When He was arrested in the Garden of Gethsemane, He was praying. He had taken the disciples with Him, and sensing the magnitude of what was ahead, He asked Peter, James, and John to stay with Him and keep watch. He went into the garden and fell with His face to the ground, praying, "My Father, if it is possible, may this cup be taken from me. Yet not as I will, but as you will" (Matthew 26:39).

We pray so haphazardly. Snatches of memorized verses are hastily spoken in the morning. Then we say good-bye to God for the rest of the day, until we sleepily push through a few closing petitions at night, like leaving a wake-up call at the hotel switchboard. That is not the example of prayer that Jesus gave. He prayed long and repeatedly. He spent at least one entire night in prayer (Luke 6:12).

He prayed briefly when He was in a crowd; He prayed a little longer when He was with His disciples; and He prayed all night when He was alone. Today, many in the ministry tend to reverse that process.

The Scriptures say, "Pray without ceasing" (1 Thessalonians 5:17 KJV). This should be the motto of every true follower of Jesus. No matter how dark and hopeless a situation might seem, never stop praying. It's not only to resolve our problems that we should pray, but to share in the strength of God's friendship. For us, prayer should be not merely an act, but an attitude of life.

Do we pray for God's will, or demand our own way? Prayer needs to be an integral part of our lives, so that when a crisis comes we have the strength and faith to pray for God's will. Someone said that strength in prayer is better than length in prayer. However, Martin Luther said, "I have so much to do today that I shall spend the first three hours in prayer."

A Friend Who Cares

Years ago a student was killed in a fraternity hazing accident at a southern university. John, the star football player at the school, was returning to his dorm on the morning after the tragedy when he saw three athletes mercilessly confront one of the dead boy's friends. That friend later recalled:

> I wanted to make my classes that day, and I was about to break down crying from the taunts of my fellow classmen. I felt like a ten-year-old kid surrounded by high school bullies. I don't think those guys realized what they were doing, but they had me boxed in and they weren't going to let me pass until I broke. One said that at least they didn't kill their pledges! My friend was dead, and these guys wanted to put the blame for his death on me.
>
> Suddenly, there was a hand on my shoulder. It was John. He stood

there while I told the story of what had happened, and faced their critical and derisive response. John squeezed my shoulder and gently pushed me on past them.

He walked clear across the campus with me to class. Though we had no classes together, he quietly checked on me during the rest of the day. Perhaps I could have made it through the day, without John, but his being there not only made it easier, but also helped shape my understanding of Christian ministry for the last twenty-two years. John was there when everyone else seemed against me.

Not to share fellowship with Jesus through prayer is sadder than it would have been for that young man to turn to John, his strong and ready friend, and reject him in that painful time. Not unlike that student, when we turn in prayer to our friend Jesus in time of crisis, sometimes our lives are strengthened forever. In the midst of our trials, He is quietly checking on us.

Pattern for Prayer

Jesus frequently prayed alone, separating Himself from every earthly distraction. I would strongly urge you to select a place—a room or corner in your home, place of work, or in your yard or garden—where you can regularly meet God alone. This does not contradict "Pray without ceasing" (1 Thessalonians 5:17), but expands it.

Jesus prayed with great earnestness. At Gethsemane, in the earnestness of His praying, He fell to the ground and agonized with God until His sweat became "like drops of blood" (Luke 22:44). The force of His prayers was increased during times of extreme suffering.

When we see the need of someone else, pray. When we know someone is in pain, pray. Let someone know you have prayed for them, and ask others to pray for you.

A missionary and his family were forced to camp outside on a hill. They had money with them and were fearful of an attack by roving thieves. After praying, they went to sleep. Months later an injured man was brought into the mission hospital. He asked the missionary if he had soldiers guarding him on that special night. "We intended to rob you," he said, "but we were afraid of the twenty-seven soldiers."

When the missionary returned to his homeland, he related this strange story, and a member of his church said, "We had a prayer meeting that night, and I took the roll. There were just twenty-seven of us present." Prayers have no boundaries. They can leap miles and continents and be translated instantly into any language.

So we not only pray through our pain, but for others as well. Some years ago, the writer and social critic Tom Wolfe coined the phrase the "Me Generation." Each generation tends to be a "me" generation, since selfishness is part of human nature. A child says, "It's mine." A teenager centers on his problems. An adult proclaims, "Look out for Number One." Selfishness is part of human nature, but today advertising and "pop" psychology may have raised self-centeredness to state-of-the-art levels. Jesus, on the other hand, tells us to pray not only for ourselves, but even "for those who persecute you" (Matthew 5:44).

We are to plead for our enemies, asking God to lead them to Christ and for His sake to forgive them. Persecution, whether it is physical, social, or mental, is one of the worst types of pain, but those who persecute us are to be the objects of our prayers.

The daughter and son-in-law of Doug Sparks were killed by a drunk driver, and their little boy was injured so badly that his brain will never function normally. A friend said to him after the accident, "Doug, it's going to work out for good for you and your family."

Sparks answered angrily, "Yes, but at what price?"

Sparks said, "For several days I wrestled with the price. I was angry. There's nothing wrong with being angry when something like this strikes you. You just need to stay in contact with God and deal with your anger."

In a time of prayer, it seemed to Sparks that God was saying, "Doug, I know how much this is costing you. I know the price you're paying. But I also know the price I paid."

Sparks continued, "In times of tragedy we must always look to the

Cross; the price God paid for a suffering, dying world. Immediately the Spirit witnessed to me that I must go to the driver who had caused the tragedy and forgive him."[2]

He visited the hospital where the driver, an illegal alien, lay strapped down with a broken neck and back and a spirit that was broken even more, sure that God had forsaken him. Sparks shared the Gospel with him and told him, "Because Christ loved me and forgave me, I love you and forgive you." At that moment, Sparks said he experienced the love of Christ for this man. Ordinary human love could not cause that kind of forgiveness for a man who had killed your loved ones, only the prayers of forgiveness could accomplish that miracle.

In His first words uttered from the cross after the nails had been hammered through His hands and feet, Jesus said, "Father, forgive them, for they do not know what they are doing" (Luke 23:34). I have often thought that because of His prayer we will see the men who nailed Jesus to the cross in Heaven. No prayer that Jesus ever prayed to the Father went unanswered.

Christian teachers through the ages have urged the importance of prayer in the lives of believers. One wise man said, "If Christians spent as much time praying as they do grumbling, they would soon have nothing to grumble about."

Someone said, "If there are any tears in Heaven, they will be over the fact that we prayed so little." Cameron Thompson said, "Heaven must be full of answers for which no one ever bothered to ask."[3]

The Power of Prayer

Few of us have learned how to develop the power of prayer. We have not yet learned that a man has more strength when he is at prayer than when he is in control of the most powerful military weapons ever developed. I was pleased to hear General Norman Schwarzkopf in an interview with Barbara Walters after the end of the Gulf War say that he prayed for the men in his command.

Effective prayer is offered in faith. From one end of the Bible to the other, we find the record of people whose prayers have been answered—people who turned the tide of history by prayer, men who prayed fervently and whom God answered.

David gave some powerful prayer patterns in his Psalms for those who are going through difficult times.

When you are distressed: "Answer me when I call to you, O my righteous God, *Give me relief from my distress;* be merciful to me and hear my prayer" (Psalm 4:1, emphasis added).

When you need mercy: "The Lord has heard my cry for *mercy;* the Lord accepts my prayer" (Psalm 6:9, emphasis added).

When you need help: "O Lord my God, I called to you for *help* and you healed me!" (Psalm 30:2, emphasis added).

Prayer is powerful, but if our prayers are aimless, meaningless, and mingled with doubt, they will be of little hope to us. Prayer is more than a wish; it is the voice of faith directed to God. One of my favorite verses is: "If any of you lacks wisdom, he should ask God, who gives generously to all without finding fault, and it will be given to him. But when he asks, he must believe and not doubt, because he who doubts is like a wave of the sea, blown and tossed by the wind" (James 1:5–6).

The Bible says, "The prayer of a righteous man is powerful and effective" (James 5:16). Jesus said, "I tell you, whatever you ask for in prayer, believe that you have received it, and it will be yours" (Mark 11:24). I have heard many stories of prayers being answered for a loved one miles away. One mother told about a time when she clearly heard one of her daughters cry, "Mom, Mom!" in the middle of the night. But her daughter was a married woman, traveling halfway around the world with her husband. The mother picked up her Bible from the nightstand and went into the family room to pray. She had a real sense of urgency that her daughter needed help. She prayed that God would show her what to do, and then she read Psalm 91 over and over again.

A few weeks later she received a letter from her daughter. This is what had happened. The daughter was in Borneo when she became very sick and feverish. Her husband could not find a good doctor, but after some time located one who took them into his home where he and his housekeeper nursed the woman back to health. The letter ended, "Remember when I was a girl and I would call out, 'Mom,' and you would come rushing down the hall? That night in Borneo, in my fever, I called, 'Mom, Mom' . . . and then I could hear you rushing down the hall."[4]

God sometimes causes us pain so that we may pray for others. Bible teaching, church history, and Christian experience all confirm that prayer does work.

Pray, Don't Panic

When we're in a threatening situation, the normal tendency is to panic. Many stories could be told of fear being replaced by calm through the power of prayer.

Carol is a victim of multiple sclerosis, which is a disease of the central nervous system. Everyone has different symptoms of MS, some more debilitating than others. Over the years this once active and vibrant woman gradually lost a great deal of her muscular ability and was confined to a wheelchair.

Her husband always saw that she was comfortably situated before leaving for work. Being a methodical man, he was used to returning home at a certain time each afternoon.

One day Carol was attempting to get from her wheelchair into her bed, and somehow she fell and her head became wedged between the wall and the wheels of her chair. She was trapped and couldn't move to reach the phone. She began to pray for help, knowing that the longer she lay on the cold, hard floor, the more difficult it would be to regain any muscular strength. Only a short time passed before she heard the door open and her husband calling to her. He had arrived hours before his normal time.

"I seemed to have someone telling me to come home," he told his wife as he lifted her into bed.

Carol said, "And I know who that Someone was. I prayed for help."

Our prayers are not always answered as quickly and specifically as

Carol's. If we remain calm, placing faith in God and believing that we will receive God's direction, we will eventually find the answer to our problem.

Creative Silence

The story is told about Robert LeTourneau, the industrialist, who received an order from the government for a very complicated machine to be used in lifting airplanes. No machine of this type had ever been designed. LeTourneau and his engineers could not come up with a plan. After some time everyone was becoming tense and nervous. Finally, on a Wednesday night, LeTourneau told his staff that he was not going to work, that he was going to a prayer meeting. The engineers were upset, because they had a deadline and the boss was deserting them.

"But," he said, "I've got a deadline with God." He went to the prayer meeting, sang the hymns, and prayed. Afterward, as he was walking home, the design of the machine in complete detail came into his mind. He needed time with God and creative silence to bring it to the surface.[5]

Sometimes we try so hard to solve the problems of our health, our children, our business, or our future that we become agitated or depressed. "Be still, and know that I am God" (Psalm 46:10).

Prayer Is a Place in Your Heart

Prayer is more than a plea, it is a place where we must spend time if we are to learn its power.

A minister had gradually lost his faith. In a world of great suffering, he could no longer feel the presence of the Lord in his own life. He was embittered that he had spent so much of his life in studying and pursuing an understanding of God. Now he had only a sense of betrayal and emptiness. Even his prayers seemed to bounce off an invisible barrier.

He expressed his anguish to an old friend he had known since his childhood. He told his friend that he thought he knew what Moses would have felt like if the burning bush had suddenly stopped burning and went up in a pale, gritty puff of smoke. He said that for him there was no more burning bush or sense of the presence of God in his life.

His friend, a rancher, confided that he, too, often felt that way. "But you know, Jack, I realized a while back that the burning bush is always there, always burning. It's just that I hadn't been spending much time in that part of the pasture."

Prayer is "that part of the pasture" where the bush is burning. If we are to be powerful in prayer, we must spend time there.

Thy Will Be Done

As we face problems and personal suffering, we must not forget that our prayers are subject to His will. This takes the burden off of us and gives it to the Lord. His will is always best. The difficulty most of us face is knowing the will of God. As believers, we cannot find true peace outside the will of God.

In our computerized society, many people have learned the value of using these amazing machines. A computer, however, has no worth unless it is programmed. When the proper data is put into it, it will do more work accurately than many people. The believer has tremendous potential, but that potential cannot be used until he is programmed with the Word of God.

J. Grant Howard said: "God has given every believer a handbook with many of the basic rules and regulations for life. If and when a believer follows these rules, he is in the will of God. When he consciously violates them, he is out of the will of God. Therefore I must know the precepts taught in the Word if I am going to do the will of God."[6]

Prayers that are selfish, vengeful, or mean are not in the will of God. However, we may be sure that God is true to His word and answers all sincere prayers offered in the name of the Lord Jesus Christ. His answer may be yes, or it may be no, or it may be "Wait." If it is no or "Wait," we cannot say that God has not answered our prayer. It simply means that the answer is different from what we expected.

When we pray for help in trouble, or for healing in sickness, or for deliverance in persecution, God may not give us what we ask for because that may not be His wise and loving will for us. He will answer our prayer in His own way, and He will not let us down in our hour of need.

Margaret Clarkson said, "It's not wrong to pray for miracles. But it is wrong to insist upon our own will rather than God's. We may not demand miracles of a sovereign God. Unfortunately, such demands are made in all too many Christian circles today."[7]

True prayer is a way of life, not just for use in cases of emergency. Make it a habit, and when the need arises you will be in practice.

You cannot suddenly fabricate foundations of strength; they must have been building all along.
Philip Yancey

CHAPTER TWELVE

Storing Up for the Storms

TOM LANDRY, FORMER coach of the Dallas Cowboys, has spoken at our Crusades and is a man I greatly admire. Because he was well known to many, his Christian testimony influenced thousands, particularly when it was known that he was in a tight spot.

Landry did not become a Christian until he was thirty-three years old, even though he had been a churchgoer all his life. One of his biographers wrote: "There would be shaky times, frustrating times that would follow, some of which would have deeply scarred those with less faith. But Landry's faith would help sustain him. It is doubtful he would have gotten through the ordeal of being fired when he was looking forward to trying to bring the team back if his faith had not been so strong. It is also doubtful he would have gotten through the Dallas Cowboys' formative years, which were much worse than he could have imagined."[1]

What guides a man like Tom Landry, giving him the resources to store up for the storms in life? Repeatedly, we hear the word "faith." Faith in Jesus Christ.

An athlete does not try out for the Olympics without hours and hours, years and years of training. An actor doesn't go onstage without memorizing his lines. A cook can't bake a cake without the necessary ingredients. Why, then, do we expect to meet life and its painful twists without the strengthening resources we need?

What Would You Do?

What would you do if the major cities in your country were suddenly leveled by guided missiles or enemy bombers? How would you react if an earthquake cut off all communication, water, and electrical sources? Suppose a group of terrorists kept you hostage? If you have never experienced such extreme horrors, you probably have no answers.

We should not live our lives anticipating disasters. I have known people who build up such fears for what might happen that they never enjoy what is happening. However, like national defense, we need to arm ourselves. George Washington said, "To be prepared for war is one of the most effectual means of preserving peace."

However, we in America, in comparison with Christians in many other countries, have experienced very little sacrifice and suffering. I know of the plight of the homeless and the poor and am not insensitive to their needs. For most of us, any persecution we may have undergone has been minor.

Christianity in America has at times become almost popular. Walk into any Christian bookstore and see the hundreds of books that are published. Well-known people openly profess their Christian belief. However, I believe that as secular materialism becomes increasingly prevalent in our educational system, the time of popularity will soon come to an end. Already we are experiencing the curtailment of prayer and Bible study. And our young people are paying the price. Christ warned His followers that to believe in Him would not make them popular, and that they should be prepared to face affliction for His sake.

Will We Escape Religious Persecution?

Some anti-abortion groups have been put in jail, some have been mistreated. In our schools, parents who have opposed objectionable material in the classroom have been called extremists or worse. Can we compare these with the persecutions in countries where Christians have been jailed, tortured, or killed?

The Bible says that all who want "to live a godly life in Christ Jesus will be persecuted" (2 Timothy 3:12). Jesus said that as the time of His return comes closer, "They will lay hands on you and persecute you" (Luke 21:12).

The fact that we are not being persecuted for Christ's sake is an abnormal situation. I am not suggesting America is about to undergo torture for Christ, but even subtle persecution for our faith is likely to cause many believers to deny Him.

Are we too soft, too used to the luxuries of freedom, that we would be unable to stand up to persecution? Most of us would do no more, no less, than we are doing right now. Some of us who wear our Christianity on our sleeves would probably be the first to surrender. Many would be modern-day Peters who would say, "Though all others deny Christ, yet I will never deny him." But he did. Three times.

Others, quietly storing up their resources of strength and power, would be strong and courageous as Paul described, "My power is made perfect in weakness" (2 Corinthians 12:9).

Persecutions of the Heart

Claudia was a newlywed in her twenties when she was diagnosed with Hodgkin's disease and was given only a 50 percent chance of survival. Rapidly she was operated on and began cobalt treatments that transformed her almost overnight from a young, beautiful woman to a wreck.

Her Christian friends came with confusing, not consoling, words of help. All the comforters with their conflicting voices only added to her misery. Her husband was a chaplain's assistant in a hospital and had seen many sides of suffering. He said, "I had seen sick and dying patients. In the movies, couples who have fought for years, suddenly in the face of danger forget their differences and come together. But it doesn't work that way in real life.

"When a couple encounters a crisis," he said, "it magnifies what's already present in the relationship. Since Claudia and I happened to love each other deeply, and had worked on open communication, the crisis drove us to each other. Feelings of blame and anger against each other did not creep in. The crisis of her illness merely brought to the surface and intensified feelings already present."[2]

Problems magnify what is already present in our relationship with those close to us. Claudia and her husband may not have realized that they were prepared for this crisis in their life, but their solid love bonded them as a fortress to meet the storm. Fortunately, Claudia was eventually cured by treatments that destroyed the cancerous cells.

Other couples and families are driven apart by troubles. Like a tree with shallow roots, they are flattened when the winds come. Some get divorces, some have family splits that never seem to heal. Accusations, bitterness, hatred, and guilt destroy relationships that should have grown stronger like a healthy tree.

If we want to have resources in our possession for a day of disaster, each one of us must have a personal survival kit.

God's Storehouse

Before Easter many of the television channels showed the film classic *The Ten Commandments.* There is one scene where Moses opens Pharaoh's grain house and the starving Jews swarm in with their baskets and fill them from the steady stream of life-giving grain that poured out of giant bins.

God has just such a storehouse of supplies. But there are some requirements for us to meet before we can receive the abundance. First, we must make sure of our relationship to God. We must be prepared to meet God at any moment.

Isn't it strange how we prepare for so many things except meeting God? Some girls spend months preparing for their wedding, down to the details of how many layers on the cake and what flavor. Do they prepare for the life after the wedding?

Getting to know God and being able to call on Him is the most important step in storing up for the storms. Knowing God is more than just treating Him as a casual acquaintance, but developing a deeper relationship with Him every day.

Second, we should learn how to walk with God in our daily life. Have you ever been asked, "How is your walk?" Some Christians will know immediately that you are asking about their walk with God, but many will probably say, "Well, I do about two miles a day."

I know people who seem to be holding the hand of God throughout their life's journey. I also know people who are lagging far behind. We have some friends in the Old Testament who have given us vivid examples of walking with God.

Abraham walked with God and was called a friend of God. Noah walked with God, and when the flood came he was saved. Moses walked with God in the desert, and when the hour of judgment fell upon Egypt, he was prepared to lead his people to victory. David walked with God as a shepherd boy, and when he was called upon to rule his people, he was prepared for the task of being a king. Daniel was saved from the lions' den, and his friends were spared from the fiery furnace.

God does not always pull his children out of deep water. Stephen was a young man "full of faith and of the Holy Spirit" (Acts 6:5). He was stoned to death, but his entry into Heaven was triumphal.

Wouldn't you think that the apostles would have fared better than some of the scoundrels that surrounded Jesus? Just look at some of their fates: Peter was crucified upside down; Andrew was tied to a cross with thick ropes for three days before he died; John was a prisoner on a desolate island; Bartholomew was beaten and then beheaded; Thomas was murdered while he was preaching. Amy Carmichael said, "For John, the beloved disciple, was reserved the long martyrdom of life."

These men literally walked with God. Although we were not present two thousand years ago, we have access to the same strength as the apostles.

Take Your Bible off the Shelf

What has happened to Bible memorization? Children in Sunday school used to have verses to memorize in order to win a Bible. Bible studies used to have passages to commit to memory. Today there are more people who know the words to a television commercial than know the words in the Bible.

Many stories have come out of prison camps about Christians who had no Bibles but who had committed portions of the Scripture to memory and shared them with others. One Christian who was in a prison camp for three years told me that during his imprisonment his greatest regret was not having memorized more of the Bible.

A Chinese missionary was imprisoned by the Japanese during World War II. She managed to take a forbidden Gospel of John with her. When she went to bed, she pulled the covers over her head, and memorized one verse each night for three years.

When the prisoners were released, most of them shuffled out, but the missionary was so chipper that someone said she must have been brainwashed. A *Life* magazine reporter, who had interviewed her, said, "She's been brainwashed for sure. God washed her brain."

People have told me that when they were suffering that sometimes they could only remember small parts of Scripture. One woman, upon hearing bad news, repeated over and over again, "I can do everything through him who gives me strength" (Philippians 4:13).

What verses have you stored up for the future?

Be a Prayer Warrior Before the Battle Begins

We have talked about the importance of prayer before, but it seems as if we pray during a crisis and neglect it in-between. In the weeks since the end of the war in the Persian Gulf, I have heard or read very little about prayers for our country. On the other hand, we have so many battles going on in America today that we should be a people of prayer. Our government needs prayer. Our leaders need prayer. Our schools need prayer. Our youth need our prayers. Our families need our prayers.

If Christianity is to survive in a godless and materialistic world, we must repent of our prayerlessness. We must make prayer our priority. Even our churches today have gotten away from prayer meetings. Potlucks and fund-raising seem to have taken precedence.

Are we spiritually prepared as individuals or as a nation for the increasing attacks upon us? I believe in military preparation, but it cannot take the place of spiritual preparedness.

We do not have wicked men at the head of our government. In fact, many of them are godly people, devoted to their families and to the protection of our nation. However, we do have "spiritual forces of evil" at work in our world. The daily news tells us of increasing depravity every year. We must be prayer warriors against these "powers of darkness."

A story about the weapon of prayer being used against a wicked ruler is told in the Bible. Sennacherib was an Assyrian leader who had boasted that he would defeat God's people and take over their land. His propaganda machine was powerful. He sent messages to Israel, taunting the people about their weakness and boasting of his strength. In the arms race of their day, the Assyrians were definitely ahead. When Sennacherib spoke, the whole world trembled!

Israel's king, Hezekiah, was a man of faith. He knew that on a purely human level the Assyrians could destroy them. But Hezekiah had a secret weapon. He called the prophet Isaiah in, and they fell to their knees in prayer.

Look what happened: "And the Lord sent an angel, who annihilated all the fighting men and the leaders and officers in the camp of the Assyrian king. So he [Sennacherib] withdrew to his own land in disgrace. . . . So the Lord saved Hezekiah and the people of Jerusalem. . . . He took care of them on every side" (2 Chronicles 32:21–22).

Miracles have happened when God's people turned to Him in prayer. We should not pray for God to be on our side, but pray that we may be on God's side. God does not always deliver His children out of a catastrophe, but promises to be with us throughout.

Practice the Presence of Christ

How do we experience the nearness of the Lord at all times? Do we need a picture drawn by some creative artist to be able to imagine Him with us? Charles Spurgeon once said that there had never been fifteen minutes in his life when he did not sense the presence of Christ. I wish I could make that statement, but I regret that I cannot. What strength we would have, not only during days of testing and suffering, if we trained for life with Christ walking alongside of us.

In His Steps was a bestseller that told of a challenge given by a pastor to his people to pledge for one year not to do anything without first asking the question, "What would Jesus do?" This challenge was provoked when a shabby man, mourning his wife who had died in poverty, stumbled into this wealthy church and addressed the congregation. He said,

> I heard some people singing at a church prayer meeting the other night,
>
> All for Jesus, all for Jesus;
> All my being's ransomed powers;
> All my thoughts and all my doings,
> All my days and all my hours;
>
> I kept wondering as I sat on the steps outside just what they meant by it. It seems to me there's an awful lot of trouble in the world that somehow wouldn't exist if all the people who sing such songs went and lived them out.[3]

If that tramp had posed the same question to us, what would be our response? Do we live our lives with the thought, "What would Jesus do?" Do we practice the presence of Christ every day?

In the story, the tramp died, but he struck the conscience of the minister so profoundly that the lives of many people in the town were changed, just as our lives would change if we truly followed "in His steps" and asked, "What would Jesus have me do?"

Christ promised His disciples, "And surely I will be with you always, to the very end of the age" (Matthew 28:20). What great reassurance that is! The fact of His presence is there because He promised. We need to cultivate the sense of His presence, as we go about the daily routine of our lives.

Christ must be vitally real to us if we are to remain faithful to Him in the hour of crisis. Who knows when that hour might be? Things are happening so fast that the need for turning to God has never been more urgent.

I have told this story many times, and I ask my wife to forgive me for repeating it again. However, it is such a great example of "storing up for the storms," that I cannot leave it out.

Several years ago Ruth had a terrible fall and suffered a concussion. She was unconscious for nearly a week, broke her foot in five places, broke a rib, cracked a vertebra, and injured her hip. Some of those injuries have lingered with her. When she regained consciousness, she found she had lost a great deal of her memory. Most disturbing to her was that she had forgotten all of the Scriptures she had learned throughout the years. The verses of a lifetime were more precious to her than any of her material possessions.

One night when she was praying, she said, "Lord, take anything I have, but please bring back my Bible verses."

Immediately this verse came to mind, "I have loved thee with an everlasting love: therefore with lovingkindness have I drawn thee." Strangely, she did not remember memorizing that verse, but the Lord brought it back to her.

She has continued to memorize, although she finds as she gets older that it takes longer. One of the most recent passages has been Romans 8:31–39.

I want to include this passage here, urging you to memorize it and hide it away in your heart. When persecution, trouble, and adversity arise, these verses will come back to you and give you hope and strength.

> What, then, shall we say in response to this? If God is for us, who can be against us? He who did not spare his own Son, but gave him up for us all—how will he not also, along with him, graciously give us all things?

> Who will bring any charge against those whom God has chosen? It is God who justifies. Who is he that condemns? Christ Jesus, who died—more than that, who was raised to life—is at the right hand of God and is also interceding for us. Who shall separate us from the love of Christ? Shall trouble or hardship or persecution or famine or nakedness or danger or sword? As it is written:
>
> "For your sake we face death all day long;
> we are considered as sheep to be slaughtered."
>
> No, in all these things we are more than conquerors through him who loved us. For I am convinced that neither death nor life, neither angels nor demons, neither the present nor the future, nor any powers, neither height nor depth, nor anything else in all creation, will be able to separate us from the love of God that is in Christ Jesus our Lord.

What a great storehouse we will have when those thoughts are in our hearts!

Family Power

A few years ago I had not heard the term "dysfunctional family" used as it is today. Now the concept is applied to so many that I begin to wonder how the family is functioning. In most parts of the world, it is not operating too well. I am not speaking only of the immediate family unit, but of the extended family and also the family of God. There is no need to review all the problems. You know them. In fact, you may be a part of the problem. Only the strong Christian family unit can survive the increasing world crises.

The previous points in our discussion of the storehouse apply to the family also. First, we need to place God at the center of our family. Second, as a family we need to walk with God daily. Third, consulting and memorizing Scripture as a family is vital. Together the family should read, mark, and learn the Scriptures as an essential preparation for the persecution ahead.

Family prayer is a fourth vital link in the chain of spiritual strength—a strength we are trying to build to protect us from a world gone mad. Practicing prayer as a family, not just a flippant blessing before a meal, can give us the security we need.

If a family is fragmented, divided into factions or unforgiving in its attitude toward its members, it will have painful times when trouble hits. Many times it takes just one member of a family to initiate the action to bring a family back together again.

One couple we know was remarried after their son finally approached his father and said, "I think you and Mother ought to get back together again." At the ceremony, the boy took a quantity of Kleenex, thinking his mother would need it, but it was the father to whom he had to keep passing the tissues as he stood with tears streaming down his face. Through the intervention of a child, the years of hurt, pain, and fragmentation of that broken family were brought to an end with a new beginning.

Family includes those small, intimate groups that are springing up inside and outside the church today. In an impersonal society, where often we don't know our next-door neighbor, there is a basic need for support groups. Many people don't have it within their family. When brothers and sisters in Christ unite in a home Bible class or a study group, their faith and witness can be strengthened. Scripture urges us to "Bear ye one another's burdens, and so fulfil the law of Christ" (Galatians 6:2 KJV). When this is done in small Christian groups, amazing things can happen.

One group of Christian business people met to pray for a friend who had suffered a severe stroke. Gradually, the prayer group became a true support group, where they openly shared their feelings and read the Scriptures together. The man who had had the stroke came to thank them for their prayers and stayed to accept Christ. Soon his wife came to a potluck they were having, and she eventually was born again. Amazing things can happen when the family of God bands together.

Ruth and I have learned that the church in China has survived after many years of severe restrictions. How could this be? It is because of small groups of believers, who, though often driven "underground" during the Cultural Revolution, managed to meet regularly around the Word. Despite the concerted effort to destroy all the Bibles in China, some copies survived. Small groups of Christians met around these and were also nurtured by the verses memorized by other believers. Chinese Christians in prisons and labor camps have allowed the flame of their faith to burn brightly and have been used to lead other Chinese to the Lord. Consequently, the number of Christians has multiplied under persecution.

What about us? Are we preparing for the storms of suffering, or will we be caught without resources? The best way to prepare is to deepen our spiritual lives—and by that I mean to deepen our life in the Spirit.

Being filled with the Spirit is not a one-time affair but an ongoing experience. When Paul said, "Be filled with the Spirit" (Ephesians 5:18), he conveyed the idea that we "keep on being filled with the Spirit." This is not a pond of water, but an ever-flowing spring. We are to have these storehouses that are available for our use at all times. When the resources are needed, they will be there.

So be prepared. When the "evil day" comes, we do not have to be dependent upon the circumstances around us, but rather on the resources of God!

In order to console, there is no need to say much.
It is enough to listen, to understand, to love.
Paul Tournier

CHAPTER THIRTEEN

How to Help the Hurting People

AN ANCIENT PHILOSOPHER, who was the wisest man of his time, wrote: "Two are better than one, because they have a good return for their work: If one falls down, his friend can help him up. But pity the man who falls and has no one to help him up" (Ecclesiastes 4:9–10).

Hurting people are lonely people. It may seem like the whole world goes on, and nobody cares. It has been said that loneliness is the disease of our time. Loneliness lingers in the hospital bed and sits with the wife whose husband spends more time at work than at home. Loneliness strikes the divorced husband or wife and the children who are left behind. Loneliness isolates the aged and impersonalizes the poor. Cities are often the loneliest places in the world.

David Jeremiah wrote: "What is loneliness? Some describe it in physical terms. It's an empty feeling in the pit of one's stomach, almost to the point of nausea. Others describe it as an underlying anxiety, 'a big black pit.' Some say loneliness is a sharp ache in moments of grief or separation. For others it's a long period of stress that wears them down until they're discouraged and defeated."[1]

Lonely people, hurting people need someone to help them up. To encourage them, to support them, to let them know they're not alone. Who are the helpers, the comforters for the times when we're bleeding and need a transfusion of love?

We can talk about God being our Comforter, but that doesn't absolve us of our responsibility. He has given us a special assignment. The Apostle Paul said: "Praise be to the God and Father of our Lord Jesus Christ, the Father of compassion and the God of all comfort, who comforts us in all our troubles, so that we can comfort those in any trouble with the comfort we ourselves have received from God" (2 Corinthians 1:3–4).

We don't have to be psychologists or trained counselors or ministers to be comforters. At some time we are all called to be comforters. Even a child can comfort with a pat or a dog with a lick.

Are We Approachable?

Does someone who is hurting feel free to tell us their problem, to cry on our shoulders, if necessary, or to ask for help? Or do we change the subject, tell a joke, or quote a Bible verse to make everything better?

Teri was a young bride when she invited Phyllis, an older Christian career woman, to have lunch. Teri was very disturbed and needed help. Phyllis, on the other hand, was someone who faced many problems every day in her business and brushed them off with positive affirmations. Instead of being open to Teri, she replied with all of the clichés, such as, "Just turn a lemon into lemonade," or "Let's look at the bright side." There's nothing wrong with those concepts, except that Teri needed someone to help her up, not give her platitudes that made her feel guilty for being discouraged.

If people feel safe disclosing their problems to us, most likely we are approachable. Confidentiality is the essence of being trusted. If our non-Christian friends don't feel that they can trust us with their hurts, we may never be able to approach them with their need for Jesus Christ.

Are You Available?

"When I lost my husband, I saw people I had known for years pretend not to see me in the market, or walk on the other side of the street if they saw me coming. I felt like a leper." This is how a woman described her feeling of isolation when she needed conversation and comfort. Deliberate avoidance is practiced when we don't know what to say. It is an insensitive attitude toward a hurting person. Don't be afraid to approach a person in pain. If he or she doesn't want to talk about it, you'll know. Chances are, they want someone to listen. Inside, they may be like the Psalmist who cried, "Turn to me and be gracious to me, for I am lonely and afflicted" (Psalm 25:16).

Being available is difficult, because it takes time, but being sensitive to the small amounts of time we can give could reap large rewards in someone's life. It doesn't really matter what we say to comfort people during a time of suffering, it's our concern and availability that count.

When my wife's father died, her mother was left incapacitated by a stroke, confined to a wheelchair and limited in her speech. Friends and neighbors dropped by to comfort her. Those who comforted the most, said the least. They were widows themselves. All they did was put their arms around her and weep together briefly. But Mother was comforted. One day a group of college students came from the local college. They gathered around her on the floor—wall to wall—and accompanied by a guitar, they sang hymns. That was all.

Philip Yancey tells about a man who said nothing when he heard about a family tragedy, and yet spoke volumes. "A story is told about Beethoven, a man not known for social grace. Because of his deafness, he found conversation difficult and humiliating. When he heard of the death of a friend's son, Beethoven hurried to the house, overcome with grief. He had no words of comfort to offer. But he saw a piano in the room. For the next half hour he played the piano, pouring out his emotions in the most eloquent way he could. When he finished playing, he left. The friend later remarked that no one else's visit had meant so much."[2]

During the Persian Gulf War, Isaac Stern was playing in Tel Aviv with the symphony. Suddenly, sirens began to wail, alerting everyone to an incoming missile attack from Iraq. Afraid of the possibility of a poison gas attack, the government had issued gas masks to everyone. So in the middle of the concert, the people in the audience grabbed their masks and put them on. Everyone wore a mask, except the maestro. One cannot easily forget the picture that flashed across our television screens of Isaac Stern playing his heart out to an audience of faceless masks.

Being available is not a statement, it's an action.

Don't Add to the Hurt

Sometimes instead of helping the hurting, we hinder them. We may hurt others deliberately and sometimes inadvertently. Some churches are accused of "shooting their wounded." This may happen when all the blame for the break-up of a marriage is put upon one member of the couple. A child may go astray, and the parents are made to feel guilty. A businessman files for bankruptcy, and people begin to question his honesty. There are so many ways we can add to another's hurt.

Tony had taken a bad fall off a roof and broken his neck. For more than a week it was not known whether he would be completely paralyzed or not. He looked terrible as he lay in bed with metal pins through his skull and surrounded by sandbags, his face bruised and swollen. The family feared for their father's recovery and needed loving support themselves.

A daughter said,

> People from the church came to visit and the moment they saw Dad, the shock of his appearance made their stay very brief. They patted me on the shoulder and headed for the door as fast as they could. We had the impression that they came because it was the "thing to do."
>
> But there was one man who was not a Christian. He was a poor immigrant, not eloquent, but a man Dad had talked to about the Lord. He came in the room and simply said, "I know that your God will take care of you." He would look at Dad, pat his hand, and walk out. But he came every day, and always said the same thing. He comforted us, because he shared with us the faith we knew Dad had.

We flourish with kindness and shrivel with unkindness. Few Christians are deliberately unkind, but some do not realize the effect they may have by the look on their faces or the tone of their voices. Someone said, "The nicest thing we can do for our heavenly Father is to be kind to one of His children." How true that is. I know how grateful I am when someone is kind to one of my children.

Gossip is another way in which we hurt others. "May the absent always feel safe with us" is a motto to be remembered. Even in prayer meetings, gossip may be transmitted in the form of prayers.

We add to the hurt when we are critical. Criticism has a withering effect upon people, especially our children. They need guidance and correcting, but constant criticism will destroy their spirit and their ability to succeed.

Dr. James Dobson has probably helped more parents and teachers understand how to bring up their children in the way they should go than anyone in our current society. He wrote in his classic, *Dare to Discipline:* "Too often our parental instruction consists of a million 'don'ts' which are jammed down the child's throat. We should spend more time rewarding him for the behavior we do admire, even if our 'reward' is nothing more than a sincere compliment. Remembering the child's need for self-esteem and acceptance, the wise parent can satisfy those important longings while using them to teach valued concepts and behavior."[3]

In David's prayer for his son Solomon, he said, "Prayer also shall be made for him continually; and daily shall he be praised" (Psalm 72:15 KJV). What a great suggestion for parents! Pray continually and praise daily. Failure to do this will cause more damage than we may be able to repair.

Failure to encourage is one of the commonest ways to hurt other people. There are so many hurts that circumstances and the world inflict upon us, we need the constant reinforcement of encouragement.

My mother was one of my greatest encouragers. In my book *Facing Death,* I said, "Mother always told me to preach the gospel, and keep it simple. Two weeks before she went to be with the Lord she admonished me with the same words. I said, 'Mother, I'm going to preach His birth, death, and resurrection. I'll preach it until Jesus comes.'

"She squeezed my hand and said, 'I believe it.'

"What a blessing it is for parents to believe in their children."

Another way to hurt people is by being too busy. Too busy to notice their needs. Too busy to drop that note of comfort or encouragement or assurance of love. Too busy to listen when someone needs to talk. Too busy to simply care. When Alan Redpath was pastor at the Moody Church in Chicago, he had this saying on the wall of his study: "Beware of the barrenness of a busy life."

It's amazing how we can hurt others, especially those close to us. We see examples all the time of the subtle and not-so-subtle ways in which wives belittle husbands and vice versa. One incident was related to me about a woman who was constantly berating her husband about being a little overweight. They were having dinner at a home where there were other guests present. The hostess served the dessert, a delectable looking chocolate mousse. The wife looked at it, reached for the salt shaker which had remained on the table, and proceeded to douse her husband's dessert with the salt. "Now you won't be tempted," she announced smugly. I heard later that they had divorced.

One incident that greatly amused Ruth in her childhood was the time when two missionaries had to journey through Shanghai and stayed in the "Missionary Home," then run by two English ladies. Dr. Patterson, quite a large woman, was a medical doctor, and her husband was a slight, rather frail man. He was not very well, being allergic to certain foods that his wife knew he should not eat. The lady who ran the Home became increasingly indignant when she noticed that whenever anything particularly good was put before Mr. Patterson, his wife quickly removed it to her plate and ate it. Mr. Patterson had a great sense of humor. He noticed his hostess' growing indignation. One day when the dessert was served, he amused and gratified her as, with eyes twinkling, he gobbled it down before his wife could object, even though he knew it would make him sick and he would pay for it later!

A keen sense of humor helps us to overlook the unbecoming, understand the unconventional, tolerate the unpleasant, overcome the unexpected, and outlast the unbearable.

We never gain in life by hurting others. Sometimes we try to elevate our own insecure egos by degrading and belittling those around us. Yet this produces only a false sense of self-esteem.

The Bible teaches us to be more concerned about the needs and feelings of others than our own. We are to encourage and build self-confidence in our loved ones, friends, and associates. A true servant of God is someone who helps another succeed. "Therefore encourage one another and build each other up" (1 Thessalonians 5:11). Someone said, "You can never speak a fine word too soon, for you never know how soon it will be too late."

Bear One Another's Burdens

Bob Pierce was a man who knew what it was to bear another's burdens. He was one of the most remarkable men I have ever known, a great evangelical humanitarian, co-founder of Youth for Christ, founder of World Vision, and, later in his life, founder of Samaritan's Purse, which is now headed by my son, Franklin. I loved and admired this amazing man who was a friend of the "little" people, the forgotten, the hurting people who are unheard of and unsung except in the courts of Heaven.

He once told Franklin, "The only measurement I had in assessing what we should be involved in was 'Is this something Jesus would do? Something God would want done?' Ultimately it boiled down to something I wrote in my Bible on Kojedo Island: 'Let my heart be broken with the things that break the heart of God.'"

I remember one story about Dr. Bob Pierce that exemplified the ability to be a bearer of someone's burdens. "Borneo Bob" Williams was a missionary who started hundreds of churches in Kaliminatan, which is now a part of Indonesia. Dr. Bob was dying of leukemia, and, knowing that he only had a short time to live, he went to Kaliminatan to say goodbye to Borneo Bob. Here's the story:

> While he was there (in Kaliminatan), on his way down to the river, he noticed a girl lying on a bamboo mat and asked Bob Williams what she

was doing there. Bob Williams explained that she was dying of a form of cancer and had very few days to live. Dr. Bob's anger flared. "How come this girl is lying down there in the mud when she could be up there in that nice, clean clinic?" he stormed.

Borneo Bob explained that this girl was a jungle girl and preferred to be near the river where it was cooler, that she had specifically asked to be placed there for the day. Bob Pierce's heart broke. He went over to the girl, knelt down beside her, held her hand, and, rubbing her forehead, he prayed for her. After he prayed, she looked up and said something to him. He turned to Borneo Bob, who translated what she had said, explaining that with her disease and the unbearable pain she was unable to sleep and was dying, "If I could only sleep again, if I could only sleep again!" Bob Pierce began to cry, for he himself was dying of leukemia and had less than a year to live, and he knew what it was to be unable to sleep. He reached into his pocket and grabbed his bottle of sleeping pills. He gave it to Bob Williams and said, "You make sure she gets a good night's sleep from now on." Dr. Bob knew that he would have to go another ten days before he could get to Singapore and replace his medication—he knew that he would have to forfeit ten nights of sleep for this little girl.[4]

When the Good Samaritan found a man robbed, beaten, and left for dead, he didn't continue on his trip and "report the accident." He didn't call 911 and leave the scene, nor pay someone else to go back and care for the man. The Samaritan himself got involved.

He tenderly lifted the wounded body onto his own donkey and continued on the journey to Jericho. When he reached the city, he found a place to stay, and probably cared for the patient. The next day, he made arrangements with the innkeeper to pay all financial debts that the patient would incur.

That is what bearing one another's burdens is all about. It's so easy to give to a charity or a ministry and feel good about it. It's not so easy to provide the personal charity. It's easier to give to someone overseas than it is to take a casserole next door.

May God give us the sensitivity to recognize the needs of those around us and lend a helping hand.

Pray for Those Who Hurt

A simple prayer, a Scripture that has meant something to you, these can be a great comfort to a hurting person. The Word of God is where we "find grace to help us in our time of need" (Hebrews 4:16).

Rather than giving personal advice, how much better would it be for Christians to share God's loving promises. It is a comfort to hear the words of God in times of stress. If you have problems remembering proper verses, there are some fine little booklets that you can carry in your pocket or purse which give verses for many different situations.

I remember a time in my late teens when I had a case of "puppy love," which was very real to the "puppy." We were even talking about marriage, although we were both much too young. However, she felt the Lord was leading her to another young man who was one of my best friends. I felt like my heart would break, so I went to a clergyman friend of mine for help. He turned to 2 Corinthians 1:3–4, 6. The passage not only tells us we are comforted in our trials, but that our trials can equip us to comfort others. I was comforted by those words of the Apostle Paul, just as many others have been. The Lord knew that young romance was not His will for my life, and that I would find in Ruth the perfect wife for me.

Pious Platitudes Don't Help

An overdose of Scripture at the wrong time may do more harm than good. Hearing verses on "counting trials as joy," in the midst of someone's difficulty can be like throwing gasoline on a fire or rubbing salt in a wound. A person needs time to assimilate what has happened, to assess the physical or emotional damage. Hearing something like "God must love you very much to put you through this," is not the bandage a person needs.

We need to build trust through listening, through caring in a tangible way. Perhaps your friend doesn't know the Lord, and you feel awkward bringing up the subject of God as the one who comforts perfectly. You might say, "I wish I could do more for you. When you feel like it, let me take you to lunch."

If you cannot find examples in your life that might relate to a sufferer, the perfect example is Jesus. He experienced people who betrayed Him. He knows what it is like to suffer. You can explain how your hurting friend can have a relationship with Him. Pray for the right words, pray for the way to comfort. Pray, don't preach.

Who Are the Best Comforters?

Those who have suffered most are often best able to comfort others. I know of pastors whose ministries have been enriched by suffering. Through their trials they have learned to live through the difficulties of people in their church family.

Someone who has experienced the same sort of pain is the one who can minister best. However, to say, "I know how you feel," is usually an unnecessary and frequently unwelcome approach. No one knows exactly how another feels. One couple who had lost their oldest son in an accident tried to comfort another couple whose child had died after lingering for many months. The comfort was only in the loss, not in the circumstances. Better to say, "I don't know how you feel, I can't really put myself in your shoes, but this is how I was comforted . . ." Our sufferings may be hard to bear, but they teach us lessons which, in turn, equip and enable us to help others.

Only God's spirit can truly mend a broken heart, but we can be a part of the healing process. We don't have to be a priest or preacher, a trained counselor or psychiatrist to be a comforter. We just need to be available, as Christ is available to us. When He was comforting His disciples before He left them, they were confused, questioning, and frightened. He said, "Now is your time of grief, but I will see you again and you will rejoice, and no one will take away your joy" (John 16:22).

Our attitude toward suffering should not be, "Grit your teeth and bear it," hoping it will pass as quickly as possible. Our goal should be to learn all we can from our personal problems, so that we can fulfill a ministry of comfort, just as Jesus did. "Because he himself suffered when he was tempted, he is able to help those who are being tempted" (Hebrews 2:18).

We are surrounded by hurting people. Some may wear a plastic mask, but beneath the mask is a scarred soul. Are we approachable and available, even when we may be hurting, too? God does not comfort us to make us comfortable, but to make us comforters.

Why, you do not even know what will happen tomorrow. What is your life? You are a mist that appears for a little while and then vanishes.

James 4:14

CHAPTER FOURTEEN

Schoolroom for Heaven

IN MILAN, ITALY, a city known for its art, there is an impressive cathedral that has some significant words inscribed around its entrance. To the right of the door is a sculptured wreath of roses. Underneath it says: "All that pleases us is only for a moment." On the left is a sculptured cross of thorns with these words beneath: "All that troubles us is only for a moment." Over the top are the words, "Nothing is important but that which is eternal."

Our pleasures are so brief. The vacation is over too soon, the fashionable suit wears out, the ice cream cone melts. Likewise, we may believe that our pain will never stop, the pressure in our lives will have no end. But someday, both the pleasures and the pain of life on earth will be over.

Someone said, "Live each day as if it's your last. It may be." A group of people were sitting on a bench at the Los Angeles airport. They were waiting for the shuttle to take them to the parking lot where they had left their cars. Suddenly the brakes gave way on the bus they were to board, and it plunged into the benches, killing one woman and injuring others. The husband of the dead woman, who had been sitting beside her, jumped clear and was saved.

I sometimes wonder, when I hear of sudden fatalities, if the victims were prepared for death. Every day we hear of such happenings. People who in an instant of time are transferred from this life to the next. The

Bible has much to say about the brevity of life and the necessity of preparing for eternity. We all need to prepare for the final exams in the schoolroom for Heaven.

I Don't Want to Think About It

When Scarlet O'Hara wanted to avoid a decision, she would say, "I'll think about it tomorrow." Too many Christians avoid thinking about death, because somehow they think the subject is unpleasant. Death is Satan's weapon, for he uses the thought of it to bring confusion and fear into the hearts of those facing it.

We need to remember that death is not of God, it is part of the curse sin brought on this world and which has the universe in its grasp. The good news is that for Christians death is not final. It is another phase of life. When a Christian dies, he moves immediately into a glorious eternal life. The Bible says, "Death has been swallowed up in victory" (1 Corinthians 15:54). I believe that if people paid more attention to death, eternity, and judgment, there would be more holy living on earth.

Surrounded by the violence and devastation of our present age, we see death on every hand, but it never seems real until we stare it in the face ourselves, or hold the hand of someone who is slipping into eternity.

The Christian knows he has eternal life, "And this is the testimony: God has given us eternal life, and this life is in his Son. He who has the Son has life; he who does not have the Son of God does not have life" (1 John 5:11–12).

Those who do not have Jesus Christ in their hearts will spend eternity separated from God. The Bible has a great deal to say about Hell, although until recent times the subject has all but disappeared from our modern pulpits. However, it was reported in a major newsmagazine that Hell is making a major comeback in American thinking.

A poll showed that of the younger Americans (between the ages of eighteen and twenty-nine), 84 percent believed in Heaven and 71 percent believed in Hell. Older Americans, aged fifty and up, were not so definite; 74 percent believed in Heaven, and 54 percent believed in Hell. It was said that three out of five Americans now believe in Hell. This is a decided increase over similar polls taken in previous years. Why this comeback? Martin Marty, a chronicler of American religious trends, said, "If people really believed in hell . . . they'd be out rescuing people."[1]

Many who are cynical about the Christian faith think deeply about life and eternity. The same Gallup poll revealed that 61 percent of those who claimed to have no religion believed they were going to Heaven and 83 percent of those who attend church believed they would be in Heaven.

We have seen thousands accept Christ for the first time who have been attending church for years. It has been said that being born in a garage does not make you an automobile, or, as Corrie ten Boom so colorfully said, "A mouse in a cookie jar isn't a cookie."

The schoolroom for Heaven has some wonderful classes and inspiring teachers. Some of the courses should be required for credit.

Is Your House in Order?

If we accept that someday, sooner or later, we are going to face death, should we be making preparations while we are living? Hezekiah, a king of Israel, was a very sick man when Isaiah the prophet went to him and said, "Put your house in order, because you are going to die" (Isaiah 38:1).

I am not a prophet, but that was certainly good advice. Too many have neglected to put their houses in order, and as a result, those who are left have had burdens added to heartache. From a practical standpoint, if we have any earthly possessions, have we made our wills? How old are they? A will should be updated every few years as children grow and circumstances change. When my father-in-law, Dr. Nelson Bell, died, his estate was in such order, with documents neatly filed in folders and explicit instructions for the distribution of his possessions, that there was no confusion. He was a great inspiration to me both in life and in his preparation for death.

How much time do we have? King Hezekiah was given a fifteen-year extension on his life. Many of us are given reprieves. The doctor may say, "You'll probably live another twenty years or more." God may not be finished with us yet. But even the best of medical knowledge cannot determine the days of our lives.

The Scripture teaches us that God knows the exact moment when each person is to die. "All the days ordained for me were written in your book before one of them came to be" (Psalm 139:16). And Job 14:5 reads, "Man's days are determined; you have decreed the number of his months and have set limits he cannot exceed."

Our days are numbered. One of the primary goals in our lives should be to prepare for the day on which our number is up. The legacy we leave is not just in our possessions, but in the quality of our lives. What preparations should we be making now? The greatest waste in all of our earth, which cannot be recycled or reclaimed, is our waste of the time God has given us each day.

Golden Minutes of Opportunity

We are told to "Be very careful, then, how you live—not as unwise but as wise, making the most of every opportunity, because the days are evil" (Ephesians 5:15–16). If we knew this was our last day on earth, what opportunities would we use? Call a friend who was hurting? Say "I'm sorry" to someone we've slighted? Encourage a young person who was struggling with a school or job? Tell our husband or wife, parents or children, how much we love them? Most important, would we tell someone about Jesus Christ and how they could have eternal life through Him? How would we spend those final twenty-four hours?

One woman who knew the exact time of her death was Velma Barfield. Velma was a convicted murderer, a woman who had committed heinous crimes while under the addiction of many different drugs. She was in a security prison, awaiting trial, when she heard a radio evangelist who said that no matter what she had done, Jesus loved her and wanted to come into her heart and give her a new spirit. Although she had heard those words all of her life, for the first time she truly understood them. Velma became a new creature in Christ while waiting for her death sentence.

For the next six years, through the love of people who cared, Velma grew in her knowledge of God. It was during this time that she wrote my wife Ruth, and they began to correspond. Our daughter Anne, who lives in the same city where the prison was located, went to visit Velma, and she was present at her execution in 1984.

Velma Barfield was a great influence for good on many people in and outside of prison. Anne told us, "On three separate occasions Velma told me, 'If I had the choice of living free on the outside without my Lord, or living on death row with Him, I would choose death row.' As November 2 (the day of her execution) drew closer, her increasing desire to see the face of her beloved Lord took the sting of fear away."[2]

Anne and Ruth told me that Velma had been praying for a year and a half for a revival to take place within the prison population. A month after her execution I led a service at the prison. And 210 inmates and staff members responded to the invitation to receive Christ. Afterward I walked into the very cellblock where Velma had been housed for three years. I found the inmates, who did not know that I was coming, with their Bibles open, watching a television broadcast of one of our Crusades. Velma's witness, even after her death, continued to permeate the place where she lived. Today a woman's Bible class carries on—a result of Velma's life.

What an Opportunity!

I didn't breeze through school. Studying was hard for me, and exam time was terrifying. But when I got my diploma, it looked just like the one that the valedictorian received. Perhaps his had a few more ribbons on it, but I graduated just the same.

Life is a glorious schoolroom to prepare us for graduation. It may be very tough, and we may fail some of the tests. But all the preparation is worth it to get the rewards at the end.

Fanny Cosby was a woman who was given a difficult course. She was blinded in infancy as the result of negligence on the part of a doctor. To compensate for the loss of her sight, she keenly developed other senses, and she became one of the greatest hymn writers ever. One of her most beautiful hymns, "I Shall See Him Face to Face," might never have been written were it not for the fact that she had never looked upon green fields, an evening sunset, or her mother's face. It was the loss of her vision that helped her gain her remarkable spiritual discernment.

The Living Bible says, "These troubles and suffering of ours are, after all, quite small and won't last very long. Yet this short time of distress will result in God's richest blessing upon us forever and ever!" (2 Corinthians 4:17).

I can still remember how long school seemed to be. Would summer vacation ever come? Would finals ever be over? Summer always came, and finals always ended. Life is just a schoolroom with a glorious opportunity to prepare us for eternity. If we fail in this, though we succeed in everything else, our life will have been a failure.

What Is Death?

The question, "What is life all about?" is frequently heard, especially by young people who are just beginning their lives. Seldom do we hear people ask, "What is death all about?" And yet one follows the other. In *King Lear,* Shakespeare said, "Fear of death is worse than death itself."

I have faced death many times, and my reactions have not always been the same. One time I had an operation that almost ended me. I knew this could be serious, so before they wheeled me into the operating room I called two of my closest friends and gave them instructions about my wife, my family, and my ministry. Ruth had gone to be with the children, and I tried to keep the seriousness of the situation from her. Whether this was right or wrong, I don't know. At least I'm living to tell the story.

I remember alternating between two feelings. First, the complete peace I had, knowing that I would be with my Lord Jesus Christ, and second, the fear of leaving my loved ones. I certainly thought I was going to die.

But the Lord wasn't finished with me. Death for a Christian is not an accident. The Bible says, "Precious in the sight of the Lord is the death of his saints" (Psalm 116:15 KJV).

How could there be anything precious about death? When a child or a young person dies, the tragedy seems so much greater than for someone who has lived a long life. People begin to question why God would allow such a thing. Do you think that God, whose "eye is on the sparrow" and who knows the very numbers of the hairs on our heads, would turn His back on one of His children in the hour of peril?

Paul lived most of his life on the brink of death. When his tired, bruised body began to weaken under the punishment he received, he said triumphantly, "We know that if the earthly tent we live in is destroyed, we have a building from God, an eternal house in heaven, not built by human hands" (2 Corinthians 5:1).

One of my dear friends had a son who was killed at the age of eighteen in a plane crash. On his gravestone are the words, "To me, to live is Christ and to die is gain" (Philippians 1:21).

What is death? For the Christian, death is a friend rather than an enemy. It is another step on the pathway to Heaven rather than a leap into some dark unknown.

How Do We Know There Is Life After Death?

If we have never died, how do we know there is hope for eternal life? Can we be certain there is life after death? Yes! There is one great fact that gives the Christian assurance in the face of death: *the resurrection of Jesus Christ*. This truth is the basis for our belief, for our living, and for our hope. The resurrection of Christ is the central event of all history.

One of the great biblical scholars was my friend, Wilbur Smith. He wrote:

> If you or I should say to any group of friends that we expected to die, either by violence or naturally, at a certain time, but that, three days after

death, we would rise again, we would be quietly taken away by friends and confined to an institution until our minds became clear and sound again.

This would be right, for only a foolish man would go around talking about rising from the dead on the third day, only a foolish man, unless he knew that this was going to take place, and no one in the world has ever known that about himself except One Christ, the Son of God.[3]

Because Christ rose from the dead, we know that sin and death and Satan have been defeated. Because Christ rose from the dead, we know there is life after death, and that if we belong to Him we need not fear death. Jesus said, "I am the resurrection and the life. He who believes in me will live, even though he dies; and whoever lives and believes in me will never die" (John 11:25–26).

Christians do not die. They go on living in another realm; a place so wonderful that I can only try to describe it in the next chapter. In fact, that's what life after death is: another chapter in our personal biography, written by "Jesus, the author and perfecter of our faith" (Hebrews 12:2).

Someone has said that death is not a period, but a comma in the story of life.

Death Is the Coronation of a Christian

Once there was a prince who went into a foreign land and fought a fierce enemy. He conquered the foe who was a threat to his country and returned home to be crowned and honored for what he had done. It was a magnificent coronation!

The Bible says that as long as we are here on earth, we are strangers in a foreign land. There are enemies to be conquered before we return home. This world is not our home; our citizenship is in Heaven.

There is a time coming when all Christians will stand before God and give an account of the way they used the gifts God has given them. It will be a time of truth for all believers. There are different crowns that are available, and these are given according to the quality of work we have done on earth.

For those who have endured trials and suffering with patience, there is a special crown of life. James 1:12 says, "Blessed is the man who perseveres under trial, because when he has stood the test, he will receive the crown of life."

For those who believe the only rewards worth desiring are measured by what money can buy, there will be surprises in Heaven to see who will receive some of the special crowns.

Death Is a Rest

God's people do not enjoy much rest here on earth. In recent years we have heard the term "burn-out" more often. Some accomplish more in a few years than others do in a lifetime, but someday their toil will come to an end. The Bible says, "There remains, then, a Sabbath-rest for the people of God; for anyone who enters God's rest also rests from his own work, just as God did from his" (Hebrews 4:9–10).

We may get some rest on earth, but heavenly rest will be so refreshing that we will never feel that exhaustion of mind and body we so frequently experience now. I'm really looking forward to that.

Death Is a Departure

Ruth and I have said good-bye many times in our life together. Sometimes we were separated by oceans and time differences. When I leave her there is always a tinge of sadness, because she is the one I love more than any other person on earth. But we part in the sure hope that we shall meet again.

The word *departure* literally means to pull up anchor and set sail. Everything that happens prior to death is a preparation for the final voyage. Death marks the beginning, not the end. It is our journey to God.

The believing Christian has hope as he stands at the grave of a loved one who is with the Lord, for he knows that the separation is not forever.

It is a glorious truth that those who are in Christ never see each other for the last time.

A poet said:

> Wish me "Bon Voyage!"
> As you do a friend
> Whose joyous visit finds its happy end.
> And bid me both "a Dieu!"
> And "au revoir!"
> Since, though I come no more,
> I shall be waiting there to greet you,
> At His Door.[4]

Death Is a Transition

When former President John Quincy Adams was eighty years old, he was met by an old friend who shook his trembling hand and said, "Good morning. How is John Quincy Adams today?"

The retired chief executive looked at him for a moment and then said, "John Quincy Adams himself is quite well, sir, quite well, but the house in which he lives at present is becoming dilapidated. It is tottering upon its foundations. Time and the seasons have almost destroyed it. Its roof is pretty worn out. Its walls are much shattered, and it crumbles with every wind. The old tenement is becoming almost uninhabitable, and I think that John Quincy Adams will have to move out of it soon. But he himself is well, sir, quite well!"

It was not long afterward that he had his second and fatal stroke, and John Quincy Adams moved from his "shaky tabernacle," as he called it, to his "house not made with hands."

To the Christian, death is the exchanging of a tent for a building. If our earthly tent is disintegrating, or if it has many structural imperfections, someday we will be given the title to a home that will never deteriorate.

Joni Eareckson Tada will walk and run again. Helen Keller will see and hear. The child who died of cancer will have rosy cheeks and a strong body. The man crippled with arthritis will stand upright. The woman who was disfigured in a fiery car crash will have a face without blemish. Everything that we try to change, paint, and correct on earth will have a glorious new look. And yet we will know each other in our heavenly bodies!

Death Is Different for the Believer

C. S. Lewis said, "I have seen great beauty of spirit in some who were great sufferers. I have seen men, for the most part, grow better not worse with advancing years, and I have seen the last illness produce treasures of fortitude and meekness from most unpromising subjects."[5]

There is something decidedly different about the death of a believer. No wonder Paul said, "I desire to depart and be with Christ, which is better by far" (Philippians 1:23).

I have talked to doctors and nurses who have held the hands of dying people, and they say there is often as much difference between the death of a Christian and a non-Christian as there is between Heaven and Hell.

The words said by dying saints before they went to Heaven have inspired me. My grandmother sat up in her bed, smiled, and said, "I see Jesus and His hand outstretched to me. And there is Ben, and he has both of his eyes and both of his legs." (Ben, my grandfather, had lost a leg and an eye at the battle of Gettysburg.)

John Knox said, "Live in Christ, die in Christ, and the flesh need not fear death."

John Wesley said, "The best of all is, God is with us."

When Joseph Everett was dying, he said, "Glory! Glory! Glory!" and he continued exclaiming glory for over twenty-five minutes. What do you suppose he was experiencing?

Victor Hugo said, "The nearer I approach to the end, the plainer I hear around me the immortal symphonies of the worlds which invite me."

The writer of "Rock of Ages," Augustus Toplady, was triumphant as he lay dying at the age of thirty-eight. "I enjoy Heaven already in my soul," he said, "my prayers are all converted into praises."

The Rev. and Mrs. R. Porteous were taken prisoners by Chinese communist bandits in 1931, and led to a lonely spot on top of a hill where they were to be executed. The leader said, "This is the place." The executioner took a long knife from its holder and raised it above the necks of the courageous couple. Certain death seemed imminent. However, instead of cringing and begging for mercy, the couple began to sing. The bandits stared open-mouthed as they heard this hymn:

> Face to face with Christ, my Savior,
> Face to face—what will it be?
> When with rapture I behold him,
> Jesus Christ who died for me.

These two saintly souls were ready for death and thought that would be their last song. But to their surprise, no order was given. The executioner returned the knife to its place, and the couple was released. Subsequently, they told the story of the perfect peace that the Lord Jesus gave to them in the face of certain death.

Jesus Gave Us the Key

John Milton said, "Death is the golden key that opens the palace of eternity." What is that place like? Is Heaven worth dying for?

One hour of eternity, one moment with the Lord, will make us utterly forget a lifetime of desolations. Horatius Bonar

CHAPTER FIFTEEN

No More Troubles

HE WAS JUST a little boy, only ten years old, but Russell Davis knew what it was to live a life of pain. For four years he fought a battle with cancer. One Saturday, when he was back in the hospital again, he wrote this note to his best friend:

> Dear Brian. How are you doing? I'm alright in the hospital but a little sleepy. I know that you worry about me some but don't worry too much. Also if it will help you feel better you can come see me if you have time.
>
> When I die, if I do soon, don't worry 'cause I'll be somewhere special in Heaven. And sooner than I know it you'll be up in Heaven with me 'cause a thousand years on earth is a minute in Heaven.
>
> I know you'll miss me when I'm gone but just accept it like you did with your uncle. My mom will give you something of mine so you can remember me always. So don't worry too much. Love, Russell.

Three days later, Russell asked for a sip of water and said, "I love you, Mom. I love you, Dad." And he went home to be with the Lord. Some people write better sermons when they die than others do in a lifetime of speaking.

We often look at a child or a young person and wonder why they weren't allowed to live out a normal life span on earth. I believe God prepares some of his precious young ones in order that they may have an influence on their peers at an age when they are forming the direction of their lives. The Bible says, "His loved ones are very precious to him and he does not lightly let them die" (Psalm 116:15 TLB).

We wonder, how can there be anything precious about death? God knows that after we've served our purpose here there is something much greater waiting for us. The younger God takes one of His children, the more dramatically it points people to the reality of Christ.

Where Is Heaven?

Heaven is a place, not just an experience. We hear of so many things being heavenly, from a chocolate soufflé to an exotic island. But the real Heaven is our eternal home.

Jesus said, "I am going there to prepare a place for you. And if I go . . . I will come back and take you to be with me that you also may be where I am" (John 14:2–3). That place is beyond anything we have on earth or anything man can build. Heaven is "my Father's house." Before Jesus went to the cross, He gathered His disciples in the upper room and talked about a home. He said, "In my Father's house are many rooms" (John 14:2). In the King James Version, it says "many mansions." This does not mean an imposing house, but a resting place. Heaven is a place of rest. If I tell the Lord I'm tired when I arrive in His house, He'll say, "Rest, Billy." God rested on the seventh day of Creation, so it is not incompatible with His will to tell us to rest. But there will be activity, too. My idea of Heaven is working forever and never getting tired. Heaven will not be an eternal Sunday afternoon nap.

When we are young we may long to get away from home and be out on our own. We want freedom from parental rules and restrictions. But when the storms of life flatten us, we may yearn to go back to the security of home. The home of our memories may not exist, or the safety we once knew in that place may be gone. Heaven will give us security and safety forever.

Some believers are lying on hospital beds today. Some may be suffering from terrible diseases or be in prisons or labor camps. They long for home, where they may find relief from their pain and a new sense of love in their lives. The home and the love that is waiting for them is Jesus Christ Himself, and because of Him, Heaven at last and forever!

When death stares us in the face, our life after death takes on new importance. Phil Manly, the chaplain of the huge USC Medical Center in Los Angeles, has hundreds of stories about the harvest of souls at hospitals. He said, "A fifty-eight-year-old lady with cancer, whose life nearly ended twice during a medical crisis, asked the Lord to change her into His image; another young man who was terrified upon learning that he had AIDS, asked to speak with the Chaplain and received the Lord that same evening; a young man and his wife received the Lord in the burn ward. He had attempted to set an individual's car on fire as an act of revenge and ended up badly burned himself."

All of us must prepare to meet God while we are still living. Someday everyone will stand before His throne and give an account of himself or herself. The saddest words I can ever imagine would be to hear the Lord say, "I never knew you. Away from me" (Matthew 7:23).

Beautiful Home and Gardens

When spring comes to our mountain home, my wife heads for the garden. She has always kept a home of comfort and beauty for our family. When I am in yet another hotel room in some city around the world, I often think of our mountain home, filled with a lifetime of memories and love.

Imagine some of the most beautiful places in the world. Switzerland when the sun breaks over the snow-capped peaks and spills onto the slopes filled with wildflowers. A crystal clear lake, nestled among pine trees. A beach with white sand and the gentle lapping of warm Caribbean waters. A night in the desert west with a million stars against a velvet backdrop. An autumn day on a quiet road in New England. An easy chair, a good book, a cup of hot chocolate, and a glowing fire when the snow is falling at home.

Heaven will be more than that, because it is the Father's house, and He is a God of beauty. The same hand that made the beauty of this world has a more beautiful place prepared for us.

Man has polluted so much of our earth, but in Heaven there will be no environmental concerns. The water will be pure, the air clean, and there will be no need for landfills or recycled paper and cans.

In Revelation, when John caught a glimpse of Heaven, the only thing he could think to compare it to was a bride on her wedding day. I have three daughters and two daughters-in-law, and every one was a beautiful bride, but their beauty was just a dim reflection of Heaven.

If we are amazed and thrilled when we view some of the beauty the Lord gave us on earth, I'm sure we are in for some wonderful surprises in Heaven.

Happiness Is Heaven

I know many beautiful homes that are unhappy. If we look around us, or look within us, we know that we are basically living on an unhappy planet. Stand on any street corner in the large cities of the world and watch faces. When we get to Heaven, all the elements that made for unhappiness on earth will be gone. Think of a place where there is no sin, no sorrow, no insecurities, no quarrels, no selfishness, no racism, no misunderstandings, no hurt feelings, no worries, no pain, no sickness, no suffering, no death.

Heaven will be filled with music and song. Its citizens will sing a "new song," giving glory to Jesus Christ, who was slain and redeemed "men for God from every tribe and language and people and nation" (Revelation 5:9).

We are told that a mighty chorus will sing, "Hallelujah! For our Lord God Almighty reigns" (Revelation 19:6). Handel's Messiah sung by the greatest choirs on earth cannot compare with the heavenly chorus. When Bev Shea sings at our Crusades, as he has since the beginning, I am blessed as no other singer blesses me. Heaven will resound with voices like his.

No Boredom

Heaven will be a place where we have work to do. It may be the kind of work we have never experienced on earth. No frustrations, no freeways, no failure or fatigue. Cliff Barrows, our song director, and Bev Shea, our special soloist, have been with me for forty years. They occasionally tease me by saying that when we get to Heaven, I'll be out of work, but they won't!

Have you ever done anything that was so exhilarating, so rewarding, that you hoped it would never end? It's been said that no work is so wearisome as doing nothing. In Heaven our work will be stimulating and rewarding.

In Revelation 22:3, John wrote: "His servants will serve him." Each one of us will be given some task that we will enjoy doing. Some may be the cooks who prepare heavenly dishes, some may play with the children. Perhaps we will be called upon to tend the gardens or polish the rainbows. Our imaginations are limitless. Whatever we do, the Bible says we will serve Him. Just think—loving the work you are doing and never getting tired!

The Ultimate Family Reunion

Have you ever been in a strange place and had the joy of seeing a familiar face? No one who enters the Father's house will feel lonely or strange, for our friends will be there. We may be very surprised by whom we meet.

My wife is fond of the following little poem she picked up somewhere. She has no idea who wrote it, or where it comes from.

When you get to Heaven
You will doubtless view
Many whose presence there
Will be a shock to you.
Do not look around
Do not even stare

Doubtless there'll be many
Surprised to see you there.

If you are a believer, you will see those friends and family who accepted Christ. Our family reunion will have all the people from the Bible you always wanted to know. The Old and New Testament saints will be there to greet you and answer some of those questions you always wanted to ask. We won't have to rush or stand in line, for we will have all of eternity to enjoy.

The Head of the House

God's house will be happy because Christ will be there. Life with Christ is endless love; without Him it is a loveless end. In Revelation 22 we are told that we "will see his face." We have looked at paintings and seen movies that have tried to depict the face and body of Jesus. No one knows what He looks like, except those believers who are now with Him.

Have you ever been in a crowd and stretched to see some important dignitary? Have you been at a meeting or a retreat where you hoped the speaker would recognize you? There will be millions of Christians in Heaven, but Jesus will know each one of us personally, and we shall know Him in a deeper way than ever before. "Now we see but a poor reflection as in a mirror; then we shall see face to face. Now I know in part; then I shall know fully, even as I am fully known" (1 Corinthians 13:12).

God knows our hearts. Nothing is hidden from His sight. We are "fully known" by Him, but many times He seems so remote from us. He is the "God who is there," but He does not seem real. In Heaven we will know Him in all of His glory.

But I Love Earth

There is nothing wrong with loving life, in fact we should enjoy it to the hilt. In Heaven, we will enjoy everything more. Paul said, "For to me, to live is Christ and to die is gain" (Philippians 1:21).

What will we gain? I can only imagine that whatever we loved on earth will be magnified in its pleasure in Heaven.

We may not be married in Heaven. Some of us who love our wives or husbands very much may find that sad, but the more I think about the promises of Heaven, the more I believe whatever God has in store for us will be unbelievably more joyous, more delightful, and more wonderful than what we now enjoy.

I trust Jesus with my eternal tomorrows and know that He will solve all of the questions we have now. We will be able to understand one another, for there will be one universal language, the language of love, that will enable us to talk freely with people who lived in other earth countries. The "communication gap" will be closed.

Night comes on earth, filled with darkness and peril. In many cities on our planet we are warned not to go out on the streets at night. But in Heaven, there is no night. We will not need to sleep, because on earth sleep is to restore our strength. But in Heaven there will be no energy drains, so sleep will not be necessary.

Night is a time when many crimes are committed. In Heaven, evil is gone and the light that will surround us will be a reflection of the light of the world, Jesus Christ.

Will we miss our life on earth? We won't even remember it! Isaiah said: "Behold, I will create new heavens and a new earth. *The former things will not be remembered, nor will they come to mind*" (65:17, emphasis added).

Heaven Is a City

When the Book of Revelation was written, cities were places of refuge, companionship, and security. Today, they speak of crowding, crime, and corruption. Heaven as a city is the former description, not our modern concept of a city.

Revelation pictures Heaven as a city, the new Jerusalem. This is the city where we will live forever. It will be large enough to house all believers without being crowded.

For centuries women have loved jewels. The New Jerusalem will have gates of pearl, streets of gold, and the foundations of the city walls will be like a display case at Tiffany's, multiplied many times in their magnificence.

On Main Street in New Jerusalem, the Tree of Life will be growing. Everyone will have access to it. John describes the Tree of Life as "bearing twelve crops of fruit, yielding its fruit every month. And the leaves of the tree are for the healing of the nations" (Revelation 22:2). The Tree of Life will accomplish what the United Nations, heads of state, ambassadors, and peace-making missions have never been able to do. Harmony will reign in Heaven.

My wife and I do not like cities. We do not care for "mansions." We love log houses, on the primitive side, with simple comforts. Could it be that each will see through his or her own eyes, differently from others—what will look like a jeweled city to some will appear to others like log cabins scattered over mountains and coves?

The struggle to support our families has been increasingly difficult. Inflation, taxes, high insurance rates, and many other drains on our personal finances have had damaging effects on our lives. Money will not be a worry in Heaven, in fact, there won't be any. The Bible tells us to "drink without cost from the spring of the water of life" (Revelation 21:6). We will not work for wages, but for the sheer joy of creating and producing.

Full Potential

One of man's greatest insecurities is his fear of failure. Life is not a series of successes, for we fail in employment, business, personal relationships, and professional endeavors. In Heaven we will never fail. We will succeed in whatever we undertake, for "no longer will there be any curse" (Revelation 22:3). The person who never got an "A" on his report card, or a parking place with his name on it, will be just as important as the corporate executive or the concert star.

Spiritually, we will be close to God, for His people will live in His presence and praise Him continually. There will be no "dry periods" in our spiritual experience, for we shall live joyfully forever with the Lord.

I think that when we reach Heaven, we will have our potentials fully realized. When God is allowed to have full control of our lives, we will know the kind of people we can really be. On earth we use only a small part of our potential, but in Heaven we will have our God-given talents released.

Together Forever

An unknown poet wrote:

> In this dark world of sin and pain
> We only meet to part again;
> But when we reach the heavenly shore,
> We there shall meet to part no more.
> The joy that we shall see that day
> Shall chase our present griefs away.

All the glories of Heaven will be multiplied because of the people we will know there. On earth, whenever we have a great experience, we want to share it with someone else. Won't it be thrilling to share Heaven with our children, our parents, our friends, and all of the great people who have gone before us?

The Final Victory

In this present world we are in the midst of a battlefield. We can understand Paul when he spoke of being harassed at every turn—conflicts on the outside, fears within (2 Corinthians 7:5).

In the battle of life, we are in a wrestling match, not only with flesh and blood, but also with principalities and powers, with the rulers of darkness and spiritual wickedness. We wonder if we will ever be "on top of it." All children of God will find songs of victory at the end. All war-weary soldiers will be able to rest.

Whenever I see an athlete come from behind and take the gold medal, or a team that is the underdog score the winning points with only seconds to go, I think of what Paul said. "I have fought the good fight, I have finished the race, I have kept the faith. Now there is in store for me the crown of righteousness, which the Lord, the righteous Judge, will award to me on that day" (2 Timothy 4:7–8).

Many stories are told and books written about aliens visiting our planet. Christians are really aliens who land for a while on this earth and then go to their true home. In the days before his death, Paul looked forward with great anticipation to the time when he would finally receive his crown of glory. We should live as Paul did, serving faithfully and anticipating Christ's return, whether that be to catch us up to be with Him in the clouds, or whether we go to see Him before that.

A few more days may dawn and darken and we will know the unending day. A few brief years, or brief moments, and we shall enter that eternal city, sit in the shadow of the Tree of Life, and drink the crystal clear water. We have only had a foretaste on earth of what it means to love and be loved.

Are you ready? I know that I am prepared to meet the Master, not because of preaching or books, but because one day, many years ago, I confessed my sins and asked the Lord to come into my life and make of me what He wanted.

That is one decision no one will regret, either in this life or in the one to come. "I consider that our present sufferings are not worth comparing with the glory that will be revealed in us" (Romans 8:18).

A Voice from Beyond

We were in Seattle for a Crusade after the end of the war in the Persian Gulf. President Bush had proclaimed March 7, 1991, as a day of celebration for the liberation of Kuwait and the end of hostilities in the Gulf. We had invited a lady to speak to the thousands of people at that meeting. I'm sure she must have been nervous, but she told a story that touched us all.

Here is part of what Mrs. Shirley Lansing said:

I come with a story about my son, John Kendall Morgan, Warrant Officer One, United States Army, serving in Operation Desert Storm. Jack committed his life to Jesus when he was young. . . . At the time it didn't seem terribly important, but it was. A few weeks ago, two officers came to our door and told us they regretted to inform us that our son had been killed in action when his helicopter was shot down by hostile Iraqi fire.

When Jack got on the airplane to leave for Saudi Arabia, he gave Lisa, his fiancé, a bride's book, so they could be planning the wedding. I speak to you only from my heart, and out of my pain, because only God can give me the strength to stand here before you and say these words. But they're so important. Each of you has the decision to make that my son made. And this is a time when you have a choice and we never know how long we'll have to make that decision.

Three weeks before he was killed, Jack wrote two letters, to be opened "just in case." After we got the news, we opened our letter and it said, "In case you have to open this, please don't worry. I am all right. . . . *Now I know something you don't know—what heaven's like!*"

And someday *we* will know, too.

Notes

CHAPTER 1—World in Pain

1. *Time,* 3 December 1990, 45.
2. Ibid., 46.
3. *U.S. News & World Report,* 24 September 1990, 37.
4. *Time,* 7 May 1990, 92.
5. Ibid., 99.
6. Francis Schaeffer, *Pollution and the Death of Man* (Wheaton, Ill.: Tyndale House, 1970), 10–11.
7. Aleksandr Solzhenitsyn, *The Gulag Archipelago* (New York: Harper & Row, 1973), 3–4.
8. *Los Angeles Times,* 12 October 1990, A13.
9. Russell Chandler, *Understanding the New Age* (Dallas: Word Publishing, 1988), 104.
10. Horatius Bonar, *When God's Children Suffer* (Grand Rapids, Mich.: Kregel Publications, 1981), preface.

CHAPTER 2—His Unfailing Love

1. Lloyd Ogilvie, *Ask Him Anything* (Dallas: Word Publishing, 1981), 13.
2. Francis Schaeffer, *The Mark of the Christian* (Downers Grove, Ill.: Inter-Varsity, 1976), 28.
3. Richard Wurmbrand, *In God's Underground* (New York: Fawcett World Library, 1968), 249.

CHAPTER 3—Into Each Life Some Rain . . .

1. Charles Colson, *Against the Night* (Ann Arbor, Mich.: Servant Books, 1989), 165.

CHAPTER 5—Why Jesus Suffered

1. Philip Yancey, *Where Is God When It Hurts?* (Grand Rapids, Mich.: Zondervan, 1990), 156.

CHAPTER 6—Who Sinned?

1. H. L. Ellison, *A Study of Job* (Grand Rapids, Mich.: Zondervan, 1971), 19.
2. Philip Yancey, *Where Is God When It Hurts?* (Grand Rapids, Mich.: Zondervan, 1990), 89.
3. Charles Colson, *The God of Stones and Spiders* (Wheaton, Ill.: Crossway Books, 1990), 99.

CHAPTER 7—Why God's Children Suffer

1. C. S. Lewis, *The Problem of Pain* (New York: Macmillan, 1955), 93.
2. Horatius Bonar, *When God's Children Suffer* (Grand Rapids, Mich.: Kregel Publications, 1981), 28.
3. Clebe McClary with Diane Barker, *Living Proof* (Pawleys Island, S.C.: Clebe McClary, 1978), 140.
4. *Lines to Live By* (Nashville: Thomas Nelson, 1972), 162.
5. Corrie ten Boom, *A Prisoner and Yet* (London: Christian Literature Crusade, 1954).

CHAPTER 8—What Do I Do When I Hurt?

1. Oswald Chambers, *My Utmost for His Highest* (Westwood, N.J.: Barbour & Co., 1963), 32.
2. *Los Angeles Times,* 16 February, 1990, C9.
3. Amy Carmichael, *Rose from Brier* (Fort Washington, Pa.: Christian Literature Crusade, 1973), 12.

CHAPTER 9—When Your Heart Is Breaking

1. Doug Sparks, *Hope for the Hurting* (Colorado Springs, Colo.: Navpress, 1990), 6.

2. Barbara Johnson, *Stick a Geranium in Your Hat and Be Happy* (Dallas: Word Publishing, 1990), 41.
3. Ibid., 57.
4. *Los Angeles Times,* 16 February, 1991, A5.
5. David Jeremiah with C. C. Carlson, *Exposing the Myths of Parenthood* (Dallas: Word Publishing, 1988), 4.
6. David Jacobsen, "Remember Them," *Guideposts,* March 1991.
7. Mrs. Charles E. Cowman, *Streams in the Desert* (Grand Rapids, Mich.: Zondervan, 1966), 314.
8. Jay Kesler, *The Strong Weak People* (Wheaton, Ill.: Victor Books, 1977), 17.

CHAPTER 10—The Fourth Man in the Fire

1. Corrie ten Boom, *He Sets the Captive Free* (Old Tappan, N.J.: Fleming H. Revell, 1977), 18–19.
2. Dale Evans Rogers, *Trials, Tears, and Triumphs* (Old Tappan, N.J.: Fleming H. Revell, 1977), 118.

CHAPTER 11—How to Pray Through the Pain

1. Amy Carmichael, *Edges of His Ways* (London: Christian Literature Crusade, 1955), 92.
2. Doug Sparks, *Hope for the Hurting* (Colorado Springs, Colo.: Navpress, 1990), 16, 17.
3. Ruth Bell Graham, *Legacy of a Pack Rat* (Nashville, Tenn.: Oliver-Nelson Books, 1989), 151.
4. *Guideposts,* July 1990, 9.
5. Norman Vincent Peale, *How to Handle Tough Times* (Pawling, N.Y.: Foundation for Christian Living, 1990), 28–29.
6. J. Grant Howard, *Knowing God's Will and Doing It!* (Grand Rapids, Mich.: Zondervan, 1976), 29–30.
7. Margaret Clarkson, *The Meaning of Suffering* (Grand Rapids, Mich.: Eerdmans, 1983), 98.

CHAPTER 12—Storing Up for the Storms

1. Bob St. John, *The Landry Legend* (Dallas: Word Publishing, 1989), 163.

2. Philip Yancey, *Where Is God When It Hurts?* (Grand Rapids, Mich.: Zondervan, 1990), 164.
3. Charles Sheldon, *In His Steps* (Grand Rapids, Mich.: Zondervan, 1967), 9.

CHAPTER 13—How to Help the Hurting People

1. David Jeremiah, *Overcoming Loneliness* (San Bernardino, Calif.: Here's Life Publishers, 1983), 12.
2. Philip Yancey, *Helping the Hurting* (Portland, Oreg.: Multnomah Press, 1984), 9.
3. Dr. James Dobson, *Dare to Discipline* (Wheaton, Ill.: Tyndale House, 1981), 77.
4. Franklin Graham with Jeanette Lockerbie, *Bob Pierce* (Waco, Tex.: Word Publishing, 1983), 77, 180.

CHAPTER 14—Schoolroom for Heaven

1. *U.S. News & World Report*, 25 March 1991, 56.
2. Velma Barfield, *Woman on Death Row* (Nashville, Tenn.: Oliver-Nelson Books, 1985), 169.
3. Wilbur Smith, *Therefore Stand: Christian Apologetics* (Grand Rapids, Mich.: Baker Book House, 1965), 364.
4. John Oxenham, "A Dieu! and Au Revoir" *Lines to Live By* (Nashville: Thomas Nelson, 1972), 81.
5. C. S. Lewis, *The Problem of Pain* (New York: Macmillan, 1955), 108.

DEATH *and the* LIFE AFTER

BILLY GRAHAM

W PUBLISHING GROUP
A Division of Thomas Nelson Publishers
Since 1798

www.wpublishinggroup.com

Unless otherwise indicated, Scripture quotations
are from the New International Version of the Bible, published
by the Zondervan Corporation, copyright © 1973 by the New York Bible
Society. Used by permission. Those marked NASB are from the New American
Standard Bible, copyright © 1960, 1962, 1963, 1968, 1971 by the Lockman Foundation.
Those marked KJV are from the King James Version.
Those marked LB are from the Living Bible, © 1971 Tyndale
House Publishers. Used by permission.

Excerpt from "Lament" by Edna St. Vincent Millay.
From *Collected Poems,* Harper & Row. Copyright © 1921,
1948 by Edna St. Vincent Millay. Reprinted by permission.

Library of Congress Cataloging-in-Publication Data

Graham, Billy, 1918–
Death and the life after / Billy Graham
p. cm.
ISBN 0-8499-5034-1
ISBN 0-8499-3520-2 (mpa)
1. Death—Religious aspects—Christianity.
2. Future life—Christianity. I. Title.
bt825.c64 1987 236'.1 87-15930

Printed in the United States of America

06 07 08 BVG 9 8 7 6 5 4

Then I heard a voice from heaven say,

"Write: Blessed are the dead who die in the Lord from now on."

"Yes," says the Spirit, "they will rest from their labor, for their deeds will follow them."

Revelation 14:13

Contents

Man is destined to die once, and after that to face judgment.
Hebrews 9:27

Introduction

THE 563 MEN, women and children who boarded *The Herald of Free Enterprise* ferry on March 6, 1987, in Zeebrugge, Belgium, for a trip across the English Channel to Dover, England, had no inkling of what awaited them shortly after leaving the harbor.

Without warning, the four-thousand-ton vessel began to list and within seconds, the happy passengers were transformed into desperate, terrified people as they plunged beneath the icy cold waters and began to battle for their lives.

Two hundred passengers and crew members went to a watery grave. The only reason the toll was not much higher was the quick work by rescue crews who risked their own lives to save others.

More recently, thirty-seven men lost their lives on the USS *Stark* in the Persian Gulf, and some twenty-nine people died when a tornado struck the little town of Saragosa in West Texas. We have grown used to hearing about (and even seeing) such tragedies reported on our television newscasts and tend to treat them as mere statistics unless one of our loved ones is involved.

It is an axiom that there are just two certainties in life: death and taxes, but that is not true. With the right deductions and a good accountant, millionaires have managed to avoid paying any taxes at all. But everyone, millionaires and paupers, will face the ultimate certainty: death.

It is doubtful that any of the passengers aboard the ferry thought about the possibility of their being dead within minutes after boarding the vessel. That is largely because we live in a death-denying society.

Even the language and atmosphere of funeral homes denies death. A person who has died is said to have "departed." The person is stripped of his or her name and referred to as a "loved one." There are persons who are specialists in applying makeup to a dead body to make it appear as if the person is only sleeping.

Advertisers do all they can to help us deny the ultimate fact of life. Billions of dollars are spent on a cosmetic industry that promises creams and lotions will slow the aging process and make the user look younger. Joggers line the roads, often before dawn; and workouts at health clubs have become popular ways to keep the body in shape to prolong life. Fiber is an increasingly prevalent part of some people's diets as physicians tell us of its ability to reduce the risk of cancer. Many people are giving up smoking to reduce the possibility of heart and lung disease.

But the irreversible fact is that no matter what your diet, no matter how much you exercise, no matter how many vitamins or health foods you eat, no matter how low your cholesterol, you will still die—someday, some way. You may add a year, or even a few years to a life that could be shorter had you not been concerned about your health, but in the end death will conquer you as it has every person who has ever lived.

If you knew the moment and manner of your death in advance, would you order your life differently? If so, when would you do it . . . right now, or would you wait until the day before? And then what would you do to right the mistakes you made during your life?

Unfortunately, no one knows the day or the hour of his death, which is why it is best, in the words of the scout motto, to "be prepared."

It is my prayer that this book may be a source of support and blessing for every reader, and that each of us will have the comfort of God's love as we face the issues discussed here. For those who do not know Christ, I pray they will meet Him in these pages.

Naturally, I have not written this book alone. Others have helped immensely. Especially do I owe a deep debt of gratitude to my longtime friend Carole Carlson. She did so much research for the first of many drafts of the manuscript. Without her this book would have been almost impossible to finish on time. Then, as always, I want to thank my wife, Ruth, for her part in helping to plan and shape this book and for sharing a number of touching moments from her own life. For years she has kept a file of material on the subject of death (as she does on many subjects, to help me in my preaching and writing). Some of the stories and statistics in this book came from her files. I also want to thank Dr. John Akers, the Reverend Jack Black, Mrs. Millie Dienert, and Dr. Harold Lindsell who read and made helpful comments and additions to sections of the book.

Further, I want to thank each of the other men and women who have supported me in researching and developing this work and in preparing it for publication. Likewise, a word of appreciation to my publisher, Ernie Owen, and my editors, Al Bryant and Dr. Jim Black of Word Publishing. And, last but not least, a special thank you to my secretary, Stephanie Wills, for her tireless effort and unflagging support.

"If we are in a battle with this enemy called Death, I believe we should learn about it, in order to know how to confront the dying experience. We need to know how to face that enemy on our own behalf, and how to deal with the inevitable deaths of loved ones and friends."

The last enemy that will be abolished is death.

1 Corinthians 15:26, NASB

CHAPTER ONE

The Last Enemy

A TWISTED PILE of metal and shattered glass lay like a broken toy in the left lane of the freeway. The flares, police cars, ambulances, and flashing red lights created a scene of sudden and ominous dread. An expensive sports car, once an object of pride, now lay twisted beyond repair. A limp body sprawled in the front seat, wedged beneath the steering wheel. Was the victim alive or dead? Could the mangled body be stitched together by the hands of a skilled surgeon, or would it be hastily covered with a plastic sheet and transported unceremoniously to the city morgue, "DOA, dead on arrival"?

For all of the shock and anguish for the loved ones and families affected by such tragedies, scenes like this one are repeated every day on America's highways. The grief we feel at the sudden death of a loved one can be crushing; yet, such accidents are all too common. Only spectacular disasters make the headlines any more, and families whose lives have been suddenly shattered and their futures dramatically changed, discover too late that they are unprepared.

What about that anonymous driver? Was he prepared for the sudden change in his future plans? Had he arranged his affairs for such a possibility, and had he considered his options for eternity?

How we deal with death and tragedy says a lot about what kind of people we are. All too often we glance at the newspaper and notice that another celebrity has died; a phone call or letter brings sad news about a friend's death. We hurt for our loved ones and mourn our own losses, but how prepared are we to face death as a reality and deal with the difficult challenges it creates?

I remember an incident in Paris in September of 1986, just before the beginning of our crusade. We were having a fairly normal day of business when, suddenly, it seemed like this beautiful city was under siege. A bomb exploded in a busy department store during the noon rush hour, killing and wounding women and children. We discovered we had arrived during a series of terrorist attacks, an onslaught which *Time* magazine decried, calling the new wave of terrorism "this leprosy of modern times."[1]

As it turned out, we were never seriously threatened by that wave of sudden violence, and I have my own feelings about why that might be, but, nevertheless, we had to think about the dire possibilities and what consequences our crusade team might have to anticipate. By nature, the human mind does not want to deal with distasteful facts. We want to forget the unpleasant or painful and concentrate on the "positive." We persuade ourselves that sudden death happens to others, not to us. But that is not always so.

Death: the Final Certainty

Death tolls in wars and epidemics, and the news we read of famine in foreign lands, draw our attention to the fatal aspects of the world around us. Reports from Africa and South America tell of millions of affected citizens, thousands of casualties, miles of affected territory, months and years of suffering, and all the tragedy that can be summed up in statistical fashion. But statistics, and the ways they are fed to us by the media, can be misleading. Death is perennial. During World War II, C. S. Lewis pointed out that war does not increase death; death is total in every generation. It takes every one of us. George Bernard Shaw wryly wrote, "The statistics on death are quite impressive. One out of one people die."

During family week at a Christian conference center, a message came that one of the couples who had been teachers for many of the children at the camp had walked into their four-month-old baby's room and found him blue and lifeless—a victim of crib death. A pall came over everyone as the news spread. Why did this happen to people like Ben and Sally? She was in her late thirties and this was their first child. She taught her kindergarten class until shortly before her baby was due, and every day her little pupils prayed for that baby. Ben and Sally's students and members of their church were excited when little Benjamin was born. Why did the Lord take him?

Death is so often accompanied by those heartbreaking questions, "Why me? Why now? Why this?"

Why must we die? The Bible says, "It is appointed unto men once to die" (Hebrews 9:27, KJV). It is the most democratic of all experiences. Over 400 years ago the English author John Heywood noted, "Death makes equal the high and low." We can fight it, and the will to fight it is instinctive. We can even avoid it for a time, and common sense allows us that privilege. We can argue, plead, and bargain, but death is the one universal enemy. Saying "I don't want to think about it" won't make the reality disappear. Death ultimately intrudes into our well-planned lives and changes things around, absolutely.

We want to deny death. We cover our awkwardness around the subject by speaking of the deceased as if they did not die. "He departed this life," we say. "He passed away," or "He's gone up yonder." The fact that the body is now in the ground and the soul of the deceased has departed is more than we like to admit.

In asking if one's father is still living, the Chinese say, "Is your father still located?" The reply would be, "He's located," or "He's not located," whichever is the case. The word "death" is rarely used, even in the world's most ancient culture.

Today we are confronted with so many voices telling us how to live. We are told how to look young, stay trim, keep healthy, have a good image, think positively, make more money, have more friends. All these are reasonable ambitions, but they indicate that we are trying desperately to cling to this present world. The truth is, life is transitory. "What is your life? You are a mist that appears for a little while and then vanishes" (James 4:14b). The psalmist said, "Each man's life is but a breath" (Psalm 39:5). If we want to make the most of life, we need to face the fact that it is going to end.

My father-in-law, Dr. L. Nelson Bell, wrote many years ago, "Only those who are prepared to die are really prepared to live." The uncertainty is not the dying, it's the preparation.

Facing Reality

If we are in a battle with this enemy called Death, I believe we should learn about it, in order to know how to confront the dying experience. We need to know how to face that enemy on our own behalf, and how to deal with the inevitable deaths of loved ones and friends.

Can you imagine any military strategist saying, "Well, if there really is an enemy out there, perhaps I should find out something about him . . . later"? It reminds me of the situation at the beginning of World War II. As long as history is recorded, the attack on Pearl Harbor on December 7, 1941, will be remembered. The Japanese High Command code-named the attack "Operation Z," and its planning took place more than a year before the launch of warplanes that would destroy the battleships and aircraft carriers at Pearl Harbor, the heart of the U.S. Pacific Fleet.

In the summer of 1941 I went to Washington, D.C., with my wife Ruth's family. Dr. Bell was intent on meeting with officials at the State Department to alert them to an imminent Japanese attack. He was politely ignored. Other warnings had been heard, but also went unheeded; America was unprepared for what happened at Pearl Harbor, blindly refusing to face the encroaching danger.

Can we afford to ignore the warnings of our ultimate enemy? We need to break the conspiracy of silence about the subject with a biblically sound, realistic approach. Years ago there was a popular play called *Death Takes a Holiday*. The idea was provocative and made good drama with its impossible theme; however, while death was not a part of God's original plan, we cannot escape it. Death *never* takes a holiday (with one possible exception which we will consider later).

Adolescents are notorious for denying the reality of death; it is the farthest thing from their minds. In the vigor of youth they take life for granted, and perhaps they should at that age; but all of us tend to take life for granted when times are good, when there is plenty, when the economy is strong, when things are getting better. Death is the last thing on our minds when we have full stomachs. But let a person who is reasonably intelligent ponder slightly the reality of death and that person is on his or her way to an existential crisis. That person starts asking questions like, "Who am I?" "Why am I here?" "Where am I going from here?" Sometimes the questions come on the heels of a serious setback or sudden loss, when the good times disappear, when the party's over, and he or she has to face the morning after. If the individual has a mind and feelings, there is no way to deny the reality.

There are signs that some people are trying to develop a more informed approach to the subject. In fact, some educators are saying death has come out of the closet and into the classroom. I have been told that sex is the only subject which is more popular on the campus these days. Students are visiting morgues, even making their own funeral arrangements. For whatever reasons death as a topic is in vogue, but the mature Christian perspective is still something less than hot news.

I suspect that modern society, with the potential for nuclear incineration, military holocaust, and natural disaster puts the spotlight on the subject for these young people. But I also suspect that the constant bombardment of TV violence is a factor.

Discussing death scientifically may help us become more capable of discussing the personal aspects of dying; and facing the fact of our own death can help us cope with our neurotic fears of dying. But most important, we can come to grips with the need to get our life's priorities in order. However, we cannot begin to understand the riddle of death without the guiding knowledge of the Word of God. Outside of the Bible, death will forever remain an unknown phantom, stalking helpless human victims.

Throughout this book it is my desire to approach the fact of death objectively and compassionately as God has revealed it to us through the Scriptures.

Although death is, as the apostle Paul claimed, the last enemy, one of the main purposes of this book is to show that it need not be feared.

Death: Our Mortal Enemy

The Bible stresses that death is an enemy, not a friend—both of God and of us.

Why is death our enemy? I'm not thinking of the death which is a release from pain, debilitating disease, or advanced age, but death the enemy who snatches a child before he learns to play in the sunshine. It is the enemy who takes the young couple before they can be married, stops the youth who wants to be a pilot, or kills the young father and leaves orphaned children and a destitute wife. As you read this sentence, one person will die. Death, like an unfinished symphony, leaves fragments of many promising careers and lives.

One woman wrote me about the death of her husband. She called it an "untimely death."

"He had called me twice that morning," she said, "after supposedly recovering after a week's stay for heart treatment in the hospital. He told me he was 'coming home.' The doctor scheduled him for a 'mild' treadmill test, and thirty minutes later the hospital called to say he died on the treadmill. The shock has been almost unbearable. Please pray that I will be able to accept this part of the Lord's plan."

Although we think of the death of a young person, or one in the prime of life, as being the most difficult for loved ones, that is not always true. I heard from one woman who said, "Please pray for me, I feel so lost without my husband. He was my life. We were married for sixty years."

Frank Coy was in Cleveland talking to his wife by long distance telephone to their home near Phoenix, Arizona. She had not been feeling very well. Frank and Virginia were extremely close and had been married for many years. They had looked forward to his retirement as president of the May Company in Cleveland, and were traveling about the country, though he still served on many boards including ours. During the conversation she said she had a pain. He said, "Well, honey, I think you ought to go to the hospital." All of a sudden he heard the phone drop. He immediately called a hospital in Phoenix and within four minutes the paramedics were there, but it was too late. She had died while talking to her husband on the phone. It absolutely crushed Frank. Except for the companionship of the Lord, he seems to be totally lost without Virginia. Heaven is much closer to him now.

Death: Enemy of God's Plan

"But, Lord, I don't want to die." And the Lord, as it were, answers: I didn't plan the world that way, but someday, even this enemy will be destroyed. God reminds us of that through the apostle Paul. "For he must reign until he has put all his enemies under his feet. The last enemy to be destroyed is death" (1 Corinthians 15:25–26).

Why is death an enemy of God? Because it destroys life, in contrast to God, the creator and author of life. In fact, the Bible tells us that neither sin nor pain, disease nor death were part of God's original plan for man. Death was the penalty for sin, and Adam and Eve made the choice of their own free wills. When they did not obey God, He told the first man and woman if they ate from the fruit of the tree of the knowledge of good and evil, they would die. But Satan scoffed at God's warning and told them they surely would not die. Adam and Eve chose to ignore God's warning and to believe Satan's lie. "For the wages of sin is death, but the gift of God is eternal life in Christ Jesus our Lord" (Romans 6:23).

Death is the common lot of every human being and of every other living thing—both plants and animals. Sin and death, the Bible tells us, have afflicted the whole of God's creation, including the natural world, and only when Christ comes in His glory at the end of the present era will sin be eradicated and creation be restored to God's original plan.

"The creation waits in eager expectation for the sons of God to be revealed. For the creation was subjected to frustration, not by its own choice, but by the will of the one who subjected it, in hope that the creation itself will be liberated from its bondage to decay and brought into the glorious freedom of the children of God" (Romans 8:19–21).

Did you ever wonder what would have happened to man if he hadn't sinned? We certainly don't know, because the Scriptures don't tell us. But perhaps man would have been translated to heaven without passing through death, just as Enoch and Elijah were. There *will* be a generation of believers who will not know physical death. Those who are still alive when Jesus Christ returns in glory for His own will not die but will be changed "in a flash, in the twinkling of an eye" (1 Corinthians 15:52).

A child asked his mother, "Where would I be if I hadn't been born?" How can we answer that? It's like asking what would have happened if Eve hadn't taken a bite of the forbidden fruit and Adam hadn't succumbed to her invitation. We just don't know.

Some Reactions to Death

People encounter death from different perspectives. Some defy death, as did my friend Steve McQueen, until it consumed him with cancer. They laugh at death, as did Will Rogers, until the day his plane crashed. George Burns says, "I don't believe in death." But they invite death when life becomes unbearable, as did Marilyn Monroe. Sometimes they are resigned to death, as was the hapless Anne Boleyn, second queen consort of Henry VIII. She wrote these poignant final words:

> *Oh, death, rock me asleep! Bring me to quiet and rest*
> *Let me pass my weary, guiltless life*
> *out of my careful breast.*
> *Toll on the passing bell, ring out my doleful knell;*
> *Let thy sound my death tell; Death doth draw me,*
> *Death doth draw me; There is no remedy.*[2]

Still others have a fatalistic attitude toward death or reject it, claiming we should not worry about it because there is no life after death and there is nothing we can do about death anyway.

The Greek philosopher, Epicurus, lived three centuries before Christ and wrote in a seriocomic tone about death, as we have a tendency to do when we are nervous about a subject. He said, "Death, feared as the most awful of evils, is really nothing. For so long as we are, death has not come, and when it has come we are not."

Others go to the opposite extreme and live in constant, paralyzing fear of death. Because they have no security and assurance of God's love and protection in the midst of death, their lives are preoccupied with fear and often filled with attempts to win God's favor and avoid His anger.

Christians are not immune to the fear of death. Death is not always a "beautiful release," but an enemy which separates. There is a certain mystery to it. It does not respect the young or the old, the good or the evil, the Christian or the heathen.

Our individual responses to death cannot be placed in neat categories and given labels. However, our experiences with life and death are generally similar to those of others around us. The Bible says, "No temptation has seized you except what is common to man" (1 Corinthians 10:13).

But we need not give way to defiance, or rejection, or fear, or any of the other attitudes people adopt in the face of the reality of death. There is another way—the way of Christ—by which we know that while the experience of death is certain, so also is the fact of heaven. For the Christian death can be faced realistically and with victory, because he knows that "neither death nor life, neither angels nor demons, neither the present nor the future, nor any powers, neither height nor depth, nor anything else in all creation, will be able to separate us from the love of God that is in Christ Jesus our Lord" (Romans 8:38–39).

Now, I am not anxious to die, nor am I writing this book with any knowledge of my imminent departure. And just because the Bible tells us that believers have a blessed hope of conquering death, we don't run to the door and say to the enemy, "Come on in, I've been waiting anxiously for you." It is not a sign of weak faith for the Christian to face death with reluctance. The apostle Paul confessed that he was torn between the desire to die and be with Christ and the need to continue his work in the churches. He wrote to the believers in Philippi, "I am torn between the two: I desire to depart and be with Christ, which is better by far; but it is more necessary for you that I remain in the body" (Philippians 1:23–24).

Can we be realistic, without being morbid? Can we find peace, assurance, triumph, and even humor, in a subject which is avoided by many but vitally important and inevitable to everyone? I am convinced we can.

"Now that the taboo has been lifted, it is more important than ever for Christians to get involved in some of the great questions about the process of dying. The Bible has the answers to the fear of death, but we need the principles in God's Word about the dying experience."

> *There is a time for everything, and a season for every activity under heaven: a time to be born and a time to die. . . .* Ecclesiastes 3:1–2

CHAPTER TWO

Death: No More Taboos

I MAJORED IN anthropology in college. That may not seem to be a good educational foundation for a clergyman. At the time, however, I thought it would give me a greater understanding of other cultures and peoples, never dreaming how useful it would become when my future ministry would be worldwide.

It is fascinating to me how customs and traditions reflect the way people really think. Hold a mirror to history and we see the art, music, literature, and manners of each era. Sometimes those of us who have lived five or more decades reach the stage where we shake our heads and say, "In my day it was different." Of course it was. And someday our children may mimic us when they tell our grandchildren, "When I was your age . . ."

Attitudes toward death have changed more than styles in clothing. We have passed from the ceremonial to the unmentionable and have reached the present "gloom boom." More books have been written about death in the last ten years than in the previous century.

A few hundred years ago, death was a ritual. Knowing that his end was near, the dying person prepared for death, as Sir Lancelot did in the Knights of the Round Table. After he was wounded in battle he believed he was about to die. He spread out his arms, his body forming a cross. He turned his head so that he faced east, toward Jerusalem. He was ready for death.

Death had its own protocol. If the dying person was unable to remember what it was, those present would remind him what the proper custom was. One historian who carefully studied the attitudes toward death in the Middle Ages, wrote, "The dying man, according to Guillaume Durand, bishop of Mende, must lie on his back so that his face is always turned toward heaven."[1]

Today on television our dying heroes fall over with a few "ughs!" if allowed that much. They jerk, explode, or topple over with no chance to leave another generation quotable words. "His last words were . . ." has been replaced by the gut reaction.

In the more romantic tradition of the past, phrases such as Hamlet's words, "To be or not to be, that is the question," masked the ugliness of death in lyrical language.

Deathbed scenes in past centuries were a public ceremony, many times including friends, relatives, and children. Illustrations in old books frequently pictured a high canopied bed on which rested the wasted form of its occupant surrounded by people in various stages of grief, concern, or even indifference. A dying man's bedroom was like Grand Central Station. However, toward the end of the eighteenth century, physicians were increasingly concerned with basic principles of hygiene and were unhappy about overcrowded conditions in the bedrooms of the dying.

Those final days when a person needed to commune with God or with loved ones were regarded as a right for the dying. People prepared to die. The language of wills documented a person's careful last plan, including his statement of faith. For instance, here is what Patrick Henry wrote in his will:

> I have now disposed of all my property to my family. There is one thing more I wish I could give them, and that is faith in Jesus Christ. If they had that and I had not given them one shilling, they would be rich; and if I had not given them that, and had given them all the world, they would be poor indeed.

However, the second half of the eighteenth century saw a considerable change in wills. "The pious clauses, the choice of a tomb, the funding of religious services, and the giving of alms all disappeared; the will was reduced to the document we find today, a legal act distributing the estate, small or large. Thus the will was completely secularized.[2]

The historian commented, "It has been thought that this secularization was one of the signs of the de-Christianization of society."

What interests me is that the return to the concept of Christian wills is being seen in our day.

In the nineteenth century came a new preoccupation with the decor of death. There were funeral processions, mourning clothes, the spread of cemeteries, regular visits, and pilgrimages to tombs. There was a pomp connected with the departure from life which was elaborate and prolonged.

But customs changed. As the twentieth century, with its rapid changes in technology, communication, and lifestyles, began its breathless race into the future, death became an unmentionable topic (perhaps due in part to increasing secularism). Over a period of time people began to exclude children from deathbed scenes, or even viewing the dead. Death became a private affair; eventually even the family was excluded as the hospitalization of the terminally ill became widespread.

With this came the rejection of mourning during much of this century. The community felt less and less involved in the death of its members. Geoffrey Gorer, an Englishman, began a study of this change in attitudes toward death and mourning as a result of a series of personal experiences. He lost his father on the *Lusitania* in 1915, so was never able to see his body. It was 1931 before he first viewed a dead body and could experience and observe the conventions of mourning. However, in the late 1940s he experienced the deaths of two close friends, and was struck by the rejection of traditional ways of mourning. In 1955 he published an article called "The Pornography of Death." In it he showed how death had become as shameful in the modern age as sex was to the Victorians. One taboo had been substituted for another.

Children were excluded from funeral services, sometimes even those of their own parents. Gorer, reflecting on his own life, told about the death of his brother in 1961. In speaking of his nephews he said, "Their father's death was quite unmarked for them by ritual of any kind, and was even nearly treated as a secret, for it was many months before Elizabeth (his wife) could bear to mention him or have him mentioned in her presence.[3]

In a questionnaire published by *Psychology Today* in 1971, a woman of twenty-five wrote, "When I was twelve, my mother died of leukemia. She was there when I went to bed and when I woke up the next morning, my parents were gone. My father came home, took my brother and me on his knee, and burst into screeching sobs and said, 'Jesus took your mother.' Then we never talked about it again. It was too painful for all of us."[4]

How unfortunate it is when Jesus is depicted to children as the person who "took" mommy or daddy, without the child having a previous understanding of the hope of heaven and eternal life. It is no wonder that the young woman just mentioned had to undergo counseling therapy in later years.

In contrast, my wife Ruth tells about the death of her former Wheaton College roommate, Ann King Blocher, who died surrounded by her husband and all five of her children. Another friend, Helen Morken, was dying of cancer when she said to Ruth in a telephone conversation that "The prayers of God's people are the extension of His loving arms." Ruth sent her a cassette of hymns and sacred music she had put together for her own mother and later produced for distribution, called "Looking Homeward." Helen played it by the hour. As she died, her entire family stood around her bed and literally sang her into the glory of heaven.

Whatever Happened to Hell?

As attitudes toward death and dying changed, another significant shift began to take place within the human family. The reality of Satan was ignored increasingly or discarded as a myth. Even many who believed in a personal devil were not allowed to acknowledge his power in this world, nor did they believe in hell.

Hell, in the eyes of unbelievers and even some believers, was abandoned. Or it was relegated to some vague concept of "evil in the world." Even some theologians chose to reject the Bible's clear teaching on hell.

Certainly war, hunger, terrorism, greed, and hatred are hell on earth, but, except for the Bible believer, a future hell became part of the ash heap of ancient history. As hell was becoming for many no more than a swear word, sin was also an accepted way of life. People began to look to science, education, and social and moral programs as possible solutions to the growing chaos of an insane world. If people can ignore what the Bible calls sin, then they can quite logically discount what it says about the reality of hell.

Whoever chooses to deny that there is a hell must then face certain questions: "Where do I go when I die?" "Who goes to heaven, and who doesn't?" And, "If I don't go to heaven, what is the alternative?"

In contemporary society hell is not a popular subject. George Gallup made a survey on hell and there were some interesting results. In his national poll 53 percent of the general population of the United States said they believe in hell. The percentage goes down dramatically among people with a college education and those with high incomes. Simply stated, the Gallup poll showed that the more education and money people had, the less likely they were to believe in hell.

What about heaven? In the Gallup survey 66 percent of the general population said they believe in "a heaven where people who have led good lives are eternally rewarded." More people are confident that there is a heaven than are concerned about hell. I was especially interested that those who believed in heaven were asked a further question, "How would you describe your own chances of going to heaven—excellent, good, fair, or poor?"

Among the Protestant denominations only 26 percent of the Baptists, 20 percent of the Lutherans, and 16 percent of the Methodists thought their chances of attaining heaven were excellent. The survey further revealed that while only 24 percent of the Protestants said they were sure of a place in heaven, 41 percent of the Catholics had this assurance.[5]

Why did members of organized churches, or those professing to be either Protestant or Catholic, have such a low assurance of heaven? Could it be that in our descriptions of heaven we have failed to mention the horrors of its alternative? Have we overreacted to the old "hell-fire and brimstone" preaching by discarding or at least watering down the clear teaching of the Bible? Jesus spoke of hell as "darkness, where there will be weeping and gnashing of teeth" (Matthew 8:12). Or have we even neglected the whole question of life after death by emphasizing only this life?

Jesus used the strongest words possible to describe the horrors of hell.

Having traveled widely and spoken with multitudes of people in many countries where the Christian faith is no longer as strong as it once was, I was not surprised to learn from the Gallup poll that more Americans believe in hell than do those in any of the other countries where Christianity is the major organized religion. In Sweden, for instance, only 17 percent believe in hell; France, 22 percent; Great Britain, 23 percent; West Germany, 24 percent; Switzerland, 25 percent; the Netherlands, 28 percent. Other countries in Europe were equally low.

Gallup surmises, and I tend to agree, that some of the reasons why more people believe in heaven than in hell is that "Hell is like death—people try not to think about it.[6] Jackie Gleason appearing on *60 Minutes* with Morley Safer indicated that he believed there was eternal life ahead either in heaven or hell. I remember talking to Jackie on several occasions in years past on this very theme.

Just because people do not believe in hell doesn't mean it doesn't exist! Jesus warned, "Be afraid of the One who can destroy both soul and body in hell" (Matthew 10:28). If there is no hell, then Jesus lied.

Some people who believe in the passages in the Bible about heaven utterly reject the references to hell. Robert Ingersoll, a famous lawyer and atheist in the latter part of the nineteenth century, once delivered a blistering lecture on hell. He called hell the "scarecrow of religion" and told his audience how unscientific it was, and how all intelligent people had decided there was no such place. A drunk in the audience came up to him afterward and said, "Bob, I liked your lecture; I liked what you said about hell. But, Bob, I want you to be sure about it, because I'm depending on you." [7]

In World War I, British soldiers had a popular song that went like this:

Oh Death, where is thy sting-a-ling-a-ling,
Oh Grave, thy victoree?
The bells of Hell go ting-a-ling-a-ling
For you but not for me.[8]

A lot of people talk about hell, use it to tell others where to go, but do not want to be confronted with the thought that it might be their destination. Hell, for them, is only where the Hitlers and Stalins should end up, along with murderers, rapists, or child pornographers. But most think that "Good People" who mind their own business, pay their taxes, and put a few dollars in the collection plate will have some "eternal rewards."

However, if the Bible is true, we know there is abundant life after death for the followers of Christ. Those who have accepted His grace and been saved will be with Him in heaven. And what about the others? "Surely a loving God would not punish good people!" says the humanitarian or the religious person who wants to ignore the uncomfortable and unpopular descriptions of hell in the Bible. Yes, they are right in some ways, for a loving God does not want anyone to perish. The Lord is not slow in keeping His promise, as some understand slowness. "He is patient with you, not wanting anyone to perish, but everyone to come to repentance" (2 Peter 3:9).

However, the Scriptures are very clear. Jesus told His disciples not to fear the killers of men, because they only cause physical death. He did not mean, of course, that we are not to be concerned about murderers, but His point was a warning of something more serious than the death of our bodies. Jesus said, "But I will show you whom you should fear: Fear him who, after the killing of the body, has power to throw you into hell" (Luke 12:5).

Let's clarify a few things about that verse in Luke. First of all, it refers to God, not to Satan; for Satan cannot determine the destiny of a human soul.

Also, I know many people stumble over the idea of "fearing God." Fear does not imply a crippling dread, but a healthy, reverent respect. All through the Bible we read about fearing the Lord. If we substitute "have deep reverence for," we may be closer to understanding the meaning of the word.

The problem is not that hell exists, because it must if God is holy and we distinguish between the biblical meaning of good and evil. The problem is that men don't understand how evil sin is in the eyes of a supremely holy God. Sin is not rated on a sliding scale, like a report card. Sin is eternal separation from God and can only be pardoned by a truly supreme sacrifice: the death of the Son of God, on the cross.

In Our Time

Today the dying experience is more openly discussed; however, many of the accounts I've heard or read of those last moments tend to confuse the biblical doctrines and raise more questions than they answer. A good example is the popularity of accounts of "near-death" experiences, in which a person claims to have approached death (or even died) and then come back to life.

It is not my purpose to doubt the sincerity of those people who have recounted their "out-of-body" experiences.

Many describe near-death encounters after a cardiac arrest or other medical crisis and tell how they seemed to rise and watch as the medical team tried to revive them. Nor do I question those who tell about seeing spirits of relatives and friends who have already died, or others who have encountered a "being of light" which brings them through a tunnel into an overwhelming, ecstatic experience of such intensity that they find it difficult to describe. I have heard many such stories offered in vivid detail, and, without exception, these life-after-death experiences seem to reduce the fear of dying.

Most of the supernatural experiences we hear or read about have classic similarities. The person who is "dead" (and we'll discuss the meaning of that word shortly) rises out of his or her body, hears strange sounds, seems to be going down a long, dark tunnel and recognizes himself hovering somewhere between life and death, and then encounters someone or something in white, or a diffusion of light. Those who return from this journey are changed persons.

These kinds of stories are not an American phenomenon. They are described by people of other cultures and nations. In addition, psychic literature and cultic practices are full of such occurrences.

U.S. News and World Report, July 11, 1983, said, "While critics have labeled these experiences mere dreams, fabrications or hallucinations brought on by pain-killing drugs or release of chemicals in the brain, at least a half-dozen books have been written attempting to give scientific evidence of the phenomenon. The International Association for Near Death Studies also has been set up at the University of Connecticut to foster research in this area. Whatever the explanation, we know from extensive studies that something extraordinarily interesting happens to many people at the moment of death, says Connecticut psychologist Kenneth Ring, who stresses that near-death experiences do not prove the existence of an afterlife but merely show that the act of dying may not be the agonizing event many people fear."

But these experiences are not the bases for eternal truths nor are they a solid foundation for our confidence in life after death. They may be dangerously deceptive. They must be examined in the context of God's Word.

The Bible does prove there is life after death, and the biblical explanation of death is very clear. Each man dies once, and there are two possible results and destinations. "Just as man is destined to die once, and after that to face judgment" (Hebrews 9:27). What bothers me about the life-after-death stories is that regardless of whether the person is a believer or not, seldom in these experiences does death appear to have any negative consequences—which is a direct contradiction of the Bible's teaching. If all death experiences are the same, there is no judgment or hell, and the Word of God is a lie. We do not presently know for certain what the source is for these "out of body" experiences. Some have even suggested they are sometimes satanic in origin, since they can deceive people about the true nature of death and salvation, and (in this view) are a satanic counterfeit of the Christian's assurance of heavenly rest.

The desire to gain a better understanding of death has been called the "new obsession." I certainly don't want to be unbalanced in thinking about the subject, but I am convinced that when we know where death leads, we will know the "hope of glory" spoken of by Paul in Colossians 1:27.

What Is Death, Anyway?

"Can doctors agree with God on the time to die?" This difficult question was asked by an assistant professor in the Department of Medicine, Medical College of Wisconsin. Many of us will be confronted with that question and we need to face it with an understanding of its complexity.

The Bible tells us precisely what death is. Physical death is separation of the spirit and soul from the body: "The body without the spirit is dead" (James 2:26). But there is a far worse death, and that is spiritual death. Spiritual death is separation from God.

To the materialistic thinker death means complete annihilation. For the Hindu and the Buddhist, death means reincarnation. To the terrorist death provides a way to be rewarded for his cause. Many Shiite Moslems believe that for every infidel they kill (especially Christians and Jews), they will have incomparable sexual pleasures in paradise.

Today, the whole question of "When is a person dead?" is being discussed more ardently than at any other time in recent history. A relatively new discipline called thanatology (from the Greek *thanatos,* or death) has entered our language and classrooms. Thanatology is the study, or science, of death.

Making his investigation of death and dying in America today, David Dempsey wrote that "Our society has secularized life. In so doing it has removed death from its traditional religious context, the belief that it is part of the natural order of things. When death was viewed more theologically, when suffering itself was thought of as spiritually purifying, when men believed in some kind of afterlife that justified suffering, death was more acceptable."[9]

What is death? One man who has stood beside hundreds of dying persons is Chaplain Phil Manly, a compassionate man who has served at the University of Southern California Medical Center in Los Angeles for many years. With his beeper always on his belt, he is on call for any doctor whose patient is terminally ill. He has held the hands of men, women, and children at the moment of their deaths, and consoled loved ones in the midst of their grief. On the wall of his cramped office, which is in one of the largest medical facilities in the world (a center which employs some eight thousand people), Chaplain Manly keeps a chart of the number of deaths each day. He describes the medical definitions which most experts would use to pronounce a person dead.

Clinical death is when the heart stops beating, blood pressure is unreadable, and the body temperature drops. It is generally agreed that a patient is dead when the vital functions utterly fail.

Sure death is the total absence of brainwave activity. A committee of physicians, lawyers, theologians, and scientists at Harvard determined what was to be considered "brain death." Four criteria were listed:

1. Unreceptivity and unresponsivity
2. No movements or breathing
3. No reflexes
4. Flat electroencephalogram[10]

The most complete definition of death seems to be "an irreversible loss of the vital functions." Death, then, is defined as the state in which physical resuscitation is impossible.

Not all physicians, lawyers, and laymen agree, however, on the definitions for the precise moment or process of death.

To complicate matters, some people have been resuscitated who were considered "clinically dead." A friend of mine was in a hospital in Tucson with pulmonary fibrosis and Russian flu. Three times during his stay in the intensive care unit he stopped breathing and had all of the signs of being "clinically dead." Three times he was revived by a mechanical respirator. When he was released from the hospital, the headline in the *Arizona Daily Star* said, "Nearly dead, now he's home, and nurses believe in miracles."

We know that doctors can often postpone death. The American Medical Association says, "The social commitment of the physician is to sustain life and relieve suffering" (*AMA Judicial Counsel,* March 1986). Today, even doctors struggle with decisions about when to sustain life.

Those who have been brought back to life after being considered dead include more than just the current examples of medical wizardry. For instance, Elijah revived a child whose "sickness was so severe, that there was no breath left in him" (1 Kings 17:17, NASB). In fact, faithful Elijah could have used what we call artificial respiration on the boy, because it says that he "stretched himself upon the child three times, and called to the Lord, and said, 'Oh Lord my God, I pray Thee, let this child's life return to him'" (1 Kings 17:21, NASB).

Elisha was another biblical character who never had a Red Cross CPR course. Yet he went into the home of the lad who was laid out on his bed and proclaimed dead, prayed, and then "went up and lay on the child, and put his mouth on his mouth and his eyes on his eyes and his hands on his hands, and he stretched himself on him; and the flesh of the child became warm" (2 Kings 4:34, NASB).

I have the greatest respect for the medical profession, having been in the competent care of fine doctors, especially at the Mayo Clinic where I get my annual physical. However, I also realize that sometimes they are in the unenviable position of not being able to determine a true definition of death. While the physicians cannot have the final power over death, they can achieve temporary power over it. This is the doctor's dilemma—and the patient's, too.

Sometimes the issues of death become so complicated that we are again reminded of Job's question in the midst of all his extreme suffering. He asked, "But where can wisdom be found? Where does understanding dwell? Man does not comprehend its worth; it cannot be found in the land of the living" (Job 28:12–13).

Here is a sample of the many instances where man's wisdom is severely taxed:

> In 1968, a sixty-two-year-old man named John Stuckwish received a transplanted heart from Dr. Denton Cooley and his team at St. Luke's Hospital in Houston. The donor was a thirty-six-year-old man named Clarence Nicks. Nicks' brain had been damaged beyond any possibility of returning to its normal functions by a beating he had received at the hands of a group of attackers. There were no signs of electrical activity in the brain and there was no spontaneous respiration. It is critical, however, that his heart continued to beat for some time. Dr. Cooley and his team took the heart from Nicks' body and placed it in that of Mr. Stuckwish. The ethical questions arise when one begins to reflect on the relationship of the surgeon, the donor, and the donor's attackers. The people who beat up this donor have now been arrested. They pleaded in their defense that Nicks was not dead at the time the heart was given; his heart was still beating. The attackers even went beyond that to accuse the physician who removed the heart of murdering Nicks. To complicate matters, one physician had pronounced Nicks dead at the time his brain stopped and his respiratory functions stopped, while another physician specifically disagreed.[11]

Surely, the definition of physical death is a complicated, delicate decision—and I would not pretend to give a final scientific answer to that question. We know God may occasionally add time to a person's life, even when others determine he has gone. What some may think is the conclusion of a life may only be the closing of a chapter, not the end of the book. For instance, in the Old Testament, King Hezekiah was mortally ill, but the Lord said He would heal him and add fifteen years to his life. Jesus brought the daughter of Jairus back to life, and Lazarus was raised from the dead after being in his tomb for four days.

I believe God allows physicians to use their modern technology to extend physical life today in a way that is unprecedented in human history. I am constantly in awe of the tenacious qualities in the human spirit, and also of the ability of skilled physicians to treat crisis after crisis and somehow manage to pull the patient through. At the same time death is a reality, and is still the ultimate event we must all face.

Is it any wonder that people study, discuss, and evaluate death today? A young minister told about a series of seminars that were held in a Los Angeles church. Out of the five different subject areas offered, the one with the largest attendance dealt with "Death and Dying." At the University of Southern California, a very popular course is "Religious and Ethical Issues in Death and Dying." *U.S. News and World Report* did a special report on a "New Understanding about Death" (July 11, 1983).

Now that the taboo has been lifted, it is more important than ever for Christians to get involved in some of the great questions about the process of dying. The Bible has the answer to the fear of death, but we also need to understand and apply the principles in God's Word about the dying experience.

The time to understand is now, while we are healthy and alert. Those in the mental health field, the philosophers, psychologists, sociologists, and even physicians, do not have the answers. The Bible says, "so that your faith might not rest on men's wisdom, but on God's power" (1 Corinthians 2:5).

John Trapp, a great theologian from England, lived over three hundred years ago. He said, "There is a perfect time for a man to die, which, if he knew all there was to know about life he would choose that time and no other."

Thank God that we can have an open, realistic discussion of death. We need the wisdom of God to live our complicated lives, and even more so for the inevitable conclusion.

"The truth is that all of us have our time to die, and the conspiracy of silence that so often surrounds death today cannot change that fact . . . within most of us is a strong desire to hold on to physical life as long as possible."

> *He is torn from the security of his tent and marched off to the king of terrors.*
> Job 18:14

CHAPTER THREE

King of Terrors

THE CONVERSATION AT the party became hushed as someone reported that a friend had just been told he had incurable cancer. A psychiatrist—a strong, handsome man who was a prominent member of the social and professional community—said, "I'm scared to death of dying." He smiled sheepishly at his feeble pun, but he had honestly expressed what so many people feel.

In spite of rapid and ever-increasing advances in medical technology and pain relief, no one has found a way to lessen people's fear of dying. This is not some new psychosis but a condition as old as man. David, the bold youth who defied the giant Goliath, the king who pursued his enemies and destroyed them, is the same man who cried out, "My heart is in anguish within me; the terrors of death assail me. Fear and trembling have beset me; horror has overwhelmed me" (Psalm 55:4–5).

Age and circumstances often dictate the degree of fear a person may feel when facing death. David did not say those words when he was a teenager facing Goliath, but when he was older and had experienced sickness and betrayal by friends. Sometimes the fear of death grows significantly with age.

Jesus' disciples were rugged men, physically toughened by living outdoors and traveling long distances on foot. And yet when they were caught in a sudden storm so common in the area of Galilee, they shouted in desperate fear, "Lord, save us! We're going to drown!" (Matthew 8:25). They were terrified that they were going to die.

My friend, Jack Black, has defined fear as "an emotion that speaks of dread, fright, alarm, panic, trepidation, and consternation." All human beings capable of thinking manifest these emotions. Thus, fear is universal in all times and places. It is a normal, human response to the unknown. And death, the experience of death, is an unknown.

Is there more fear of death today than there was before technology enabled us to prolong life? Many people think so—although we try (as we have seen) to hide it or suppress it. Some psychiatrists say that fear of death fosters a variety of psychoses. Others believe that fear is intensified by the medical emergencies which cause them to be treated more like a thing than a human.

Another indication that the fear of death has become more prevalent comes from the fact that 80 percent of the people in the United States die in hospitals or convalescent centers instead of at home. Dying can be a lonely business. David Dempsey says, "Most hospitals in this country share at least two characteristics: they do their best to conceal from the patient the fact that he might be dying, and when the fateful time draws near they isolate him from family and friends."

Conspiracy of Silence

Some believe that telling the truth to a person who may be dying is destructive to his morale. The patient's resigned comment, "I think I'm going to die," may likely be met by the reassuring deception, "Now don't talk like that. You'll probably outlive us all." This kind of deception is practiced by medical personnel as well as by family, thinking they are being kind and acting in the patient's best interest. The "conspiracy of silence" is based upon the assumption that people don't want to think about death, especially their own. However, studies indicate that most people *are* willing to think and talk about dying, even though they may be frightened by the idea. Certainly I wouldn't want anyone to give me forced cheerfulness when what I need is honesty and love.

My wife Ruth told me about a pastor's wife who was dying of cancer. She knew it, and so did her family. But they kept telling her she was going to recover. One day a friend called on her, and the sick woman said, "I know I'm dying, but nobody will talk to me about it. Please tell me about heaven." For more than an hour they had a marvelous time, laughing and talking about her heavenly home.

Another woman told me about a visit with her brother who was in an isolation ward in intensive care. She was gowned and masked to help shield him from possible infection, so he could not see her smile or feel the touch of her hand. Nor could he move from one position because of the tubes attached to his body. She thought she should keep a positive attitude, so she said to him, "You're going to walk out of here someday, Bert." Tears flooded his eyes as he shook his head feebly and pointed one finger up. He was trying to tell her that he was on his way to heaven.

The man died two days later, and his sister said she regretted she hadn't given him reassuring words about his eternal home, rather than offering him false expectations. There is a fine line between hope and compassionate honesty. Only the wisdom of God can guide us in moments like these.

The truth is that all of us have our time to die. The conspiracy of silence which so often surrounds death today cannot change that fact. Of course, within most of us is a strong desire to hold on to physical life as long as possible. I could relate many of the stories I've heard about how the timing of death is often determined by a person's desire to live for a certain goal. One of my friends told me that when he and his wife, Joannie, were on an extended trip in Europe, his wife's father in Illinois was given only a few days to live. He rallied long enough to say, "I want to see Joannie again." He asked that his daughter and son-in-law not be told how serious his condition was, because he didn't want to spoil their trip. They returned home as scheduled, and ten days later her father died peacefully in his daughter's loving arms.

A sociologist, David Phillips of the State University of New York at Stony Brook, reported that terminally ill people tend to hang on to life until they reach some date that is important to them—a wedding anniversary, a birthday, a religious holiday. "This appears to be particularly true for the famous because of the attention they receive on such occasions. Phillips found that these notables were less likely to die in the months preceding their birthdays, and more likely to die in the three months following them. It is interesting, for instance, that both Thomas Jefferson and John Adams died on July 4, fifty years to the day after they had signed the Declaration of Independence."[2]

I remember when I heard of the death of Corrie ten Boom, the remarkable Dutch woman who hid Jews from the Gestapo during World War II and later was sent to the infamous Ravensbruck concentration camp. Her sister died in camp, but Corrie was released, and for more than thirty years she traveled the world, telling her experiences and writing books. Corrie's story received national attention in the movie, *The Hiding Place,* and in the many books she wrote. For the last few years of her life her friends and co-workers made quite an occasion of her birthdays. She was bedridden and unable to speak for the last five years of her life, but she truly loved parties. Corrie died on her ninety-first birthday, April 15, 1983. As one friend said, "What a birthday party she must have had!"

Corrie died in God's good time, at the end of a long life lived for the glory of God.

On the other hand, there are many who die prematurely, having reached a point in their lives when they feel they have no more goals left. Idle retired people reportedly have a shorter life span than those who continue with purposeful activity. We have all heard stories of a bereaved husband or wife surviving less than a year after the death of a spouse. When love is gone, life is gone. And unless we can feel needed by someone, life seems meaningless.

David Dempsey's study relates that "one survey of 260 persons sixty and over found that only 10 percent answered the question, 'Are you afraid to die?' in the affimative. The authors believe that the high percentage of those who said they were not afraid can be accounted for by an almost as high (77 percent) number of persons who professed a belief in some kind of afterlife."[3]

That is an interesting statistic. It shows the peace of mind we gain through faith, even when the vigor of life is somewhat diminished. The challenge we have as believers is to do our best to ensure that the "afterlife" in which so many put their trust is the genuine article and not a false front, like a house on a movie set.

The fear of death is not universal. Many factors such as age, physical health, family, social, and religious backgrounds make a difference. There are times when you hear people say, "Oh, I wish I could die." And yet, after a bout in the hospital or a near brush with death, the same person might say, "It's great to be alive!"

More than likely it is the process of dying that frightens people—not death itself. Chaplain Phil Manly said that as a hospital chaplain he has seen many people die very peacefully. Physicians have told me that while the body is fighting for survival, there may be severe suffering, but in life's closing moments the words "He died peacefully" have real significance.

G. K. Chesterton said, "The Lord of compassion seems to pity people for living, rather than for dying." Isn't it true that many of the experiences in life we fear because of the anticipation, but when we actually encounter them they lose much of their terror? I have watched people become physically pale and weak at the thought of speaking before a group. Then, after their initial fright, the feeling of having conquered that fear is exhilarating. I suspect death is like that. Its power to terrorize fades as we near the actual moment of passing.

Attitudes Toward Death: The World and the Cults

One of the most common attitudes toward death is denial, which says, "I don't want to think about it." The attitude is not necessarily bad, unless it means we never come around to facing the facts. It is certainly not my intention to have my daily thoughts caught up in the subject of death. In some cases doctors have said that death denial may be therapeutic. An attitude of "I'm not going to die!" may be an affirmation which prolongs life.

Another approach to death is to laugh. Some of the most soft-hearted people are the ones who say, "I'm too mean to die." Humor becomes the protective mechanism that allows us to laugh at ourselves and defy the specter of death. We can hide the fear with a chuckle, which may not always be such a bad idea!

Then there is irrational fear. It can take the form of anxiety that cripples our spirit of daring, or develops into an emotional illness, or phobia, very much like the fear of high places, or crowds, or travel. "Necrophobia," the pathological fear of death, is a fear that stifles ambition and can smother spouse and children through overprotectiveness. It was this sort of intense fear that the writer to the Hebrews addressed when he told how Christ, through His death on the cross, broke the power of the devil to "free those who all their lives were held in slavery by their fear of death" (Hebrews 2:15). The man or woman without Christ can become a slave to fear.

Another common attitude toward death is that it is like a bridge. The principle is that death is a transitional state, a state best seen in the idea of some cults that death is a transition into a happy, bright spirit world of souls who have "crossed over" to a "cosmic" eternity. Spiritism, Eastern mysticism, reincarnation, and countless other occult beliefs offer seductive answers which remove the fear of death but at the expense of denying God's truth.

It is not my purpose in this book to discuss the various beliefs of the cults in detail, or the dangers of believing in a "mystical transition" into another existence, or another life. I want to show that there is a better, surer way to life after death, and that is God's way. Without that assurance you will never have permanent peace in your life. The cults offer seductive answers that are not grounded in truth. Some are so ludicrous that we wonder how any rational person can believe them.

Dr. Sheldon B. Zablow, a San Diego psychiatrist who treats former cult members, said there are over 2,500 cults operating in the United States. He said that some people do see improvement in their lives for a brief time after entering a cult. "They sometimes give up drugs and alcohol but sacrifice the ability to think and reason. The group becomes the focus of their entire lives. The most disturbing thing is, these are people with serious emotional problems."[4]

A story in a West Coast newspaper told of a cult that has thousands of devotees who believe in reincarnation. Its founder believes she is Mary Magdalene and claims to have lived former lives as Bathsheba, Mona Lisa, and Maria Theresa of Austria. If people can believe they will return as another person, then their responsibility for this life is no longer so important. After all, they believe, we get another chance . . . and another, and another.

It becomes increasingly evident that the way we view death determines, to a surprising degree, the way we live our llves.

Is Fear Unreasonable?

I once heard a man describe his life on a sheep ranch in New Zealand. As he told about the unusual stupidity of sheep, I could see how the frequent references to sheep in the Bible really do apply to us. We follow the crowd. We are helpless when we are attacked, especially if we are attacked by fear. No wonder Christ, the Good Shepherd, continues to assure us, "Fear not, little flock." It may not be a flattering picture, but without His guidance we "baa baa" and wander aimlessly through life, searching for green pastures and stumbling over rocks. "For you were like sheep going astray, but now you have returned to the Shepherd and Overseer of your souls" (1 Peter 2:25).

In the great classic, *Pilgrim's Progress,* Mr. Honest is asked by Mr. Great-heart about one of the Pilgrims. "Did you know Mr. Fearing, who came on the pilgrimage?" Mr. Great-heart asks. Honest replies, "Yes, very well. He was one of the most troublesome pilgrims that I ever met in all my days."

Granted, Mr. Fearing is, as John Bunyan described him, "a troublesome man." But there is something of Mr. Fearing in all of us. Fear is a very painful emotion, one which may immobilize us or cause more pain than a physical blow.

The greatest fear comes when God is a stranger—when our voices and hearts cry out, "God, help me," but our words are muffled because we do not know Him. What do sheep do without a shepherd? They stumble in the darkness. The Bible says, "We all, like sheep, have gone astray, each of us has turned to his own way" (Isaiah 53:6). And that's our picture: going in all directions, bumping into each other, and not being able to find our way home. Fear stalks our every turn.

Reflecting on his years as a pastor, the Rev. Jack Black once told me, "My ministry was filled with persons who feared death; not a natural fear but an anxious fear almost becoming hysterical. Inevitably those persons so described had little or no religious identification, had no close family, had massive egos but low self-esteem, and were bored with life. Compare this human tragedy to the passing of a poor soul, leaving this world surrounded by family and loved ones. Our culture trains us to prepare for almost everything but death. And I include the churches because I have rarely ever heard any public utterance on the subject."

The Bible refers to fear more than 500 times, generally telling us *not* to be afraid. There are so many "fear nots" that we could probably have one for every day in the year—and then some! Look at a few of them:

> "Fear none of those things" (Revelation 2:10, KJV).
>
> "Fear not, for I am with thee" (Genesis 26:24, KJV).
>
> "Fear ye not, stand still, and see the salvation of the Lord" (Exodus 14:13, KJV).
>
> "Fear not [your enemies]" (Deuteronomy 3:2, 22, KJV).
>
> "Fear not them which kill the body" (Matthew 10:28, KJV).
>
> "Fear not: believe only" (Luke 8:50, KJV).
>
> "Fear not; I am the first and the last" (Revelation 1:17, KJV).

But wait. What do we do with the "fear of the Lord"? If the Bible says "fear not," and yet it also says "fear," which does it mean? The answer is: both. Fear is a twofold word. It refers to an emotion marked by dread and anxious concern. But it is also the word that means awe and profound reverence. This is the fear that inspires trust and confidence.

When we fear God, we don't cringe before Him like a prisoner robbed of his freedom by a ruthless dictator. Our fear is a love which causes us to treat Him with respect. This is what the prophet Isaiah meant when he said, "The fear of the Lord is the key to this treasure" (Isaiah 33:6). It is a reverence that comes when we see the majesty and holiness of our loving heavenly Father.

There is no shame in being afraid; we're all afraid from time to time. But there's an interesting paradox here, in that if we fear God with all our hearts, there will be nothing else to fear. When I see a child placing his little hand confidently in the bigger hand of his father, I recognize the sort of fear that fosters trust.

When it rains and then freezes over in our mountains in North Carolina, the winding roads become treacherous. I can remember walking with my children, slipping and sliding through the woods. When they held my hand, the children were less afraid. It was up to me not to let them fall down. Our heavenly Father asks us to place our trust in Him and He will steady us.

Was Jesus Afraid?

We know that Jesus was the only person in history who was born without sin, who lived without sin, and who died sinless. Since that is so, why did He display such anguish, sorrow, and fear in the Garden of Gethsemane? There are few episodes in the history of man more dramatic than what took place in that little garden during Christ's final hours on earth.

It might help to imagine ourselves there and try to understand the overwhelming emotion He must have experienced.

Gethsemane means "oil press." Most of us are familiar with olive oil as an ingredient in salads or cooking. In Palestine it was, and is, a valued staple. The Mount of Olives is frequently mentioned in the New Testament and is intimately connected with the devotional life of Jesus.

It was on the Mount of Olives that He often sat with His disciples, telling them of events yet to come. And it was to the Mount of Olives that He retired each evening for prayer and rest, after the weary work of the day.

The oldest olive trees in Palestine today are those which are enclosed in the Garden of Gethsemane. Visitors to Jerusalem today can look at them, but they can't get close enough to touch them. Too many curious people have tried to deface those ancient, gnarled trees as they sought a special souvenir from the Holy Land.

When olives are harvested, they are squeezed, pressed, and pulverized under an enormous revolving stone which mashes the fruit to pulp and recovers the valuable oil. It was in the Garden of Gethsemane that the wheel of humiliation, defeat, and eventually death would grind Jesus to the point of His greatest personal agony. Emotional torment is many times more difficult to bear than physical torment. At Gethsemane, the place of the press, the mental anguish was so intense that Jesus pleaded with His Holy Father for release. But only if it was the Father's will.

How we need friends in time of testing! Jesus demonstrated His humanity when He asked His disciples to stay with Him. He wanted and needed them in His time of greatest trial. "My soul is overwhelmed with sorrow to the point of death. Stay here and keep watch with me" (Matthew 26:38). Jesus moved a short distance from His friends, the ones who confidently said they would follow Him, the ones who said they would never deny Him, and He fell on the ground to pray. It couldn't have been too long before His heavy-lidded friends dozed off. The sleepy disciples who had said they would do anything for Him couldn't even sit up and console Him.

As Jesus prayed, His agony was great, "and being in anguish, he prayed more earnestly, and his sweat was like drops of blood falling to the ground" (Luke 22:44). Does that seem impossible? Medical dictionaries describe this condition as "chromidrosis," a state in which intense emotional stress may actually cause the blood vessels to expand so much that they break where they come in contact with the sweat glands. Personally, I cannot begin to comprehend such overpowering emotion.

Jesus prayed three times, "My Father, if it is possible, may this cup be taken from me. Yet not as I will, but as you will" (Matthew 26:39).

Was there a way out? Could Jesus be delivered from the horrors of such a death—at least for a time?

Jesus did not take delight in His approaching crucifixion; He loved life on this earth. He enjoyed the pleasures of walking with His disciples, holding children on His knees, attending a wedding, eating with friends, riding in a boat, or working in the temple at Passover time. To Jesus death was the enemy. When He prayed, "if it is possible," He wanted to confirm once again if His imminent death were truly the Father's will. Was there some other way?

But what did He mean by His plea to "let this cup pass from me"?

In the Scriptures "cup" is used figuratively to describe either God's blessing (Psalm 23:5) or God's wrath (Psalm 75:8). Since Jesus would not have prayed for God's blessing to be taken from Him, it is obvious that His use of "cup" here speaks of the divine wrath that Christ would suffer at the Cross as He bore the sins of mankind upon Himself.

How unthinkable it seems to us for Jesus, who knew no sin, to have to bear the sin and guilt of all men. "God made him who had no sin to be sin for us" (2 Corinthians 5:21). Was there no other way of accomplishing the will of the Father without drinking that cup of wrath?

This was the question Jesus was asking—and in complete obedience to the Father's sovereign will, Jesus voluntarily accepted the answer. No, there was no other way for a just and loving God to deal with our sins.

Sin must be punished; if God were simply to forgive our sins without judging them, then there would be no justice, no accountability for wrongdoing, and God is not truly holy and just. And if God were simply to judge us for our sins as we deserve to be judged, then there would be no hope of eternal life and salvation for any of us—for "all have sinned and fall short of the glory of God" (Romans 3:23). His love would have failed to provide a way for our salvation.

The cross was the only way to resolve this awesome dilemma. The conflict of the ages was about to reach its climax. On one hand, our sins were about to be placed on Christ, the sinless One. He would be "clothed" in our sins like a filthy, tattered old garment, and on the cross those sins would be judged—your sins, my sins. He would be the final atoning sacrifice for sin. On the other hand, however, Christ's perfect righteousness would be given to us, like a spotless, gleaming set of new clothes. Sin was therefore judged, and God's justice was satisfied. The door of forgiveness and salvation was opened, and God's love was satisfied. "God made him who had no sin to be sin for us, so that in him we might become the righteousness of God" (2 Corinthians 5:21).

Even as Jesus, in His humanity, struggled within Himself over this awesome predicament, He finally prayed, "Thy will be done." This was not a prayer spoken with a sigh of resignation, but with a strong voice of complete trust. Jesus knew this meant total and absolute surrender to the will of the Father and to the needs of others. Yet, there is a mystery here that we cannot fully understand. Jesus surely experienced the overwhelming awareness of His inevitable sacrifice for the sins of the world. He knew this was His primary mission on earth, for He had said, "For even the Son of Man did not come to be served, but to serve, and to give his life as a ransom for many" (Mark 10:45).

The Garden of Gethsemane is the place where Jesus was revealed to be a true man. He was face to face with the choice between obedience or disobedience. He was not a robot programmed to obey God automatically. He can sympathize with our weaknesses, "For we do not have a high priest who is unable to sympathize with our weaknesses, but we have one who has been tempted in every way, just as we are—yet was without sin" (Hebrews 4:15). Satan tempted Jesus all through His ministry, but the temptations in the wilderness at the beginning of His ministry can scarcely compare to those in the garden. After three years of selfless giving and the stress of that final week, Jesus was never more vulnerable than at this moment of time.

Some skeptics have said that Jesus' suffering in Gethsemane was a sign of weakness. They point out that many martyrs, for instance, died without the intense emotional wrestling of Jesus.

But it is one thing to die for a cause, or to die for country or for another person. It is quite another to die for an entire world, all the accumulated sins of generations past and generations to come. Jesus was to become guilty of murder, adultery, cheating, lying, and all other evil human behavior. It's more than our finite minds can ever comprehend.

One critic of the faith said to a college audience, "Look at Socrates. He didn't anguish over his impending death. He stoically took the hemlock. He proudly held his head high to the end."

Socrates, a great teacher-philosopher of ancient Greece, willingly accepted the death penalty in order to remain true to his convictions. But he died only for himself. No other death in the history of mankind can be compared to the death of Jesus Christ. Many may have suffered as much or more physically, but no one suffered more spiritually. His battle against the powers of darkness, in its essence, meant the triumph of God over Satan. No mere man could defeat Satan—only the Godman, Jesus Christ.

Jesus' Choice: Our Choice

Socrates said, "I go to die, you remain to live. God alone knows which of us goes the better way." As I compare the differences between the deaths of Socrates and Christ, I am struck by a curious contrast. Socrates died by suicide; Jesus by crucifixion. The death of Socrates saved no one, not even himself. Christ's death can save everyone who believes in Him. You and I must also choose between crucifixion and suicide. God has given each of us one life and one time to die. We may live for others or perish in our own selfishness.

If the thought of dying for others is startling, think of what it means to say "Yes" to Jesus, just as He said "Yes" to the Father. When we accept Christ as our Savior and know that He died on the cross for our sins, we have been crucified with Him. Our sins hung on that cross, just as our Lord did.

A friend of mine walks every morning and has been memorizing Bible verses as he walks. He told me that one morning he began to repeat the following verse, and for the first time understood what it meant to be crucified. Here is that verse:

"I am crucified with Christ: nevertheless I live; yet not I, but Christ liveth in me: and the life which I now live in the flesh I live by the faith of the Son of God, who loved me, and gave himself for me" (Galatians 2:20, KJV).

What is the alternative? Instead of Christ living in us, it would be self. To die without Christ is to take one's own life.

Jesus had a choice, and so do we. Did He have fear? Was the "King of Terrors" with Him in that grove of olive trees, stalking Him as He prayed on the damp ground, His sweat mixed with blood? How can we contemplate such intense suffering?

But He has taken away the fear of death for those who trust in Him. We do not need to be ashamed of our fear, but we can rest assured that He will give us strength when we have none of our own, courage when we are cowardly, and comfort when we are hurting.

When fear enters one's life, which it will, the faith which God supplies will defeat the terror and give us victory. Just as knowledge is one of the greatest deterrents to fear, so will our understanding of death enable us to combat fear. The key to victory is found in Solomon's words, "The fear of the Lord is the beginning of knowledge" (Proverbs 1:7).

We fear the unknown, but we can explore that together while we are still in the land of the living.

"We don't own our children. God has given them to us in trust, and normally we spend eighteen to twenty years providing for their training, which represents the period of time we have to fulfill that trust. . . . However, God may transfer our children to His home at any time."

Precious in the sight of the Lord is the death of his saints.
Psalm 116:15

CHAPTER FOUR

Why Do Some Die So Soon?

MY HEART ACHES for the people who suffer when a child, a young person, or a loved one in the prime of life is snatched away by death. I have tried to comfort grieving members of my family or associates and friends who have experienced tragic loss. We expect the old to die, but death seems to be a cruel thief when it steals the young. Carl Jung said it is "a period placed before the end of the sentence."

A young man whose best friend was killed in a plane crash began a poem with these words: "It is hard to contain so great an emptiness." Those words could be echoed by many throughout the ages.

There are no easy replies to the question of why some die an untimely death, but the Bible does provide us some answers. If we could not find in the Bible solutions to the most difficult questions of life, there would be little worth to this Book.

And the Bible's answers do make a difference in the lives of those confronted with the tragedy of life cut short. In this chapter, I have also tried to gather some of the most meaningful stories of those who have had firsthand experience. Out of their suffering we can discover some of the answers they have found.

Ruth's Little Brother

People keep what is precious to them. My wife has a letter written by her father in 1925 that has been a source of comfort to her for many years. Dr. Bell was a medical missionary in China, where he and another doctor helped build and develop a hospital despite civil wars, bandits, and Japanese occupation. Ruth was born in North China, and it was from there her father wrote this important letter.

How amazing it is to discover that the small things we do in our lifetime may be the very touch someone needs in generations to come. Ruth and I believe her father and mother would have wanted this intimate letter to be shared with you.

Little Nelson Bell, Jr., died at the age of ten months, after an illness of just eighteen days. Dr. Bell wrote:

> Virginia and I realized that he was going and we were with him alone when the end came. It was so sweet and so peaceful, no struggle and no evidence of pain, just quietly leaving us and going back to Him.
>
> His going has left an ache in our hearts and our arms feel very empty, but oh the joy of knowing he is safe. It has but drawn us closer to Him and given us a new tie and joy to look forward to in Heaven. We would not have him back for we know it was His will that he should go. There is no repining, wishing we had used other medicines, etc. We feel that everything that could have possibly been done was done. We had the joy of caring for him ourselves while he was sick and the memory is very sweet. He had been such a perfectly healthy baby, in some ways one of the best developed children I have ever seen and so full of life that he was a favorite with the foreigners and Chinese alike.
>
> Virginia and I had the privilege of fixing him ourselves when he died and then Virginia immediately went to the Talbots where Rosa and Ruth were at school. She wanted to tell them herself, rather than have them hear the news thru the Chinese. They were nearly heartbroken, but it was a wonderful opportunity to bring the great hope that is ours very close and plain to them.
>
> We laid him to rest just at sunset and the service was such a sweet one and we pray was a blessing to the large number of Chinese friends who came. Virginia expressed my feelings exactly as we were leaving the little cemetery (owned by our hospital) when she said, "I have a song in my

> heart, but it is hard to keep the tears from my eyes." At the grave we sang "Praise God from Whom All Blessings Flow" for this had made the wonderful hope of eternity doubly precious to us. Were it not for that hope we would not be here in China.

A child is born, he may live for a short time, and then die. What good can possibly come from a short life which never was allowed to bloom, from a mind which was never permitted to learn, from a body which was placed in a grave before it had time to grow? I believe God wants us to ask questions, for only then can we find answers. The *Living Bible* says, "Yes, if you want better insight and discernment, and are searching for them as you would for lost money or hidden treasure, then wisdom will be given you, and knowledge of God himself; you will soon learn the importance of reverence for the Lord and of trusting him" (Proverbs 2:3–5).

Trusting Him in life and, yes, in death.

Like a Vapor

Our actions would trouble us much less if we knew God's reason for sending them. This is not always the case, however. Sometimes we will never understand during our lifetime why God permits some things to happen. But sometimes we are given precise answers to the meaning of a personal tragedy.

The following story is about friends of mine who discovered, after the sudden death of their eighteen-year-old son, how God can work all things together for good.

The Bible says, "Why, you do not even know what will happen tomorrow. What is your life? You are a mist that appears for a little while and then vanishes" (James 4:14). Kent left home one afternoon to take his buddy for a flight in his new airplane. He never returned. His plane crashed on takeoff, and two young lives were instantly cut short.

Kent was about to enter college to study aeronautical engineering, and he had aspirations of becoming a pilot with Missionary Aviation Fellowship. His parents told me that he accepted Christ as his Savior at our Los Angeles crusade in 1963. He was then nine years old, and when he was eighteen he went to be with the Lord he loved.

However, in those nine short years this young man had matured in his Christian life more than many others do in a far longer lifetime. He wrote a theme paper in his senior year in high school which showed that he had a clear understanding of what it meant to be a Christian.

In that school assignment, he recounted how he had gone to the crusade and become convicted that "this spiritual element was absent in my life because of what the Bible calls sin. . . . It was at that point in Graham's talk that I decided to acknowledge what Christ had done for me by dying on the cross. I asked Him through prayer to make my life what He would have it. . . ."

Yes, Kent's life was cut short before he had fulfilled any of his greater ambitions. But had God answered his prayer to make his life "what He would have it?" His family and friends, in the years that followed that fatal crash, have seen some of the results. Many of his friends, captured by the realization of the uncertainties of life, dedicated themselves to God. One prominent doctor who attended the memorial services was so convicted that his entire life was changed. He later founded a worldwide association of Christian doctors.

Kent's parents went on to develop a ministry to those whose children were suddenly taken by accident or disease.

Clearly, God can turn tragedy into triumph.

When death comes swiftly, especially to a child, the shock can be overwhelming. Without the comfort only God can provide, it is quite difficult to console the stricken loved ones. One woman wrote about finding her six-year-old son crushed beneath a pile of logs behind a sawmill. She said, "Being a nurse, I knew immediately that he was critically injured. I asked the country doctor, who had been summoned from a nearby camp, if we shouldn't get him to a hospital. Standing up, and speaking with a slow Vermont accent, he replied, 'A hospital's not going to do him any good—might better take him to a morgue.' It was then that I realized as I knelt beside his broken, bleeding body, that Craig had gone Home.

"I looked up at the friends and folk who had gathered around and said, 'Do you know where Craig is now? He's up in Heaven with the Lord. He took the Lord as his Savior last spring, and I know he's safe in the arms of Jesus.'

"Humanly speaking, I would have been down hysterically beating the ground and sobbing my heart out, but the Lord gave me peace and strength when I needed it most. Through every minute of the days that followed, my husband and I felt His presence continuously. 'Underneath are the everlasting arms'" (Deuteronomy 33:27)[1]

I had a handsome, bright young nephew by the name of Sandy, the son of Leighton and Jean Ford. An outstanding and fiercely competitive athlete, he almost collapsed at the end of a race his senior year in high school; the newspapers had a picture of him stumbling and falling across the finish line to beat the competition. Upon examination it was discovered he had a rare heart condition which caused his heart to beat far too fast on occasion. Determined not to let it handicap him, Sandy went on to the University of North Carolina. There he became a campus leader and president of the InterVarsity Christian Fellowship, and touched many lives for Christ through his witness. But the old problem with his heart erupted, and after much discussion and prayer the decision was made to operate.

I will never forget visiting him in the hospital one Sunday afternoon on my way from New York to my home in Montreat, North Carolina. My sister Jean came in, as well as Sandy's girlfriend, and we had a wonderful time of talking, praying, and laughing. Later I went to Winston-Salem to visit his father Leighton, who was holding a week of meetings in a church there, and we prayed and committed Sandy to the Lord. On Thursday the doctors operated, and everyone was optimistic that his problem would be solved. But they could not get his heart started again. Sandy's vibrant young life, so full of promise and potential and dedication to Christ, had come to an end.

Our family could not help but wonder "Why?" How could we

reconcile Sandy's death with the purposes of a loving God? Ultimately we had to confess that we did not know the full answer—but God did, and He could be trusted. My wife Ruth came up with the best answer, however, by pointing out that the work God had given to Sandy was completed. Since that time a book about his life and death has become a best seller, inspiring and challenging thousands. A fund set up in his memory provides scholarships for dozens of students each year who are preparing for careers in missions and evangelism. God has used Sandy's death to touch lives in a way no one could ever have envisioned.

As I said at the memorial service for my nephew, Sandy, "His life was not cut short, it was completed."

The late Joe Bayly wrote about the death of the young from firsthand experience. He lost three children: one at eighteen days, after surgery; another at five years, with leukemia; the third at eighteen years, after a sledding accident complicated by mild hemophilia. Joe said, "Of all deaths, that of a child is most unnatural and hardest to bear." He did not underestimate the grief of parents. He added, "When a child dies, part of the parents is buried."

For others to assess "the peace of God, which transcends all understanding" (Philippians 4:7) as being an attitude of indifference or callousness is a mistake. Intense emotions well up in the hearts and minds of those who suffer the loss of a child or a young person. But the Christian does have the sure promise from Jesus that "I will not leave you comfortless: I will come to you" (John 14:18, KJV).

"You cannot imagine what it is like to live with a dying child," a mother told us. Faith is tested to a degree that those of us who have never experienced such a trial cannot imagine.

Joe Bayly, who knew that testing, said, "To spoil a child at a time of serious illness is to do him no favor. Few things are more liable to give away the fact that we are uptight about him than special treatment to a child. This is the time for treatment as usual, including—hard as it may be—necessary discipline. Of course we will spend more time with the sick child."[2]

Erika's Story

Erika was Lauren and Dave's first baby. She was the picture of a beautiful child, welcomed by the congregation of the church where Dave was youth pastor. After a few months a concern began to grow because little Erika had trouble holding her head up. She was unable to control her arms, and her other physical skills were not improving. At one year of age it was obvious that she hadn't grown as she should. Her worried young parents took her to medical specialists and neurologists for diagnosis. The consensus was that she had a rare disease for which there was no known cure.

During her second year Erika was susceptible to any illness that came her way. She had pneumonia several times and was in and out of hospitals. Lauren began to stay away from church activities, gave up her Bible study group, and devoted all her time to caring for Erika. She thought if she guarded the child from possible infection she might get stronger.

Erika's battle for life was frustrating for Lauren and Dave, because there didn't seem to be anything the medical profession could do for her. Lauren recalled how she reached one of her lowest emotional points when someone thoughtlessly said to her, "It is because of your lack of faith that Erika isn't being healed."

Early one morning Dave went to check on his little girl. He noticed that her skin was a brownish gray rather than her normal pink tone, and her doctor advised him to rush Erika to the hospital emergency room. By the time they arrived she had gone into shock, and immediate attempts were made to resuscitate her. The chances for her survival were slim. However, she was revived, and when they heard she was improving Dave said, "The time was not ripe for God to take her home. Thankful, we were trusting His care and His timing."

Lauren was pregnant with their second child, and as the nature of Erika's illness became known to the staff doctors at the hospital, that unborn child became the object of increasing concern. A genetics specialist told Lauren and Dave that any of their future children would have a one in four chance of being born with the same disease.

One day when Dave was out of the hospital, Erika's doctor suggested to Lauren that she should think about having an abortion. "At least consider amniocentesis to know whether you want to terminate this pregnancy," he said. Dave was angry when he heard that abortion had been recommended. "That suggestion is from the pit!" he wrote in his diary. "What else can be expected from someone with no spiritual receiver?"

During the next two weeks the young couple experienced a roller coaster of emotions. One day Dave wrote, "Overall we are very encouraged and feel that perhaps Erika still has a fighting chance." But within a couple of days, he and Lauren were asked the big question: What measures should be taken to resuscitate Erika if a seizure sends her into failure? "This is agony," wrote Dave. "How can we be involved in making such choices? We are praying that we will have God's supernatural wisdom regarding this trial. Nothing else can possibly suffice."

The doctor who had suggested the abortion told Dave and Lauren that their stability helped him do his job. But he wondered if they were suppressing their feelings and would suffer later as a result. "We admitted openly," Dave said, "that we cry together and hurt together when we are alone . . . sometimes with others, too. But we know a real peace in believing that God is sovereignly controlling this situation."

On the last day of little Erika's earthly life, her parents were faced with major decisions that had to be made immediately. The doctors asked if they wanted them to employ extraordinary measures to keep Erika alive. Her parents decided it was time to say "no." As Lauren held Erika in her arms and softly sang to her, they watched their child's life slip away.

Erika touched lives because of her mother and father, because of the friends who visited the hospital and the churches that prayed. And Lauren and Dave have had two more healthy little daughters since Erika died. What if they had listened to medical advice to abort?

Erika's story is not a closed chapter. Her parents saw that many witnessed about God with new boldness during the time Erika was in the hospital. Lauren said, "Time doesn't heal. . . . It's what you do with the time that heals." As Jack Black has said, "A long life or a short life are of equal importance to God."

Robin's Story

Millions of people throughout the world have been touched over the years by the life of a little girl who lived two short years. Her name was Robin and she was born with borderline Down's syndrome. She also suffered from a heart condition that gave her a very small chance of surviving for long.

One day Robin's mother received a phone call from a minister she had never met. He said to her, "You and your husband will soon begin to receive what our Lord wants you to learn from this child. In my opinion these little children are allowed to come into this world to bless lives. Their presence teaches patience and understanding that makes those around them more godly. Mrs. Rogers, you are truly blessed by the Lord, and you may be sure that your sweet Robin will one day be rewarded handsomely in the hereafter."[3]

Robin's parents are my long-time friends, Roy Rogers and Dale Evans, and the book Dale wrote, *Angel Unaware,* became a bestseller. Dale told of the agonizing visits to doctors, only to be told there was no hope. She told of the heart-wrenching feelings of watching a helpless child suffer.

When Dale wrote that amazing little book, it wasn't from her own viewpoint, but as if the baby, Robin, were speaking from heaven. Robin talked about her Daddy, and how seeing crippled children always hurt him and caused him to question why a loving God would allow children to suffer. And so Roy began to read his Bible, "as though he had never seen it before." From the experience of having an exceptional child, a new Roy Rogers was born.

Dale has said that she is grateful that the Lord sent Robin to them, for it made her walk closer to God.

It has not been an easy time for Roy and Dale: two other children died at an early age. But through the lessons they have learned, the good they have done for other sufferers, and their sincere commitment to the Lord, they're able to sing "Peace in the Valley" from the heart.

The Guilt Syndrome

Often when a child is suffering, parents will ask themselves, "What did I do wrong? How did I sin?" Guilt begins to accentuate the pain. Sometimes guilt comes in the guise of, "If only I had . . . " and then they review again and again all of the things they think might have been done to avoid the illness or the accident. I was told of one woman who spent years blaming herself because she had taken her little daughter to a park and allowed her to play in a stream. The child caught a cold which developed into a fatal bout with pneumonia. The mother allowed her own sense of blame and guilt to plague her for the rest of her life.

Even the disciples asked Jesus, "Who sinned, this man or his parents, that he was born blind?" (John 9:2). They, too, thought that affliiction was something always brought about by sin.

Granted, there are diseases and deaths that are the direct result of man's sin. We are surrounded by these every day. However, in the example of the blind man, and in the case of innocent children, Jesus had the answer. He said, "Neither this man nor his parents sinned . . . but this happened so that the work of God might be displayed in his life" (John 9:3).

I don't mean that parents of children who are born with an affliction, or become ill, or have an accident and die, are not sinners. We all are. However, if we believe that God punishes our children or loved ones because we have sinned, we have fallen into a cruel fallacy. Blaming ourselves leads to depression and unjustified guilt, and blaming a husband or wife may cause a breakdown in a marriage at a time when a sick child or other children desperately need the security of the family.

It may shock some parents to learn that we don't own our children. God has given them to us in trust, and normally we spend eighteen to twenty years providing for their training, which represents the period of time we have to fulfill that trust. (Don't misunderstand me—we don't cut them off at that point. Even when they are adults, they are our children. Relationships don't change, only obligations.)

However, God may transfer our children to His home at any time. If Jesus were to come today and say, "I want to take over all the teaching and training of your little boy," you would gladly let go of his hand and place it in the hand of Jesus, wouldn't you? That is what happens when He takes a child to heaven.

Why "Suffer Little Children"?

Jesus' disciples were irritated. The Master was tired from teaching all day, and here were all of these little kids pushing Him around. Can't you imagine the scene? Their mothers wanted the boys and girls to touch Him, and the disciples sought to shoo the children away. But Jesus reached out and said, "Suffer little children, and forbid them not, to come unto me; for of such is the kingdom of heaven" (Matthew 19:14, KJV).

Translated into modern vernacular, that meant, "Let the children alone, don't stop them from coming to Me. Don't you know that the kingdom of heaven belongs to children?"

We must all enter the kingdom of heaven with the simple faith and trust of a child, but a special place is reserved in the heart of the Lord for the young ones. One mother of a child who died said, "I thank God for loaning us the little fellow for a few years, and for the knowledge that we will see him again when we are united with Christ after death. What a joyous reunion. What a wonderful Savior, to provide the gift of eternal life!"

How true it is that the Lord must love little children, because He calls so many of them home. Our hope that those who die as children are lovingly taken by God to heaven was expressed beautifully by King David when his infant son died: "I will go to him, but he will not return to me" (2 Samuel 12:23).

If I Should Die Before I Wake

When children mumble that little prayer, I doubt if most of them think much about it. "I pray the Lord my soul to take," is the way it ends. Today that prayer has been neglected by most modern parents, and even banned by some. But what do we tell our children about death?

When I was growing up on a farm, death was an ever-present reality. The animals gave birth and some died. Death was not a secret. My children were reared with a menagerie of pets. Inevitably, some of them died. Somehow, without a long, psychological explanation, our kids became aware that death is part of the human experience and can be expected.

Our daughter Anne Lotz is one of the great Bible teachers in the country today. But I can remember she had a wonderful police dog when she was about thirteen years of age. The dog died. Anne, of course, was in tears. How she loved that dog. I remember taking her into my study and explaining to her that God was training her and teaching her for events that might happen in her life to come, and this would make her depend upon the Lord far more. We got down and prayed. And I remember that extra-special little time with Anne, never dreaming what she was to become as her life was strengthened by such events and the study of Scripture.

In fact, pets are a very good way of teaching children about death. The death of a pet may be a child's dress rehearsal for other losses. If we treat that death with respect and dignity, answering the child's questions, we will probably help prepare him for the inevitable encounters with the death of a friend or relative. Of course, the death of a person is a very different matter: friends and loved ones are not so easily replaced.

When a child has a pet that dies, the wise parent sometimes goes out and gets a new puppy or kitten to replace the beloved pet. The child is not given the chance to grieve too long and unnecessarily. A wonderful, faithful pet becomes part of a family, and when it is gone, it is sure to be missed. But given time, a new pet can bring his own special love into a child's life.

When Ruth was a child in China, she had a mongrel dog named Tar

Baby. When he died, he was buried beside a wall in the compound. In 1980, when she returned to her birthplace with her brother, Clayton, and two sisters, Rosa and Virginia, one of the first things she did was look for Tar Baby's grave. Fifty years later she remembered where that little dog's grave was.

Whenever a child encounters death, it is important that he or she be able to talk about it. I am concerned when the members of a family keep their feelings to themselves. When our children were growing up, I was not always around to share all of their daily challenges (though I was there more than most people think). But they all tell how their mom would be available to listen to their problems, and if she wasn't around, her parents, Dr. and Mrs. Bell, were.

To tell children about the death of someone they love may be one of the most difficult tasks of life. But even well-intended misinformation can do more damage than the blunt truth.

Seven-year-old John was told that his uncle had gone to sleep. For many nights John refused to go to sleep, afraid of what lurked in the darkness of his room. It took months for that little boy to return to his natural sleeping habits.

It is equally cruel to tell a child that the dead person has taken a trip. Death is not a trip, but a destination. Taking a trip implies that the person who died abandoned his loved ones without a good-bye, and it holds out the false hope that he may be returning.

Christians must be careful to tell a child about death without making God sound cruel. "God took Aunt Betsy" may cause a child to ask, "What kind of a God would take someone away like that?" When I told my nephew Kevin that his brother, Sandy, had died, I remember saying, "Sandy is in heaven."

The best thing we can do for a child is tell him about death without hiding facts. Visualizing heaven will give comfort, and describing a place where there is no more suffering or problems is something even the smallest child can understand. We shouldn't be afraid to talk openly about the person who has died, especially recalling good times or funny stories about them.

The Facts of Death

Kids tend to think of death as a game to play. "Shoot 'em dead!" is not a serious command. Our children played many games of cops and robbers or cowboys and Indians in the hills surrounding our North Carolina home. Today's kids don their camouflage outfits and pocket their Rambo knives for the great "search and destroy."

As they grow older, we talk about teaching "the facts of life." The "facts of death" are natural counterparts. However, in these days of "megadeath," with news of earthquakes in South America, plane crashes in our capital cities, hurricanes on Atlantic beaches, or starvation in Africa, we have been bombarded with images of death to the point of indifference. It is estimated that children may see as many as 15,000 graphic depictions of death before reaching adolescence. Psychologists are saying the increasing violence on television is already having serious consequences in the lives of children as they grow up.

However, newspaper accounts and images on the screen seem remote until someone you know dies. This is when we need to talk, not hide the facts. And how we talk about it is more important than the exact words we say.

After the tragic explosion of the *Challenger* spaceship in 1986, the students in Christa McAuliffe's class had a particularly rough time coping with their grief and the reality of their teacher's death. The difficulty of accepting the deaths of the crew members was magnified by the impact of seeing the fateful explosion being replayed over and over on television. Those who watched the news that day will have a hard time forgetting it.

However sad it may be, truth is easier for a child to handle than evasiveness. A Christian needs to deal honestly with a child's questions about birth, the body, and the soul.

A psychologist wrote in the *Los Angeles Times,* "Before an adult can help a child, though, it is necessary for the adult to understand the mourning process, be able to speak about death, face one's own mortality and understand that the most important thing is to be able to feel and express those feelings with tears, words and physical activity as an outlet for anger."[4]

In *Children's Letters to God* a little boy wrote, "Dear God, What is it like when a person dies? Nobody will tell me. I just want to know, I don't want to do it. Your friend, Mike."[5]

If I could answer Mike, I would first sit down with my arms around him and say, "Mike, everything must die sometime. When someone is dead, the body they have lived in stops breathing and moving, and seeing, and hearing. The person who had that body doesn't hurt or worry any longer. That is his earthly body. But we also have a spirit, Mike, and when we ask Jesus to come into our hearts, we will have a spiritual body from heaven. You see, son, God tells us that we will have new bodies that are strong and healthy, that are supernatural, spiritual bodies."

Losing a Loved One

Mike, and all the children like him, need simple, honest answers and lots of love. If Mike should have someone he loves die, he needs to be able to express himself without being judged for his actions. He may show indifference or anger. He may revert to baby habits.

One friend told me about his eleven-year-old son, who developed a clinging attitude after the death of his big brother. The boy would cry if his parents wanted to go out for the evening. He wouldn't go anywhere without Mom or Dad. He left for a weekend with the Boy Scouts and became sick to his stomach before the troop reached their campsite. Fortunately, an understanding counselor brought him home without forcing him to stay.

Losing a parent through death is experienced by about one in six young people before they reach eighteen, and the statistics today on the number of children of divorce indicate that millions of young people are victims of a loss sometimes worse than death.

One of the burdens on my heart is for the churches to provide the extended arms of love to kids who are victims. A hurting, resentful child will grow into an adult who believes no one cares, and he continues the cycle of pain. Most of all, adults need to recognize that the Bible tells us to care for widows and orphans: "Religion that God our

Father accepts as pure and faultless is this: to look after orphans and widows in their distress and to keep oneself from being polluted by the world" (James 1:27), and it is the obligation of the entire Christian community.

Children feel the need to talk about the death of a loved one, just as adults do. Stephen was eleven when his father died. He said in an interview, "I stayed home from school for two weeks and when I went back I wasn't crying anymore. My friends said, 'It doesn't seem like you're very sad your father died. It doesn't seem like you miss him.' I did feel sad, but I just didn't want to cry in front of them, you know. One kid even said, 'You must be glad your father died because you're not crying.' That remark really got me so upset that I told my mom about it when I got home. She said it was because when they saw me, it made them all think how sad they would be if their fathers died and they didn't realize I had done all my crying at home."

Stephen continued, "I don't know if I'll ever see my father again. No one really knows about heaven because they haven't been dead yet. But I think part of my father is still with me. His body isn't, but his spirit is. If he's anywhere, I guess he's in heaven with my grandfather. At night I usually pray to God and say, 'Please help Dad and Grandpop to have a fun time up there.'"[6]

I would like to tell all the Stephens out there that, yes, there really is a heaven. Jesus came from there and He died and has gone back to prepare a place for us.

What Happens to the Family?

When a child or young person dies, parents sometimes elevate him or her to a pedestal never attained in life. The one who is gone may become the most perfect son or daughter who ever lived, at least in the memory of mother and father. One woman told me of resenting her dead sister all her life, because her mother always talked about "little Lucille" as if she had been a saint.

It is unfair to attribute virtues beyond a person's true character. On the other hand, it can be healing to blot out the bitter memories and grasp the happy ones.

A family either comes closer together as a result of death or is driven farther apart. Nothing ever seems to remain the same. The death of a child, especially a firstborn or an only child, can place severe strains on a marriage. A psychiatrist said, "No adequate studies have been carried out, but some authorities estimate that as many as 75 percent of couples may separate after the death of a child, especially if they do not seek competent help."[7]

But there is help. C. S. Lewis says, "God whispers to us in our pleasures, speaks in our conscience, but shouts in our pains: it is His megaphone to rouse a deaf world."[8]

No one likes to be shouted at, and yet God loves us so much that when troubles come, He is there to call us closer to Him.

Children may be the little trumpet players who bring us to our senses, and to our knees. "Jesus said, 'Let the little children come to me, and do not hinder them, for the kingdom of heaven belongs to such as these'" (Matthew 19:14).

"Many people say they do not fear death, but the process *of dying. It's not the destination, but the trip that they dread."*

> *Even though I walk through the valley of the shadow of death, I will fear no evil, for you are with me. . . .* Psalm 23:4

CHAPTER FIVE

Journey Through the Valley

DR. DONALD GREY BARNHOUSE was one of America's great preachers. His first wife died from cancer when she was in her thirties, leaving three children under the age of twelve. Barnhouse chose to preach the funeral sermon himself. What does a father tell his motherless children at a time like that?

On his way to the service, he was driving with his little family when a large truck passed them on the highway, casting a shadow over their car. Barnhouse turned to his oldest daughter who was staring disconsolately out the window, and asked, "Tell me, sweetheart, would you rather be run over by that truck or its shadow?"

The little girl looked curiously at her father and said, "By the shadow, I guess. It can't hurt you."

Dr. Barnhouse said quietly to the three children, "Your mother has not been overrun by death, but by the shadow of death. That is nothing to fear." At the funeral he used the text from the Twenty-third Psalm, which so eloquently expresses this truth. That illustration from Dr. Barnhouse's own experience has been used by countless preachers to help other families face their fear of death.

Many people say they do not fear death, but the *process* of dying. It's not the destination, but the trip that they dread.

John Newton, a one-time slave trader, was converted and became a great preacher and hymn writer in the Church of England. Two years before his death, in 1807, he was so weak that he could hardly stand in his pulpit; someone had to support him as he preached. Shortly before he died, when he was confined to his room and unable to move, he told a friend, "I am like a person going on a journey in a stagecoach, who expects its arrival every hour and is frequently looking out of the window for it. . . . I am packed and sealed, and ready for the post."[1]

You may have heard of Newton; he wrote some words which are sung around the world: "Amazing grace, how sweet the sound."

The Dangers of Denial

Whether our last trip is by stagecoach, slow and arduous, or by jet, swift and smooth, the journey through the valley eventually comes to a stop. How should we travel, and how can we help the ones we love along the way?

As Christians we are constantly bombarded with attitudes and values which are contrary to biblical teaching. Even though the subject of death has come out of the closet, the denial of one's own mortality is instinctive in most of us. No matter how well we take care of ourselves, there may come a time when we face a severe health problem. Sometimes we are not given a choice about our physical or mental condition. How can we live in a basically non-Christian culture and cope with the despair that may come when death seems near?

In her inimitable bravado Katherine Hepburn said, "I think we're finally at a point where we've learned to see death with a sense of humor. I have to. When you're my age, it's as if you're a car. First a tire blows, and you get that fixed. Then a headlight goes, and you get that fixed. And then one day, you drive into a shop, and the man says, 'Sorry, Miss, they don't have this make anymore.'"[2]

But a time comes when the humor becomes deadly serious. Anyone who is told he has a fatal illness cannot just laugh it off. The first reaction is, "You must be wrong." "Not me." Bad news is all too frequently met, first, with disbelief.

Denial can be very dangerous. A prominent urologist endured

severe lower back pains over a long period of time; although he had diagnosed patients with similar conditions, he refused to get treatment until his own condition was beyond hope of a medical cure. He did not want to hear the bad news, so he opted for no news.

Dr. Ruth Kopp, a Christian doctor specializing in clinical oncology, has had many years of experience with terminally ill patients. She wrote: "The first important effect of denial I've seen in my relationships with patients is that it produces a partial deafness. Although the hospital staff told Jesse (the patient) that he had widespread, inoperable cancer, he was deaf to much of what he had heard. He was not unique in that respect!"[3]

A terminally ill patient may reject what he has heard, and then deny the need for treatment. Some will listen to the doctor's diagnosis and then begin a round of searching for other doctors who will give them happier news. Of course, there is nothing wrong with getting other qualified opinions; this should not be considered denial. Others look for unorthodox methods and spend time and money for temporary, often fraudulent, cures for their symptoms instead of facing the reality of their condition.

Denial isn't necessarily a sign of weakness, but a normal emotion that needs to be voiced. Sometimes it can serve as a protective mechanism to shield a person from threatening situations before the individual is emotionally ready to handle them. If we persist in denial, however, we are cutting ourselves off from the help we need—from others and from God.

The prophet Jeremiah said, "You can't heal a wound by saying it's not there" (Jeremiah 6:14, LB). And yet we want to ignore a diagnosis about our physical state if it is unpleasant.

Chaplain Phil Manly tells a story that illustrates the force that denial can play in masking the truth. A badly burned baby was admitted to the USC Medical Center burn ward in Los Angeles. The mother was with the baby when the child died. The next day the nurse on the ward received a call from the mother asking how her baby was and what time she could visit. The nurse and Chaplain Manly were able to bring her lovingly to accept the reality of her baby's death.

Jesus had a difficult time with the attitude of denial in His disciples.

He told them repeatedly that He would be betrayed and crucified, but they refused to listen. Peter even rebuked Him for saying that He was going to be killed and after three days rise again: "From that time on Jesus began to explain to his disciples that he must go to Jerusalem and suffer many things at the hands of the elders, chief priests and teachers of the law, and that he must be killed and on the third day be raised to life. Peter took him aside and began to rebuke him. 'Never, Lord!' he said. 'This shall never happen to you!'" (Matthew 16:21–22).

Peter knew Jesus told the truth, but he did not want to hear it.

When Truth Hurts—Or Heals

The Bible tells us to "speak the truth in love," and yet there are times when the truth seems so harsh that we play games. One way to respond when a terminally ill person is in the denial stage is to join him in the ostrich attitude. But Dr. Ruth Kopp warns, "If your response is behavior that is harmful to the individual, it is inappropriate."[4] Most people can't face the fact of their own deaths twenty-four hours a day, and need to pretend, at least for a while, that the situation may be just a bad dream.

We may respond to someone's denial by avoiding it. Many people who have been told they have just a few weeks or months left have lived to laugh at the diagnosis years later. A Christian may have complete confidence that God has healed him or her, despite medical reports to the contrary. A realistic answer, given with gentleness and love, might be, "We know that God can heal, and He does. But we don't know what He has in store for you or for me. Let's trust the doctors for treatment, and continue to pray for healing, asking for God's will." One doctor said he used the "wait and see" response whenever a terminally ill person said that God had healed him or her. If He hasn't, then they will face that reality later.

No One Wins

Some types of denial can be dangerous for the patient and loved ones. I refer specifically to the "Let's Spare Them" game. The patient knows he or she is terminally ill. There are important things such a person wants to say to his wife and children, but he is afraid they cannot accept the fact that he may soon die, so he spares them any painful conversations. His wife, knowing her husband's time is short, wants to keep the atmosphere cheerful, so she doesn't ask the questions she needs to ask about the family and finances that are a burden on her heart. His family would like to tell him some of the things they never got around to saying when he was well, but they're afraid to upset him. Everyone plays the game, and no one is a winner.

What if, instead, dying people were urged to express themselves and talk openly about their illness? And what if the loved ones listened to such concerns, instead of ignoring them? Nothing soothes loneliness or depression as much as being able to talk about those fears and concerns.

Job's Friends: Who Needs Enemies?

Job was affliicted with so many physical and emotional problems that his name is always associated with suffering. His wealth was taken from him, and his sons and daughters were crushed when a great wind demolished the house where they were dining. Job was struck with terrible boils from head to foot. His wife and brothers shunned him and children ran from the sight of him. Those who loved him turned against him. He became a joke among the people who had once respected him.

Along came those "well-meaning friends" who tried to explain the cause of his pain. One "friend" told him he was being punished by God less than he deserved. Another argued if he had been pure and good, God would hear his prayers and answer him.

In various modern guises many of "Job's friends" are still among us today. There is nothing more dangerous than a half-truth, so let's examine what the Bible says about the sickness, disease, and pain which usually precede all but sudden, accidental deaths.

We know that when God created Adam and Eve, they were holy and healthy. They were created in His perfect image and were to remain perfect human specimens. More than that, they were not meant to experience death. But Satan ruined these two divine masterpieces, and as a result of their decision to disobey God, sin, sickness, and death entered paradise. So, human sin was the first cause of sickness and death. Since that moment in the Garden of Eden, pain and death have been the heritage of the entire human race. "Sin entered the world through one man, and death through sin, and in this way death came to all men, because all sinned" (Romans 5:12).

Even the strain of Christian service can result in sickness. Daniel was a devoted servant of the Lord, and when he saw a vision of things to come, he fainted and was ill for many days (Daniel 8:26–27).

The apostle Paul likewise experienced frequent bouts of illness and physical weakness. He recalled to the Corinthians, "I came to you in weakness" (1 Corinthians 2:3). He prayed also that God would take his problem away: "There was given me a thorn in my flesh, a messenger of Satan, to torment me. Three times I pleaded with the Lord to take it away from me. But he said to me, 'My grace is sufficient for you, for my power is made perfect in weakness.' Therefore I will boast all the more gladly about my weaknesses, so that Christ's power may rest on me. That is why, for Christ's sake, I delight in weaknesses, in insults, in hardships, in persecutions, in difficulties. For when I am weak, then I am strong" (2 Corinthians 12:7b–10). I have known many Christian workers who have risked their lives and their health in serving the Lord, although I have known others whose ministries would have lasted longer if they had taken better care of themselves and learned to relax.

A leading cause of sickness today is our high-pressure lifestyle. Heart disease, ulcers, and some types of cancer often may be attributable to our ambitious pursuits and reckless living. We know that neglecting our need for good diet, rest, and mental habits can lead to serious physical problems. The Bible says, "My people are destroyed from lack of knowledge" (Hosea 4:6).

We cannot always know or understand God's purpose in allowing us to endure physical or mental trials. I must admit that when I see someone suffer who has devoted his life to the Lord and has led an exemplary life, I find it difficult to understand. Nevertheless, we know we can trust God and His love, even when we do not understand.

My friend of many years, the late Herbert Lockyer, in his book, *All the Promises of the Bible,* illuminates some of his discoveries from the Bible concerning the purposes of sickness.[5]

One purpose is to teach us God's laws. The psalmist said, "It was good for me to be afflicted so that I might learn your decrees" (Psalm 119:71).

Another purpose of sickness and suffering is to perfect the person who sins. It's the idea that God will pull us up short to strengthen us for His purpose. "And the God of all grace, who called you to his eternal glory in Christ, after you have suffered a little while, will himself restore you and make you strong, firm and steadfast" (1 Peter 5: 10).

Suffering is also meant to prepare us for a coming glory. Peter writes, "Dear friends, do not be surprised at the painful trial you are suffering, as though something strange were happening to you. But rejoice that you participate in the sufferings of Christ, so that you may be overjoyed when his glory is revealed" (1 Peter 4:12–13). Also, suffering equips us to comfort others ". . . so that we can comfort those in any trouble with the comfort we ourselves have received from God" (2 Corinthians 1:4).

God doesn't comfort us to make us comfortable, but to make us comforters.

In addition, suffering can give us opportunities to witness. The world is a gigantic hospital; nowhere is there a greater chance to see the peace and joy of the Lord than when the journey through the valley is the darkest.

Gene and Helen Poole were Christians who had been married for sixty-five years. When Helen was in the final weeks of her life, unable to move or speak, it was the witness of her faithful husband, spending all day beside her bed in his wheelchair, that touched the lives of the staff and visitors at the convalescent home.

Perhaps you are going through a period of suffering right now. It may be because of some physical illness which has afflicted you, or it may be because of a broken relationship, a financial difficulty, or some other reason. What is your reaction to it? Are you resentful and bitter, demanding that God change your situation or lashing out at those around you for what you consider unjust treatment? Or have you yielded your life—including your suffering—to Christ and asked Him to work for His glory through your suffering, even if you do not fully understand it?

When the word came of the illness of Lazarus (who would die and then be raised from the dead by Jesus), Jesus declared, "This sickness will not end in death. No, it is for God's glory so that God's Son may be glorified through it" (John 11:4). The same could be said of much of our suffering, as we seek God's will and strength.

The Bible warns that bitterness never solves anything, but only hurts both us and those around us: "See to it . . . that no bitter root grows up to cause trouble and defile many" (Hebrews 12:15). It also promises us that God can bring a harvest of good in our lives through our suffering, if we will let Him. "No discipline seems pleasant at the time, but painful. Later on, however, it produces a harvest of righteousness and peace for those who have been trained by it" (Hebrews 12:11).

William W. Kinsley has written, "Just as soon as we turn toward Him with loving confidence, and say, 'Thy will be done,' whatever chills or cripples or enslaves our spirits, clogs their powers, or hinders their development, melts away in the sunshine of His sympathy. He does not free us from the pain, but from its power."

Yes, God is with us in the midst of our suffering, and He can bless us in ways we could never have imagined. Lay your burden of suffering at the feet of Christ—who suffered on the cross for you—and ask Him to help you not only bear it but experience His victory and peace in the midst of it.

Do We Go Through Stages?

Elisabeth Kubler-Ross was one of the first secular psychologists to observe that there are five stages that patients and their loved ones may go through in the dying process. Most people in the medical and psychological fields agree that a person doesn't march through the five stages of denial, anger, bargaining, depression, and acceptance like a programmed robot. These stages may coexist, be reversed, or be skipped, but the pattern is common in many sufferers.

Marian Holten cared for terminally ill patients for more than forty years and had many experiences seeing her patients through the valley. She had been a student nurse in the 1940s when her first assignment was to sit with a dying, comatose patient. She said those were the days when there was more personal than machine care. She pulled up a chair by the bedside, prepared for a long, tedious vigil. Suddenly she was startled when her patient, who had been unable to move or speak for weeks, opened his eyes, sat up in bed and looked around. A beautiful expression came over his face, and then he fell back on his pillow, dead.

From that time on, Marian asked to be assigned to the terminally ill. She wanted to know more about the dying experience, what happened at the moment of death, and how to help her patients through those final hours.

Denial is so strong that patients will insist they are going to do things they are incapable of doing. Marian told of a young girl who was in the last stages of acute leukemia and kept insisting that she was going to Canada. How do caring people respond when they know the desire cannot be carried out? We do not need to lie, but we must be supportive. Marian taught her student nurses to make a statement which was positive. She would say, "I can see that's something you are happy about. Tell me about Canada. Is it someplace you've always wanted to go?" Taking someone's mind off his or her illness, without supporting his or her denial, is the honest way.

When my mother was in her final days, Rose Adams would get her dressed to go out, even when she knew Mother would not be able to go. It was a game, but it made Mother happy, and that was the most important thing.

Denial Through Anger and Indifference

Anger is another very human response from those who are very ill. One patient became so angry that when the nurse came in to take his temperature in the morning, he shouted at her, "Get out of here, I can't stand your face." Marian Holten remembered another time when a patient threw a full urinal at her. How can caring people handle other people's anger? One way is with humor. Later Marian who was on the receiving end of the outburst poked her head cautiously in the door and said, "Hey, is it OK to come in now?" He laughed, realizing how unreasonably hard he had been on her, and soon they were friends.

Another type of denial is to ignore those we think are past understanding. We should never assume that people do not hear what we are saying. Among the "living dead" are those who are very much alive. Nurses report that family members, and even hospital personnel, talk around a comatose patient as if he or she were already dead. At first all the family members come to the bedside of their dying loved one. Then, they begin to return to their other activities and, just when the patient needs them the most, there is no one around. "It's taking him so long to die," someone says in his presence; or, "I just wish the Lord would take him and get it over with."

One nurse told how she talked quietly and encouragingly to her patient all the time she was caring for his needs, even though the doctors said he didn't know anything that was happening. He miraculously came out of his coma and upon hearing the voice of this nurse said, "Oh, you're the one who talked to me."

Denial Through Bargaining

Another of the stages is bargaining. A Las Vegas showgirl was admitted to the hospital and it was discovered that she was in the final stages of cancer. A year before she had discovered a lump on her breast, but she chose to ignore the symptoms. Her body was her fortune, and she refused to have it "mutilated," as she described it. When she had to have surgery to save her life she was angry. Soon she thought her beauty was gone, but she still propped herself up in bed and spent hours every day applying make-up. She became garish looking and increasingly bitter. One day a beautiful student nurse came into the room and the showgirl looked at her and remarked to Nurse Nolten, "I would give anything if I could be like . . ." and then she cut off her bargaining plea and ended pathetically, "But I don't have anything left to give, do I?"

Ironically, at that point she was finally past denying and bargaining and at last able to accept her position. It was then she said, "I can't handle this alone."

When we have "nothing left to give," God says, "All I want is you, beloved. Trust Me." The Great Physician is willing and able to take our burdens, if we will just hand them over to Him. Life and death is not a do-it-yourself project.

Divine Healing: Truth and Consequences

When little Erika was on life-support systems, hundreds of people were praying for her healing. Instead, the Lord took Erika to be with Himself. At the same time, in another hospital, Ron Stokes was in intensive care after a severe stroke. Hundreds of people all over the country were praying for Ron. He recovered, and as a result of caring Christian friends, accepted Christ. Why did God cure Ron and not Erika? Were prayers any less fervent or the faith of loved ones any weaker in one case than the other? No, not at all. Does God heal today? Of course He does, but not always. He can heal in response to prayer and faith; He can heal through the skill of physicians or the effectiveness of medicines.

When Ruth's sister, Rosa, was a senior at Wheaton College, she collapsed in chapel and was rushed to the hospital. They thought she had appendicitis. Dr. Ken Gieser, who had interned in Dr. Bell's hospital in China, went to the hospital with her. When they operated on Rosa they discovered her abdominal cavity was filled with tubercular nodules. She had to have several months of complete bed rest. The housemother where Ruth and Rosa lived turned over the sunporch to the young patient and Ruth dropped out of school to care for her. She seemed to improve until just before she was to resume normal life when she hemorrhaged from her lungs and they knew she had tuberculosis all through her system. At the small hospital to which she was transferred, the surgeons proposed doing a phrenichotomy on one lung, permanently crushing the phrenic nerve, and a weekly pneumo–thorax treatment to rest the other.

At that time the Bells returned from China and moved Rosa to a drier climate at a hospital in New Mexico. Ruth stayed with Rosa and watched her attitude with interest. As Ruth said in later years, "There are two kinds of hypocrites in the world, one who wants you to think that they are better than they are and one who wants you to think they are worse than they are. Rosa was one of the latter. She delighted in shocking people. She read her Bible like some people read *Playboy* magazine, shoving it under her pillow when someone came into the room. However, she began to read her Bible in earnest and learned that while Jesus was here on earth, no one came to Him for healing without Jesus healing them. She read where James says, 'Is any one of you sick? He should call the elders of the church to pray over him and anoint him with oil in the name of the Lord. And the prayer offered in faith will make the sick person well' (James 5:14–15). Rosa inquired and found a little church that followed those instructions; she called for the elders and they came and prayed for her. Rosa decided she could get up and lead a normal life and stopped the hospital treatments. Medically speaking, she should have hemorrhaged to death."

Ruth remembers her father's reaction to Rosa's decision: "Daddy was concerned. Being a doctor, he knew the dangers involved, but being a man of God he didn't want to discourage Rosa if God was leading her. He talked to the godly superintendent, Mrs. Van Devanter, who ran the hospital, and she said, 'Dr. Bell, there is something special happening in Rosa's life. I would be careful not to discourage it.'

"Rosa resumed a normal life, her lungs expanded, and to all appearances, she was healed. Later, the two doctors who had been treating her in New Mexico, both agnostics, said to Daddy, 'Dr. Bell, your daughter's explanation that God healed her is the only adequate one.'"

Ruth has said that, to her knowledge, from that day until this Rosa has never had a serious illness.

God does heal today and He often spares lives of some who, by human standards, would be dead. Our son, Franklin, has survived many harrowing circumstances, but one is especially vivid to us. This happened while he was a student at Le Tourneau College in Texas. He was taking flight instruction and during a spring break his flight instructor and wife, another buddy, and he flew down to Florida to join us for a few days' vacation. When they took off to return, it was overcast. As they flew above the clouds, something happened to the electrical system and they lost all the lights on the plane. They descended beneath the cloud cover where they could see the lights of Jackson, Mississippi, and circled until they spotted a small airport. All the lights went on, the strobe lights were flashing, and they made a safe landing.

When the pilot walked over to thank the men in the tower for being so cooperative, they said, "We didn't even know you were coming. . . . We were just showing some friends around the airport and they wanted to know what would happen if someone came in late at night. We told them we'd turn on the strobe lights, so we demonstrated them. At that moment you came in sight and we couldn't believe it, because we didn't know there was a plane in the area."

God knew Franklin was not ready to go at that time. About two years later his flight instructor was killed in a crash. Sometimes God delivers us from death, and sometimes He doesn't. Only God knows the reason.

Ruth has a friend in England, Jennifer Larcombe, who had developed multiple sclerosis. She prayed for healing, but continued to get worse. She was besieged by people who told her that if everything was right between her and the Lord she would be healed, otherwise she must have some secret sin which she hadn't confessed. This advice was devastating to her, because she loved the Lord with all her heart. Finally, the British publishers, Hodder & Stoughton, asked her to write a book about her experiences. The book was eventually published and was called *Beyond Healing*. Ruth was asked to write the foreword, and when she read the manuscript she was deeply moved. Clearly, when God said no to Jennifer, He gave her another ministry.

James said, "And the prayer offered in faith will make the sick person well" (James 5:15). And, yet, James himself was beheaded. He trusted God, whatever the outcome.

Soon after James was put to death, Peter was arrested and put in prison. The believers prayed earnestly for Peter, and the night before he was to be brought to trial, an angel rescued him (Acts 12:5–11). In that situation God said "yes" to Peter.

Christians know that God answers prayer in three ways: yes, no, and later. The apostles of Jesus illustrate this beautifully. After Pentecost, the early church was persecuted severely, but they trusted God in all circumstances. All but one of these apostles died as martyrs, but they were as faithful in their deaths as in their lives, understanding that death is the believer's translation to the presence of the Almighty.

Divine healing or deliverance from death is in His hands.

Sam was a devoted Christian who discovered that he had cancer of the mouth. As the dreadful disease developed, multiple operations took so much of his tongue and face that soon he had very little face left. His wife took him to a healing service and when they returned she told everyone triumphantly that Sam had been healed. It would be impossible to imagine what went on in Sam's mind as his suffering became worse. He hated to have anyone see him, and yet his wife would invite friends and neighbors in and announce that Sam was healed. Instead, he died. In such a case an unrealistic faith in divine healing can be another form of denial: a belief that comes from disbelief in our own mortality.

Christians should have another view of divine healing, and that is to acknowledge God's ability to heal—but to be willing to accept a yes or no answer. Job was God's great example of this belief when he said, "Though he slay me, yet will I hope in him" (Job 13:15).

To face the awfulness of disease or illness, knowing that unless God intervenes we will die, is simply being honest.

The psalmist says, "The Lord will sustain him on his sickbed and restore him from his bed of illness" (Psalm 41:3). What a wonderful promise to know that God is with us, caring for us in the room where we are in pain. I have visited Christians in sickrooms where the presence of Christ was so real that, even in the midst of unbelievable suffering and facing death, the patient had serenity.

The Remarkable Amy Carmichael

In 1956 I was in India and visited the Tinnevelly district of South India where Amy Carmichael had lived. Amy was the first missionary to be supported by the Keswick Convention and a woman who wrote forty books during her lifetime. She labored in the land of her adoption for over fifty-six years, never once returning to her home in England on furlough.

I had the honor of visiting the place where she spent the last twenty years of her life, bedridden due to a leg injury from an accident. It was a modest little room, with red tile floor, very few pieces of furniture, and an enormous bird cage outside the window where she could watch the birds.

She had ministered and written from her bed for all those years, and I had a feeling of awe being shown the premises by the woman who had cared for her. As I stood in that simple place, the presence of Christ was very real. Amy went through the valley of the shadow and in spite of pain and physical weakness caused a great light to be spread around the world. It was during those years she did most of her writing—books that still bring blessing to millions across the world. Elisabeth Elliot has recently written her story in a challenging book entitled *A Chance to Die.*

All Prayers Answered

Christians in desperate situations search the Scriptures for the many wonderful promises of God. One of our favorites is the statement made by Jesus that "You may ask me for anything in my name, and I will do it" (John 14:14). We claim that promise and ask the Lord to heal our loved one. But what happens if healing doesn't come? It's easy for Christians to feel guilty or believe our faith is weak if we pray for healing and it doesn't take place. Believers throughout the ages have had to face the fact that God does not heal everyone who prays for healing. But our lack of faith does not determine God's decision on healing. If that were so, He would have to apologize to all of His great servants in the Hebrews 11 Hall of Fame. Look at that cast of characters: Abel, Enoch, Noah, Abraham, Sarah, Isaac, Jacob, Joseph, Moses, Rahab, Gideon, Barak, Samson, Jephtah, David, Samuel, and all the prophets! All of these received great deliverance from God and endured incredible hardships through faith. What happened to them? "Some faced jeers and flogging, while still others were chained and put in prison. They were stoned; they were sawed in two; they were put to death by the sword. They went about in sheepskins and goatskins, destitute, persecuted and mistreated" (Hebrews 11:36–37).

Even though God was pleased because of their faith, they didn't receive much of the world's pleasures. Why? Because God had a better destination, a heavenly city, waiting for them. It was not because of lack of faith or as a punishment for sin that these men and women of God were not delivered from suffering and death. We have the faith to believe that God has a special glory for those who suffer and die for the sake of Christ.

The Pulpit On Death Row

Velma Barfield was a woman from rural North Carolina who was charged with first degree murder; no one could have surmised the effect her life and death would have upon so many people. In 1978 she was arrested for murdering four people, including her mother and fiance. She never denied her guilt, but told the chilling story of her drug-dazed life, beginning with the tranquilizers which were prescribed following a painful injury.

Velma was a victim of incest as a child and the abuse of prescription drugs as an adult. After she admitted her guilt, she was taken to prison and confined in a cell by herself. One night the guard tuned in to a twenty-four hour gospel station. Down the gray hall, desperate and alone in her cell, Velma heard the words of an evangelist and allowed

Jesus Christ to enter her life. She wrote, "I had been in and out of churches all my life and I could explain all about God. But I had never understood before that Jesus had died for me."

Her conversion was genuine. For six years on death row she ministered to many of her cellmates. The outside world began to hear about Velma Barfield as the story of her remarkable rehabilitation became known.

Velma wrote to Ruth and there developed a real friendship between them. In one letter Ruth wrote to Velma, "God has turned your cell on Death Row into a most unusual pulpit. There are people who will listen to what you have to say because of where you are. As long as God has a ministry for you here, He will keep you here. When I compare the dreariness, isolation, and difficulty of your cell to the glory that lies ahead of you, I could wish for your sake that God would say, 'Come on Home.'"[6]

My daughter, Anne, received special permission to visit Velma Barfield many times and was touched by the sadness of her story and the sincerity of her love for Christ as well as the beauty of her Christian witness in that prison.

Before her final sentence, Velma wrote to Ruth: "If I am executed on August 31, I know the Lord will give me dying grace, just as He gave me saving grace, and has given me living grace." On the night she was executed, Ruth and I knelt and prayed together for her till we knew she was safe in Glory.

Velma Barfield was the first woman in twenty-two years to be executed in the United States. She walked through the valley of the shadow for many years and at her memorial service the Reverend Hugh Hoyle said, "She died with dignity and she died with purpose. Velma is a living demonstration of 'by the grace of God you shall be saved.'"

Ruth wrote the following poem which was read for the benediction at Velma's funeral service:

As the eager parents wait
the homing of their child
from far lands desolate,

from living wild;
wounded and wounding along the way,
their sorrow for sin ignored,
from stain and strain of night and day
to home assured.
So the Heavenly Father waits
the homing of His child;
thrown wide those Heavenly Gates
in welcome glorious-wild,
His, His the joy by right
—once crucified, reviled—
So precious in God's sight
is the death of His child.

Who Cares?

As Christians we are responsible for one another. "Carry each other's burdens, and in this way you will fulfill the law of Christ. . . . Therefore, as we have opportunity, let us do good to all people, especially to those who belong to the family of believers" (Galatians 6:2, 10). At no time is this more true than when suffering and death touch someone around us.

Often the friends and family who care for a sick loved one touch more lives by their example than they will ever know. But many times we are at a loss to know what to do or what to say. We stumble in awkward embarrassment or ignore an unpleasant situation by staying away from someone who is seriously ill. However, members of a family are not meant to suffer alone.

Most of us will have times in our lives when we are with people who are going through the valley of the shadow. How can we show the love of Christ? How would we like others to treat us if we were in similar circumstances? Remember the words of Jesus: "In everything, do to others what you would have them do to you, for this sums up the Law and the Prophets" (Matthew 7:12).

Margaret Vermeer served as a missionary in Nigeria. When she was seven months pregnant, she received the report that a biopsy of a small tumor was malignant. Five weeks after the surgery to remove the tumors, she gave birth to a son, then began chemotherapy and radiation treatments. For two years she had a miraculous remission, but then gradually more tumors appeared. As her condition grew increasingly serious, she became more sensitive about the way people viewed her. Six months before she died she was speaking for women's church groups, sharing her insights on how to care for others as she wanted to be cared for. Here are some of her thoughts:

First, be honest in sharing your feelings. Don't bounce into the room with false cheerfulness, but admit your helplessness and concern. "I would like to help you, but I don't know how," is a straightforward expression of concern. Don't play games and be evasive. Even children can cope better when people talk to them honestly.

Don't preach a well-thought-out sermon. Christians who bring out their Bibles and read lengthy passages are not being sensitive. To share a verse that means something to you may be helpful, but wait for the signals before plunging into a lengthy spiritual discussion.

Be a good listener. People will tell you what they are ready to talk about. Sickness can be a very lonely journey. When Jesus was agonizing in the Garden of Gethsemane, He didn't want to face death alone. He asked three disciples to wait and pray with Him, but they fell asleep. What good were they?

Treat a dying person as a human being. Sometimes we treat a dying person in such a way that we make it harder on that person emotionally. We shut the people up in hospitals, whisper behind their backs, and deprive them of all the things that had made their lives rich. Familiar things *are* important.

One woman told me that when her mother was in a coma, she put a picture of her father, who had died many years before, on the nightstand beside her mother's bed. Whenever the comatose woman was turned to the other side, she struggled unconsciously to face the photograph of her husband. Finally, her daughter gave instructions to the nurse that whenever her mother was turned she was to move the picture, too. The woman never regained consciousness, but she died with a smile on her face, looking at the picture.

Provide spiritual support. When you quote a Bible verse to comfort a person, be sure you know what the verse means. When Margaret Vermeer knew that she only had a short time to live, she said that she was told by her Christian friends to "give thanks in all circumstances, for this is God's will for you in Christ Jesus" (1 Thessalonians 5:18). Does that mean to thank God for cancer? Didn't Jesus see sickness and disease as part of Satan's work? Look at the verse carefully. It doesn't say give thanks for everything, it says to give thanks in everything. There is a vast difference.

When we are told that "God causes everything to work together for good," it doesn't mean that all things are good in themselves, but that God is making them work out for good.

Always have hope. God is greater than the situations we face. Sometimes it's hard to find that which is positive and hopeful, but there is always something to be thankful for. Help the patient look forward to something . . . a visit from someone special . . . a time when you will be returning.

My mother loved to anticipate celebrations. A few months before she died, one of her granddaughters was going to be married. Her nurse knew that Mother was too weak to go to the wedding, but she helped her get dressed, anyhow, giving her the hope of that occasion. When Mother realized she couldn't go, she was at peace about it. If she had been told from the beginning that she couldn't make it, she would probably have been resentful.

Elisabeth Kubler-Ross made a great contribution to the understanding of death and dying, but her conclusions stand in stark contrast to the hope of the Christian. In an interview she was asked if a patient's religious orientation affected his view toward resignation in the end. She answered, "I have very few really religious people. The few I have—and I mean those with a deep intrinsic faith—have it much easier, but they are extremely few. Many patients become more religious in the end, but it is not really effective."[7]

My father-in-law, who had seen many die, said there was a vast difference between the reactions of believers and nonbelievers at the time of death.

In contrast to the anguish and anxiety of the person with no eternal hope, Christians can look to Christ for hope and encouragement. Because of our faith in Christ we do not "Grieve like the rest of men, who have no hope" (1 Thessalonians 4:13b).

Whatever suffering and agony we must endure, either in our own body or for someone we love, we are assured of His presence. And ultimately we will be resurrected with a body free of pain, an incorruptible and immortal body like His. This is our future hope.

The journey through the valley may be extremely difficult, but what a glorious destination awaits us when we travel with Jesus Christ!

"There has always been a 'time to live and a time to die.' Today, with the ability to prolong life, each one of us will probably have to face this issue ourselves or with someone we love. . . . How long is too long?"

> *For the soul of every living thing is in the hand of God, and the breath of all mankind.* Job 12:10, LB

CHAPTER SIX

How Long Is Borrowed Time?

"IF I EVER become so ill that only machines can keep me alive, please instruct the doctors to pull the plug."

Jacqueline Cole was forty-four years old when her husband, Presbyterian Minister Harry Cole, had to honor or ignore that agonizing request. Jacqueline had suffered a cerebral hemorrhage in the spring of 1986 and had been in a coma for forty-one days. When her case seemed hopeless, her husband reluctantly asked a Maryland judge to order doctors to let his comatose wife die, according to her own wishes. The judge determined that it was too soon to give up hope, and six days later Jacqueline opened her eyes, smiled, and returned her husband's joyous kiss. "Miracles can and do occur," said the happy minister. "I guess we've muddied the waters surrounding the question of a person's right to die."[1]

Never before in human history has there been the urgency to debate such a vital and complex issue. There has always been a "time to be born and a time to die" (Ecclesiastes 3:2). Today, however, with the ability to prolong life, each one of us will probably have to face this issue ourselves or with someone we love. How long should we live on "borrowed time"? How long is too long? What are the medical, legal, and moral principles involved? What are the guidelines?

The issues of euthanasia and "right to die" have joined the abortion issue as among the most vital and complicated concerns of our age.

We Have the Right to Die

Somehow we have confused the right to die with the subject of euthanasia (the deliberate killing of those who are suffering). They are not the same thing. The "right to die" is defined as the individual's right to determine whether unusual or "heroic" measures should be taken—normally involving expensive and mechanical means of life support—to prolong life in cases where death is almost certainly inevitable. Life is sacred and given to us by God; for that reason we must never condone the deliberate, unnatural taking of life. This is a major reason most Christians who take the Bible seriously oppose abortion and euthanasia. At the same time, allowing the natural process of death to run its course is not necessarily wrong, when life can only be sustained by extreme medical measures. There is a difference between the prolongation of life and the postponement of death.

Standing at the bedside of someone who has lifesustaining tubes intruding into many parts of the anatomy, we can understand how humane medical treatment could be viewed as inhumane. When the treatment of humans becomes, for all appearances, inhuman, most of us want the right to refuse such treatment.

Could you make a decision for yourself on whether or not life-sustaining procedures should be used? Members of the medical profession, the Los Angeles Bar Association, and the California Hospital Association gave some recommendations on withholding and withdrawing life-sustaining treatment. The first principle applies to each one of us. They said:

> It is the right of a person capable of giving informed consent to make his or her own decision regarding medical care after having been fully informed about the benefits, risks and consequences of available treatment, even if such a decision may result in shortening the individual's life.[2]

If we are able, we have the right to say, "Stop, no more."

A statement issued by American Catholic bishops in June 1986 said, "We also recognize and defend a patient's right to refuse 'extraordinary' means—that is, means which provide no benefit or which involve too grave a burden."[3]

But the right of choice by an individual is clouded. For instance, many people advocate drawing up a "living will" in anticipation of a time when they can no longer make decisions about sustaining or prolonging their lives. What is a living will? Is it something we should seriously consider in anticipation of a time when we cannot make a life or death decision for ourselves?

A living will is a document written and signed by a person at a time when he or she has the mental capacity to dictate final requests. Usually the living will states that "heroic measures" or artificial means should not be used if it has been determined that the person would remain in a vegetative state or in an irreversible coma.

On the surface this sounds like a good idea. Before such difficult decisions need to be made, why not clarify in advance how we wish to be treated? Unfortunately, it's not so simple. Right now I'm in reasonably good health. If I were to write a living will, it would be from the perspective of how I think I would feel under more drastic circumstances. But when that time actually arrives, I might feel quite differently. Also, the guidelines set forth by the Joint Ad-Hoc Committee on Biomedical Ethics in California wisely say that "even when a competent patient has directed withholding or withdrawing of life-sustaining procedures, it is advisable to consult with the patient's immediate family and to give great weight to their wishes."

Finally, there is the question of whether living wills might not justify more questionable practices, such as euthanasia and suicide. The Bishops' Committee for Pro-Life Activities referred to such a possibility when they made their chilling statement: "Some living will proposals have been formulated and promoted by right-to-die groups which see them as stepping-stones to the eventual legalization of euthanasia."[4]

Our states do not agree upon the validity of living wills. Proposals have been made, therefore, for uniform laws to eliminate the differences. But is federal legislation the answer? I cannot propose or evaluate such legislation, except to comment on ethical concerns. Would such legislation be in the interests of preserving life, preventing suicide and homicide, and maintaining sound ethics in the medical profession? That's a tall order! Would legislation encourage communication among patient, family, and physician in the decision-making process? Most important, are all of the considerations strongly biased toward life? All of these questions would need to be answered with a resounding "yes" before considering any so-called "right-to-die" legislation.

Each one of us needs to consider these subjects carefully and prayerfully and be alert to such issues as they become public matters. Also, we must each consider whether a living will is a document that we, ourselves, would want to write. And since these decisions affect our loved ones and families, it is important to discuss our feelings with them. And finally we must understand that, as it was for Jacqueline Cole, the final determination is in God's hand.

What Is "Passive Euthanasia"?

The phone rang and all conversation stopped. A friend of our family, who was at a bon voyage party for her upcoming departure for Europe for a writing assignment, had just finished telling of her concern for her mother who was on life-support systems in a distant state. Our friend had been assured by the doctors and members of her family that there was nothing she could do and that she should go on her trip as she had planned. Now the doctor was calling her long distance. "Your mother is in extreme discomfort, and it is the opinion of myself and the staff at the hospital that her condition is irreversible." He continued to describe her mother's condition and then asked the dreaded question, "Do you wish to have heroic efforts continued?"

"I don't know. I'll have to consult my brother," choked the distraught daughter. "Please tell me what 'heroic measures' means."

The doctor described the purpose and result of each tube, injection, and treatment. As the medical terminology was quoted, my friend began to shake and grow cold. "You're asking me to make a decision about killing my own mother," she cried.

Later, however, with the consent of her brother, the counsel of her minister, and a circle of prayer with her friends, the daughter told the doctor to discontinue the life-sustaining or "heroic" measures.

What my friend was forced to decide was when to permit what is termed today as "passive euthanasia." Although those words send shudders through most of us, the definition is important to understand. Passive or negative euthanasia means to discontinue or desist from the use of "extraordinary" life-sustaining measures or "heroic" efforts to prolong life in cases judged hopeless. It is refraining from action that would probably delay death and, instead, permitting death to occur naturally.

My friend's mother was then eighty-seven years old. To everyone's surprise, without the life-support systems she lived to be ninety-three. Even when we think we "play God," we may be fooled. The wisdom of God is greater than the foolishness of man.

Even the definitions of "life-sustaining measures" vary. A committee on biomedical ethics comprised of members of the medical and legal professions said: "Life-sustaining procedures are defined as interventions which artificially sustain, restore, or supplant a vital function and which serve only to artificially prolong the moment of death where, in the judgment of the attending physician, death is imminent whether or not such procedures are utilized."

In March of 1986 the American Medical Association Judicial Counsel gave the following opinion of "Withholding or Withdrawing Life-Prolonging Medical Treatment." Since most of us as laymen would not have access to this information, I think it is important to include it. This information was printed in the *Christian Medical Society Journal,* summer 1986.

> The social commitment of the physician is to sustain life and relieve suffering. Where the performance of one duty conflicts with the other, the choice of the patient, or his family or legal representative if the patient is incompetent to act in his own behalf, should prevail. In the absence of the patient's choice or an authorized proxy, the physician must act in the best interest of the patient.

> For humane reasons, with informed consent, a physician may do what is medically necessary to alleviate severe pain, or cease or omit treatment to permit a terminally ill patient whose death is imminent to die. However, he should not intentionally cause death. In deciding whether the administration of potentially life-prolonging medical treatment is in the best interest of the patient who is incompetent to act in his own behalf, the physician should determine what the possibility is for extending life under humane and comfortable conditions and what are the prior expressed wishes of the patient and attitudes of the family or those who have responsibility for the custody of the patient.
>
> Even if death is not imminent but a patient's coma is beyond doubt irreversible and there are adequate safeguards to confirm the accuracy of the diagnosis and with the concurrence of those who have responsibility for the care of the patient, it is not unethical to discontinue all means of life-prolonging medical treatment.
>
> Life-prolonging medical treatment includes medication and artificially or technologically supplied respiration, nutrition or hydration. In treating a terminally ill or irreversibly comatose patient, the physician should determine whether the benefits of treatment outweigh its burdens. At all times, the dignity of the patient should be maintained.[5]

These legal guidelines are, according to a Christian doctor, "very permissive toward withdrawal of all life-sustaining measures."

Most of the time I see issues as right or wrong, black or white. However, searching for God's will in the matter of life-sustaining measures is perhaps one of the most difficult decisions we will ever have to make. The prestigious *New England Journal of Medicine* said, "Few topics in medicine are more complicated, more controversial, and more emotionally charged than treatment of the hopelessly ill. Technology competes with compassion, legal precedent lags, and controversy is inevitable" ("The Physician's Responsibility toward Hopelessly Ill Patients," 310:955–959).

The doctors' dilemma is our dilemma too. It is a complicated, emotionally charged issue which many of us may encounter in our lifetimes.

What Is "Active Euthanasia"?

Active euthanasia is an act of commission, rather than omission. Its proponents contend it is a positive merciful act taken deliberately to end futile suffering or a meaningless existence; it could involve lethal drugs or the withholding of nourishment. Christians, however, would strongly disagree with this view.

In most cases this constitutes a criminal act. But not always. Take the case of author Betty Rollin, who revealed her role in helping her mother commit suicide.

In the spring of 1986 the New York writer told a luncheon meeting of women how she provided the capsules which ended her mother's life. The elder woman had ovarian cancer and had pleaded with her daughter to help her die. Rollin and her husband called dozens of doctors across the country before an Amsterdam physician gave them a combination of pills that would be "lethal, yet painless."[6]

In her book about this experience, Betty Rollin wrote about how she came to make such a decision and how she dealt with the implications of it. Later, it was reported, "Rollin calmly said, 'I knew that at worst I would be arrested. And that at best I wouldn't be arrested.'" As far as I know, she was never arrested, nor did she face much opposition in her act.

Where do we go from here? Are we just a breath away from euthanasia on demand? There are groups in America and many other nations who vocally support it as a means of preserving "human dignity" and eliminating needless suffering.

Some doctors have also gone on record in support of active euthanasia. Dr. Christiaan Barnard gained a great deal of notoriety after performing the first heart transplant. His views on euthanasia and suicide were published in a book, *Good Life, Good Death.* He writes, "I have no deep conviction in the existence of a personal God or in the geography of an actual heaven or hell. To that I must add, on the other hand, that I have not dismissed the possibility of life after death."[7]

Dr. Barnard said that he never practiced active euthanasia, since in his country it is regarded as murder and could merit the death penalty. But, on the other hand, he says, "I believe that in the clinical practice of medicine, active euthanasia has a definite place."[8]

Ten thousand irreversibly comatose patients are currently institutionalized in America, according to medical estimates. When the AMA stated its guidelines on the discontinuance of life-prolonging treatment, one of the statements included withdrawal of medication and artificially or technologically supplied respiration, nutrition, or hydration. Now we are talking about food and water.

Elizabeth Bouvia, a quadriplegic cerebral palsy patient, made national headlines in her fight to be allowed to starve to death. At first a judge refused her request. She became the object of bitter legal battling. While hospital officials and the American Civil Liberties Union took sides, the public debate brought the issue into the open. Finally a California appeals court ordered the removal of her feeding tube. As of this writing, however, she is still alive by her own choice.

But there is more at stake here than the life of one individual. Some have said that removal of food and fluids is frighteningly reminiscent of Nazi Germany where "useless mouths" weren't fed. Dr. Leo Alexander, consultant to the office of the Chief of Counsel for War Crimes wrote about how German physicians started a trend which resulted in the euthanasia of 275,000 people before the war began:

> It started with the acceptance of the attitude, basic in the euthanasia movement, that there is such a thing as a life not worthy to be lived. This attitude in its early stages concerned itself merely with the severely and chronically sick. Gradually the sphere of those to be included in this category was enlarged to encompass the socially unproductive, the ideologically unwanted, the racially unwanted, and finally all non-Germans. But it is important to realize that the infinitely small wedged-in lever from which this entire trend of mind received its impetus was the attitude toward the nonrehabilitatable sick.[9]

I am not so sure it couldn't happen again. Even the possibility is enough to keep us ever vigilant against attempts to encourage or promote euthanasia.

The Inevitable Will of God

There is a rising tide of opinion in favor of active euthanasia. Prominent physicians are heard to say that "prolonging life is cruel." As compassionate as this observation may seem on the surface, there are important biblical standards which both Christians and non-Christians must consider.

From the biblical perspective we know that death is inevitable, but not to be hastened. Human life is given by God and is precious. "I praise you because I am fearfully and wonderfully made; your works are wonderful, I know that full well" (Psalm 139:14). God can and may intervene to restore someone who was considered a terminal patient. "I put to death and I bring to life, I have wounded and I will heal, and no one can deliver out of my hand" (Deuteronomy 32:39).

"Lord, let me die," is a prayer and a plea offered to God by many throughout the ages. Moses was not ill, but he was grieved about the burden the Lord had given him. He looked at his people grumbling about their food and their living conditions, complaining until Moses must have reached his limit. He'd had it. He said to God, "If this is how you are going to treat me, put me to death right now" (Numbers 11:15).

But the Lord was not finished with Moses yet! He went on to lead his people through the wilderness and to the boundaries of the Promised Land.

Elijah had killed the prophets of Baal, yet when the evil Queen Jezebel swore she was going to get even, the fearless Elijah ran into the wilderness, sat down under a juniper tree, and cried out, "I have had enough, Lord," he said. "Take my life; I am no better than my ancestors" (1 Kings 19:4).

But the Lord sent an angel to supply him with food and water; essential ingredients for life!

The Lord was not finished with Elijah yet.

And think about Job. He had boils all over his body. His flesh was eaten by worms. His skin was oozing and decaying like rotten turnips. He was so shriveled and thin that his bones were sticking out and he had gnawing pains and frightening dreams. Under such circumstances most of us would cry out, as Job did, "that God would be willing to crush me, to let loose his hand and cut me off!" (Job 6:9).

But the Lord was not finished with Job yet, either.

If we had been with Job in his pain-wracked, miserable situation, would we have taken away his food and water, and allowed him to starve and dehydrate?

The Bible does not give us clear-cut answers on how to treat people in a "vegetative" state. However, the Scriptures are very clear about caring for the weak and defenseless. While "pulling the plug" may not result in death, denying food and water means certain death.

Dr. David Schiedermayer, from the Center for Clinical Ethics, Pritzer School of Medicine, University of Chicago, said, "Our courts and our society are rapidly moving toward approving the withdrawal of food and water from patients. As a clinician and as a Christian I share the concerns of many who feel this is morally wrong. If this is not the time to speak up, then there will never be a time. Food and water have always been worth fighting about."[10]

While all must sympathize with human suffering, practicing "active euthanasia," either through the use of lethal drugs or denial of food and water, violates the Judeo-Christian code of moral conduct.

Is Suicide the Way to Go?

The old Eskimo is sick and knows he is dying. He walks out into the cold, killing world and falls into a freezing slumber. His family did not abandon him. They supported him in this act of suicide. It was their way of life—and death.

To many peoples of the earth death is intimately related to group survival. Legends from Iceland, Greenland, and Siberia tell us that suicide is normal when life has no other meaning.

Ritual suicide was practiced by peoples of Africa and South America where the deaths of wives, servants, and members of the court would follow the death of the king. Of the major world religions Shintoism,

Buddhism, and Hinduism allow suicide, but Catholicism and Judaism condemn it.

Today, suicide is committed in startling numbers by teenagers, cutting short promising young lives. Men and women take their own lives to avoid the problems or responsibilities of living. In many cases serious emotional illness is involved, in which the person may not be fully rational or responsible for his or her actions. Others, a smaller percentage, are the people who are severely ill and near death, who seek a way of escape.

Suicide is a crime in America, as is attempted suicide. Aiding a suicide is tantamount to homicide. But there are those who lobby to make it a legal and acceptable possibility.

A few years ago *Time* magazine had a story about a British society which issued a pamphlet on "How to Commit Suicide." It listed methods, gave specific drugs, and advised against such methods as shooting, slashing wrists, or jumping from buildings.

This is a painful issue for many people who struggle with feelings of despair and hopelessness. And while the Bible does not give us detailed direction on this subject, it does come down firmly on the side of life and hope, and that should inform us as we consider this and the many related issues.

In many cases the real burden of suicide falls upon those who are left behind. Anne-Grace Scheinin, a woman who had attempted suicide many times, wrote a strong argument against taking one's own life. She spoke from personal experience, using the example of her own mother who had committed suicide: "There is something about suicide that, even when done as an escape from an agonizing terminal illness, signals complete and utter defeat. It is without any semblance of nobility or pride. Life can become too heavy a burden to bear, but the release that suicide offers is not a triumph of life, the ultimate mastery of self over fate, but a grim renunciation of hope and a failure of the human spirit."

This California woman wrote, "No matter how bad the pain is, it's never so bad that suicide is the only answer. . . . Suicide doesn't end pain. It only lays it on the broken shoulders of the survivors." And she ends her story. "By the way: to all the doctors, nurses and psychiatrists who forced me to live when I didn't want to—thank you for keeping breath in my lungs and my heart beating and encouraging hope in me when I didn't have any hope."[11]

If we are made in God's image, do we have the human right to destroy our own bodies? Every day we commit little acts of suicide in the manner in which we care for those bodies, but these are not the overt acts of taking our own lives.

A Broadway and London hit play, *Whose Life Is It Anyway?* treated suicide and mercy killing in a sympathetic manner.[12]

This issue is a struggle against "the powers of this dark world and against the spiritual forces of evil" described in Ephesians 6:12. Little by little, the sanctity of life is being eroded. Will survival of the fittest be our elitist philosophy? I pray not!

Questions to Ask

In his poignant book, which he called *Mother's Song,* John Sherrill relates the decision he had to make concerning the life and death of his mother. When her death seemed imminent and he could not bear to see her suffer, he asked the doctor, "What would happen if we asked for those IVs to come out?"

Sherrill said he tensed for what he expected as an outraged reaction from the doctor. Instead, the doctor gave him some yardsticks to consider. With the prayerful agreement of the entire family and the concurrence of the doctor, he eventually asked to have his mother's life-prolonging measures removed. He summed up some important questions to ask ourselves now, while we are healthy and alert. This is what he listed:

1. If doctors are able to help an elderly person through a health crisis, what does he return to? Will it be to a life of reason and tolerable health, or will it be to new breakdown and deterioration and pain?

2. What does the person himself want? Has he expressed a desire to live just as long as possible, no matter what the means? Or does he want to be allowed to die without using the extraordinary aids that are available to us today?

3. What is the person's attitude now? Our feelings may change as death approaches. Even if we are unable to speak, there are innumerable ways to communicate.

4. What is the attitude of the family?

5. What is God's timing? We found that His signature is beauty, even in the midst of pain and sorrow. In Mother's passing we encountered example after example (coincidences, kindnesses, unusual provisions). They were His encouragements, we believe now, that we had correctly interpreted the signs of His time.

Is death the end? This is the question, of course, that affects all the others. Facing death is entirely different for someone who believes that there is an afterlife.[13]

Yes, we need to know the right questions to ask, for we live on borrowed time, and we want to use our inheritance as wisely as we can. Since God has given us sound minds, we must exercise them while they are able to function. This is not morbid; this is one of the greatest challenges we may ever face.

When death comes
will it come quietly
—one might say creep—
as after a hard and tiring day, one lies
and longs for sleep—
ending age and sorrow
or youth and pain?
Who dies in Christ
has all to gain

—and a Tomorrow!
Why weep?
Death may be savage.
We cannot be sure:
the godly may be slaughtered,
evil men endure;
however death may strike,
or whom,
who knows the risen Lord
knows, too, the empty tomb.

—Ruth Bell Graham[14]

"Most of us have a subliminal desire to leave this world with some degree of dignity . . . quick, quiet, easy. But life doesn't follow the pattern we have so clumsily designed. . . . Death has many faces and voices."

> *If any of you lacks wisdom, he should ask God, who gives generously to all without finding fault, and it will be given to him.* James 1:5

CHAPTER SEVEN

Life and Death Choices

WISDOM TO MAKE choices in life . . . and in approaching death. How we need God's wisdom. For instance, most of us have a subliminal desire to leave this world with some degree of dignity . . . perhaps at the age of ninety-five, sitting in an easy chair before a fire . . . just close our eyes and the next thing we know we're in eternity. Quick, quiet, and easy.

But life doesn't follow the pattern we have so clumsily designed. "Why, you do not even know what will happen tomorrow. What is your life? You are a mist that appears for a little while and then vanishes" (James 4:14).

Most of us would like to say something quotable to be remembered by our family. But what if disease or age ravages our body and the person in the mirror shows little resemblance to the snapshot in the family album? Is it possible to say good-bye to earthly life with some degree of honor?

A doctor painted two verbal portraits of undignified death for me. The first he described in this way: "The ICU death: comatose, respirator keeping the shell of a body alive indefinitely, a few EEG waves flickering here and there keeping it going, two or three IVs, tubes in the nose and bladder, multiple consultants making daily adjustments to keep the numbers balanced, and the bill increasing by $2,000 a day with no end in sight."

A grim thought! And yet it happens with increasing frequency. Alan's case is one example. For months Alan was sustained in just that manner. His insurance was used up and his money all gone. At that point his wife prayed for his death and, finally, stopped coming to see him altogether. When Alan died he left her a legacy of bitterness and regret.

The cases are legion on hospital records. Death's sting may be cruel and lingering and financially devastating.

The second portrait of undignified death may be viewed on occasion in a nursing home. For weeks, months, or years the patient depends upon employees of an institution, who may or may not have much interest in her comfort. Her surroundings consist of a bed, bed table, the moans and babblings from the next room (or the next bed), the aroma of disinfectant trying to cover the unpleasant odors. When death finally comes, a distant relative is notified, who then puts on a sad voice and makes the arrangements over the phone.

Unfortunately, the description, and the fact, is too common. Ask any nursing home manager and he will tell you about Mrs. Thomas or Mr. Peters who has been in the home for years, with only token visits from anyone who cares. Many people are abandoned socially long before they die physically.

Nursing homes can be a great blessing to people who find it impossible to care for their elderly or infirm family members at home. However, careful investigation should be made to assure the family and patient that dignified treatment is the order of the day. One friend told me how his mother had died in a "rest home" and when he went to pick up her belongings he was directed to a storage room where he found a plastic trash bag stuffed with her pictures, plants, and clothing. His grief was compounded by those thoughtless actions.

This is not an indictment of nursing homes. Most are wonderful, run by caring, compassionate personnel. I visited Vance Havner, the noted Bible preacher, who was in a fine establishment in his last days.

However, in contrast to abandonment or undignified treatment, picture homey surroundings, with a few friends or close family members nearby, personal affairs settled, and a certainty of a future with a loving God.

After Ruth's father died, her mother found it increasingly difficult to take care of herself. She was partly paralyzed by a stroke, dependent upon help for most of her physical needs. Ruth had her brought up to our mountain home for a while, but she wanted her own home, so that's where she was returned.

Ruth said, "All her life Mother loved music—both playing the piano and singing, as well as listening to others make music."

Then during her final days we suddenly realized that hymns enjoyed by the living do not necessarily appeal to the dying. Ruth went through her favorite record albums, marking hymns she felt her mother would enjoy, and our local radio station graciously lifted them off onto tapes. As Ruth recalled those days, she said, "Mother had a simple tape player and was able to push the on and off button at will, so beautiful old hymns ministered to her hour after hour the last few weeks she was with us."

Harder Decisions

We did not have to make the difficult decision with Ruth's mother whether to sustain or prolong her life. She was not on life-support systems, but she needed complete and loving care. There was no question in our minds that this was what she would have.

We have a close friend who had to make the decision for her husband whether his life would be sustained by machines or not. Fortunately, they had discussed the possibility of this choice before the time of crucial need.

Edith Schaeffer, the widow of my friend, the late Francis Schaeffer, was called into the hospital room of her husband who was dying of cancer. Six doctors told her there was little hope for Francis, and they asked her if she wanted him placed in intensive care on machines. One doctor, acting as spokesman, said, "Once a person is on machines, I would never pull the plug. I need to know what your viewpoint is."

Edith knew that for years she and Francis had talked about the preciousness of life and that even a few minutes could make a difference if something needed to be said or done. "But," she said, "there is no point in simply prolonging death. It is a fine line; it is not an absolute one-two-three process. There are differences from person to person, and it requires great wisdom."

Edith Schaeffer chose to have her husband brought home. She said, "I believe when my husband leaves his body, he will be with the Lord. I don't want him to leave me until he's with the Lord. Therefore, I am sure he would want to go to the house he asked me to buy and be there for the time he has left."

The doctors agreed with her and told her they wished more people would do things the same way. Fran was taken home, and Edith surrounded his bed with the things he loved, and had music playing in his room. She said, "One after another, we played his favorite records: Beethoven, Bach, Schubert, and Handel. Ten days later, on May 15, 1984, with the music of Handel's *Messiah* still in the air, Fran breathed his last breath."[1]

A Public Death

I remember a man who added a new dimension to the idea of dying with dignity. Hubert Humphrey was vice president of the United States under Lyndon Johnson. He established his career and reputation as a Senator, and later as the Democratic party's unsuccessful presidential candidate. However, Humphrey made some of his greatest public statements in his dying months when he became a role model for the American public.

Do you remember when cancer was too often a whispered word? Perhaps more than anyone else, Humphrey brought the dreaded subject out of the closet. In 1977 his doctors made public the diagnosis, and we understand it was with his approval. He had an inoperable tumor and his situation was terminal. One of the nation's leading writers and teachers on death and dying, Edwin Shneidman, wrote, "Thereafter, the world either had to shun Humphrey as a leper and pariah (because of the social stigma of terminal cancer) or, because of who he was and the way in which he conducted himself, accept him as he was."[2]

The public accepted Humphrey, and watched his attitude as he approached death openly and with wry humor. "The extraordinary public death from cancer of Hubert Humphrey can be a guiding example to some of one kind of 'appropriate death.' His published utterances about his cancer, his state of health, and his death probably can stimulate many of us to think about our own way of dying."[3]

Humphrey's remarks on the floor of the Senate express so beautifully the qualities that make for a dignified, graceful death. He said, "The greatest healing therapy is friendship and love, and over this land I have sensed it. Doctors, chemicals, radiation, pills, nurses, therapists are all very, very helpful. But without faith in yourself and your own ability to overcome your own difficulties, faith in divine providence, and without the friendship and kindness and generosity of friends, there is no healing."[4]

He knew he would not be healed, but he expressed what is needed by all of us . . . friendship, kindness, and faith in God.

Different People, Different Choices

We know that death has many faces and voices. Paul Tournier wrote, "Rare is the death that is truly conscious, lucid, serene, and accepted. But how impressive such a death is! A young woman with whom I have worked for a long time falls seriously ill in the flower of life. From the start she feels intuitively that she will not recover. She makes out a list of the relatives and friends whom she wants to see once more before she goes, and invites them one by one to her bedside. She prays that she will be able to give to each the message she has in her heart for them, and dies the day after the last visit. I have myself been called for in this way by several of my best friends, when they knew their days to be numbered. At such times how profound the dialogue between us becomes!"[5]

Most people die somewhere between the two extremes of death: the dignified and the utterly undignified. Increasing longevity, advances in public health, and improved sanitation, along with the likelihood of a reasonably safe environment for older citizens in recent decades mean that the most common causes of death among the elderly are degenerative illnesses such as cardiovascular disease, cancer, strokes, diabetic complications, and other disorders.

But we're seeing two trends in major medical care. One is a tendency for doctors to overtreat the patient with cautious but expensive care in order to protect themselves against the potential threat of malpractice suits. This can lead to "heroic medical treatment" in some cases. At the opposite extreme there is the pragmatic approach which says if the person is not useful, withhold even minimal care. A Christian doctor said, "The latter is going to become more tempting as money becomes tighter and as individual human life becomes devalued."

So, what is the answer? Can we find a moderate and loving position which guarantees the dignity of the patient during the period of disease and convalescence without destroying that dignity with expensive, exhaustive, and unproductive treatment?

Dr. C. Everett Koop, surgeon general of the United States, said, "All such talk has different connotations for the Christian than for the non-Christian. My wife knows I do not believe in being ushered out of this life with a lethal injection. I want to hang around long enough to be sure my family is taken care of. But after that, I don't want my life prolonged in great discomfort when it is fruitless."[6] Dr. Koop is also a great Bible student.

God's Wisdom and our Responsibility

A sick person has God-given worth. God is concerned about the way we treat people who may not have much to offer us. An influential or public figure may have little trouble getting kind and loving treatment. But when Jesus was teaching His disciples He said, "For I was hungry and you gave me something to eat, I was thirsty and you gave me something to drink, I was a stranger and you invited me in, I needed clothes and you clothed me, I was sick and you looked after me, I was in prison and you came to visit me" (Matthew 25:35–36).

His followers were baffled. When had they done all of those noble deeds? Jesus told them, "I tell you the truth, whatever you did for one of the least of these brothers of mine, you did for me" (Matthew 25:40).

Let's take a look at some of the ways we can contribute to the God-given worth of a human life . . . and how we would want to be treated ourselves.

Please Don't Leave Me

I have often said that loneliness is the predominant attitude in our culture. A person can be lonely in the midst of a party; he can be lonely in a crowd or lonely in the country. Loneliness may be experienced by the rich and famous or the poor and unknown. Loneliness may engulf the dying and make their last hours a torture chamber of abandonment. How can this be? It is because of certain attitudes others assume.

First, there is the monologue attitude. "How are you today, Bill? You look fine." Bill is ready to tell how he feels and needs to express some of his concerns, but the "stiff upper lip" syndrome has been imposed upon him by his doctor or his friends. They inform him how he ought to feel and then may say, "I'll be back to see you again." The promise is made, but not kept, in the same way some Christians say piously, "I'll pray for you," and then never do.

Another attitude promotes a sense of abandonment. A person may be treated as though disease or an accident has turned him into a non-person. Just as we sometimes do to children, we talk in front of them as if they weren't even there. Even my dogs have the intelligence to know when we are talking about them. They will turn their heads to one side and their ears will prick up. Jesus was talking about "the least of these," and even animal lovers will agree that humans have higher intelligence than dogs.

People who are asking for help give cues. We need to be sensitive to them. "I think I'm going to die soon," is a plea for understanding, not a statement to disregard.

Too many times we respond with nonsense, such as, "You're going to live many years more," when all of the indications are to the contrary. Honesty seems to fly out of many sickroom windows.

Sometimes people in nursing homes, as well as terminally ill patients, are truly abandoned. "I'd rather remember her as she was," is the rationalization. Another indication of this abandonment has to do with physical contact. First, the loved one is kissed on the lips, then the kiss drops lightly on the forehead, the next time it is blown from across the room, and loneliness grows.

I wonder what would have happened if Jacob's family had abandoned him? In his last days he gathered all of his sons around him and prophesied what would happen to each one of them. Some of them received strong admonitions, others blessings. When he was finished, the Bible says that Jacob "breathed his last and was gathered to his people" (Genesis 49:33).

One Choice for the Terminally Ill

Several years ago Columnist George Will wrote a *Newsweek* article called "A Good Death." I cut the piece out and kept it because I wanted to know what he considered a *good* death and a *bad* one, and I found some of his commentary indicative of popular American attitudes on human dignity.

Will said, "There comes a point in a degenerative disease when further 'aggressive' treatment would intensify the patient's suffering without substantial benefit. Then concern for the patient should become concern for a dignified death."[7]

The article continued with a description of the hospice program. This is a new-old concept that is growing rapidly in the Western world. It is comparatively new in America, but old in following the Christian principles of the Golden Rule.

During the Middle Ages medieval hospices were refuges where pilgrims were sheltered and fed along their long journey to the Holy Land. Sometimes hospices were located near monasteries. One of the most famous was the hospice of St. Bernard in the Swiss Alps. (We think of the massive St. Bernard with the flask around his huge neck as being a dog that saved lives, and that was true at one time.)

The modern hospice movement began in England, where a caring woman, Dr. Cicely Saunders, founded St. Christopher's, the model upon which so many others have been based. A hospice provides care for terminally ill patients and their loved ones; its primary purpose is to alleviate chronic pain. One hospice medical director said, "There is never a time when nothing more can be done. There may be nothing more that can be done to cure the disease, but there are always further measures to be taken for the comfort of the patient."

The purpose of St. Christopher's is to render loving care, using medicine with a humane dimension in the treatment of all aspects of pain: physical, social, emotional, and spiritual. The hospice is a therapeutic community within the community, helping the dying to live until they die and helping families to live on.

George Will commented, "With hospice care as an alternative, there would be little demand for euthanasia. Without the hospice alternative, legalization of euthanasia would exert vicious pressure on people who are old and frail and believe society does not think much of them. When incurably ill, such people would think of an administered death as the only alternative to terrible suffering for themselves and terrible cost to their families, so their right to die would come to seem like a 'duty to die.'"[8]

What does a dying person want? The material things which were once so important become insignificant. Tournier said, "The pursuit of success, the hard struggle to avoid failure, is appropriate enough in the prime of life. But whatever fruit this long effort has borne, it will seem of small account in the face of approaching death. What counts then is serenity."[9]

Serenity is the "quiet waters" of the Twenty-third Psalm. Serenity is what the old man, Simeon, expressed when the child Jesus was presented to him: "Lord," he said, "now I can die content" (Luke 2:29, LB).

Serenity is what the devoted people in the hospice movement wish to bring to the dying. Serenity and dignity.

Special Care for Special People

The hospice movement continues to grow. If you know someone in a life-threatening or terminal illness, you may find that a hospice offers a reasonable and considerate alternative for care.

What qualifies someone for hospice care? When a physician determines there is nothing more that he can do to save a person's life, he may recommend a hospice instead of hospital care. Anyone can refer a patient to hospice care. In most cases the dying person stays at home and a support team, consisting of doctors, nurses, medical social workers, chaplains, home health aides, and trained volunteers, provides individualized, comprehensive care. The teamwork does not cease with death, but continues to help the family during bereavement.

San Diego has a hospice program which was started by sixty people who were concerned for dying patients and their families. In less than ten years the concept continued to grow until more than 3,200 patients and families had been served. Today, if the criteria have been met—which simply means a person must be diagnosed as having a terminal illness, with only days, weeks, or, at the most, months left to live—anyone can get help. Color, creed, or financial status is neither a deterrent nor a qualification for admission to such a facility.

Deep human needs surface when someone is dying. Sometimes the family feels helpless, and at other times they are angry. Emotions may be hidden, only to surface in painful outbursts. "The hospice goal is to assist in the emergence of these positive and natural feelings so that one's last passage is as it should be—free from pain and stress, in an atmosphere of love and caring."[10]

The public relations director of the San Diego Hospice, and the chaplain, emphasized that the role of all the team and volunteers is to combine care with caring.

Among some of the home care services are daily home visits, assistance in personal and business affairs, nursing care, running errands, and spiritual and psychological support. After the death of the patient the hospice continues offering help to the family during their grief.

One story was told about an attitude change brought about by a member of a hospice team. I heard about a grandfather who was dying. His four-year-old granddaughter was ordered to go to another part of the house to play, and told not to go near Grandpa's room. The adult members of the family sat and cried in the living room, and the teenage grandsons wandered in and out of the house aimlessly. A hospice worker found the little girl sobbing in the corner of her room. "What's the matter, honey?" she asked.

"They won't let me see Grandpa, and I'm scared," she whimpered. "I think they're going to do something awful to him."

The hospice nurse went to the family and said, "It's wrong not to allow the children to see their grandfather and tell him good-bye. Don't keep them away."

Reluctantly, the mother and father told their children they could go into the room. The little girl stood on her tiptoes and kissed her Grandpa, and then, not satisfied that he knew she was there, she pulled herself up on the bed and snuggled next to him. The boys sat in chairs beside his bed, and a smile came to Grandpa's face—and he died peacefully.

That little girl will never forget the experience, her love for her grandfather, or being there beside him the last few minutes of his life.

Experience in England shows that hospice care has other good effects. Depression, anxiety, and anger are reduced, with those who are cared for in homes. One of the things that has happened in areas where the hospice movement is working is that more people are now dying at home. In New Haven, Connecticut, for instance, the statistics changed from about 10 percent dying at home to over 70 percent. A positive direction has been added to our society with the staffs and volunteers in this outstanding effort. I hope many more Christians will become involved in this movement, as a means of witnessing to Christ's love.

Opportunity to Show Christ's Love

Remember the story of Jesus and the blind man told in the ninth chapter of John? Here is a model of needs being met and eyes opened to a personal relationship with the Lord. The man was blind and Jesus healed him. The Pharisees were shocked that Jesus healed him on the Sabbath, and they scorned him. But the once-blind man knew that the man who healed him had a special relationship with God, and he wanted to know more about this source of comfort and love.

When a person's needs are met, it may open his eyes or improve his vision to what God can accomplish in his life. God gives us the example through Jesus, and we are following Him when we get involved with something as positive as this recent trend on the American caring scene. It is Christ ministering to others through His own. If the current dire predictions come true concerning deaths from the aids virus, the need for more programs like this will become urgent.

Many times the dying child unwittingly directs his parents toward the Lord. The chaplain of one hospice said that he wished older persons could have the insight which dying children often have. "Children are so open to talking about God. They are more willing to talk about dying than their elders."

At some point terminal patients have to come to grips with their condition. However, in the past the families and the patients were usually left to tough it out with little support, especially when they had no religious background or involvement. Now that this is changing, the Christian community should take note and do something. For instance, direct care volunteers are needed by all hospices. They are called "The Heart of the Hospice."

The direct care volunteer is a special friend to patients and their families.

Patient care volunteers are trained in such topics as communication, pain and symptom control, grief and bereavement support, spiritual care, ethical issues, and terminal care. Although these skills may sound complicated, they are essential human qualities, talents we all possess to some degree. They are an expression of the compassion which can help many thousands of people (as people live longer in this latter part of the twentieth century) to attain some degree of dignity in their last days.

Most important of all, we should be willing to pray with those in their final days and hours and read to them from the Scriptures. Remember that it is through "the encouragement of the Scriptures we might have hope" (Romans 15:4).

Jesus is walking the earth today in the hearts of those who believe in Him. More good has been done, more people loved, more comfort brought by His people than by the humanistic philosophy that displays a caring philosophy without His saving grace.

"Christians Who Care" should be the slogan, and the banner, for the body of believers. When others see the compassion we express for the suffering and bereaved, they will truly believe our faith means something. In the words of the song, "They will know we are Christians by our love, by our love; yes, they'll know we are Christians by our love."

"The facade of grief may be indifference, preoccupation, anger, cheerfulness, or any variety of emotions. But if we try to understand it, we may learn how to cope with it."

That their hearts might be comforted, being knit together in love.
Colossians 2:2, KJV

CHAPTER EIGHT

Groping Through Grief

HER SON WAS dead, killed in a tragic accident only a few days before. She sat in the front row of the church, listening quietly as the minister spoke at the memorial service, her face composed, one might almost say serene. When the final prayer ended, friends filed by the casket, hugging members of the family through tears. Later it was said, "They are taking it so well." "His mother is a real brick." At the home afterward the parents greeted dozens of people with smiles and words of encouragement.

A few days later her husband found his wife sitting on the kitchen floor, banging her fists and sobbing uncontrollably. The woman others thought was "so brave" was sick to the core of her being with an emotion common to every living person.

A neighbor of ours, whom we'll call Frances North, lost her husband through a tragic accident. Again, everyone commented on the widow's bravery—even cheerfulness.

"Only the Lord can give such victory," was the general opinion. Perhaps poor Frances felt trapped. How could she express her grief without letting the Lord down?

Months passed, and Ruth got a phone call. A friend was concerned. Frances was withdrawing more and more into herself.

So Ruth, having been friends with Frances for years, drove over. She found Frances sitting alone, staring at the floor. Gently, Ruth talked with her and received either no response or one in monosyllables. Finally, realizing Frances was worse off than she had thought, Ruth asked if she would like her to call the doctor. Frances nodded numbly. Ruth called and was told to bring her right over.

The doctor, an understanding, compassionate Christian, recognized the danger signals of unresolved, long suppressed grief, and took her under his care.

Today Frances is the normal, happy, outgoing person she was before tragedy struck.

How wrong we may be when we draw conclusions about others based on their outward appearance or attitude. Peel away the smile and you may uncover a desperate need. Grief hides under many masquerades. It takes many forms. The façade of grief may be indifference, preoccupation, anger, cheerfulness, or any variety of emotions. But if we try to understand it, we may learn how to cope with it. When we experience it, we may be able to help others.

Grief is a Fact

Grief comes with many losses. It may be the loss of a job or a friend, a pet or a possession. The loss of a marriage relationship may cause grief as wrenching as death. Whatever its cause, grief will come to all of us.

Statistics reveal that grief-causing sorrow affects ten families out of every 250 each year in America. Since we are studying the subject of death and dying, we will look particularly at personal grief, and how to comfort someone who is grieving, in relation to a loss by death. Many of the principles we will discuss can, however, be applied to help those who are grieving because of another type of loss, such as a broken marriage.

Grief which is not dealt with properly can cause us to lose our perspective on life. A friend told me about his mother who mourned the death of her husband so keenly that seventeen years after he died she would cry every time he was mentioned. My friend's wife told her husband, "Honey, I love you very much, but I will never grieve for you for seventeen years!"

Edna St. Vincent Millay expressed the type of hopelessness that many feel in facing a loss. In her poem "Lament," she wrote:

Life must go on,
and the dead be forgotten;
Life must go on,
Though good men die;
Anne, eat your breakfast;
Dan, take your medicine;
Life must go on;
I forget just why.

Jesus was no stranger to grief. Isaiah 53:3, 4 foretold that Christ would be "despised and forsaken of men, a man of sorrows, and acquainted with grief" (NASB).

Happiness is a choice, but grief is a certainty. When Jacob thought that Joseph had been torn apart by wild beasts, the Bible says he "tore his clothes and mourned for his son many days." When King David heard that his son had been killed, he expressed his grief in words which have echoed throughout the ages: "O my son Absalom, my son, my son Absalom! would God I had died for thee, O Absalom, my son, my son!" (2 Samuel 18:33, KJV).

When death separates us from someone we love, there is a time when we think no one has suffered as we have. But grief is universal. The method of handling grief is personal and vital.

The Emotions of Grief

Guilt is a gripping force that comes when a loved one dies. It's easy to begin the chorus of "if onlys" sung to ourselves or someone else. "If only the paramedics hadn't been so slow." "If only I had been there, I could have done something." "If only I hadn't given him that car." "If only I had spent more time with her and told her how much I cared."

There are two kinds of guilt: real and false. Sometimes they are so entwined that we don't know which one we are experiencing. Real guilt comes when we feel or know that we have disobeyed God's commandments or transgressed His standards. False guilt is one of the normal emotions of grief, when someone is feeling guilty for something over which he had no control.

Velma Barfield, the woman executed for the crimes she committed, knew and experienced real guilt. King David must have suffered from real guilt after he had ordered the murder of Uriah, Bathsheba's husband. He cried, "For I know my transgressions, and my sin is always before me" (Psalm 51:3).

We are all imperfect human beings, with imperfect relationships. Nobody's love for friends or family is perfect. The less perfect that love, the more necessary it may seem to those who survive to ritualize grief. Elaborate caskets and burials, beyond the means of the family, may be a way to "atone" for feelings of guilt. However, I don't want to criticize funeral practices; I believe they need to be a matter of personal and thoughtful choice for each family.

Sometimes guilt comes as a result of felt relief when someone who has endured a prolonged illness finally dies. We may say, "We're thankful he's out of his pain." Then afterward guilt creeps in because of such thankfulness.

When neglect or hate have become a part of a relationship, the death of the person who has generated those feelings may result in self-inflicted grief by the survivor. I was told of a young man who had lost both his mother and father as a child. The young man was raised by an aunt who was indifferent to him. He was visited only occasionally by an older brother, who also neglected him. The young man died when he was only twenty-one, and suddenly the aunt and the brother cried foul play against the doctors, demanded retribution from everyone who had been associated with their relative, and mourned loudly and vocally. Guilt as a result of previous neglect was disguised as grief.

The pain of grief often causes people to become resentful, blaming, or condemning toward others for things they did or did not do. Remember what Martha said to Jesus when Lazarus died? She said,

"Lord, if you had been here, my brother would not have died" (John 11:32). I wonder if she later wished she had never said those words when Jesus brought Lazarus out of his tomb.

Christians are not immune to guilt feelings. However, they have an advantage over the nonbeliever because of God's grace and forgiveness. The Lord tells us to confess our sins and He will forgive them. Guilt, real or false, is a burden too heavy to carry. Confession brings forgiveness and forgiveness brings freedom.

Some of the most healing words in any language are, "I'm sorry. Will you forgive me?" How much more we need that confession to our Father in heaven, in order to have a spirit which is unbound by stifling self-accusations.

If God willingly forgives us, we must be willing to forgive ourselves.

Grief also quenches the normal zest for living. "I just don't feel like doing anything." In his heart-wrenching book, *A Severe Mercy,* Sheldon Vanauken wrote after his young wife died, "How could things go on when the world had come to an end? How could things—how could I—go on in this void? How could one person, not very big, leave an emptiness that was galaxy-wide?"[1]

After a personal loss people think that nothing looks the same. Food loses its flavor, music seems hollow, and nothing satisfies. Tears come at strange times, often for no apparent reason. The bereaved person may see someone walking down the street who looks like the person who died, and pain comes without warning.

Another emotion of grief is anger. One woman told how she went into the ladies' room at a gathering of Christian women and tried to speak compassionately to someone whose husband had recently died. The young widow shocked the bystanders when she bitterly retorted, "Why did he do this to me? I have two children to raise. We'll probably have to move and find a cheaper place to live. He died and left me in a mess." She was venting feelings that many others have suppressed. Later she may have regretted that tongue-lashing of her deceased husband, but she expressed a common emotion that many have felt.

When a mourner cannot express anger toward the deceased, he or she may look for another scapegoat. In grief, people tend to become critical of others who are continuing life as usual. Blame the doctor, the nurse, the hospital, relatives. . . . Find someone to blame! Why not blame God? These feelings aren't new. David cried out, "Why are you downcast, O my soul? Why so disturbed within me? . . . I say to God my Rock, 'Why have you forgotten me?'" (Psalm 42:5, 9).

Jesus didn't reason or argue with Martha when she accused Him of neglect. He patiently understood. If we are on the receiving end of anger, we should not take it personally. Wait until the person has had time to stabilize, and then we may be able to discuss it.

Interwoven with the emotions of grief there is a resistance to returning to normal activities. Nothing seems to matter. The closer the grieving person was to the one who died, the more difficult it is to see life in anything but tones of gray. The griever resents those who want him to pick up the pieces and go on as if life had not collapsed. Friends seem callous and thoughtless.

Christians are not stoics like the Greeks of ancient times. The Scriptures see grief as a normal part of the life process. Out of grief often comes depression. Depression is like a dark day when the clouds block out the sun and we say it isn't shining. When someone says he's "in the pits" it is a very appropriate description.

Groping through your own grief is an emotional, physical, and spiritual effort. Faith gives us the power to pass through grief, not avoid it.

The Sun is Shining . . . Somewhere

We cannot give pat answers or "three easy steps to work through your personal grief." A friend sent us some quotes from W. Graham Scroggie, words which had helped her cope with the loss of her mother. "Let grief do its work. Tramp every inch of the sorrowful way. Drink every drop of the bitter cup. Draw from memory and hope all that they can offer. To see the things our loved ones have left behind will give us daily pain—the clothes they wore, the letters they wrote, the books they read, the chairs in which they sat, the music they loved, the hymns they sang, the walks they took, the games they played, their seat in church, and much beside—but what would we be without these reminders? Would we like quickly to break with the past in order to assuage grief? Those who truly love will say that they have found in sorrow a new joy, a joy which only the broken-hearted can know."

Today we are so health-conscious, and yet when it comes to the sickness of grief, we entertain many misconceptions. First of all, to be emotionally healthy, we should be encouraged to grieve. I believe God gave us tear glands for a good reason and we should not be embarrassed to use them, though mine don't work, even though I have emotions that would make normal tear glands shed tears. It's too bad that courage and tears are seen as opposites. Men, especially, should not see tears as a sign of weakness. In the Old Testament stout-hearted men "lifted up their voice, and wept" (Job 2:12, KJV). Tears were not considered unmanly. David wept over the death of Saul (2 Samuel 1:12); King Jehoash wept as the prophet Elisha's death approached (2 Kings 13:14).

If someone is embarrassed over tears in public, he should feel free to cry it out in privacy. The psalmist said, "My tears have been my food day and night" (Psalm 42:3).

Without an emotional outlet, trying to "keep up appearances" and demonstrate strength, a person may be inflicting great physical harm. In a book called *Good Grief* Granger Westberg wrote, "As a clergyman in a medical center, where I have worked closely with doctors and their patients for many years, I have slowly become aware of the fact that many of the patients I see are ill because of some unresolved grief situation. Usually the patient first went to see the doctor with a physical complaint. In an increasing number of cases these people tell me about some great loss they have sustained during the past months or year or two. As we talk, it is clear they have not yet worked through some of the central problems related to that loss. I see this so often that I cannot help drawing the conclusion that there is a stronger relationship than we have ever thought between illness and the way in which a person handles a great loss."[2]

Chaplain Phil Manly at the USC Medical Center says there is great evidence that a fourth of all patients hospitalized are there because of unresolved grief in their lives. The Reverend Jack Black has said that when a person breaks down and cries over the loss of a loved one, "that person is behaving and responding as a human being. Crying at the loss of a loved one is a demonstration of love, not weakness. Expressing grief is a witness of our humanity, not an absence of bravery."

Physically, one of the frightening symptoms of grief is the feeling of tightness in the throat. One woman said, "I just can't eat. Everything sticks in my throat." Later she was heard to remark, "The only good thing to come out of my husband's death is that I lost the weight I have been trying to lose for years. I wish he could see me now." A friend remarked, "I think he can, Sally."

Others may experience a shortness of breath, or an empty feeling in the abdomen. One authority on grief said there is "a rather vague misery that we feel everywhere at once and nowhere in particular."

None of these reactions is abnormal. Grievers in this stage should endeavor to take good care of their bodies, eating a proper diet, getting adequate rest, and trying to have a good mental attitude—even if they don't particularly feel like it.

Panic is another emotion that may confront the griever. "I can't think of anything else. . . . I think I'm losing my mind." By dwelling on morbid fears and anxieties, the grief-stricken person does, in fact, lose the ability to concentrate, which only intensifies the panic. Panic, in turn, creates a sort of emotional paralysis.

Frankly, I don't know how anyone overcomes the deep, agonizing emotions of the loss of someone very near and dear without the sustaining hand of God. We can help ourselves through periods of grief or panic or fear by believing His promises. He has told us He will be with us always and never leave us or forsake us (Hebrews 13:5). We are told to give Him all of our cares and concerns.

The prophet Micah said, "Though I sit in darkness, the Lord will be my light" (7:8).

A Christian has access to that light. One woman who was grieving over the death of her child, told about claiming a simple verse and repeating it under every circumstance. When she thought she didn't have the strength to get supper she said, "I can do everything through him who gives me strength" (Philippians 4:13). When she needed to be with other people, but wanted to isolate herself in her room, she would open the door and repeat, "I can do all things through Christ." Those words, she said, became her life's verse. They have helped her through many crises since then.

Best of all, there is ultimate and justifiable hope for the Christian. A griever knows when he or she is reaching the reconstruction stage of the grief process when, little by little, hope becomes more of a reality. The time between periods of extreme grief grow longer. The memories become sweeter and less painful. Laughter is genuine, instead of forced. Great verses of hope leap out of the Bible to bring peace and even joy.

"We believe that Jesus died and rose again and so we believe that God will bring with Jesus those who have fallen asleep in him" (1 Thessalonians 4:14). We can rest in the assurance that we will be reunited with our loved ones at the resurrection, as well as being with our Lord and Savior.

"Therefore we are always confident and know that as long as we are at home in the body we are away from the Lord" (2 Corinthians 5:6).

There is no greater comfort than that offered by the promises the God of the universe gives to us. However, anyone who goes through any intense grief experience is never quite the same afterward. He becomes either stronger or weaker, and ultimately he chooses which it will be.

In today's society we feel a sense of urgency to finish one project and move on quickly to another. Most of us don't realize that it takes time to work through losses. The days of mourning and black armbands are ancient history. One of the last prominent personalities to wear the black armband was President Franklin Delano Roosevelt, at the death of his mother. But today we get the impression that any evidence of grief is out of place. Only the one who is grieving knows how long or how severe it may be. No two people are alike and no two grief situations are identical.

Those best prepared for grief are men and women with a deep faith who accepted and trusted God's promises before they had need to claim them. They nurtured their faith by reading and believing the Bible, by observing others in situations of grief, and by building spiritual strength when the sun was yet shining. Someone observed that we tend to buy umbrellas after it starts to rain. How much better to have the umbrella at hand *before* we need it.

But we need help from friends, too, and we must be willing to be receivers of love and hope as well as givers. As we have been comforted, we will know how to comfort. "Praise be to the God and Father of our Lord Jesus Christ, the Father of compassion and the God of all comfort, who comforts us in all our troubles, so that we can comfort those in any trouble with the comfort we ourselves have received from God" (2 Corinthians 1:3–4).

The story is told of the rich, old widow who acted in a strange manner after the death of her musician husband. Twenty years after he died, she still kept his music studio just as he left it. She locked the keyboard of his piano and did not allow anyone to play it or enter the room. Every day she stood in the doorway of that room, reliving memories and dwelling on the past.

Very likely she had no one to stand by her and help her through the grieving process when her husband died. How badly she needed people to care enough to be there to love and understand, and to help her resume life on her own.

Comfort, O Comfort My People

My wife says that the ones who comforted her mother the most after her father died were the widows who came to the house, put their arms around Mother Bell, and wept with her. They didn't need to say a thing.

But how can we have a ministry of comfort if we have never experienced deep sorrow ourselves? What could we say to the girl whose mother, father, brother, and grandmother were all killed in an automobile accident? What comfort could we offer the parents who have spent two years with a dying child? How could we understand the emotions of a mother and father whose only daughter was a victim of rape-murder by the Hillside Strangler? They are beyond our ability to understand.

And yet God does not suggest, He commands us to "Comfort my people" (Isaiah 40:1). However, allow me to make some general observations and suggestions for those who want to obey that command and be a source of support and comfort for the grief-stricken.

The first suggestion is to ask God to give us a tender heart. David asked the Lord, "Create in me a pure heart" (Psalm 51:10). We could add, an understanding heart, an aching heart, a considerate heart. "Finally, all of you, live in harmony with one another; be sympathetic, love as brothers, be compassionate and humble" (1 Peter 3:8). It was told that St. Patrick had this prayer inscribed on his breastplate:

God be in my head,
And in my understanding; God be in my eyes,
And in my looking; God be in my mouth,
And in my speaking; God be in my heart,
And in my thinking; God be at mine end,
And at my departing.

Sometimes well-meaning Christians will approach a mourner with long Scriptures, a series of small sermons, or pious speeches. An example of this took place at the home of a young couple whose baby had just died in that mysterious manner called "crib death." Friends and relatives gathered at their home. One young man, an unmarried seminary student, began to recite all of the recently learned verses of triumph and assurance. His anxiety to repeat all the right phrases, though essentially well intentioned, was as irritating as a fingernail scraping on a blackboard. One by one, people walked out of the room, leaving only the mourning parents to endure the insensitive seminarian's preaching.

Second, use the gift of listening. Somehow this is very difficult for all of us. We talk, many times, because we think we need to say something.

Listening is hard. The sound of our own voices may be therapy for us, but it is not necessarily healing for the wounded griever. During a time of shock, people need to repeat their story over and over again. You may think they would grow weary of giving details, or telling what happened, but that isn't the case at all.

A woman told me about her Bible teacher who came to her home after a loved one had died. She expected him to offer some profound truths, to quote Scripture, or to tell stories from the Bible. Instead, he sat on the couch as people came and went. While food was served and removed, and long after everyone was gone, he remained on the couch. Exhausted from the strain, she sat down beside him, and he said, "Tell me how you feel." Years later the woman recalled that one of the people who made the most profound impressions upon her during her stage of grief and shock was that quiet Bible teacher.

It often takes discipline to listen to the same events repeated over and over again. But by listening, we show we love. Remember how God shows His love for us by listening to the cries of our hearts.

In his book, *Comforting Those Who Grieve,* Doug Manning said, "A good listener becomes a walking, touching, personal, intensive care unit. That is what I want to be."[3]

Third, we shouldn't be shocked by whatever the grief-stricken person may say. Death can be a nightmare, and while visitors are there, life and reality may be distorted. A perfectly rational person may say irrational things. One man returned to his home from the hospital where his daughter had died, and saw his best friend sitting in his kitchen, wearing a worn sweater the friend had taken from the closet. The distraught father snapped at his friend, "Why are you wearing that? It's my fishing sweater."

The understanding friend took off the sweater without a word. Did the father make an issue over a trivial matter? Of course he did, but in later years he remembered every detail of that night and thanked his friend for being there when he needed him.

Fourth, let the bereaved one decide if he or she wants Bible reading or prayer. "Would you like to have me pray with you?" is a simple request.

But keep it simple and short, for a mind in agony cannot grasp lengthy prayers that circle the globe.

Fifth, anticipate needs without being told. Be the one who asks, "May I answer the phone for you?" Or "I would like to drive you to the funeral home to make the arrangements." Or, "Don't worry about anything in the kitchen, I'll handle it."

One of the worst things to say is, "Call me if you need anything."

Finally, don't stop being a comforter when the wounds seem to be healed. A wedding anniversary, a birthday, holidays, the anniversary of a death, these are hard times to grope through. Remembering those times with an invitation to dinner, a phone call, or a little note, will provide thoughtful comfort.

One loving Christian couple called or sent flowers on the anniversary of the death of their friend's son, every year for several years. They showed their love by not forgetting.

Hope . . . The Most Important Ingredient

Even in the midst of grieving, the mourner sooner or later begins to see little glimmers of hope. First an hour will go by when he does not think of his loss, then a few hours, then a day. He has a good night's sleep for the first time. A meal tastes good. Slowly, reconstruction begins.

For believers in Jesus Christ verses of hope seem to appear in the Bible, verses they had previously passed over. Passages they have read many times before suddenly stand out with new clarity, with new, deeper meanings. A daughter called her grieving mother long distance and said, just as if no one had ever discovered this verse before, "Listen, Mom, to what Romans 14:8 says: 'For if we live, we live for the Lord, or if we die, we die for the Lord; therefore whether we live or die, we are the Lord's.' Isn't that great?"

One of the reasons I am writing this book is my gratefulness for the fact that my mother, and others like her, taught me the truth of the verse, "For to me, to live is Christ and to die is gain" (Philippians 1:21).

The Bible says we have a God of hope. In the Scripture we find our hope. Having faith and hope does not mean that we bypass grief, but we can work through it and be strengthened by the experience.

At the beginning of the book we spoke of death as being an enemy. Its companion, grief, does not need to be an enemy, but a process of life through which we can have a closer relationship with Jesus Christ, a stronger bond with other believers, and a greater outreach to others.

Learning How to Live, and Die

During the first few years of my life, I lived in a frame farmhouse near Charlotte, North Carolina. When I was about nine years old we moved to our new red brick home, built for $9,000, a roomy, rambling house filled with laughter, books, the smells of cooking and canning, and most of all, an atmosphere of love. That wonderful house reminds me of the proverb, "By wisdom a house is built, and through understanding it is established; through knowledge its rooms are filled with rare and beautiful treasures" (Proverbs 24:3–4).

My father, Frank Graham, was a farmer whose strength and integrity made him admired, and sometimes feared, by the farmhands and us children. I can still remember the sting of his belt when I had carried some prank to the edge of disobedience. He did not, in my memory, ever punish in anger or desperation, but it pained my mother, nevertheless, and she wrote in later years, "More than once I wiped tears from my eyes and turned my head so the children wouldn't see, but I always stood behind my husband when he administered discipline."[4]

And this country boy certainly needed and deserved the discipline.

My mother, Morrow Coffey Graham, was country bred and country raised. A picture of her at eighteen showed a beautiful young woman, with a Gibson Girl hairdo, an enviable figure, a tiny waist, and a shy smile. She was one of the most beautiful women I have ever known, and she instilled in me a love for the Bible, even when it didn't seem to interest me. She began to read to my brother and sisters from devotionals and many times I thought them extremely boring. However, I listened, probably fidgeting and gazing out the window or cracking my knuckles.

My mother told how one day she took me to the family doctor and said, "Billy Frank has too much energy. He never slows down." I've sometimes wondered if she sought advice because of my excess activity or because I simply wore her out.

Mother was a very busy woman with four children and her duties as a farmer's wife. The day I was born she spent much of the afternoon picking beans and then stood in the kitchen, stringing them to prepare for canning. I still remember all the rows of canned fruit and vegetables she lined up on the shelves. She would have at least five hundred jars in the pantry after the canning season, or she wouldn't think it was enough.

Most of all, she loved the Bible. When I was in my teens, she and my father were attending a Brethren Bible class and fervently studied their Scofield Bibles. She began to order Christian books from a New York mail order house, becoming an avid reader. There were always good books lying around the house for us to read.

Mother prepared me for the lovely woman who was to become my wife. One letter I wrote said, "The reason I like Ruth so much is that she looks and reminds me of you." Mother told me later that when she finally met Ruth she was so touched, for she felt that Ruth was far above her.

My father and mother influenced and helped direct me toward the Lord. Although the testimony of my mother's life helped mold me and taught me how to live, the testimony of her last years and her death gave me insight into how to die.

She lived in our family home until the end of her life and ministered with her wonderful spirit.

We rarely had family prayers when I was young—only when I was about fourteen or fifteen did we begin. She wrote, "None of us will ever forget the time when we knelt to pray without my husband there beside us. Mr. Graham [she was very formal in referring to him] was struck in the face by a piece of wood flying from a saw. He hovered between life and death for two days. I remember going up to our bedroom and just laying hold of the Lord. I know I groaned as I pleaded with God to restore my husband to us, once again in perfect health. We needed him so!"[5]

My father did live many years after that lifethreatening time; he died in 1962 and my mother lost her beloved husband of forty-six years. Although her life as a wife and mother was productive, the following nineteen years were not lost in sorrowing or useless activity. She was a beautiful example of how Christians should serve the Lord in their latter years. She wrote, "Since the children have married and gone their separate ways, and since my husband's death, I have found myself with more time to devote to prayer. I pray without ceasing for Billy and the tremendous responsibility that God has given to him; but also for my other children, my grandchildren and great-grandchildren, and for worldwide needs."[6]

What comfort it was for me to know that no matter where I was in the world, my mother was praying for me.

The Tender Heart

An eminent psychiatrist said that the chief duty of a human being is to endure life. In contrast, the Westminster Shorter Catechism says, "Man's chief end is to glorify God, and to enjoy Him forever." My mother did just that.

The last two years my mother lived she was cared for by a wonderful Christian woman, Rose Adams. Rose often said that she had a seminary course, living with Mother, and I can believe it. Mother could quote and remember Scriptures and apply them to everyday living better than most ministers. She never had formal training in a Bible college, but said she learned as the Bible says, "For it is: do and do, do and do, rule on rule, rule on rule; a little here, a little theren (Isaiah 28:10). Put all of these bits of learning together and you have a woman whose knowledge touched an untold number of lives.

She was one of my greatest encouragers. The first sermon she ever heard me preach was in an old synagogue, about forty miles from Charlotte. I was home from Bible school for the Christmas holidays and my parents drove me to the service. Mother said later she was so nervous for me that she was wet with cold perspiration. She never remembered what I said that day, but she thought I was very loud. She was right.

While I was in college Mother and Father prayed every day for me and claimed the verse: "Study to shew thyself approved unto God, a workman that needeth not to be ashamed, rightly dividing the word of truth" (2 Timothy 2:15, KJV).

Mother always told me to preach the gospel, and keep it simple. Two weeks before she went to be with the Lord she admonished me with the same words.

I said, "Mother, I'm going to preach His birth, death, and resurrection. I'll preach it until Jesus comes."

She squeezed my hand and said, "I believe it."

What a blessing it is for parents to believe in their children.

As I remembered my mother's last years, and heard from Rose Adams of the thoughts that she shared, I realized that other lives could be blessed by her example.

At one time it was thought that Mother would have to have her leg amputated. When the infection finally cleared and she was sent home from the hospital, she said, "God never uses a person's life until first he has been broken." She was no stranger to mental and physical suffering. She endured pain, but enjoyed life. She said the Lord had dealt with her through heartaches, but said, "God doesn't comfort us to make us comfortable, but to make us comforters."

Rose, a fun-loving, ebullient woman, with a laugh as big as her heart, came to stay with Mother on a full-time basis the last two years of her life. When Rose's husband died, Mother wrote her this note:

> Dear Precious One, When this storm shall pass, the brightness for which He is preparing you will appear unclouded, and it shall be Himself.

Rose and Mother had a routine for their devotions each morning. During this time Mother would quote Scripture and give Rose an application. It was the spiritual food that sustained her through the pain and weakness of her last days.

One of the first Scriptures my mother taught all her children was Ecclesiastes 12:1. "Remember now thy Creator in the days of thy youth, while the evil days come not, nor the years draw nigh, when thou shalt say, I have no pleasure in them" (KJV). She told her grandchildren and great-grandchildren the same thing, urging all of us to learn to love God and study the Bible when we were young. She never stopped studying and told her pastor, Dr. Ross Rhoads, "I just want to study more and more and do what the Bible says." He commented, "Isn't it something . . . here she is eighty-nine years old and the most perfect person I know living by the Word, and yet she says she wants to study more and more."

Rose Adams told us how Mother would say a verse, in that gentle, expressive manner of hers, and then give an illustration of what it meant to her. These gems were not lost, since Rose recorded them in the margin of *Streams in the Desert* or wrote them in her journal. Here are some of her thoughts shortly before she died.

An Understanding Heart

"For I reckon that the sufferings of this present time are not worthy to be compared with the glory which shall be revealed in us" (Romans 8:18, KJV).

Mother commented, "When God afflicts us He hews a rugged stone. It must be shaped, or else we will be thrown aside, useless. What comforts me is this precious thought: we are being shaped into stones for His heavenly temple. To be made like Him is the very object of our earthly existence. He is the shaper and carpenter of the heavenly temple. He must work us into shape. Our part is to be still in His dear hand. Every vexation is a little chip. We must not be in a hurry to go out of the quarry, for there is a certain place for each stone. We must wait until the building is ready for that stone."

"The angel of the Lord encampeth round about them that fear him, and delivereth them" (Psalm 34:7, KJV).

She was very weak the day she read that verse, but said to Rose, "I always wanted to grow old gracefully and have a sweet spirit. . . . I don't want to complain, but sometimes I think Satan is trying to use my suffering to force me to complain. but the Lord has given me such great promise to send an angel to surround me."

From the time when she finally quit struggling with her weakness she developed a certain serenity and a peace. She said, "Do not be afraid to enter the cloud which is settling down on your life, for God is in it. The other side is radiant with His glory. If we are to wear a crown we must first bear a cross. We all have a Gethsemane. . . . Jesus did." Mother couldn't understand people who taught that if you are filled with the Spirit and walk with the Lord you won't suffer. She believed that was a cruel teaching.

Was she afraid to die? Not really. And yet she told Rose she was afraid of being left alone in her last moments. She had not been with my father when he went to be with the Lord and always regretted her absence. Rose promised to be with her, and she kept that promise.

The Last Mile

After a series of minor strokes, Mother would become confused at times. When she was lucid she told Rose, "If I get so I don't know what I'm doing, you make sure that I'm fixed. . . . Put a little color on my face, but don't make me look worldly. I just don't want the children to see me look poorly."

Gracious to the last, this dear lady wanted to be attractive for us. We always thought she was beautiful, and age only enhanced her charm.

She believed the only reason the Lord was delaying His coming for her was so she could pray for others. "That's about all I'm able to do now," she would say. But what an amazing ministry that was. Until the very last few months, whenever she heard of someone in need she would have Rose write a little note and send a few dollars, as had been her habit for so many years. One of her greatest joys was to listen to the records of George Beverly Shea. She played them almost every day and especially loved it when he sang "Be Still My Soul," "He Will Give His Angels Charge Over Thee," and "Amazing Grace."

In the last months she began to dread seeing the approach of evening. "Nights are so long," she would tell Rose in her fading voice. But she quoted Revelation 22:5 which speaks about heaven and says, "And there shall be no night there; and they need no candle, neither light of the sun; for the Lord God giveth them light: and they shall reign for ever and ever" (KJV).

In May of 1981 she said, "Rose, I feel it won't be long until the Lord takes me home. I don't want any mourning or sad spirits. It says in Acts 27:22, 'And now I exhort you to be of good cheer: for there shall be no loss of any man's life among you, but of the ship'" (KJV).

In June of 1981 I was holding a crusade in Baltimore. I called every day to see how Mother was doing and Rose said she listened to the tapes of the hymns Ruth had recorded a few years before for her mother.

My wife knew the comfort in music and compiled some of the great old songs into a cassette which was called "Looking Homeward." Ruth's mother had a tape recorder on her bed and would switch it on and off to hear the inspiring music. A few years later we had those tapes sent to our television audience and received one of the largest responses to any book or tape we ever gave away. The comfort our mothers found resulted in comfort for many thousands.

On June 15 I called from France, and Rose said Mother had given her the Scripture for the day, Colossians 1:9: "For this cause we also, since the day we heard it, do not cease to pray for you, and to desire that ye might be filled with the knowledge of his will in all wisdom and spiritual understanding" (KJV).

While I was concerned about my dear mother, thousands of miles away on a bed of weakness and pain, she had a verse of encouragement for me. What would the world be like if there were more mothers like her? She didn't make great speeches or write clever books. She didn't have any great causes to espouse, except the cause of Jesus Christ. She didn't have university degrees, nor was she mentioned in society columns. But she knew how to pray.

The Lord seems to prepare His children for their homecoming in most unique ways. Toward the end of July Mother constantly talked about going to heaven. Rose asked her if she could come to her mansion in heaven and work for her because she thought her house would be very small and she wouldn't have much to do, but Mother Graham's would be so large she'd need help.

One morning when she awoke, she told Rose there was a man at the foot of her bed. She wanted to know who he was.

Rose asked her if he looked like a good man.

"Oh yes, he has a very kind face."

"Maybe he's your guardian angel."

Mother then asked, "Who is that woman who comes in with you?"

This time Rose was startled. "There hasn't been anyone with me," she said.

"Oh, but for the last two weeks every time you came in the room there's been someone with you. She just stands beside you. She must be your guardian angel. Now, get me ready for church."

The beginning of August, 1981, Mother awoke around midnight and called to Rose, who was sleeping nearby on a pallet in the living room. "Rose, are all the children on the train?"

Rose told her everything was all right and the children were on the train. She would quiet down for a time and then try to lift herself up from the bed and call again, "Rose, are all of the children on the train?"

"Don't you worry, Mother Graham, they're all there," she said. Rose went back to bed, but soon Mother became more persistent.

"Rose, please check and see if all the children are on the train." Somehow she seemed to know she was going somewhere and wanted to be certain her children were going with her. We believe she was seeking assurance that all of her family were saved.

On August 8, my brother, Melvin, T. W. Wilson, and I went to see her. She wanted us to tell Ruth and Mary Helen (T. W.'s wife) how much she loved them. She was always so proud of the wives of our team, whose unselfish loyalty meant so much to all of us, particularly when we had to be gone so much. She urged us to continue preaching the gospel and to be faithful in winning the lost.

The next day she was in a semicoma, but woke early in the morning, long enough to announce very loudly, "No payment, no pain, no sickness, no death . . . O what a beautiful day!"

Rose hurried to her bedside, wondering why she had spoken so forcefully when she had been so weak, and said, "Mother Graham, are you all right?"

She said, "Am I in a coma yet?"

"No, Ma'am."

"Am I dead yet? Are we in heaven yet?"

"No, Ma'am," Rose answered, "you're not in heaven 'cause I'm still with you."

"Oh well," sighed Mother, "it's a beautiful day, anyhow."

When she was too weak to speak, she seemed to be moaning and trying to sing a little tune. Rose leaned down close to her mouth and she picked out the words, "Face to face." Then she said, "Psalm . . . 1 . . . 4" and would doze off.

Rose tried to figure out what she was trying to say, and then remembered Psalm 149:5 was underlined in her Bible. It says, "Let the saints be joyful in glory: let them sing aloud upon their beds" (KJV). She was trying to sing, but couldn't voice the words; however, her habit of Bible memorization recalled the proper verse at a time when she needed it.

The morning she went to be with the Lord she kept reaching up. . . . She tried to say something about hand, and Rose didn't know what she wanted. Perhaps, Rose thought, she is trying to say a verse of Scripture, but couldn't get the words out.

"Mother Graham, are you trying to say, 'Father, into Thy hands I commend my spirit'?"

Her hand dropped and a smile came upon her lips. She looked peaceful all day, and once when Rose was about to leave the room, she seemed to yawn. Rose put her arms around her and Mother went to be with her precious Lord.

"How do we prepare for that last day? Before we embark on our final trip, have we left an earthly home in a state of chaos or a condition of order?"

Set thine house in order; for thou shalt die, and not live.

2 Kings 20:1, KJV

CHAPTER NINE

Is Your House In Order?

GOING THROUGH SOME old newspaper clippings that Ruth had saved, we found one dated May 5, 1957, entitled "You must prepare for that last day." As I began to reminisce about what was happening in our lives thirty years ago, the humor and irony of that article hit me.

On May 15, 1957, we began the New York Crusade. After we had accepted the challenge to hold those important meetings, it was reported that "This invitation brought upon Graham's head some of the most violent opposition he had ever experienced."[1] I wonder if Ruth thought I was heading for my "last day" in Madison Square Garden?

Incidentally, we were there for sixteen weeks. Only on the second night did we have empty seats; it became our most successful American crusade. At Madison Square Garden we began to put our crusades on national television at prime evening times.

Preparation for the Journey

But how do we prepare for that *last day*? What if the old bedtime rhyme, "If I should die before I wake," becomes a reality? Before we embark on our final trip, have we left an earthly home in a state of chaos or a condition of order?

A young minister said that about once a year he asks his wife, "What if I had just died . . . what would you do?" He doesn't ask her to rehearse grief reactions but to go through the mechanics of saying whom she would call, where important documents are kept, what arrangements she should make with the executor of their estate. This may not be a very enjoyable exercise, but both the husband and the wife say this mock rehearsal gives them a peace of mind and an openness of communication they did not have before they set their "house in order." They are planning in their thirties what many people leave until their seventies. How many heartaches for survivors would be avoided by planning ahead.

The prophet Isaiah delivered a tough message from God to King Hezekiah: "Put your house in order, because you are going to die" (38:1). That crisp command brings into sharp focus a vital, but often neglected, aspect of Christian stewardship. It is the responsibility of every believer while he or she is alive and able to make proper preparations spiritually, as well as fiscally, for the distribution of property and possessions he leaves behind at his death.

The first step in preparation is to accept the fact that we *are* going to die. Unless we are willing to talk openly about this fact, we will never be motivated to follow through on any of the remaining steps.

I have faced death many times and my reactions have not always been the same. Many years ago I had an operation that almost ended me. As a result, a second operation was required to save my life, and before I went into the operating room I called two of my good friends. Ruth was not with me, and I tried to keep from her the seriousness of the situation. She had gone to be with the children. But I gave to these friends instructions for my wife, my family, and my ministry.

During that time, I can remember alternating between complete peace in knowing that I would be with my Lord Jesus Christ, and a fear of leaving my loved ones. Neither emotion predominated, but I seemed to vacillate back and forth. My memory of that time is clouded because of the pain, but I certainly thought I was going to die.

Another brush with death occurred on an airplane over the Atlantic, when Ruth and I were returning from Europe. It had been an uneventful flight until, suddenly, there was an explosion; the airplane began to vibrate and lose altitude. Dishes flew off trays, people were jolted in their seats, and we thought a bomb was going to finish all of us. There was some comment about turbulence, and we never found out exactly what happened, but we were all immediately aware of our mortality.

We landed safely and thanked the Lord again for giving us a little more time to be doing His work.

I remember a story the late Dr. V. Raymond Edman, former president of Wheaton College, told about his first encounter with death. As a young missionary in Ecuador, he contracted typhoid fever while working among the Indians in the Andes Mountains. After several days he was unconscious but, as he described it, fully aware that death was closing in on him. In fact, his friends had bought a coffin for him and helped his wife dye her wedding dress black for the funeral. Dr. Edman said that he experienced the overwhelming love of God and remembered the wonderful assurance that "if our earthly house of this tabernacle were dissolved, we have a building of God, an house not made with hands, eternal in the heavens" (2 Corinthians 5:1, KJV).

In remembering that story, I can't help speculating that Mrs. Edman must have rejoiced that her black wedding dress was never worn.

Author Edward Young wrote that procrastination is the thief of time. Procrastination may also be the thief of our loved ones' sense of security. None of us wants to compound someone else's grief, but many do by their failure to practice good stewardship. Stewardship is more than just giving our tithe to the church or Christian organizations. The faithful Christian steward acknowledges that God owns all he has, and it is his responsibility to manage and dispose of his possessions in a way that is acceptable to the Lord. "Now it is required that those who have been given a trust must prove faithful" (1 Corinthians 4:2).

Stewardship is not just the tithe we give during our lifetime, but a responsibility which continues after our death. We should, as did the young minister and his wife, rehearse in our minds what needs to be done.

It has been said that someone found St. Francis working in his garden and asked him, "What would you do if you knew that you would die in ten minutes?" St. Francis replied, "I'd try to finish this row."

Most of us are not that ready. We might need ten days instead of ten minutes!

Putting Things in Order

After accepting our mortality, the next step is to put our material affairs in order. Dr. Bell taught me a great lesson about that. When I was a very young man, he urged me to make a will. When he, himself, died, his papers were found to be perfectly categorized and numbered in file folders, and there was no confusion about how he wanted his earthly estate to be dispersed.

From that I learned the value of writing down instructions and leaving vital information where it could be found. This includes providing information about where bank books are kept, how insurance papers are filed, and where the key is to your safe deposit box. Our treasures may be laid up in heaven, but those things we leave on earth will mean a great deal more to those we leave behind. Many Christians today seek to include their church and other ministries in their will.

Years ago I read an article by Dr. Edman in the Wheaton College bulletin. It was called, "Facing Death Unafraid," and his description of stewardship made a lasting impression on me. He said, "To the best of my knowledge, all arrangements for the eventuality of death had been made. Just recently Mrs. Edman and I had brought our wills up to date. This was the fourth revision. Conditions had changed since the four boys were little fellows. Furthermore, we had completed a life estate plan with a Christian organization. After much prayer and planning we had sought the counsel and help of those qualified to advise the Lord's people in these matters, for it is our conviction that no matter how large or how modest the estate, plans should be laid so that nothing is wasted."[2]

I have heard so many stories of people who have spent weeks, sometimes months and years, trying to find documents and straighten out the estate of a deceased member of the family. One such story concerns a fine Christian physician who was dying of cancer. Long before his death he knew that the end was certain. He continued with his practice as long as he could, but during the final months of his life was not able to make clear decisions.

His widow believed she had been properly taken care of and would enjoy some degree of financial independence. She had never questioned her husband's arrangements, having depended upon his wisdom to leave his house in order. But within a year the distraught widow found she had been left penniless and in debt. She was forced to sell the family home, take her daughter out of college, and go to work in a menial job. As a society wife of a prominent surgeon, it had never been necessary for her to learn any earning skills, but suddenly she was faced with the need to support herself and her children.

Perhaps there should be more of us who proclaim the practical applications of Isaiah's warning to Hezekiah, "Set your house in order."

Plan Your Own Funeral

Did you make plans for your own wedding? Did you ever have a special party, an anniversary or birthday celebration, where you planned in advance what you would do? Then what's so strange about planning your own funeral?

I have preached at many funerals. It seems to me that those loved ones who have some knowledge of the wishes of the deceased move through the funeral process with less anxiety than those who have no idea what the departed one might have wanted. I remember one sincere request made by President Lyndon Johnson after he retired from public life. I had delivered the invocation at the dedication of the Johnson Library in Austin, Texas, and later LBJ took me to his ranch in the Hill Country. We walked down to the oak trees by the Pedernales River and he said, "Billy, one day you're going to be asked to preach at my funeral. You'll come right here under this tree and I'll be buried right there." And he pointed to the spot. "You'll read the Bible and preach the gospel, and

I want you to, but I hope you'll try to tell some of the things I tried to do."

President Johnson and I spoke about the brevity of life, and the fact that someday we will stand before God to give an account. We discussed the resurrection at some length.

Just fifteen minutes after I returned home from President Richard Nixon's second inauguration I heard of Mr. Johnson's death. On January 25, 1973, I preached beneath that old oak tree, as he requested, and the nation watched on television.

Though in many ways he was a rough man, and a complex man, down deep in his heart he loved God. A number of times it had been my privilege to be with him both in Washington and in Texas, and have prayer with him. I can remember seeing him climb out of bed and get down on his knees while I prayed.

So it was with a heart full of love that I told about the man I knew: his compassion for the underdog, his friendship for children of all races, his strong family life and, most importantly, his faith. My biographer, John Pollock, wrote how I spoke of death, judgment, and the Cross, and said, "Lyndon Johnson understood that. . . . for the believer who has been to the Cross, death is no frightful leap in the dark, but is the entrance into a glorious new life . . . . For the believer, the brutal fact of death has been conquered by the historical resurrection of Jesus Christ. For the person who has turned from sin and received Christ as Lord and Savior, death is not the end . . . ."[3]

That is what President Lyndon Johnson wanted me to say.

Why give instructions for your own funeral? Certainly not because you will be concerned about them. You won't attend your own funeral. However, your spouse, your children, your friends, and business associates may all be there. The survivors would want to know your wishes. Where will you be buried? Have you left instructions about cremation or a burial plot? What hymns would you want to be sung? Are there any words of assurance you would want to be said to your loved ones and friends? Are there any requests about an open or closed casket?

How often the survivors of the deceased have to struggle with those decisions when they are in no condition to be making such plans, and when it would have been so much easier to have the plans already made and settled.

If we plan our own funeral, we should keep in mind family traditions or customs in the part of the country where we live. For instance, in many places viewing the body is an important part of the grief process which allows the survivors to say farewell to the physical part of the person they loved. It gives a certain finality to the death process.

I remember when Richard Nixon's mother died. I had the privilege of participating in her funeral. I had known his father and mother before I knew him and, as was the custom in that Quaker city of Whittier, California, people filed by to see the open casket. The pastor of the church and I stood there beside the casket, then the Nixon family came in. As the future president looked at his mother, he burst into tears. He had a deep love for his mother, and for all his family.

However, for some people the cosmetic attempts upon the deceased are unseemly. It is important to be sensitive to the feelings of others when we make decisions about our own funeral or memorial service.

Personally, Ruth and I know where we will be buried and we have expressed our desires to have a homegoing "celebration," not a woeful wake.

Of course, I cannot make definitive statements about planning your own funeral since it is a subject with so many personal applications. However, biblical precedents have been set for us by some of the great Old Testament believers who gave personal burial instructions. Jacob said, "I am about to be gathered to my people. Bury me with my fathers in the cave in the field of Ephron the Hittite. . . . " After he expressed his wishes, the Bible says, he went peacefully. "When Jacob had finished giving instructions to his sons, he drew his feet up into the bed, breathed his last and was gathered to his people" (Genesis 49:29, 33).

"By faith," the writer tells us, "Joseph, when his end was near . . . gave instructions about his bones" (Hebrews 11:22).

These two great patriarchs didn't use long-range planning, but at least they had definite arrangements which were made known to their kinsmen.

It was reported that President Franklin Delano Roosevelt left exact instructions concerning his funeral in a four-page, penciled document addressed to his eldest son, James. It read, "If I should die while in office, I want a service of the utmost simplicity held in the East Room of the White House. There should be no lying in state, no gun carriage and no hearse. The casket should be of utmost simplicity in dark wood. The body should not be embalmed or hermetically sealed. The grave should not be lined with brick, cement or stones."[4]

Those directions were certainly explicit. There was only one catch. No one in the Roosevelt family knew this document existed. It was found in the President's private safe a few days after he was buried.

It may be wise for us to make arrangements for our funerals, but our most carefully drawn plans won't do any good if no one knows where they are!

Planning your own funeral is a gift from you to your survivors. No one can convey what you wish to leave as a personal testimony better than you can. Others may extol your virtues, and ignore your shortcomings, but only you can tell of your love for the Lord, your appreciation of your family, and your anticipation of heaven, if those are your personal beliefs.

Funerals Are for the Living

Every culture has had its ceremonies for meeting emotional crises. All of the major changes in life, from birth to adolescence, marriage, and death, have been dignified by rituals. A funeral should be a ritual which meets the social, emotional, and spiritual needs of the survivors.

A newspaper columnist wrote, "Funerals are for the living, not the dead, and I've never attended one that I thought did a good job of comforting the survivors, or really helped them to work through their grief."[5]

On the contrary, I have attended and officiated at many funerals where I felt that the funeral or memorial service was a turning point in the lives of some of those attending. Often, from the witness of the life and death of the deceased, or the statements made by family members, uncommitted men and women have been convicted about their own lives and have been directed to a loving God.

For believers in Jesus Christ a Christian funeral reaffirms the blessed hope of eternal life and the resurrection. Jesus said, "I tell you the truth, whoever hears my word and believes him who sent Me has eternal life and will not be condemned; he has crossed over from death to life" (John 5:24).

When Martha needed comfort about the death of her brother, Lazarus, Jesus said to her, "I am the resurrection and the life. He who believes in me will live, even though he dies; and whoever lives and believes in me will never die. Do you believe this?" (John 11:25).

At a funeral service the bereaved can be drawn closer to the Lord, experiencing His comfort, as Martha did, and as other believers have throughout the ages. The writer who said he had never attended a funeral where survivors were comforted also admitted that he didn't believe in an afterlife and doubted that his spirit would be transformed in a world elsewhere. Such skepticism only serves to rob the funeral service of anything meaningful. It leaves the bereaved with no hope.

A funeral should provide a time for relatives, friends, and church family to support the grieving loved ones and to express concern and sympathy for their loss. Even if friends never knew the deceased, it is a time to show their love for the survivors. We honor the dead at such a service, but we also are provided with a tangible way of ministering to the bereaved before, during, and after the funeral.

Years ago, a Christian wrote a letter which she instructed to be sent to friends after her memorial service was held. She was an English teacher at a small Texas college, and a devout Christian. She said, "All my lifelong study of literature has taught me that when the writer is great enough, the end is the best part of the book. I am a volume written by a divine Writer, and the climax is the best part of the book."

A Christian funeral should be a coronation ceremony, a statement to the world about eternal life.

Do You Need a Will?

Polls show that only about one in every five adults has made a will. When we see the problems created for the surviving family members whenever anyone dies without leaving one, it should convict us with our own sense of responsibility. Recently I learned of a prominent business person, head of a large company, who died without leaving a will. It is difficult to understand how anyone of that stature could have neglected such an important document; however, it is startling to me to find out how prevalent this omission really is. Such situations create needless hardships and heartache for loved ones.

The Lord's work suffers because of this lack of concern on the part of such a great number of Christians.

What is a will? Essentially, it is a legal document that names the people—family members, friends, business associates—as well as the organizations, churches, and charities that you choose to receive your property when you die.

I remember once when Charlie Riggs and I were flying late at night on the west coast of Africa in an old Ghanian Airways DC-3. We ran into a terrible thunderstorm and none of us thought that old plane could possibly survive. People all around us started screaming, and one big, strong Nigerian man sitting beside Charlie began sobbing so loudly everyone on the plane could hear him. Later, I asked Charlie why the Nigerian had been weeping so bitterly, and Charlie said the man was sure he was going to die and his body was going to fall into the water where his son could not recover it. Among his people the son could not inherit anything from the father unless his body was found.

Your estate includes personal property, such as automobiles, stocks, interest in a business, furniture, jewelry, dishes, a stamp collection or books, or other similar personal effects. I suspect my wife would say her most important possessions are her books.

When Dr. Bell, my father-in-law, died, the family went to his closet and found only two suits and one pair of shoes. He had arranged his personal effects impeccably for his departure, but even these few things which he had kept were important to his family.

Your estate also includes real property, which is land and any buildings you own or any improvements that stand on the land.

Who among us can make a will? Generally, anyone who is eighteen years of age or older can write a will. For it to be valid, you must be of sound mind, which means that you must understand what property you own, about how much it's worth, and to whom you are leaving it.

You may name your own "executor," who is the person, bank, or corporation which will handle your affairs after you die, until your property is distributed in accordance with your will or other legal settlement. The executor collects any money owed to your estate, pays your debts and taxes, and gives the remaining property to the persons or organizations named in the will.

If an executor is not named, the court will appoint someone to settle the affairs of the estate. This may not be the person you would have chosen.

Your will lets you name a guardian for your minor children. This can be important if both parents die at the same time, or if you're a single parent. If you don't name a guardian, it will be up to the court to decide where the children will live and how to spend any money you leave for their care. For anyone with minor children, this fact alone should be reason enough to get a will written now.

A will should generally be drawn up by a lawyer, but under certain conditions you may write your own will. If you have a handwritten, or "holographic" will, the law says that your signature and all important parts of the will must be in your own writing. It should be dated, but witnesses are not required. Not all states accept such handwritten wills, however, so you should be sure it is legal where you live, and if you should move to another state, don't forget to check the laws there.

Some married couples, believing that their goals and desires are the same, want to write a joint will. But lawyers and administrators warn against the perils of this practice, since in a joint will two people say what's to be done with each one's property. If both people agree that their joint will is final, it can't be changed later by the survivor. I know a woman who took the opportunity to change a joint will after the death of her husband. The couple had four children and the husband had left somewhat more money to two of them. When those two found out, a few years later, that their share had been reduced by their mother so that all the children would share equally, they were so upset that they begged, and almost threatened, the other two until they were given some of the money that had originally (and legally) been left to them.

You can imagine what complications might arise if, for instance, the spouse who survives should remarry, or children who are to receive property become irresponsible. Joint wills may sound like a noble statement that both partners are of like mind, but the actual consequences of such a will can be disturbing.

If you die without a will, the court will distribute your property to your relatives in a manner established by law. However, your property cannot go to friends, charities, or churches if you do not leave a will so stating. There can be no special provisions for heirlooms, jewelry, or the family business.

Your will remains in effect until you change it or draft a new one. Many people will be convinced they need a will, have one drawn up, and then let it sit for years without giving it another thought. "Sure, I have a will," they say, confidently. However, since that will was written, children may have grown and married, grandchildren may have been born, tax laws changed, estate size increased, and the original will may have little validity anymore. A review should be made of your will every few years. The court will follow your most recent will.

The law gives you many choices if you make a will, but none at all if you don't.

A Christian's will should be a matter of much prayer and thoughtfulness, including perhaps not only gifts to individuals but to one's church or to other religious organizations. A Christian's will may also contain more than directions on how money and possessions are to be dispersed. It can also be a testimony to those who read it. It can be a lasting memorial to faith in Christ and love for others. Someone said that he could tell better what a man had in his heart by reading his will than by reading his obituary. "For as he thinketh in his heart, so is he" (Proverbs 23:7, KJV).

Many of us who have read and loved the books written by Charles Dickens have thought that he must have been a Christian. Generations of readers have laughed and cried over his *Pickwick Papers, Oliver Twist, David Copperfield,* and *Nicholas Nickleby.* Not a Christmas goes by without many revivals of his great classic, *A Christmas Carol.* But it was not the great books he wrote nor the lengthy eulogy in the *London Times* when he died that will be recorded in eternity, but the inheritance he left in his will. He wrote: "I commit my soul to the mercy of God, through our Lord and Savior Jesus Christ, and I exhort my dear children humbly to try and guide themselves by the teaching of the New Testament."[6]

The best preparation for death is not a list of instructions about our funeral, not an up-to-date will, but an experience with Christ that gives eternal life: ". . . a faith and knowledge resting on the hope of eternal life, which God, who does not lie, promised before the beginning of time" (Titus 1:2).

The hope of eternal life becomes more precious when we increase our knowledge of what that means. Our everyday existence is so centered on what is happening to us on earth that the prospect of eternity may be perceived as overwhelming—even frightening.

What does await us in eternity? Is it a journey into the unknown, or a glorious spiritual pilgrimage to eagerly anticipate?

We will all go on the trip to eternity, and we make the choice of the type of reservations we will have to determine our destiny.

"Throughout our culture we have been led to the idea that we accept death as the end of life on earth. . . . Time bound as we are and goal oriented to achievements in our lifetime, we find it strange to anticipate heaven."

> *I consider that our present sufferings are not worth comparing with the glory that will be revealed in us.* Romans 8:18

CHAPTER TEN

Where Do I Go When I Die?

A GHOSTLY IMPERIAL guard of more than seven thousand life size clay soldiers has been unearthed in mainland China. Archaeologists recently uncovered these massive terra-cotta statues, considered one of the most spectacular finds of the age. The royal army, standing in battle formation to protect the grave of China's first emperor, Shih Huang Ti, was equipped with war chariots and weapons of wood and bronze. Their horses, harnessed in gold and silver, lay in a pit near the tomb. In this amazing discovery we see death depicted as a battleground. The emperor wanted assurance of protection in the afterworld.

Man's final destination has been pondered throughout the ages. Some have accepted the tradition of their ancestors, others have struggled with conflicting ideas. Buddhists and Hindus believe they will undergo repeated rebirths, transmigrating from existence to existence; there is no beginning and no end of a continuing life; they are reincarnated into other bodies.

The Taoist treats death with indifference; oblivion is a state of nondoing. Islamic belief recognizes seven heavens, places of carnal pleasure and spiritual bliss. American Indian culture speaks of the "Happy Hunting Ground." Most adherents to Judaism believe in a heaven where good deeds done on earth are rewarded.

The Christian has a strong hope of heaven because of what Jesus Christ has done through His death and resurrection. "Praise be to the

God and Father of our Lord Jesus Christ! In his great mercy he has given us new birth into a living hope through the resurrection of Jesus Christ from the dead, and into an inheritance that can never perish, spoil or fade—kept in heaven for you" (1 Peter 1:3–4).

At the same time there are many things about heaven we do not know for sure. "Now we see but a poor reflection (as in a mirror); then we shall see face to face. Now I know in part; then I shall know fully, even as I am fully known" (1 Corinthians 13:12).

One unknown poet expressed it this way:

When the holy angels meet us,
As we go to join their band,
Shall we know the friends that greet us,
In the glorious spirit-land?
Shall we see the same eyes shining
On us, as in days of yore?
Shall we feel their dear arms twining
Fondly 'round us as before?
Shall we know each other there?

What Right Have You to Enter Heaven?

Every man and woman who has ever lived will have to answer that question. A woman who had just experienced a death in her family told me she felt such an urgency to share Christ with someone that when a repairman came in to fix the furnace she backed him up against the wall and said, "If that furnace had blown up in your face and you had died, would you know for certain where you would spend eternity?" The repairman was so startled he forgot to leave a bill.

Why do some people believe they have a paid ticket to heaven? They give many answers, but most can be classified within three basic attitudes. The first is, "Just look at what I've done on earth. My record is pretty good, compared to some. I'll be in heaven because I lived such a good life."

That person is in trouble. The Bible says "for all have sinned and fall short of the glory of God" (Romans 3:23). So if we're placing our good deeds on a scale of 1 to 10, even a perfect 10 wouldn't make it. No one can ever live a life that is "good enough." The Bible says, "For whoever keeps the whole law and yet stumbles at just one point is guilty of breaking all of it" (James 2:10).

The second answer might be, "I really don't know, and I'm not sure that I care. I gave it some thought for a while, but there were so many other things that seemed more important."

As mothers say, "Excuses will get you nowhere." The Bible says, "For since the creation of the world God's invisible qualities—his eternal power and divine nature—have been clearly seen, being understood from what has been made, so that men are without excuse" (Romans 1:20).

Only one answer will give a person the certain privilege, the joy, of entering heaven. "Because I have believed in Jesus Christ and accepted Him as my Savior. He is the One sitting at the right hand of God and interceding for me." No one can deny the Christian his entrance into heaven.

The Heidelberg Catechism, originally written in 1563 and used by Christians of many backgrounds, was a favorite of my father-in-law. On his study wall he had the first question and answer of the Heidelberg Catechism framed, which reads,

Q 1 What is your only comfort, in life and in death?

A That I belong—body and soul, in life and death—not to myself but to my faithful Savior, Jesus Christ, who at the cost of his own blood has fully paid for all my sins and has completely freed me from the dominion of the devil; that he protects me so well that without the will of my Father in heaven not a hair can fall from my head; indeed, that everything must fit his purpose for my salvation. Therefore, by his Holy Spirit, he also assures me of eternal life, and makes me wholeheartedly willing and ready from now on to live for him."

"Who will bring any charge against those whom God has chosen? It is God who justifies. Who is he that condemns? Christ Jesus, who died—more than that, who was raised to life—is at the right hand of God and is also interceding for us" (Romans 8:33, 34).

What a magnificent thought! Jesus is our advocate, our lawyer, pleading our case before God the Father, telling Him that the person being presented for entrance into heaven must be admitted on the basis of God's grace alone, not by any good works or noble deeds done on earth.

Many people are deceived by Satan into thinking that God is a vengeful taskmaster, ready to send to hell all those who offend Him. They can see no hope. True, God does hate sin, but He loves the sinner. Since we are all sinners, our only right for admission to heaven lies in the provision God made for our sins: His Son, Jesus Christ. "For God so loved the world that he gave his one and only Son, that whoever believes in him shall not perish but have eternal life" (John 3:16).

Do We Decide to Go to Hell?

Hell has been cloaked in folklore and disguised in fiction for so long, many people deny the reality of such a place. Some think it is merely a myth. This is understandable. Our minds revolt against ugliness and suffering. However, the concept of hell is not exclusive to the Christian faith.

Centuries before Christ, the Babylonians believed in "The Land of No-Return." The Hebrews wrote about going down to the realm of Sheol, or the place of corruption; the Greeks spoke of the "Unseen Land." Classical Buddhism recognizes seven "hot hells," and the Hindu *Rig Veda* speaks of the deep abyss reserved for false men and faithless women. Islam recognizes seven hells.[1]

Jesus specifically states that nonbelievers will not be able to escape the condemnation of hell (Matthew 23:33). He told His disciples, "Do not be afraid of those who kill the body and after that can do no more. But I will show you whom you should fear: Fear him who, after the killing of the body, has power to throw you into hell" (Luke 12:4–5).

Probably one of the most graphic descriptions of hell in the Bible is given by Jesus in His parable of the rich man and Lazarus. During his life the rich man refused to help Lazarus, a poor beggar who yearned to eat crumbs which fell from the rich man's table. When the beggar died, he was carried to Abraham's side, which was what we would describe as heaven. The rich man was sent to hell and was in torment. Jesus did not imply that having wealth means being doomed to hell, nor did he say that being poor guarantees anyone the right to heaven. However, it is a graphic description of the unbeliever's suffering apart from God.

According to the parable, the rich man looked up and saw Abraham, with the beggar by his side. He spoke through cracked, parched lips and pleaded for Abraham to ask Lazarus to dip his finger in some water and bring it to him to cool his tongue. "I am in agony in this fire," he cried.

But Abraham said there was a great chasm between the two worlds and it was "fixed," or permanent. No person on one side could cross over to the other. In other words, the one in hell had been given a choice of direction during his life on earth, and now he had to suffer the consequences of his decision to live for himself instead of for God. There was no second chance.

Hell: A Controversial Subject

I am continually asked, "What about hell?" or "Is there fire in hell?" and similar questions. I cannot ignore this unpopular subject, although it makes people uncomfortable and anxious. It is probably the hardest of all Christian teachings to accept.

Some teach "universalism"—that eventually everybody will be saved and the God of love will never send anyone to hell. They believe the words "eternal" or "everlasting" do not actually mean forever. However, the same word which speaks of eternal banishment from God is also used for the eternity of heaven.

Others teach that those who refuse to accept Jesus Christ as Savior are simply annihilated; they no longer exist. I've searched the Bible and have never found convincing evidence to support this view. The Bible teaches whether we are saved or lost, there is an everlasting existence of the soul.

Some believe God gives a second chance. But the Bible says, "Now is the day of salvation" (2 Corinthians 6:2). At our crusades I invite people to accept Christ right then, for we do not know when we will pass into eternity.

The Bible teaches there is hell for every person who willingly and knowingly rejects Christ as Lord and Savior. Many passages could be quoted to support that fact.

"But anyone who says, 'you fool!' will be in danger of the fire of hell" (Matthew 5:22).

"The Son of Man will send out his angels, and they will weed out of his kingdom everything that causes sin and all who do evil. They will throw them into the fiery furnace, where there will be weeping and gnashing of teeth" (Matthew 13:41–42).

"Then death and Hades were thrown into the lake of fire. The lake of fire is the second death. If anyone's name was not found written in the book of life, he was thrown into the lake of fire" (Revelation 20:14–15).

In the Sermon on the Mount, Jesus said, "It is better for you to lose one part of your body than for your whole body to be thrown into hell" (Matthew 5:29).

Will a loving God send a man to hell? The answer from Jesus and the teachings of the Bible is, clearly, "Yes!" He does not send man willingly, but man condemns himself to eternal hell because in his blindness, stubbornness, egotism, and love of sinful pleasure, he refuses God's way of salvation and the hope of eternal life with Him.

Suppose a person is sick and goes to a doctor. The doctor diagnoses the problem and prescribes medicine. However, the advice is ignored and in a few days the person stumbles back into the doctor's office and says, "It's your fault that I'm worse. Do something."

God has prescribed the remedy for the spiritual sickness of the human race. The solution is personal faith and commitment to Jesus

Christ. Since the remedy is to be born again, if we deliberately refuse it, we must suffer the horrible consequences.

Yes, there is an alternative to heaven. No matter what your conception of it may be, we know it will be separation from God and all that is holy and good. John Milton described it in *Paradise Lost:*

> *A dungeon horrible on all sides round,*
> *As one great furnace, flamed; yet from those flames*
> *No light, but rather darkness visible*
> *Serv'd only to discover sights of woe,*
> *Regions of sorrow, doleful shades, where peace*
> *And rest can never dwell, hope never comes*
> *That comes to all; but torture without end.*[2]

Heaven Can Wait?

However glorious heaven may be, all too many Christians don't give it much thought. Philip Yancey wrote, "A strange fact about modern American life: although 71 percent of us believe in an afterlife (says George Gallup), no one much talks about it. Christians believe that we will spend eternity in a splendid place called heaven. . . . Isn't it a little bizarre that we simply ignore heaven, acting as if it doesn't matter?"[3]

We are seeing more and more articles on old age, death, AIDS, right to die, and out-of-body experiences. But rarely if ever do we read anything about heaven in the magazines or find books on the subject. When we go through a gallery of pre-twentieth century art or look at dusty anthologies of poetry and prose, we discover that heaven was a topic of greater interest in the past. What has happened to us today? Why the general lack of attention to heaven in modern thought and preaching?

If we begin to think of reasons for disinterest in heaven, here are a few conclusions. First of all, in America and most of the Western nations, we live in an affluent society. Most of us have pain relievers to rely upon, enough food, and beautiful surroundings. The biblical promises of those advantages seem to have been dulled for us. We are so caught up with the affairs of this life we give little attention to eternity.

There is another psychological problem. We see people acting fully alive on television who have been dead for years. Well-known personalities like Gary Cooper, Marilyn Monroe, John F. Kennedy, or Martin Luther King appear giving speeches or acting in films as though they were yet alive. People have an idea they *are* still alive. It makes a vast difference in the thinking of young people about death. It may be one of the reasons why the suicide rate among young people has been increasing at an alarming rate.

Throughout our culture we have been led to the idea that we accept death as the end of life on earth. Elisabeth Kubler-Ross, with her five stages of death, has indicated that the "acceptance" stage is the most healthful. The hope of heaven rarely enters into a therapy session. Philip Yancey said, "I have watched in hospital groups as dying patients worked desperately toward a calm stage of acceptance. Strangely, no one ever talked about heaven in those groups; it seemed embarrassing, somehow cowardly. What convulsion of values can have us holding up the prospect of annihilation as brave and that of blissful eternity as cowardly?"[4]

Heaven may seem vague to some of us because our experience is earthbound. How can we conceive of infinity? To imagine an existence which never ends is mindboggling. Education and the media hinder man from believing anything that cannot be proved in a test tube. At a time when knowledge of the universe is increasing at great speed through the exploration of outer space, the notion of eternity for finite creatures is an absolute mystery. And it will always be a great mystery. Even the apostle Paul did not plumb the depths of it or describe the prospect. He said, "No eye has seen, no ear has heard, no mind has conceived what God has prepared for those who love him" (1 Corinthians 2:9).

Time bound as we are and goal oriented to achievements in our lifetime, we find it strange to anticipate heaven. It sounds boring to the contemporary mind.

What do we do throughout eternity? A person who has worked hard all his life may look forward to retirement, but sometimes relief from responsibility and challenge leads to restlessness.

We live in an age when activity is equated with value and usefulness. "How are you?" "Busy, busy, busy!" When the merry-go-round slows down, will the music of life fade away?

Every day of our lives we are just a breath away from eternity. The believer in Jesus Christ has the promises of heaven. If we believe them, the anticipation of heaven will never be boring. It will be more thrilling than any of the pleasures earth can offer.

Promises of Heaven

On earth we tend to think of ourselves. But in heaven things will be different. We will experience the truth of the catechism, "Man's chief end is to glorify God, and to enjoy him forever." In heaven God, not man, will be at the center of everything. And His glory will be dominant.

Have you ever watched young couples in love communicate without words? Have you been in love yourself? People deeply in love find absolute bliss in each other's presence and wish their moments together would go on forever. If those moments could be frozen, with no sense of passing time, would that be "heaven" for them? Have you ever said, "I wish this moment could last forever"?

I suspect those feelings are a small indication of what it would be like, frozen in time and loving God, enjoying Him, forever. We will never come down from that "mountaintop" experience.

The Bible assures us that heaven is a definite place. Jesus said, "In my Father's house are many rooms; if it were not so, I would have told you. I am going there to prepare a place for you. And if I go and prepare a place for you, I will come back and take you to be with me that you also may be where I am" (John 14:2–3).

Today homeless people can be found just about everywhere throughout the world. During a recent cold spell many street people suffered, and some died. Those of us who have comfortable homes may want to help those who are less fortunate, but deep inside we may think, "I'm just glad I have a bed tonight, a warm house, and food to eat." If we have never been homeless, it's hard to understand what it would be like.

In some ways Christians are homeless. Our true home is waiting for us, prepared by the Lord Jesus Christ. "Now we know that if the earthly tent we live in is destroyed, we have a building from God, an eternal house in heaven, not built by human hands. Meanwhile we groan, longing to be clothed with our heavenly dwelling" (2 Corinthians 5:1–2). If we look at the beauty He has created on earth, can we comprehend what He has furnished for us in heaven?

When people gaze at the Grand Canyon, they are instantly captured by its blazing glory. The earth offers spectacular vistas on every continent, in every country. Many of us have a favorite place which we would describe as "heaven on earth."

It has been my privilege to preach hundreds of sermons in Europe over the years, and a number of times we have preached in Switzerland. My daughter met and married a Swiss psychologist, so we are quite well acquainted with the Alps. Time after time my wife and I have shared the glories and beauties of those mountains—a meadow filled with spring flowers, the Dent du Midi, or the Matterhorn. From Geneva we can travel by plane to the south coast of France in thirty minutes. There we see the historic Mediterranean Sea sparkling with diamond-capped waves. We have so many memories of such times together.

But all of these will pale in comparison to what the Designer and Maker of these wonders of nature has prepared for us. Like Abraham, we can be "looking forward to the city with foundations, whose architect and builder is God" (Hebrews 11:10).

Years ago, Andre Kole, the talented illusionist who traveled all over the world as a representative of a Christian youth organization, wrote about the death of his wife, Aljeana. She had an incurable brain tumor, and for two years she endured incredible suffering. She gradually lost the use of her arms and legs and couldn't move her head or body. She became totally blind. Day after day she could do nothing but lie helplessly in bed. Kole wrote, "While Aljeana was still able to do some speaking, she always shared a poem that ended with these lines: 'We should not long for heaven, if earth held only joy.'"[5]

Heaven is a place, designed by the greatest architect, and it is promised that there we will receive our glorious inheritance.

I don't exactly know what kind of an inheritance I will receive in heaven, but I know it will be magnificent. When we visit someone's home and admire beautiful silver, rugs, or paintings, we might ask, "Is that an heirloom?" The owner might say that it belonged to his mother, and was very valuable to him. My wife, Ruth, has a beautiful chest inlaid with rare pieces of wood which her grandfather built years ago. People are always admiring it and asking where she got it. "I inherited it," she says.

The silver will tarnish, the rugs will be soiled or torn, the chest could burn in a few minutes. The Bible says we will receive "an inheritance that can never perish, spoil or fade—kept in heaven for you" (1 Peter 1:4).

The things that we inherit on earth may be a great blessing or a terrible curse. Countless lives have been ruined by riches left to irresponsible heirs. However, as children of the King, our inheritance will not spoil, nor will it spoil us. What a wonderful promise!

Heaven is the city of our God. He created heaven and He possesses it. "Acknowledge and take to heart this day that the Lord is God in heaven above and on the earth below. There is no other" (Deuteronomy 4:39).

When everything on earth seems to be going wrong, and when we ache to cry out, "God, where are You?" we have the promise that God is in heaven and is in command. It may seem that no one is in charge here, but if that were true, God Himself would be a liar.

God Speaks from Heaven

What is heaven? It's the home that God created and He possesses. His throne room is His headquarters from which He issues His commands, directions, and prophecies. And Jesus sits at His Father's right hand.

I am not sure God talks audibly to us today as He did to Moses on Mt. Sinai—He certainly never has to me. The movies and stage sometimes portray God as an offstage voice, speaking in rolling bass tones, warning the characters or directing their actions. This may make an interesting scenario, but it may be theologically wrong. Moreover, God never directs in a way contrary to His character. When the Scriptures tell us that He will direct our paths, we can be assured that when He is in control, no matter how thorny the path, He will not tell us to jump off a cliff.

How does God speak from heaven? First, He speaks through the Bible, His written Word. This is why I use the phrase "the Bible says." I would not have the authority to say what I do during crusades or in sermons unless it was based upon the Word of God. "All Scripture is God-breathed and is useful for teaching, rebuking, correcting and training in righteousness" (2 Timothy 3:16). The authors of the Old Testament, for example, make it clear that God was speaking to them and through them. More than 3,000 times they said, "Thus saith the Lord," or the equivalent. And that's good enough for me!

God also speaks in nature. When He created the heavens and the earth, He gave us the most incredible, complex, beautiful, orderly universe. He has spoken in such a way that men and women are without excuse if they do not hear and understand the psalmist's praise in saying, "The heavens declare the glory of God; and the firmament showeth his handiwork" (Psalm 19:1, KJV). Because of the clarity of the message, we can also agree with his statement that "The fool says in his heart, 'There is no God'" (Psalm 14:1). As the Bible declares, "For since the creation of the world God's invisible qualities—his eternal power and divine nature—have been clearly seen, being understood from what has been made, so that men are without excuse" (Romans 1:20).

God speaks most clearly and completely through His Son, Jesus Christ, who is revealed for us in the pages of the Bible and is the Word of God incarnate. When God, the Son, stepped out of heaven onto earth in the form of man, He accomplished what God intended Him to do from eternity past. "In the past God spoke to our forefathers through the prophets at many times and in various ways, but in these last days he has spoken to us by his Son, whom he appointed heir of all things, and through whom he made the universe" (Hebrews 1:1–2).

God also speaks to us through our consciences. This may be a "still, small voice" that will not let us go until we do what we know is right, or it may be a loud, clear indication that God wants us on the path. We might even think of it as a searchlight revealing the way in which we should go, beamed from heaven itself. Proverbs says, "The lamp of the Lord searches the spirit of a man; it searches out his inmost being" (Proverbs 20:27). We must never silence that inner voice—although we must check what we think it is saying against the Scriptures, to be sure that inner voice is not simply our self-will or our emotions.

When God speaks through His Word, we may receive it clearly, or because of our human frailty it may be distorted, something like a scrambled TV signal coming in over the satellite. Sometimes our receivers are tuned. At other times we may have to wait until we can more clearly hear or "receive" the picture.

One family told a harrowing story of being caught in a blinding blizzard while cross-country skiing. Mother, father, and ten-year-old daughter were lost in a stretch of wilderness on the coldest night in January, with a wind chill factor of twenty to forty degrees below zero. They fashioned a little shelter among some fallen trees and developed a plan of survival. Father said, "We're going to pray and sing hymns, and exercise, and eat, and play games. In the morning we'll try to get back up to the ski trails."

The little family knew they faced at least twelve hours of freezing darkness. They began their plan, singing "Onward Christian Soldiers" as they jogged in place. They named all the relatives they could remember, invented stories, made grocery lists, and most important, talked to God. The mother remembered a Bible verse and repeated it so that the little girl and the father could memorize it. "The Lord is near. Do not be anxious about anything, but in everything, by prayer and petition, with thanksgiving, present your requests to God. And the peace of God, which transcends all understanding, will guard your hearts and your minds in Christ Jesus" (Philippians 4:5–7).

As the night wore on, the circumstances worsened. The father recalled later, "I was holding one of the space blankets over the others in a not-very-successful attempt to block out the wind-driven snow, and for the first time I wondered if we were going to make it. But then it was as if God spoke to me and said, 'Don't worry, I'm going to take care of you.'" And He surely did.[6]

God speaks to us from heaven when we pray. Sometimes the answers are clear; sometimes they are vague; sometimes they say "wait." However, we know that someday we will be with Him in His home, and communications will be crystal clear, because we will be with Him. "Now we see but a poor reflection (as in a mirror); then we shall see face to face. Now I know in part; then I shall know fully, even as I am fully known" (1 Corinthians 13:12).

What Will Not Be in Heaven

In heaven there will be no sectarian worship, no denominational differences, no church creeds. There will be no temple worship, for God and His Son, Jesus Christ, will be the centers of worship (Revelation 21:22).

I was brought up as a Presbyterian and later became a Baptist. But in later years I have felt that I belong to all churches. Ruth has remained a strong Presbyterian, but deep in her heart she, too, belongs to all the other churches. We have never had major differences in our theology despite these backgrounds, but many people do get into heated arguments about denominational doctrines.

God did not invent denominations; man did. When we go to His home, He will invite us in, but will not ask us for our church or Sunday school credentials. Only one question will be asked: "What did you do on earth with My Son, Jesus?" It will make no difference whether we were Catholic or Protestant, Jew or Gentile. What matters is whether we believe in Him or reject Him. Attending a particular church does not guarantee anyone admission to heaven. Corrie ten Boom used to say, "A mouse in a cookie jar isn't a cookie."

In heaven we won't get secondhand knowledge. On earth we listen to pastors, teachers, philosophers, parents, and writers, and sometimes we don't know who to believe. (That secondhand knowledge is important, of course, because God has endowed man with intellect to use and has given the gifts of teaching and preaching to some individuals to help us.)

Some men use their intellect for His glory; others use it for their own. However, in heaven our spiritual intelligence will be perfected by direct contact with the source of all knowledge. If there is a *Daily News of Heaven,* we can be sure we will be able to believe what we read there.

In heaven there will be no fear. We won't need locks on the doors, bars at the windows, or alarm systems. Everything that causes fear will be eliminated. We will walk the golden streets with no concern for danger lurking in doorways. Today, fear stalks the world. We cannot escape it on any corner. Even if we believe we have nothing to fear, our human nature will invent something to fear.

In heaven there will be no night. On earth we equate night with darkness and ignorance; we say, "I was really left in the dark." Light is a symbol of understanding; we may nod our heads as a problem is clarified and say, "Now I see the light!" "The Lord is my light and my salvation—whom shall I fear?" (Psalm 27:1).

Night hides the joyous beauty of the sun, although it has a beauty of its own. But a nightless world will be illumined by His light, making the sun, moon, and stars (and the electric lights of earth) a pale comparison to the authentic masterpiece.

Finally, in heaven there will be no more suffering or death. Think of it! "And I heard a loud voice from the throne saying, 'Now the dwelling of God is with men, and he will live with them. They will be his people, and God himself will be with them and be their God. He will wipe every tear from their eyes. There will be no more death or mourning or crying or pain, for the old order of things has passed away.' He who was seated on the throne said, 'I am making everything new!' Then he said, 'Write this down, for these words are trustworthy and true'" (Revelation 21:3–5).

Homesick for Heaven

When business recruiters visit prospective employees to tell them about their business, they put up a good front. They may woo the recruit with an expensive dinner while they paint a wonderful picture of the company. The description is so exciting that the recruit can hardly wait to begin. However, soon after being hired the new employee discovers that everything isn't quite as rosy as it was originally portrayed.

Will heaven really offer such wonderful benefits that the recruit can't wait to get started?

Vance Havner, who was one of the most quotable pulpiteers of our time, said, "I'm homesick for heaven. It's the hope of dying that has kept me alive this long."[7]

Heaven is a wonderful place and the benefits for the believer are out of this world!

THE OTHER SIDE

This isn't death—it's glory!
It is not dark—it's light!
It isn't stumbling, groping,
Or even faith—it's sight!
This isn't grief—it's having
My last tear wiped away;
It's sunrise—it's the morning
Of my eternal day!
This isn't even praying—
It's speaking face to face;
Listening and glimpsing
The wonders of His grace.
This is the end of pleading
For strength to bear my pain;
Not even pain's dark memory
Will ever live again.
How did I bear the earth-life

Before I knew this rapture
Of meeting face to face
The One who sought me, saved me,
And kept me by His grace![8]

"Even when we allow our imaginations to run wild on the joys of heaven, we find that our minds are incapable of conceiving what it will be like."

For to me, to live is Christ and to die is gain. Philippians 1:21

CHAPTER ELEVEN

Believer's Death Benefits

A LITTLE GIRL was walking with her father in the country. No neon signs, no automobile headlights or street lamps marred the stillness of the crisp evening. As she looked into the deep blue velvet sky, studded with an array of diamonds which put the most dazzling Tiffany display to shame, she said, "Daddy, if the wrong side of heaven is so beautiful, what do you think the right side will be like?"

Someday all believers in Jesus Christ will see the "right side" of heaven.

When will we go to heaven? What will it be like? What will we experience there? I have asked myself those questions and searched the Scriptures for the answers. While we are on earth, I doubt that any of us have our eyes constantly fixed on the glory to come; we have God-given responsibilities to take care of right now. However, knowing the final destination should make our daily life more vigorous, our problems on earth less troublesome.

When the apostle Paul said "to die is gain" he did not mean he wanted to escape his earthly existence. He prefaced it by saying, "For to me, to live is Christ," which is life in its most joyful form, relying upon Christ's love and guidance, strengthened by Him, and loving and being loved by Him. Paul could never be accused by the slur of being "so heavenly minded he was no earthly good."

A Christian's citizenship may be in heaven, but he has obligations as a citizen of earth. Both living with Christ and going to be with Him in death are greatly to be desired.

When Will We Go to Heaven?

The believer's passage to heaven is a direct route. As soon as we are dead, we will be with the Lord. Jesus told the repentant thief on the cross, "I tell you the truth, today you will be with me in paradise" (Luke 23:43). Paul declared, "I desire to depart and be with Christ" (Philippians 1:23). He also affirmed, "Therefore we are always confident and know that as long as we are at home in the body we are away from the Lord. We live by faith, not by sight. We are confident, I say, and would prefer to be away from the body and at home with the Lord" (2 Corinthians 5:6–8).

The moment we take our last breath on earth we take our first in heaven. We are absent from the body and immediately present with the Lord. Then in God's time we receive our glorified bodies at the Second Coming of Christ.

We will be known in our resurrection or heavenly bodies, just as Moses and Elijah were recognized when they appeared with Jesus on the Mount of Transfiguration. Moses had been dead for more than 1,400 years and Elijah had been caught up to heaven in a whirlwind over six centuries before Jesus lived. Here's what happened all those years later: "Jesus took Peter, James, and his brother John to the top of a high and lonely hill, and as they watched, his appearance changed so that his face shone like the sun and his clothing became dazzling white. Suddenly Moses and Elijah appeared and were talking with him. Peter blurted out, 'Sir, it's wonderful that we can be here! If you want me to, I'll make three shelters, one for you and one for Moses and one for Elijah'" (Matthew 17:1–4, LB).

The disciples recognized Moses and Elijah, although they did not yet have their resurrection bodies. This will be explained later. They had recognizable bodies; they were not disembodied, ghostly apparitions.

We will go to heaven immediately, and we will recognize and be recognized. Do some believers have glimpses of loved ones as they approach the gates of heaven? I believe it is possible.

Ruth tells about an experience she had in China. On the station where she lived, one of the evangelistic missionaries was Ad Talbot, whom she affectionately called Uncle Ad. Talbot had five sons and a daughter, Margaret Gay, a girl he deeply loved. Sometime after her death he was in the country with a Chinese Christian woman who was dying. As he knelt beside her bed, the old woman's face lit up and she said to Uncle Ad, "I see heaven, and Jesus is on the right hand of God, and Margaret Gay is with him." At that moment the room was filled with heavenly music and the Chinese woman was dead.

When my grandmother was dying she sat up in her bed, smiled, and said, "I see Jesus, and He has His hand outstretched to me. And there's Ben and he has both of his eyes and both of his legs!" My grandfather had lost a leg and an eye at Gettysburg.

Death has two stages: first, the separation of the body from the spirit of a person for a purely spiritual existence; and second, reunion with the body and a glorious resurrection at the Second Coming of Christ.

When our body ceases to function and we are dead, the spirit of the believer is not asleep. Our flesh and bones and all the intricate and wonderful parts God has made are the dwelling place of the spirit of the believer. When we leave our bodies, we depart to be with Christ (Philippians 1:23), and "wait eagerly for our adoption as sons, the redemption of our bodies" (Romans 8:23). Yes, some day our bodies will be renewed and changed, like that of the resurrected body of Jesus Christ.

The story is told of a missionary family who was forced to leave inland China when the enemy took over the country. Each night on their flight to the coast they slept in a different village hut. One night the missionary's wife died quite suddenly and unexpectedly. When morning came he had to explain what had happened to the grief-stricken children.

None of them would consent to leaving their mother's body behind, buried in the soil of a foreign land. If ever the missionary prayed for wisdom and the right words, he did that day as he tried to explain to his children.

He reminded them that they had stayed in a different hut every night, but when morning came and it was time to leave, they continued on their journey, leaving the hut behind. He told the children that their mother's body was the house in which she lived. During the night God told her to come home, so she went, leaving her house behind.

"That house was her body and we loved it," he said, "but Mother no longer lives in it. So we'll leave her here and put her in the ground until the Lord picks her up and takes her body home to be glorified and again restored to her spirit, which is with God now."

That settled the question for them and they left China, certain that their mother had gone on ahead of them to heaven.

If the two stages of death seem difficult to understand, Dr. H. A. Ironside explained them by using this simple illustration which may help. He noticed a shop in his town which was no longer open for business. One day while driving past the building he saw a sign in the window, "Closed for Alterations." The owner had suspended his business dealings with the public long enough to renovate the store. After a time the store was reopened with many changes and improvements. This is a picture of the death of the believer. He moves out of his body until it has been repaired, then, at the resurrection, the inward man will move into his renewed body.

Not Everyone Will Die

Many believers will go to heaven before they die a physical death. The Bible tells us that one generation of believers will never know bodily death. This miraculous and mysterious event is called the "Rapture." We are told that it is a mystery, something that has not been revealed before. Paul says, "Listen, I tell you a mystery: We will not all sleep, but we will all be changed—in a flash, in the twinkling of an eye, at the last trumpet. For the trumpet will sound, the dead will be raised imperishable, and we will be changed" (1 Corinthians 15:51–52).

What a quick transformation that will be! Scientists tell us that the winking of an eye is the quickest movement of the human body. However, in the Greek, the "twinkling of the eye" implies only half a wink; that was the expression Paul used to describe the change.

What does it mean, that we will be "changed"? Our mortal bodies will become immortal. This means we will be changed in our appearance, but not in our essence. This is why we will recognize people we knew here on earth.

When will these great events take place? Predictions about this happening and the Second Coming are not unique in our time. I would not make such predictions, because they are in complete disobedience to the Word of God: "Now, brothers, about times and dates we do not need to write to you, for you know very well that the day of the Lord will come like a thief in the night" (1 Thessalonians 5:1–2).

Jesus said, "No one knows about that day or hour, not even the angels in heaven, nor the Son, but only the Father" (Matthew 24:36). He also said that we should watch for the signs of the end of the age, and not be caught in the dark. Many Bible believers who have studied the Scriptures and the signs of our times believe that the Rapture may not be far away. Certainly in our lifetime we are seeing an acceleration of those events that Jesus said would be signs of His return.

In recent years I have spoken more and more on the Second Coming of Christ, for this glorious event has been neglected in many of our churches. Also, I cannot help being excited when I see all around me the rapidity with which the announced signs of the end times seem to be happening.

However, I try seriously to avoid two extremes: one is the arrogance of believing I have some special insight about the future and His coming, even if this knowledge seems to be based upon the Bible; the other extreme is to ignore the fact that Christ will return, and for me to live as if His coming were a meaningless myth.

In spite of the wars, the crimes, the agony of many who are living today without freedom, there is the "blessed hope" for all true believers that we could be caught up to meet Christ in the air at any moment (Titus 2:13–15).

The Rapture will take place when Jesus comes for His saints, or all true believers. This will not be seen or understood by the world of unbelievers. Only the Christians will see Him. It will take place quickly and unexpectedly; those who are left will be bewildered as they try to rationalize the sudden disappearance of millions of people.

At the Second Coming, after the Rapture, *everyone* will see Him. His return will be personal and physical. "Look, he is coming with the clouds, and every eye will see him, even those who pierced him; and all the peoples of the earth will mourn because of him" (Revelation 1:7).

The Second Coming of Christ will be sudden. It will be as electrifying as an unexpected flash of lightning. Jesus said, "For as lightning that comes from the east is visible even in the west, so will be the coming of the Son of Man" (Matthew 24:27).

Christ will be accompanied by the believers who have died, returning in immortal, glorified bodies. Who will they be? They will be all of the resurrected saints of the Old Testament and everyone who repented of their sins and received Christ by faith—those who have been saved this side of the Cross.

Many places in the Scriptures tell us of Christ's return accompanied by the "clouds of heaven." The prophet Daniel predicted, "In my vision at night I looked, and there before me was one like a son of man, coming with the clouds of heaven" (Daniel 7:13). In Hebrews 12:1 believers are admonished to serve God righteously because we are constantly surrounded by a "cloud of witnesses." Zechariah says that "the Lord my God will come, and all the holy ones with him" (Zechariah 14:5).

What a thrilling future for those of us who know that some day we will populate the kingdom of God.

Is the Trip Worth It?

Many true Christians disagree on the sequence of events in relation to the Second Coming of Christ. It is not my purpose in this book to propose a theological debate between the premillennial, amillennial, and postmillennial viewpoints. The most important issues are: Will you be in God's kingdom that is now being prepared for us? What will it be like? And how should we live in anticipation of heaven?

I have traveled all over the world and have slept in more hotel and motel rooms, endured more airline flights, and tried to understand more foreign language menus than I care to count. Resorts with year-round swimming pools, and villas with oceanfront views hold some appeal for me, but the older I get the more my idea of a great vacation is to go home, sit on the front porch with Ruth on a spring, summer, or fall evening as the sun is setting, and listen to the katydids and the night noises as they begin; or to sit in an easy chair before a crackling fire in the wintertime with Ruth and gaze out on the mountains.

I had always thought that I would have some years of retirement when I would be able to spend most of my time doing those things. However, to my surprise, God has given me extra strength to preach and write, and to have a ministry at my age that I never dreamed I would have. So I have foregone many of the pleasures of retirement to continue the ministry. This makes heaven an even greater anticipation for me.

God called me many years ago to be an evangelist, and I have never regretted His leading. I love the crusades, meeting people from every country and culture all over the world. My life has been blessed by friends from every land, and challenges from every corner.

However, I cannot help but long so many times in my travels for the serenity of our log house in the mountains of North Carolina.

When we are young and restless to be free, home is the place from which we long to escape. But if there is still a home intact when trouble arises and life becomes a battlefield, home is the place to which we yearn to return. Solomon, who was called the Teacher in Ecclesiastes, expressed this human tendency. He said, "Remember your Creator in the days of your youth, before the days of trouble come and the years approach when you will say, 'I find no pleasure in them'—before the sun and the light and the moon and stars grow dark, and the clouds return after the rain . . ." (Ecclesiastes 12:1–2).

Solomon tells us when we are stooped with age, when our teeth are gone, when our eyesight and hearing begin to fail, then "man goes to his eternal home and mourners go about the streets" (Ecclesiastes 12:5).

Our temporary homes may be palaces or hovels, but our eternal heavenly home will be bright and beautiful. How could it be any other way? The great Architect and Builder of the universe designed a permanent dwelling place for His children. Earth has its beauty, but man has spoiled so much of it. In heaven there will be no need for environmentalists to work for better air and water quality, or to decry the destruction of our land for housing developments.

When heaven was revealed to the apostle John, he found difficulty describing it, so he used the analogy of a bride, beautifully dressed for her bridegroom. What an apt description. My three daughters are married, and I believe they are all very beautiful, but they were never so radiant and beautiful as on their wedding days!

With five children and eighteen grandchildren family reunions are difficult to plan. Yet we love being together and hate it when we must part. I have dear friends with whom I enjoy talking for hours. Then we look at the clock, run to keep appointments, and sometimes don't see each other again for years.

In heaven there will be no more sorrowful separations. For many people life on earth has lost its meaning because a dear one or close friends who were a vital part of life on earth are no longer here. In heaven we will be together in Christ. We will see the mother or father, the children, brothers, and sisters who have preceded us. We will have a family reunion like no other!

Even when we allow our imaginations to run wild on the joys of heaven, we find that our minds are incapable of conceiving what it will really be like. We are imprisoned by our earthly limitations. Years ago, Rebecca Ruter Springer wrote a little book called *My Dream of Heaven.* One of my friends told me she was given a copy of that book after the death of a loved one and it consoled her by describing the glories of heaven in such a beautiful way that she could appreciate and even anticipate what wonders her loved one was enjoying. The book, in its quaint early nineteenth-century style, was fanciful, but it captured biblical truths with emotional impressions. We wonder, for instance, about some of the things we love on earth. Will we be separated from them in heaven? What about our favorite pets? Is there a place for them? I don't know the exact answers to those questions, but I trust the love of my Lord. Everything needed for our happiness will be there.

In describing her journey *intra muros,* within the gates, Mrs. Springer wrote, "Do you know I think one of the sweetest proofs we have of the Father's loving care for us is, that we so often find in this life the things which gave us great happiness below. The more unexpected this is, the greater joy it brings. I remember once seeing a beautiful little girl enter heaven, the very first to come of a large and affectionate family. I afterward learned that the sorrowful cry of her mother was, 'Oh, if only we had someone there to meet her, to care for her!' She came, lovingly nestled in the Master's own arms, and a little later, as he sat still caressing and talking to her, a remarkably fine Angora kitten, of which the child had been very fond, and which had sickened and died some weeks before, to her great sorrow, came running across the grass and sprang directly in her arms, where it lay contentedly. Such a glad cry as she recognized her little favorite, such hugging and kissing as that kitten received, made joy even in heaven!"[1]

Far-fetched? Why should it be? If to die is gain, as Paul said, then why shouldn't we enjoy even more in heaven the things we loved on earth?

It is often asked, "Will we be married in heaven?" The Sadducees of Jesus' time questioned Him about a woman who had seven husbands. They asked, "At the resurrection whose wife will she be, since the seven were married to her?" Jesus replied, "Are you not in error because you do not know the Scriptures or the power of God? When the dead rise, they will neither marry nor be given in marriage; they will be like the angels in heaven" (Mark 12:23–25).

Someone may object, "But I love my husband (or wife) so much. If we know our loved ones in heaven, why aren't we married?" Also, there are instances in which a person has had more than one marriage, as did the woman to whom the Sadducees referred. The more I meditate on the promises of heaven, the more I have faith that these questions will no longer be relevant, because they will be answered in a glorious manner. I trust Jesus with all my tomorrows, knowing that He will solve the mystery of life beyond the grave.

New Bodies for Old

Scientists have made amazing advances in giving new arms and legs for lost ones, new eyes so the blind can see. Kidney and heart transplants help people extend their life spans. But someday, we shall have complete and perfect new bodies. Today we live in a literal body, but someday "When he comes back he will take these dying bodies of ours and change them into glorious bodies like his own" (Philippians 3:21, LB).

We are guaranteed new bodies because of the resurrection of Jesus Christ from the grave. The central fact of our entire Christian theology is that Jesus rose! No amount of skepticism or alleged "Passover Plots" can blot out the fact that Jesus Christ died on the cross and that in three days He arose from the grave. He appeared to the disciples in His post-resurrection body, walked through the doors they had locked in fear. Thomas, the disciple, was not there, and he said doubtfully, "I'll believe it when I see the nail marks in his hands and in his side." A week later Jesus passed through the locked doors again and said to Thomas, "Put your finger here; see my hands. Reach out your hand and put it into my side. Stop doubting and believe" (John 20:27).

Later Jesus had a fish dinner alongside the Sea of Galilee with His disciples. When He returned in His resurrected body He performed so many miracles, "If every one of them were written down, I suppose that even the whole world would not have room for the books that would be written" (John 21:25).

The resurrection of Jesus Christ guarantees that we will someday have resurrected bodies. He will change or transfigure our bodies, as an ugly caterpillar is changed to a beautiful butterfly. We recognize the magnificent winged creature is the same living being as the fuzzy insect, yet different.

The resurrection is our great hope. In what is called "the great resurrection chapter" of the Bible, 1 Corinthians 15, Paul wrote, "But if it is preached that Christ has been raised from the dead, how can some of you say that there is no resurrection of the dead? If there is no resurrection of the dead, then not even Christ has been raised. And if Christ has not been raised, our preaching is useless and so is your faith. . . . But Christ has indeed been raised from the dead, the firstfruits of those who have fallen asleep" (1 Corinthians 15:12–14, 20).

The Christians at Corinth did not question that Christ had risen, but they evidently didn't believe others who had died would rise again. However, Paul paints a gloomy picture of what life would be like without belief in the resurrection. He said all preaching would be in vain, faith would be worthless, and all Christian belief would be false.

Kenneth Chafin wrote in his commentary on the epistles to the Corinthians, "I remember hearing a person say once that even if Christ had not been raised from the dead, he thought he would continue to live the Christian life because 'it would still be the best way to live.' But I wonder if he didn't say that because he could not conceive what it would be like to live in a world without the hope of the resurrection."[2]

A Superhuman Body

What kind of a body will a resurrected believer have? It's difficult for us to imagine what someone would be like with any other than a physical body. We can visualize a different earthly body, and many people do this. Some women put pictures of movie stars or models on the refrigerator door to remind themselves of the body they would like to have. Men imagine themselves as an athlete, or perhaps as Rocky, invincible in their physical abilities. But there are very few in the entire world who have what might be called "ideal bodies." And yet, someday, we will have them. Paul has given us a pretty good description of what those bodies will be like.

First, the resurrection body is compared to a seed planted in the ground which produces a plant or a flower. Anyone who has ever gardened knows how miraculous it is to see a towering tomato plant, with yellow blossoms that become huge tomatoes, grow from a tiny seed. The seed and the plant are the continuous life of a single entity, just as our physical body, planted in death, will have the same individuality as our resurrection body. We will be recognized as ourselves, not some genetic version without a distinctive label.

"It is sown in dishonor, it is raised in glory; it is sown in weakness, it is raised in power" (1 Corinthians 15:43). The body that lies in the grave has been neglected. It may be worn out with age, abused by disease, or broken by an accident, but in the resurrection that body is raised in glory! It will be free of all infirmities. Joni Eareckson Tada will throw away her wheelchair. Dr. Bob Pierce will be free of cancer. Helen Keller will see and hear and speak. Those who were burned or maimed in wars will be whole. Old people will be young and vigorous.

In our resurrection bodies, we will know nothing of physical weakness. Limitations imposed on us on this earth are not known in heaven. We will have a habitation from God that is incorruptible, immortal, and powerful.

"Yes, they are weak, dying bodies now, but when we live again they will be full of strength. They are just human bodies at death, but when they come back to life they will be superhuman bodies" (1 Corinthians 15:43–44, LB).

That verse makes me chuckle when I see myself today and think that someday I'll be like Superman, without the red cape and tights. However, in spite of this exciting prospect, I want to keep this present body in as good shape as I can for the work that the Lord has for me to do while I'm still on earth.

"For our earthly bodies, the ones we have now that can die, must be transformed into heavenly bodies that cannot perish but will live forever. When this happens, then at last this Scripture will come true—'Death is swallowed up in victory.' O death, where then your victory? Where then your sting? For sin—the sting that causes death—will all be gone; and the law, which reveals our sins, will no longer be our judge. How we thank God for all of this! It is He who makes us victorious through Jesus Christ our Lord!

"So, my dear brothers, since future victory is sure, be strong and steady, always abounding in the Lord's work, for you know that nothing you do for the Lord is ever wasted as it would be if there were no resurrection" (1 Corinthians 15:53–58, LB).

What a promise! Christ lives. We shall live. He has a glorious, resurrected body, and so shall we! This is how a Christian can live and die with hope. Death is swallowed up in victory.

Beyond the Body Beautiful

There is more to a Christian's death benefits than a fine body. Some people place so much emphasis upon the care and feeding of this temporary shelter that the overwhelming problems of a sick world get little or no attention. We do not have a paradise on earth; it is riddled with so much sin and disease.

The first great benefit of death for Christians is permanent freedom from evil. When Paul talked about his desire to "depart and to be with Christ" (Philippians 1:23), he was conveying the idea of leaving something permanently behind. Everything that is not useful is left—all of the pain, the care, and the anguish of the world. Crime, drugs, war, hatred, starvation, all of the horrors of man's inhumanity to man will be cancelled out of our heavenly existence.

When John was given the Revelation and had caught a glimpse of the Holy City, the New Jerusalem, he said, "There shall be nothing in the city which is evil" (Revelation 22:3, LB).

Freedom! Men have searched for it and died for it, but they will never attain it unless they know Jesus Christ. The message of the old cowboy song, "Don't Fence Me In," will be an eternal reality.

The second benefit of death to believers is that we will be like Jesus. John writes, "Dear friends, now we are children of God, and what we will be has not yet been made known. But we know that when he appears, we shall be like him, for we shall see him as he is" (1 John 3:2).

Our imaginations are so stilted. The very thought of being like Jesus is breathtaking. We will be like Him in righteousness. Our old sin nature will be forgotten, erased from our memories forever.

We shall be like Him in knowledge. We have the Holy Spirit to guide us in our understanding of the Word of God here on earth, but our "understanding" is always limited and mixed with error. We struggle to understand the Scriptures, but sometimes even great Bible scholars differ over the exact interpretation of certain passages. However, everything that puzzled us in life will be made clear. All our "whys" will be answered.

Do you have many unanswered questions today? Our IQs in heaven will far surpass those of the most brilliant people on earth.

We will also be like Jesus in love. Today we are so centered on self, but our death policy says that we will be heirs to the selfless, self-sacrificing love of Jesus Christ. We may find it difficult to love everyone on earth, but in heaven love will be freely given and freely received.

So the supreme benefit, the one which surpasses all others, is that we will be with Jesus Christ. I long to see Him face to face, to hear His voice and touch Him. In the day I go to be with Him, there will be no unfulfilled longings or disappointments. He will welcome me into His mansion, answer my questions, and teach me the wisdom of the ages.

Once we meet Him, what will happen? Will He be glad to see us?

I must ask myself, "Billy Graham, are you prepared to meet the Master at any moment?" Yes, I am—but not because I have preached or tried to help people, but solely because I am trusting Christ as my Lord and Savior.

Stop right now and ask yourself that question.

"When we build a house we lay the foundation first. After that we choose the material for the walls, floors, and roof: The believer has his foundation in Jesus Christ. Now we are to build upon this foundation, and the work we have done must stand the ultimate test. . . ."

> *For we must all appear before the judgment seat of Christ, that each one may receive what is due him for the things done while in the body, whether good or bad.* 2 Corinthians 5:10

CHAPTER TWELVE

Before I Die

IN THE LAST days before a Christian goes to be with the Lord, Satan will seek to steal his peace. The weakness caused by disease or pain, the confusion of the mind, may cause even the greatest saints to have moments of doubt.

Before one of America's greatest theologians and Bible teachers died, he called me frequently seeking assurance of his eternal salvation. At first I didn't understand how this man of God, a teacher of the Word, could be troubled with questions about his worthiness. However, I have discovered this problem is not uncommon, and loved ones should be available to offer help and hope without provoking a sense of guilt.

Few women in our generation have had greater influence upon the world than Corrie ten Boom. Her biographer wrote, "A Christian witness meets its true test in times of suffering. Pastor Chuck Mylander visited her often after her first crippling stroke, and only once did he see her upset about her own needs. As is very common in stroke patients, a wave of doubt about the Lord's nearness had swept over her. Pam Rosewell explained what Corrie couldn't fully communicate, and as he questioned Corrie, tears coursed across her wrinkled cheeks.

"Pastor Mylander took out his Bible and read from Matthew 28, where Jesus said, 'Lo, I am with you always, even to the end of the age.' He reminded Corrie that this promise was for those who gave themselves to fulfill the Great Commission, as she had done so faithfully. Her face brightened as she began to speak with confidence, 'Always, always, always.'"[1]

When the final moments come, the power of God will conquer and the believer will enjoy the comfort of His loving arms.

Signs for a Peaceful Exit

Herbert Lockyer tells about finding an ancient work called *The Book of the Craft of Dying*. The unknown writer of this early treatise discussed five principal temptations confronting the believer. Translating them into modern vernacular, they are worthy of examination.

1. *Faith must be maintained*. This is what so many seek, when doubt clouds the mind as the last hour approaches. It does not seem to matter how long the Christian has walked in the path of faith. As with Corrie the questioning sometimes comes. We are all like children who constantly need to be told that we are loved.

2. *Desperation must be avoided*. Another wile of the devil is to bring up past sins and parade them before the mind of the Christian. We have been forgiven, and there is no need to pull out the past and review it morbidly. "Everyone who believes in him receives forgiveness of sins through his name" (Acts 10:43).

3. *Impatience must be avoided*. When we come to die of old age or disease or accident, we should await the final outcome patiently. Dr. Bob Pierce, who was the founder of World Vision and Samaritan's Purse, the ministry my son, Franklin, has continued, was in the last hours of his life, suffering from leukemia. In his final letter he wrote, "Now I am living totally in 'God Room.' No known human skill can further prolong my life and I am gloriously living and working in that space reaching beyond the utmost man and science can do. This is the area

where miracles begin. If the greatest human skills and genius can do it, God is not required and it is no miracle. Miracles only begin at the point just beyond all furthest stretch of human ingenuity and possibility of accomplishment. That is God Room!"

Dr. Bob was patient, but hopeful, to the end.

4. *Complacence must not rule.* When Satan can't shake the faith of a believer, nor cause him to despair or be impatient, he may tempt him through spiritual pride. "Look how many good deeds I have done, how great my service has been for the Lord," may be the boast. We are taught in the Scriptures that we are saved by grace, through faith, it is a gift of God, so that no one can boast (Ephesians 2:9).

5. *The temporal must not dominate.* I can understand this more than any other. We are all so possessed by our possessions and absorbed in our earthly obligations that we set our minds on temporal and impermanent things, rather than fully committing ourselves to God.[2]

We may not encounter any of these temptations, but if we do we must remember that the Bible says, "No temptation has overtaken you but such as is common to man; and God is faithful, who will not allow you to be tempted beyond what you are able; but with the temptation will provide the way of escape also, that you may be able to endure it" (1 Corinthians 10:13, NASB).

Last Words of Saints

An old hymn says,

> *Teach me to live that I may dread*
> *The grave as little as my bed;*
> *Teach me to die, that so I may*
> *Rise glorious at the Judgment Day.*

Many times the dying words of believers have been recorded by family members and biographers. These expressions of faith and trust illustrate the mighty power of God at a time when human resources have been drained.

In the sixteenth century there was a bloody purge of Christians in Scotland who died for their faith. Thousands of ministers and laymen suffered for Christ's sake. Many were hanged on the gibbet or slaughtered in cold blood. Some of these believers endured the torture of burning at the stake or being beheaded. The last words of these heroes and martyrs prove the truth of Christ's promise He made to His disciples. He warned them, "I am sending you out as sheep among wolves. . . . Yes, and you must stand trial before governors and kings for my sake. This will give you the opportunity to tell them about me, yes, to witness to the world" (Matthew 10:16–18, LB).

In their final hour of agony men and women who have suffered and died for His sake are given the words to say and the courage to die.

Patrick Hamilton was a young Scotsman, twenty-four years old, when he was condemned and sentenced to die. As he was hurried to the stake and the fire was burning he pulled off his outer garments and handed them to his servant, saying, "These will not profit me in the fire, yet they will do thee some good." Hamilton was taunted by one of his persecutors to deny God, but answered, "Wicked man! Thou knowest I am not at guilt, and that it is the truth of God for which I now suffer."

As the fire burned, the young martyr called out, "How long, O Lord, shall darkness overwhelm this realm? How long wilt Thou suffer this tyranny of man?" As he was being consumed by the flames he prayed like the biblical Stephen, "Lord Jesus, receive my spirit."[3]

Donald Cargill was a bright star in the history of Scottish persecutions. He was condemned by the government as "one of the most seditious preachers and a villainous and fanatical conspirator," and sentenced to the gallows. When he came to the scaffold, Cargill said these moving words, although it was said that the drums were beaten in an attempt to drown out his voice:

> Now I am near to getting to my crown, which shall be sure; for I bless the Lord, and desire all of you to bless Him that He hath brought me here, and makes me triumph over devils, and men, and sin . . . they shall wound me no more. I forgive all men the wrongs they have done to me, and pray the Lord may forgive all the wrongs that any of the elect have done against Him. I pray that sufferers may be kept from sin, and helped to know their duty . . . farewell reading and preaching, praying and believing, wanderings, reproaches, and sufferings. Welcome joy unspeakable and full of glory.[4]

As Martin Luther was dying he repeated three times, "Into Thy hands I commend my spirit! Thou hast redeemed me, O God of Truth."

John Milton's farewell was, "Death is the great key that opens the palace of Eternity."

Lew Wallace, the author of *Ben Hur,* had a sentence from the Lord's Prayer on his lips, "Thy will be done."

In his last will and testament Shakespeare said, "I commend my soul into the hands of God my Creator, hoping and assuredly believing, through the merits of Jesus Christ my Savior, to be made partaker of life everlasting; and my body to the earth, whereof it is made."

Michelangelo's last words to those at his bedside were, "Through life remember the sufferings of Jesus."[5]

I do not know whether we will suffer for the cause of Christ. But throughout the world today there are people who are enduring cruelties and persecution because of their Christian faith. We must pray for them, and for ourselves, so that in our own dying hour God will give us grace to endure until the end, anticipating the certainty of His glory to come.

We Are Accountable

Before we die two basic issues must be resolved. The first is, "Am I ready?" Have you confessed your sins and asked Jesus Christ to come into your heart, to take possession of your life? Millions of Christians throughout the world are assured "That if you confess with your mouth,

'Jesus is Lord,' and believe in your heart that God raised him from the dead, you will be saved" (Romans 10:9).

But the Christian life doesn't end there! The next basic issue is "How then do I live?" This is to say, before you die, what service will you render to God and man? Are you investing your life in those things that will last for eternity? "So we make it our goal to please him, whether we are at home in the body or away from it. For we must all appear before the judgment seat of Christ, that each one may receive what is due him for the things done while in the body, whether good or bad" (2 Corinthians 5:9-10).

The Bible says we will all have to give account to Jesus someday (1 Peter 4:5). We will stand before the Judgment Seat of Christ (Romans 14:10). On that day, what we have done on earth will be past. Our chances to speak to the neighbor about the love of Christ, to give to missions, to help evangelism, will be over. Opportunities to share our earthly goods with the starving will be gone. Whatever gifts we were given will be worthless if we hoarded them on earth.

The Ultimate Test

When we build a house we lay the foundation first. After that we choose the material for the walls, floors, and roof. Some buildings are put up for planned obsolescence. From a distance they may look slick and modern, but they cannot stand the test of time.

The believer has his foundation in Jesus Christ. Now we are to build upon this foundation, and the work we have done must stand the ultimate test; final exams come at the Judgment Seat of Christ when we receive our rewards.

Paul explained this building process when he said:

> No one can ever lay any other real foundation than that one we already have—Jesus Christ. But there are various kinds of materials that can be used to build on that foundation. Some use gold and silver and jewels; and some build with sticks, and hay, or even straw! There is going to

> come a time of testing at Christ's Judgment Day to see what kind of material each builder has used. Everyone's work will be put through the fire so that all can see whether or not it keeps its value, and what was really accomplished. Then every workman who has built on the foundation with the right materials, and whose work still stands, will get his pay. But if the house he has built burns up, he will have a great loss. He himself will be saved, but like a man escaping through a wall of flames (1 Corinthians 3:15, LB).

We will be judged according to the secret motives and the character of our work. If we have done our work for selfish motives or personal gain, even if the results looked noble to our friends and family, God knows our hearts.

Also, we will be judged according to our ability. Some Christians are capable of more than others, physically, financially, or intellectually. The grandmother living on a small pension but faithfully teaching her little grandchild Bible verses will not be judged for her giving a pittance to missions in the same manner as the business couple with a double income, living in a house beyond their means. The retired couple who count the offering every Sunday, never divulging the amount anyone in the congregation contributes, will not be tested in the same way as the millionaire who wants an inscription on the stained glass window, so everyone will know who donated it.

Some of the most severe tests will be given to the pastors and teachers for the way in which they handled the Word of God. There will be no reward for leading others astray in lifestyle or in doctrine through false teaching.

The Judgment Seat of Christ is referred to as the Greek word *bema,* which identifies the judge's seat in the arena of the Olympic games. The *bema* was the seat where the judge sat, not to punish contestants, but to present awards to the victors. When Christians stand before the *bema* of Christ, it is for the purpose of being rewarded according to their works.

When Christ returns, every Christian will stand before the *bema,* not as spectators, but as those to be judged. The Bible doesn't say where this judgment will take place, and the logistics of millions of saints standing there are beyond comprehension. But one thing is certain, we must all appear.

The Judgment Seat of Christ will be graduation ceremonies at which time each believer will receive a reward for his works. The New Testament teaches these rewards are called "crowns."

We will surely be surprised to note who receives the crowns and who doesn't. The lowliest servant may sparkle with more jewels than the philanthropist who endowed the church and whose name is engraved on the plaque in the narthex.

We all long for appreciation, which doesn't always come from those around us; however, we have assurance that Jesus knows the intentions of our hearts and what we do in secret. "Therefore, my dear brothers, stand firm. Let nothing move you. Always give yourselves fully to the work of the Lord, because you know that your labor in the Lord is not in vain" (1 Corinthians 15:58).

Five Minutes After I'm in Heaven

My wife saved an article from *Moody Monthly,* published over thirty years ago. When she gave it to me, I was working on this book and I marveled how the Lord brings information to us just at the right moment.

At the beginning of the book I quoted my father-in-law's comment, "Only those who are prepared to die are really prepared to live." I want to know how to live so that I may learn how to die. Final exams may, in fact, be tomorrow.

Five Minutes After . . .

It may be a moment, or after months of waiting, but soon I shall stand before my Lord. Then in an instant all things will appear in new perspective.

Suddenly the things I thought important—tomorrow's tasks, the plans for the dinner at my church, my success or failure in pleasing those around me—these will matter not at all. And the things to which I gave but little thought—the word about Christ to the man next door, the moment (how short it was) of earnest prayer for the Lord's work in far-off lands, the confessing and forsaking of that secret sin—will stand as real and enduring.

Five minutes after I'm in heaven I'll be overwhelmed by the truths I've known but somehow never grasped. I'll realize then that it's what I am in Christ that comes first with God, and that when I am right with Him, I do the things which please Him.

I'll sense that it was not just how much I gave that mattered, but how I gave—and how much I withheld. In heaven I'll wish with all my heart that I could reclaim a thousandth part of the time I've let slip through my fingers, that I could call back those countless conversations which could have glorified my Lord—but didn't.

Five minutes after I'm in heaven, I believe I'll wish with all my heart that I had risen more faithfully to read the Word of God and wait on Him in prayer—that I might have known Him while still on earth as He wanted me to know Him.

A thousand thoughts will press upon me, and though overwhelmed by the grace which admits me to my heavenly home, I'll wonder at my aimless earthly life. I'll wish . . . if one may wish in heaven—but it will be too late.

Heaven is real and hell is real, and eternity is but a breath away. Soon we shall be in the presence of the Lord we claim to serve. Why should we live as though salvation were a dream—as though we did not know?

"To him that knoweth to do good, and doeth it not, to him it is sin."

There may yet be a little time. A new year dawns before us. God help us to live now in the light of a real tomorrow! [6]

Looking Homeward

I'm not afraid to die, for I know the joys of heaven are waiting. My greatest desire is to live today in anticipation of tomorrow and be ready to be welcomed into His home for all eternity. Will you be making the journey with me?

"There is no more urgent and critical question in life than that of your personal relationship with God and your eternal salvation."

A Closing Word

THROUGHOUT THIS BOOK we have faced honestly the reality of death and how we should deal with it. We have seen also the wonderful promises of God concerning eternal life, and the glory that awaits every believer on the other side of death in heaven.

Perhaps, however, as you have read this book you have had to face the fact that you are not ready to die. You do not know for sure that you will go to heaven when you die, and you have no assurance that God is with you right now as you face illness and suffering. You have never experienced the peace and security that come from a personal relationship with Him.

There is no more urgent and critical question in life than that of your personal relationship with God and your eternal salvation. But can you know—really know—that you will go to heaven when you die? Yes, you can know, and I invite you to make that discovery today.

What must you do? First, you must acknowledge that you are a sinner and repent of your sins. As we have seen in this book, there is only one thing that will keep you out of heaven, and that is your sin. The Bible says, "For all have sinned and fall short of the glory of God" (Romans 3:23). God is pure and holy, and we have no right to enter His presence because we are sinners. No matter how good we are, we can never be good enough to go to heaven on our own merit because His standard is perfection. We need to repent—to turn from our sins.

Second, you must trust Christ alone for your salvation. Christ did for us what we could never do for ourselves. He was without sin—but He took upon Himself your sin and mine when He died on the cross. We deserved only the judgment of God, but Christ willingly suffered the judgment and death we deserved. He died in your place, because He loves you. And now God offers you forgiveness and salvation as a free gift. "For the wages of sin is death, but the gift of God is eternal life in Christ Jesus our Lord" (Romans 6:23).

How do you receive Christ personally and make your decision to follow Him? The Bible says, "Yet to all who received him, to those who believed in his name, he gave the right to become children of God" (John 1:12). Notice in that verse that we are to "believe" and to "receive" Christ. We are to *believe* that He died on the cross for us and rose again from the dead so we could be saved, and we are to *receive* Him personally into our hearts. God has done everything that is necessary to make our salvation possible—but (like any other gift) we must receive it.

Right now I invite you to pray a prayer we have seen people all over the world pray, asking Christ to forgive them and inviting Him to come into their hearts as their Lord and Savior. Will you sincerely pray this prayer now?

O God, I know that I am a sinner and need Your forgiveness. I believe that You died for my sins. I want to turn from my sins. I now invite You to come into my heart and life. I want to trust You as Savior and follow You as Lord, in the fellowship of Your church. In Christ's name, Amen.

If you have asked Christ into your heart and committed your life to Him, then God has forgiven you and adopted you into His family. More than that, He has promised to save you and bring you into His heavenly kingdom forever—and God cannot lie. "God has given us eternal life, and this life is in his Son. He who has the Son has life; he who does not have the Son of God does not have life. I write these things to you who believe in the name of the Son of God so that you may know that you have eternal life" (1 John 5:11–13).

May God bless you as you commit your life to Christ and follow Him every day. And as you face that day in the future when God will call you to be with Him forever in heaven, may you say with the apostle Paul, "I know whom I have believed, and am convinced that he is able to guard what I have entrusted to him for that day" (2 Timothy 1:12).

Billy Graham

Notes

CHAPTER 1

1. *Time* Magazine, Sept. 22, 1986.
2. Mencken, H. L., *A New Dictionary of Quotations* (New York: Alfred A. Knopf, 1966) 260.

CHAPTER 2

1. Aries, Phillippe, *Western Attitudes toward Death: From the Middle Ages to the Present* (Baltimore and London: Johns Hopkins University Press, 1974) 9.
2. Ibid., 13.
3. Aries, Phillippe, *The Hour of Our Death* (New York: Alfred A. Knopf, 1981).
4. Ibid.
5. Gallup, George, Jr., with William Proctor, *Adventures in Immortality* (New York: McGraw-Hill, 1982) 185-190.
6. Ibid., 75.
7. MacArthur, Jack, *Exploring in the Next World* (Minneapolis, Minn.: Dimension Books, 1967) 91.
8. Mencken, H. L., *A New Dictionary of Quotations* (New York: Alfred A. Knopf, 1966) 548.
9. Dempsey, David, *The Way We Die* (New York: McGraw-Hill, 1977) 17.
10. Bane, J. Donald; Kutscher, Austin H.; Neal, Robert E. and Reeves, Robert, Jr., Editors, *Death and Ministry* (New York: Seabury Press, 1975) 151.
11. Ibid., 150.

CHAPTER 3

1. Dempsey, David, *The Way We Die* (New York: McGraw-Hill, 1977) 67.
2. Ibid., 53.
3. Ibid., 76.
4. *Los Angeles Times,* Sept. 29, 1986.

CHAPTER 4

1. American Tract Society, Box 191, Lake Grove, L.I. 11 10.
2. Bayly, Joseph, "When a Child Dies," *Family Life Today,* March, 1976.
3. Rogers, Dale Evans, *Angel Unaware* (Old Tappan, NJ.: Spire Books, Fleming H. Revell, 1963) 9.
4. *Los Angeles Times,* Feb. 3, 1986, Part IV.
5. Marshall, Eric, and Hample, Stuart, *Children's Letters to God* (New York: Simon & Schuster, 1966).
6. Krementz, Jill, *How It Feels When a Parent Dies* (New York: Alfred A. Knopf, 1981).
7. Simpson, Michael A., *The Facts of Death* (Englewood Cliffs, N.J.: Prentice-Hall, Inc., 1979) 184.
8. Lewis, C. S., *The Problem of Pain* (New York: Macmillan Publishing, 1962) 93.

CHAPTER 5

1. Lockyer, Herbert, *Last Words of Saints and Sinners* (Grand Rapids: Kregel Publications, 1969) 65.
2. *Reader's Digest,* Nov., 1986, p. 203.
3. Kopp, Ruth, *When Someone You Love Is Dying* (Grand Rapids: Zondervan, 1980) 20.
4. Ibid., 44.
5. Lockyer, Herbert, *All the Promises of the Bible* (Grand Rapids: Zondervan, 1962) 200.
6. Barfield, Velma, *Woman on Death Row* (Nashville: Oliver Nelson Books, 1985) 141.
7. Kubler-Ross, Elisabeth, *Therapeutic Grand Rounds,* Number 36, July 10, 1972.

CHAPTER 6

1. *Time,* Oct. 6, 1986, p. 35.
2. Bioethics Committee Report, Sept. 25, 1986.
3. NCCB Committee for Pro-Life Activities, June 1986.
4. Ibid.
5. *Christian Medical Society Journal,* Summer 1986, p. 17.
6. *Santa Monica Evening Outlook,* May 14, 1986.
7. Barnard, Dr. Christiaan, *Good Life, Good Death* (Englewood Cliffs, NJ.: Prentice-Hall, Inc., 1981) 15.
8. Barnard, op. cit., 66.
9. Alexander, L., "Medical Science Under Dictatorship," *New England Journal of Medicine,* 1949; 241:39-47.
10. "The Physician's Responsibility toward Hopelessly Ill Patients." *New England Journal of Medicine,* 1984; 310:955959.
11. *Newsweek,* Feb. 7, 1983, p. 13.
12. *Time,* July 7, 1980.
13. Sherrill, John, *Mother's Song* (Lincoln, Va.: Chosen Books, 1982) 132, 133, 144.
14. Graham, Ruth Bell, *Sitting by My Laughing Fire* (Waco, Tex.: Word Books, 1977) 178.

CHAPTER 7

1. Schaeffer, Edith, *Christianity Today,* Mar. 6, 1987, p. 20.
2. Shneidman, Edwin, *Voices of Death* (New York: Harper and Row, 1980) 138.
3. Ibid., 135.
4. Ibid., 137.
5. Tournier, Paul, *The Adventure of Living* (New York: Harper and Row, 1965) 104, 105.
6. *Christianity Today,* Mar. 6, 1987, p. 185.
7. Will, George, *Newsweek,* Jan. 9, 1978.
8. Ibid.
9. Tournier, op. cit., 104.

10. Richards, Larry; Johnson, Paul, M.D., *Death and the Caring Community* (Portland, Ore.: Multnomah Press, 1980) 158.

CHAPTER 8

1. Vanauken, Sheldon, *A Severe Mercy* (New York: Harper and Row, 1980) 180.
2. Westberg, Granger, *Good Grief* (Philadelphia: Fortress Press, 1962) 324.
3. Manning, Doug, *Comforting Those Who Grieve* (New York: Harper and Row, 1985) 71.
4. Graham, Morrow, *They Call Me Mother Graham* (Old Tappan, N.J.: Fleming H. Revell, 1977) 28.
5. Ibid., 31.
6. Ibid.

CHAPTER 9

1. Pollock, John, *Billy Graham* (Grand Rapids: Zondervan Publishing Co., 1966) 173.
2. Bulletin of Wheaton College, Nov., 1966.
3. Pollock, John, *Billy Graham* (New York: Harper and Row, 1979, Special Crusade Edition) 170-171.
4. Radio message by Dr. James T. Jeremiah, Cedarville College, Dec. 11, 1972.
5. Sanderson, Jim, *Los Angeles Times,* Mar. 5, 1986.
6. Lockyer, Herbert, *Last Words of Saints and Sinners* (Grand Rapids: Kregel Publications, 1969) 114.

CHAPTER 10

1. Encyclopedia Americana, Vol. 14 (Danbury, Conn.: Grolier, Inc., 1986) 68.
2. Mencken, H. L., *A New Dictionary of Quotations* (New York: Alfred A. Knopf, 1966) 527.
3. Yancey, Philip, "Heaven Can't Wait," *Christianity Today,* Sept. 7, 1984.
4. Ibid.

5. Kole, Andre, "To Be Continued," *Worldwide Challenge,* April, 1977, p. 27.
6. *Guideposts,* February 1987, p. 27.
7. *Christianity Today,* Nov. 7, 1986.
8. Nicholson, Martha Snell, *Christian Medical Society Journal, Vol. X,* Number 1, Winter, 1979.

CHAPTER 11

1. Springer, Rebecca Ruter, My *Dream of Heaven* (Forest Grove, Ore.: Book Searchers) 42.
2. *The Communicator's Commentary, Vol.* 7 (Waco, Tex.: Word Books, 1985) 184.

CHAPTER 12

1. Carlson, Carole, *Corrie, Her Life and Her Faith* (Old Tappan, NJ.: Fleming H. Revell, 1983) 217.
2. Lockyer, Herbert, *Last Words of Saints and Sinners* (Grand Rapids: Kregel Publications, 1969) 220, 221.
3. Ibid., 185.
4. Ibid., 196.
5. Ibid., 73, 105, 109, 110, 125.
6. *Moody Monthly,* January, 1952.